DEVELOPMENT CENTRE STUDIES

MONITORING THE WORLD ECONOMY 1820-1992

by
Angus Maddison

DEVELOPMENT CENTRE
OF THE ORGANISATION FOR ECONOMIC CO-OPERATION AND DEVELOPMENT

ORGANISATION FOR ECONOMIC CO-OPERATION AND DEVELOPMENT

Pursuant to Article 1 of the Convention signed in Paris on 14th December 1960, and which came into force on 30th September 1961, the Organisation for Economic Co-operation and Development (OECD) shall promote policies designed:

— to achieve the highest sustainable economic growth and employment and a rising standard of living in Member countries, while maintaining financial stability, and thus to contribute to the development of the world economy;
— to contribute to sound economic expansion in Member as well as non-member countries in the process of economic development; and
— to contribute to the expansion of world trade on a multilateral, non-discriminatory basis in accordance with international obligations.

The original Member countries of the OECD are Austria, Belgium, Canada, Denmark, France, Germany, Greece, Iceland, Ireland, Italy, Luxembourg, the Netherlands, Norway, Portugal, Spain, Sweden, Switzerland, Turkey, the United Kingdom and the United States. The following countries became Members subsequently through accession at the dates indicated hereafter: Japan (28th April 1964), Finland (28th January 1969), Australia (7th June 1971), New Zealand (29th May 1973) and Mexico (18th May 1994). The Commission of the European Communities takes part in the work of the OECD (Article 13 of the OECD Convention).

The Development Centre of the Organisation for Economic Co-operation and Development was established by decision of the OECD Council on 23rd October 1962 and comprises twenty-two Member countries of the OECD Austria, Belgium, Canada, Denmark, Finland, France, Germany, Greece, Iceland, Ireland, Italy, Japan, Luxembourg, Mexico, the Netherlands, Norway, Portugal, the United Kingdom, the United States, Spain, Sweden and Switzerland, as well as the Republic of Korea since April 1992 and Argentina and Brazil from March 1994.

The purpose of the Centre is to bring together the knowledge and experience available in Member countries of both economic development and the formulation and execution of general economic policies; to adapt such knowledge and experience to the actual needs of countries or regions in the process of development and to put the results at the disposal of the countries by appropriate means.

The Centre has a special and autonomous position within the OECD which enables it to enjoy scientific independence in the execution of its task. Nevertheless, the Centre can draw upon the experience and knowledge available in the OECD in the development field.

Publié en français sous le titre :
L'ÉCONOMIE MONDIALE 1820-1992
ANALYSE ET STATISTIQUES

*
* *

Foreword

This volume was produced in the context of the Development Centre's 1993/1995 research programme on financial systems, resource allocation and growth.

The OECD Development Centre would like to thank the Government of the Netherlands for its generous financial support.

Table of Contents

List of Tables

Appendix Tables

List of Figures

Acknowledgements

I am grateful to Jean Bonvin for commissioning this study, and for the freedom he gave me in writing it. Michèle Fleury-Brousse and Thai-Thanh Dang provided access to the OECD Development Centre's data files on the non-sample countries and processed them in the form I required. Remco Kouwenhoven was of great assistance in processing the estimates for the sample countries. Christine Johnson, Tineke Tadema and Monique Tjiong prepared successive drafts of a complex manuscript with great efficiency. Thai-Thanh Dang and Ly Na Tang prepared the graphs.

I received useful comments on different drafts of the study from Moses Abramovitz, Bart van Ark, Jean-Claude Berthélemy, Abram Bergson, Colm Foy, David Henderson, Ulrich Hiemenz, Christian Morrisson, Nanno Mulder and from participants in seminars of the OECD Development Centre, the International Association for Research in Income and Wealth, and the University of Groningen.

I am grateful to EUROSTAT, Alan Heston and Gyorgy Szilagyi for supplying unpublished details of ICP material on purchasing power parities.

I had advice or material help with queries for individual sample countries from Thad Alton, Geert den Bakker, Asdrubal Baptista, Carlo Bardini, Carlos Boloña Behr, Albert Carreras, José Cordeiro, Thomas David, Pierre van der Eng, Rainer Fremdling, Roland Granier, Mark Harrison, André Hofman, Richard Hooley, Kieran Kennedy, Olle Krantz, Valentin Kudrov, Pedro Lains, Maurice Levy-Leboyer, Brian Mitchell, Kevin O'Rourke, Robert P. Parker, Martyn Pearce, Dwight Perkins, Leandro Prados de la Escosura, Rossitsa Rangelova, Albrecht Ritschl, Ren Ruoen, Jan Pieter Smits, Jean-Claude Toutain, Malcolm Urquhart and Jan Luyten van Zanden. Responsibility for errors lies with the author.

University of Groningen

Preface

This book, which was written by Angus Maddison as a contribution to the Development Centre's research programme on financial systems, resource allocation and growth, represents an extension and updating of his *The World Economy in the 20th Century*, published by the Centre in 1989.

A major aspect of this work is a data base of exceptional interest for economic historians who will be able to use it to describe virtually the entire world economy over the period from 1820 to 1992. It is thus the first book systematically to document convergence and divergence trends in the standards of living in different economies. These movements are of particular interest for growth economists.

The interest of this book, however, does not end there. Angus Maddison presents his most comprehensive view of world economic growth, based upon a career which brought the author to senior posts in the OEEC in the 1950s before returning to the OECD in the 1960s and 1970s.

Maddison's study of phases in the development of the world economy, together with his comparison of relative performance between the different economies, casts light on the rôle of international economic relations and on the important rôle of national economic policies in the explanation of long-term growth trends. This is particularly useful at the present time.

I am convinced that this book will be welcomed not only by academics, but also by policy makers in both developed and developing countries who need to have their daily decisions guided by just such a study.

Jean Bonvin,
President,
OECD Development Centre
June 1995

Introduction

This study is a sequel to my *World Economy in the 20th Century*, OECD Development Centre, Paris, 1989, but it differs from it in five significant ways:

a) Its temporal scope is twice as long, i.e. 1820-1992 instead of 1900-87. The year 1900 is a turning point of chronometric convention, not a dividing line between economic epochs. World economic performance in the nineteenth century had more in common with the twentieth than with any earlier epoch. We therefore cover the whole period of modern capitalist development, characterised by rapid growth of output and international trade, unparalleled accumulation of physical and human capital, and technical progress which has penetrated all areas of economic activity, creating new patterns of demand, output and employment.

b) The present work provides complete coverage of the world economy. The earlier study covered 32 countries which accounted for 85 per cent of world output, but omitted Africa and most of Eastern Europe. This volume provides detailed treatment of a more representative and bigger sample — 56 countries — which accounted for 93 per cent of world output, 87 per cent of world population and world exports in 1992. The nature and quality of the quantitative evidence is assessed in Appendices A, B, C and D. Table 1-3 shows the gaps in the data-set which are bigger the further one goes back in time. These gaps were filled by estimating procedures described in Appendix E. Appendix F shows the derivation of the estimates for 143 non-sample countries; for 1950-92, they were taken mainly from the OECD Development Centre's data files, and for earlier years the crude estimation procedure is described as transparently as possible. Estimates for the world as a whole are contained in Appendix G. The present estimates are adjusted to eliminate the influence of changes in national boundaries, so that the growth dynamics of individual countries will not be obscured. Appendix H provides estimates for major countries without these adjustments.

c) In the past decade there has been a new wave of interest in economic growth, catch-up, convergence and divergence. Economists have been able to test new ideas empirically with relatively little effort, across a wide range of countries, as the Penn World Tables of Summers and Heston provide a data-set for the years since 1960 on income levels, growth rates and associated information on diskette, ready for regression. The present work is intended to help growth accountants and econometricians to carry out such exercises for a very much longer stretch of time. The estimates are set out in a transparent and flexible form, so that the user can amend or augment the data, or regroup the regional aggregates. The main tables cover a restricted number of macro-magnitudes (population, GDP indices, GDP and per capita GDP levels), but these are augmented by estimates of other magnitudes in Chapters 1, 2 and 3, by estimates of world trade in Appendix I, estimates of employment, working hours, and labour productivity in Appendix J, and detailed growth accounts for Japan, the UK and USA in Appendix K.

d) This work is intended to help and encourage basic research on quantitative economic history. In the first place it demonstrates what has already been accomplished. Thanks to the efforts of a whole generation of scholars, it is possible to make intertemporal and interspatial comparisons for a large fraction of world economic activity. I have described in some detail the different approaches which have been adopted to measure growth and levels of output and have indicated the types of problem where further research and sensitivity testing is needed. There is clearly a need to improve the present data-base. Amongst OECD countries, the weakest long-term GDP estimates are for Greece, Ireland, New Zealand, Portugal, Switzerland and Turkey. There is also a need for a complete overhaul of the historical estimates for the East European countries and China. In all these cases, it is reasonable to hope that potential data sources can be exploited to provide improved estimates. There is also a serious potential for developing better growth accounts for many countries.

e) As the major purpose of the present study was to provide a new and comprehensive long-term data-set for general purpose use, the interpretative analysis in the first three chapters is a modest coping stone on a pyramid of appendices. These chapters concentrate on analysing the longer-term forces which explain why growth accelerated in the capitalist era, why growth rates differed, and why such large spreads emerged in the per capita income of nations. Quantitative evidence helps greatly to illuminate these issues. It sharpens our appreciation of differences or similarities in the way nations, or distinctive groups of nations, perform. If there is enough comparative evidence it is possible to assess what is "normal", how potential and performance have changed over time, and whether particular countries have done well or badly. Quantification clarifies issues which qualitative analysis may leave fuzzy. Without it, one cannot readily separate "stylised facts" which economic theory seeks to explain from the "stylised phantasies" which are sometimes perceived to be reality.

Although quantification is important, no sensible person would claim that it can tell the whole story. One needs to probe beyond quantifiable causes to deeper layers of explanation. This is a complex task because there are many interactive causes whose individual impact is difficult to specify. Nation-states have widely different institutions, traditions and policies which have a powerful impact on the operation of atomistic market forces. Hence the need to use a blend of evidence on proximate and deeper layers of causality.

Chapter 1

Income Growth, Income Gaps and the Ranking of Nations

Three main features emerge from our quantitative evidence:

a) Economic growth was extraordinarily fast from 1820-1992, World population increased five-fold, per capita product eight-fold, world GDP forty-fold, and world trade 540-fold;

b) The rise in per capita income differed widely between countries and regions, so intercountry and interregional spreads became very much wider;

c) The momentum of growth varied significantly. The best performance was in the post-war golden age 1950-1973 when per capita income improved dramatically in all regions, the second best was 1870-1913, the third best 1973-92.

The Post-1820 Acceleration in Long-Term Perspective

Growth performance since 1820 has been dramatically superior to that in earlier history. Table 1-1 gives a very rough summary picture of the situation over the past five centuries.

Before our present "capitalist" epoch[1], economies were predominantly agrarian, and economic advance was largely extensive. In response to demographic pressure, economic activity was successful over the long term in sustaining living standards, but technology was virtually stagnant and evidence of advances in economic well-being is very meagre.

Table 1-1(a). **Levels of World Economic Performance, 1500-1992**

	1500	1820	1992
World Population (million)	425	1 068	5 441
GDP Per Capita (1990 $)	565	651	5 145
World GDP (billion 1990 $)	240	695	27 995
World Exports (billion 1990 $)	n.a.	7	3 786

Source: 1820 and 1992 figures for population, GDP and GDP per capita from Appendix G, exports from Appendix I. West European population 1500 from Maddison (1991) p. 226 (the rest of Europe assumed to move parallel); population in 1500 in China, India and Japan from sources cited for 1820 in Appendix A (other Asia and Oceania assumed to move parallel); population in 1500 in the Americas from Rosenblat (1945) p. 92. African population growth rate 1500-1820 from Bennett (1954) Table 1. Per Capita GDP growth 1500-1820 assumed to be 0.2 per cent a year in Western Europe, 0.1 per cent in the rest of Europe and Latin America, 0.0 in Asia and Africa. For Western Europe the 0.2 per cent per capita hypothesis is taken from Kuznets (1973), pp. 139-40. For the other regions anything like 0.2 per cent would imply an implausibly low 1500 level of income in societies which in most cases had incomes enough above subsistence to provide for the maintenance of governing elites in some degree of luxury. For recent research on per capita income trends 1500-1820 see Maddison and Van der Wee (1994), see also Perkins (1969) for long-term developments in China.

Table 1-1(b). **Rates of World Economic Growth, 1500-1992**
(annual average compound growth rates)

	1500-1820	1820-1992
World Population	0.29	0.95
GDP Per Capita	0.04	1.21
World GDP	0.33	2.17
World Exports	n.a.	3.73

Source: Table 1-1a.

Table 1-2. **The Performance of Major Regions, 1820-1992**

	Population (millions)		GDP per Head (1990 $)		GDP (billions 1990 $)	
	1820	1992	1820	1992	1820	1992
			Absolute Levels			
Western Europe	103	303	1 292	17 387	133	5 255
Western Offshoots	11	305	1 205	20 850	14	6 359
Southern Europe	34	123	804	8 287	27	1 016
Eastern Europe	90	431	772	4 665	69	2 011
Latin America	20	462	679	4 820	14	2 225
Asia & Oceania	736	3 163	550	3 252	405	10 287
Africa	73	656	450	1 284	33	842
World Total	1 068	5 441	651	5 145	695	27 995
			Coefficients of Multiplication (1820-1992)			
Western Europe	3		13		40	
Western Offshoots	27		17		464	
Southern Europe	4		10		38	
Eastern Europe	5		6		29	
Latin America	23		7		161	
Asia & Oceania	4		6		25	
Africa	9		3		26	
World Average	5		8		40	

Source: Derived from Appendix G. The figures for GDP per head are weighted averages for 199 countries. Those in Table 1-3 are arithmetic averages for 56 sample countries.

There were some stirrings of economic growth after 1500 when the European "discovery" of the Americas and Australasia opened up new horizons, and different parts of the world became increasingly interactive, but over three centuries performance was extremely modest. From 1500 to 1820, the average growth of world per capita income was probably only a thirtieth of that achieved since 1820. There were some advances in technology, living standards and productivity in Western Europe and its offshoots, and more limited progress in the European periphery. But the rest of the world was economically stagnant, and by 1820 the West had established a substantial leadership margin[2].

The Hierarchy of Regions

For analytical convenience, I have divided the world into seven groups of countries, ranking them in order of their developmental promise as it might have been assessed by a well informed observer at the beginning of the capitalist epoch. My hierarchy is very similar to that in Adam Smith's *Inquiry into the Nature and Causes of the Wealth of Nations*. This was published in 1776 but his criteria for ranking nations were close to mine.

The main considerations I had in mind in allocating countries to these regions were: (a) their initial level (or assumed range) of per capita income in 1820; (b) their initial resource endowment in relation to population; (c) institutional or societal characteristics likely to influence economic performance.

The intra-regional congruence of countries and the regional groupings themselves may legitimately be challenged by some readers, but the basic evidence for the 56 sample countries is presented transparently, and it is quite easy for the reader to construct alternative groupings.

Table 1-2 shows the performance of the seven different regions since 1820. They are ranked in order of their initial levels of per capita income. This ranking has not changed much over the very long run. The most prosperous have retained their privileged position, and the poorest have remained relatively poor.

Figure 1.1. **Levels of GDP per capita by region, 1820-1992**

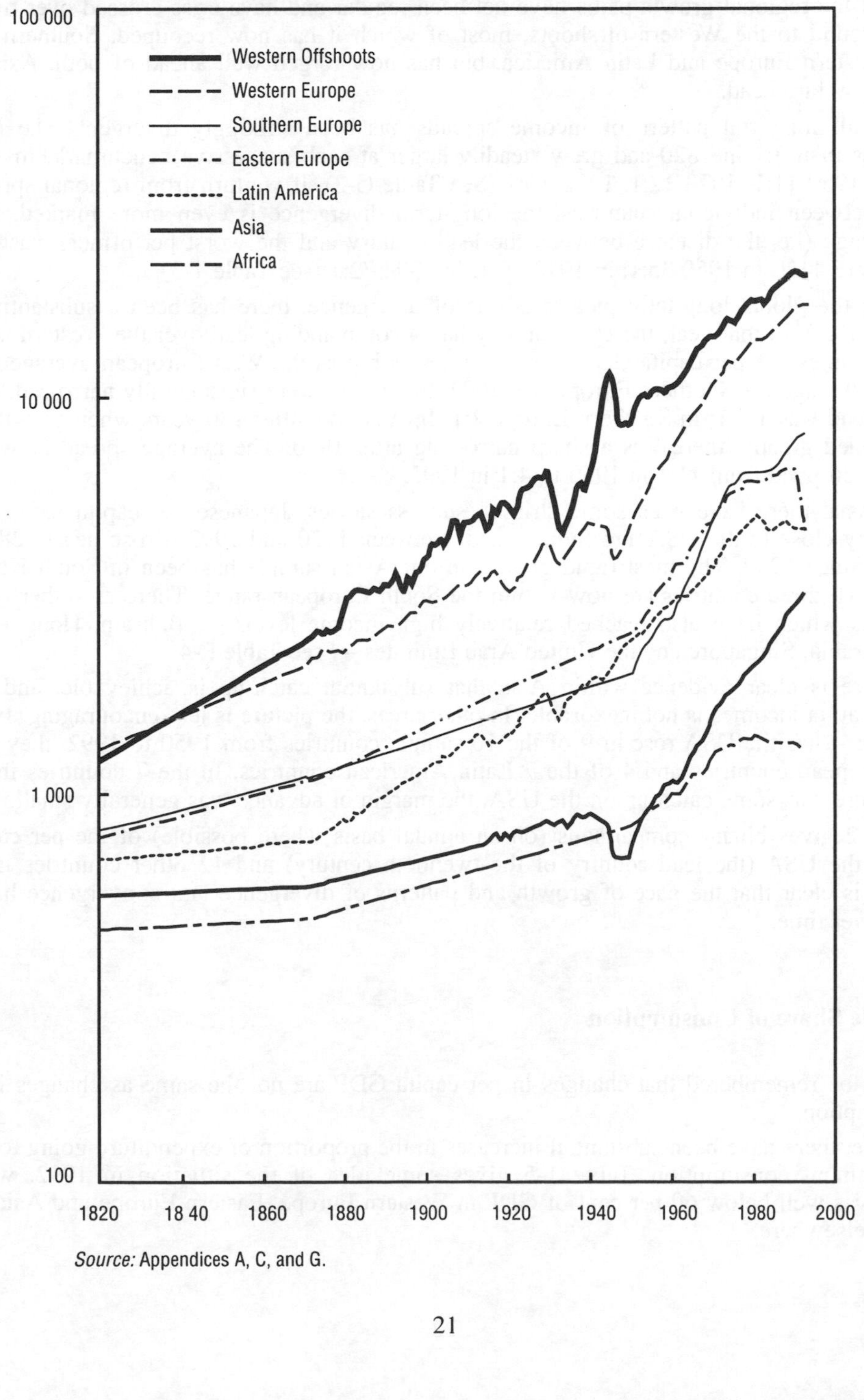

Source: Appendices A, C, and G.

Per Capita GDP Performance

Per capita growth since 1820 has been fastest in countries which were already the most prosperous in the initial year, with a 13-fold increase in Western Europe and a 17-fold increase in the Western Offshoots. The next fastest growth — a ten-fold increase — occurred in Southern Europe, which was the third most prosperous region in 1820. The fourth ranking region in 1820 was Eastern Europe. It had the fourth fastest per capita growth up to the 1980s, but with the large drop since the collapse of communism it ranks fifth in long-run per capita income gains. Latin America, the fifth most prosperous region in 1820 had a seven-fold increase in real income by 1992. Asia which had sixth rank in income in 1820, had the same ranking in 1992 with a six-fold increase in real product. Africa had the lowest per capita level in 1820. It was in the same position in 1992 with very modest gains to show. After 17 decades, its average per capita income in 1992 was about the same as Western Europe had achieved in 1820! However, it is clear from Figure 1-1 that the regional growth paths have not been regular and have criss-crossed over time. Western Europe lost ground to the Western offshoots, most of which it has now recouped. Southern Europe fell behind both Eastern Europe and Latin America, but has now forged well ahead of both. Asia fell below Africa but is now far ahead.

The overall long run pattern of income spreads has been strikingly divergent. The interregional spread was less than 3:1 in 1820 and grew steadily larger at each successive benchmark. In 1870, it was 5:1, 1913 9:1, 1950 11:1, 1973 12:1, 1992 16:1 (See Table G-3). If we turn from regional spreads to look at the range between individual countries, the long-term divergence is even more marked. In 1820 the intercountry range (i.e. the distance between the lead country and the worst performer) was over 3:1, in 1870 7:1, in 1913 11:1, in 1950 35:1, in 1973 40:1, in 1992 72:1 (see Table 1-3).

Although the global long-term picture is one of divergence, there has been a substantial degree of catch-up since 1950. In that year, the US economy had a commanding lead over the Western and Southern European economies. Its per capita GDP was 1.7 times as big as the West European average in 1950 and four times the average for Southern Europe. By 1992, these gaps were substantially narrowed. For Western Europe the spread was 1.2:1; in Southern Europe 2:1. In Asia too, after 130 years when growth was feeble and gaps widened greatly, there was a sharp narrowing after 1950. The average spread between US and Asian incomes dropped from 11:1 in 1950 to 4:1 in 1992.

Within Asia, there have been some striking success stories. Japanese per capita income is now in third place, very close to the USA and Switzerland. Between 1820 and 1992 it rose nearly 28-fold — the world record. Since 1950, The most rapid growth in our Asian sample has been in South Korea, Taiwan and Thailand. All three countries are now within the South European range. There are other (non-sample) Asian countries which have also reached relatively high income levels — Bahrain, Hong Kong, Israel, Qatar, Saudi Arabia, Singapore and the United Arab Emirates — see Table F-4.

Thus there is clear evidence within Asia that substantial catch-up is achievable, and that falling behind in per capita incomes is not inexorable. In other areas, the picture is less encouraging. In Africa, the income gaps *vis-à-vis* the USA rose in 9 of the 10 sample countries from 1950 to 1992, they rose in 4 of the 7 East European countries and 4 of the 7 Latin American countries. In the 7 countries in these three areas where there was some catch-up on the USA, the margin of advance was generally small.

Figure 1-2 gives binary comparisons (on an annual basis where possible) of the per capita income gaps between the USA (the lead country of the twentieth century) and 12 other countries in the period since 1820. It is clear that the pace of growth and patterns of divergence and convergence have changed substantially over time.

Changes in the Share of Consumption

It should be remembered that changes in per capita GDP are not the same as changes in per capita private consumption.

Over time, there have been substantial increases in the proportion of expenditure going to investment, and to government consumption. Table 1-5 gives some idea of the situation in 1992, when private consumption was well below 60 per cent of GDP in Western Europe, Eastern Europe and Asia, and below three-quarters elsewhere.

Table 1-3. **GDP per Capita in 1990 International Dollars in the 56 Country Sample**

	1820	1870	1900	1913	1950	1973	1992
12 Western European Countries							
Austria	1 295	1 875	2 901	3 488	3 731	11 308	17 160
Belgium	1 291	2 640	3 652	4 130	5 346	11 905	17 165
Denmark	1 225	1 927	2 902	3 764	6 683	13 416	18 293
Finland	759	1 107	1 620	2 050	4 131	10 768	14 646
France	1 218	1 858	2 849	3 452	5 221	12 940	17 959
Germany	1 112	1 913	3 134	3 833	4 281	13 152	19 351
Italy	1 092	1 467	1 746	2 507	3 425	10 409	16 229
Netherlands	1 561	2 640	3 533	3 950	5 850	12 763	16 898
Norway	1 004	1 303	1 762	2 275	4 969	10 229	17 543
Sweden	1 198	1 664	2 561	3 096	6 738	13 494	16 927
Switzerland	-	2 172	3 531	4 207	8 939	17 953	21 036
UK	1 756	3 263	4 593	5 032	6 847	11 992	15 738
Arith. Average	1 228	1 986	2 899	3 482	5 513	11 694	17 412
4 Western Offshoots							
Australia	1 528	3 801	4 299	5 505	7 218	12 485	16 237
Canada	893	1 620	2 758	4 213	7 047	13 644	18 159
New Zealand	-	3 115	4 320	5 178	8 495	12 575	13 947
USA	1 287	2 457	4 096	5 307	9 573	16 607	21 558
Arith. Average	1 236	2 748	3 868	5 051	8 083	13 828	17 475
5 South European Countries							
Greece	-	-	-	1 621	1 951	7 779	10 314
Ireland	954	1 773	2 495	2 733	3 518	7 023	11 711
Portugal	-	1 085	1 408	1 354	2 132	7 568	11 130
Spain	1 063	1 376	2 040	2 255	2 397	8 739	12 498
Turkey	-	-	-	979	1 299	2 739	4 422
Arith. Average	-	1 194*	1 676*	1 788	2 259	6 770	10 015
7 East European Countries							
Bulgaria	-	-	-	1 498	1 651	5 284	4 054
Czechoslovakia	849	1 164	1 729	2 096	3 501	7 036	6 845
Hungary	-	1 269	1 682	2 098	2 480	5 596	5 638
Poland	-	-	-	-	2 447	5 334	4 726
Romania	-	-	-	-	1 182	3 477	2 565
USSR	751	1 023	1 218	1 488	2 834	6 058	4 671
Yugoslavia	-	-	-	1 029	1 546	4 237	3 887
Arith. Average	-	876*	1 174*	1 527*	2 235	5 289	4 627

Table 1-3 (continued.) **GDP per Capita in 1990 International Dollars in the 56 Country Sample**

	1820	1870	1900	1913	1950	1973	1992
7 Latin American Countries							
Argentina	-	1 311	2 756	3 797	4 987	7 970	7 616
Brazil	670	740	704	839	1 673	3 913	4 637
Chile	-	-	1 949	2 653	3 827	5 028	7 238
Colombia	-	-	973	1 236	2 089	3 539	5 025
Mexico	760	710	1 157	1 467	2 085	4 189	5 112
Peru	-	-	817	1 037	2 263	3 953	2 854
Venezuela	-	-	821	1 104	7 424	10 717	9 163
Arith. Average	-	783*	1 311	1 733	3 478	5 017	5 949
11 Asian Countries							
Bangladesh	531	-	581	617	551	478	720
Burma	-	-	647[a]	635	393	589	748
China	523	523	652	688	614	1 186	3 098
India	531	558	625	663	597	853	1 348
Indonesia	614	657	745	917	874	1 538	2 749
Japan	704	741	1 135	1 334	1 873	11 017	19 425
Pakistan	531	-	687	729	650	981	1 642
Philippines	-	-	1 033	1 418	1 293	1 956	2 213
South Korea	-	-	850	948	876	2 840	10 010
Taiwan	-	-	759	794	922	3 669	11 590
Thailand	-	717	812	846	848	1 750	4 694
Arith. Average	609*	638*	775	872	863	2 442	5 294
10 African Countries							
Côte d'Ivoire	-	-	-	-	859	1 727	1 134
Egypt	-	-	509	508	517	947	1 927
Ethiopia	-	-	-	-	277	412	300
Ghana	-	-	462	648	1 193	1 260	1 007
Kenya	-	-		-	609	947	1 055
Morocco	-	-	-	-	1 611	1 651	2 327
Nigeria	-	-	-	-	547	1 120	1 152
South Africa	-	-	-	1 451	2 251	3 844	3 451
Tanzania	-	-	-	-	427	655	601
Zaire	-	-	-	-	636	757	353
Arith. Average	-	-	-	-	893	1 332	1 331

a) 1901

* hypothetical average, assumes that average movement of GDP per capita in countries of the group with data-gaps, was the same as the average for the countries remaining in the sample.

Source: Appendix D. All figures in this table are adjusted to exclude the impact of frontier changes. See Appendix H for estimates without adjustment.

Table 1-4. **Falling Behind and Catching Up: Rates of Divergence from or Convergence towards the Per Capita GDP Level of the USA, 1820-1992**

(annual average compound rate of growth)

	1820-1913	1913-50	1950-92		1820-1913	1913-50	1950-92
Austria	-0.46	-1.40	1.71	Argentina	n.a	-0.85	-0.93
Belgium	-0.27	-0.89	0.85	Brazil	-1.27	0.27	0.50
Denmark	-0.32	-0.04	0.47	Chile	n.a.	-0.60	-0.42
Finland	-0.45	0.30	1.09	Colombia	n.a.	-0.18	0.16
France	-0.40	-0.48	1.01	Mexico	-0.81	-0.64	0.20
Germany	-0.19	-1.29	1.67	Peru	n.a.	0.52	-1.37
Italy	-0.63	-0.75	1.79	Venezuela	n.a.	3.62	-1.42
Netherlands	-0.52	-0.53	0.59				
Norway	-0.64	0.52	1.08	Bangladesh	-1.35	-1.88	-1.29
Sweden	-0.50	0.51	0.26	Burma	n.a.	-2.85	-0.40
Switzerland	n.a.	0.44	0.10	China	-1.22	-1.88	1.94
UK	-0.29	-0.76	0.05	India	-1.28	-1.86	0.00
				Indonesia	-1.09	-1.71	0.80
Australia	-0.15	-0.86	0.00	Japan	-0.83	-0.67	3.70
Canada	0.14	-0.20	0.32	Pakistan	-1.18	-1.89	0.27
New Zealand	n.a.	-0.26	-0.75	Philippines	n.a.	-1.83	-0.65
				South Korea	n.a.	-1.79	3.85
Greece	n.a.	-1.08	2.05	Taiwan	n.a.	-1.18	4.18
Ireland	-0.39	-0.81	0.93	Thailand	n.a.	-1.57	2.16
Portugal	n.a.	-0.37	2.02				
Spain	-0.71	-1.42	2.02	Côte d'Ivoire	n.a.	n.a.	-1.26
Turkey	n.a.	-0.83	0.99	Egypt	n.a.	-1.53	1.33
				Ethiopia	n.a.	n.a.	-1.73
Bulgaria	n.a.	-1.32	0.21	Ghana	n.a.	0.05	-2.31
Czechoslovakia	-0.55	-0.21	-0.34	Kenya	n.a.	n.a.	-0.62
Hungary	n.a.	-1.14	0.02	Morocco	n.a.	n.a.	-1.05
Poland	n.a.	n.a.	-0.37	Nigeria	n.a.	n.a.	-0.16
Romania	n.a.	n.a.	-0.09	South Africa	n.a.	-0.41	-0.81
USSR	-0.78	0.15	-0.74	Tanzania	n.a.	n.a.	-1.11
Yugoslavia	n.a.	-0.49	0.26	Zaire	n.a.	n.a.	-3.27

Source: Derived from Table I-3.

Table 1-5. **Private Consumption as a Share of GDP at Market Prices, 1992**

(percentages)

France	60.5	Argentina	80.5c
Germany	54.0	Brazil	64.7
Netherlands	60.3	Mexico	73.9
Sweden	53.9	Average	73.0
UK	64.1		
Average	58.6	China	52.4
		India	67.1
USA	67.4	Indonesia	53.0
		Japan	57.0
Portugal	62.9	Korea	52.7
Spain	63.2	Average	56.4
Czechoslovakia	51.1a	Egypt	79.5
USSR	55.1b	Ghana	84.9
Average	53.1	Morocco	67.0
		Nigeria	70.9
		South Africa	64.9
		Average	73.4

Around 1820, the share of private consumption was around 84 per cent in France and 88 per cent in the UK. If the price movement had been the same for consumption and for GDP, this would mean that French private consumption levels in 1992 were about ten-and-a-half times as high as in 1820, compared with a per capita GDP about fourteen-and-a-half times as high. For the UK it would mean a rise in per capita consumption of six-and-a-half times compared with the nine-fold rise in per capita GDP. For the world as a whole, the average level of private consumption in 1992 was probably around five-and-a-half times higher than in 1820 compared with the eight-fold increase in per capita GDP.

The increase in the non-consumption share is a reflection of the effort required to sustain growth. A good deal of collective consumption goes to improve human capital (health and education), and a substantial savings effort was needed to finance the massive increase in physical capital.

Productivity Levels

The ranking of countries in per capita GDP is not necessarily the same as their standing in terms of productivity. In 1992, for example, Japanese per capita income was nearly 15 per cent higher than that in the Netherlands, but labour productivity was little more than two-thirds of Dutch levels.

Table 1-6 shows the difference between per capita GDP and labour productivity levels for some of the advanced capitalist countries whose performance characteristics are best documented. France and the Netherlands have attained virtually the same labour productivity levels as the USA, even though they have lower inputs of physical capital, human capital, and natural resources. This means that their level of total factor productivity is even better relative to the USA than their labour productivity. It is clear from this kind of confrontation that one cannot judge the economic performance of nations only by the yardstick of per capita GDP — a point to which we return in Chapter 2.

Table 1-6. **Factors Affecting Real Income and Productivity Performance Levels in Six Advanced Countries in 1992**
(USA = 100)

	France	Germany	Japan	Netherlands	UK	USA
GDP Per Capita	83	90	90	78	73	100
Labour Input Per Capita	82	95	131	79	89	100
GDP Per Hour Worked	102	95	69	99	82	100
Non-Residential Capital Stock Per Person Employed	92	91	101	78	58	100
Educational Level	88	67	82	74	78	100
Commodity Exports Per Person Employed	276	371	123	563	202	100
Scale of Domestic Economy	19	23	44	5	17	100
Land Area Per Person Employed	31	11	8	7	12	100

Source: Appendices C, J, K, Maddison (1995a) and sources cited in Chapters 2 and 3.

Demographic Experience in the Major Regions

In demographic terms, the most rapid long-term growth has been in places which were relatively empty in 1820 and attracted large-scale immigration from Europe. Thus the "Western Offshoots" increased their population 27-fold and Latin America 23-fold. The other relatively empty region, Africa, increased its population ninefold. Demographic expansion was below the long-term world average in Western and Southern Europe and Asia.

Population growth in Western Europe has been modest over the long run. In the nineteenth and twentieth centuries there was a gradual but substantial increase in life expectation from about 37 to 77 years. The long decline of mortality was matched by gradual reductions in fertility, and there was significant migration to the Western Offshoots and Latin America. Since 1973, the widespread availability of contraceptive techniques and changing attitudes to family size have reduced population growth to historically low levels. In Eastern Europe there have also been drops in fertility, increased emigration, and in some cases higher death rates because of worsening economic conditions. In Bulgaria and Hungary there were declines in population, a phenomenon with little historical precedent in the modern era, except in Ireland.

Table 1-7. **Vital Statistics, 1820-1992**

	Births per 100 Population			Years of Life Expectancy at Birth Average for Both Sexes		
	1820	1900	1992	1820	1900	1992
France	3.17	2.13	1.30	40	47	77
Germany	3.99	3.56	1.11	n.a.	47	76
Netherlands	3.50	3.16	1.30	32	52	77
Sweden	3.30	2.70	1.42	35	56	78
UK	3.03	2.87	1.37a	39	51	76
Canada	5.69	2.72	1.47	n.a.	n.a.	78
USA	5.52	3.23	1.59	n.a.	47	77
Spain	n.a.	3.39	1.01a	n.a.	35	77
Russia	n.a.	4.93	0.94	n.a.	32	64
Brazil	n.a.	4.60	2.67e	n.a.	37b	66
Mexico	n.a.	4.69	2.74e	n.a.	33c	70
China	n.a.	n.a.	2.17e	n.a.	n.a.	69
India	n.a.	4.60	3.00e	n.a.	24	61
Japan	n.a.	3.17	0.97	35d	44	79
Ethiopia	n.a.	n.a.	5.14a	n.a.	n.a.	49
Egypt	n.a.	4.52	3.08e	n.a.	n.a.	62

a) 1991; b) 1920; c) 1930; d) 1850; e) "most recent" estimate as given by World Bank (1992).

Source: Maddison (1991 and 1995c), World Bank *Social Indicators of Development 1991-92*, Washington, D.C., 1992, and national sources.

In the nineteenth century, population growth was very fast in the Western Offshoots because of unusually high fertility and immigration.

In Latin America, population growth was rapid by world standards from 1820 to 1950, because of rapid immigration and high fertility. The transition to lower fertility was slow when death rates began to fall. Population increase accelerated substantially to an average of 2.8 per cent a year in 1950-73. After 1973 it slowed somewhat, but was still very much faster than in Europe or North America.

Asian countries had an overall population growth rate similar to that of Europe in 1820-1950. When economic progress accelerated after 1950, mortality fell and population grew at an average rate of 2.3 per cent a year to 1973. Thereafter voluntaristic controls on fertility increased and population growth rates declined.

In Africa, evidence on long-term demographic trends is poor. Until the 1950s, fertility and mortality were probably a good deal higher than in Europe. Since then, cheap modern methods of disease control have reduced death rates quite sharply, and by 1992, life expectation was about 55 years. However, fertility remains very high and population growth accelerated to an average of 3 per cent a year in 1973-92, i.e. ten times the European rate.

The Size Ranking of Countries and Regions

There have been substantial changes in the relative size of different regions. They were most dramatic in "Western Offshoots" and Latin America. In 1820, they each represented 2 per cent of world output; in 1992, the first group accounted for 22.7 per cent and Latin America 7.9 per cent. The Asian share dropped from 58.3 per cent in 1820 to 19.3 per cent in 1950, then rose sharply to 36.7 per cent in 1992. The West European share was 19.1 per cent in 1820, peaked at 27 per cent in 1870-1913 and has

Figure 1.2. **Binary confrontation of per capita GDP levels since 1820 (1990 Geary-Khamis dollars)**

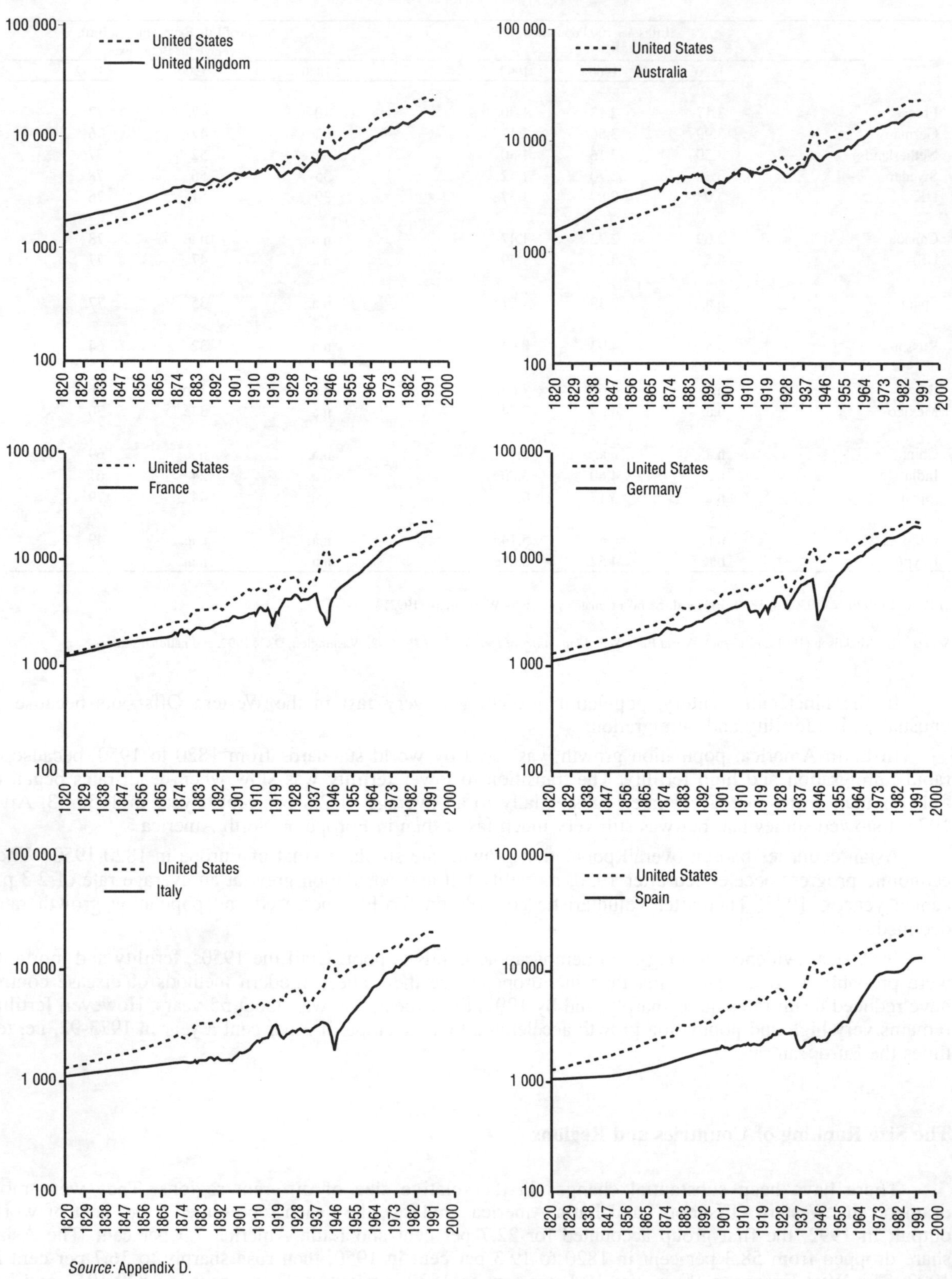

Source: Appendix D.

Figure 1.2 cont'd. **Binary confrontation of per capita GDP levels since 1820 (1990 Geary-Khamis dollars)**

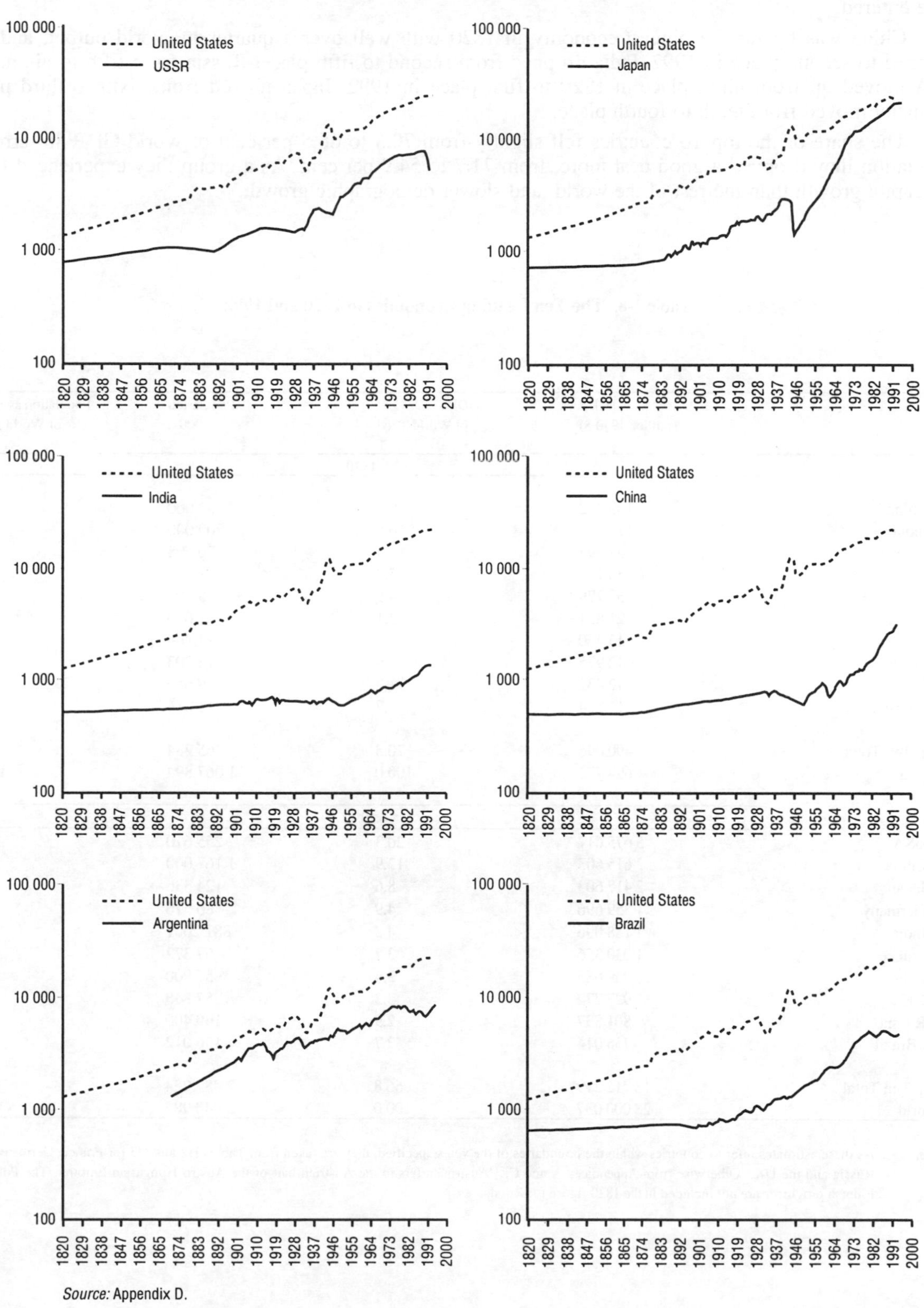

Source: Appendix D.

since fallen back to 18.9 per cent — about the same level as in 1820. The African share fell from 4.7 per cent in 1820 to 3 per cent in 1992.

Table 1-8 shows the relative standing of the 10 biggest countries in 1820 and 1992. The composition of the group was similar in the two years, except that Austria and Spain have dropped out; Brazil and Italy have entered.

China was by far the biggest economy in 1820 with well over a quarter of world output, and had dropped to second place in 1992. India dropped from second to fifth place, Russia from fifth to ninth. The USA moved up from ninth place in 1820 to first place in 1992. Japan moved from sixth to third place. Germany moved from tenth to fourth place.

The share of the top 10 countries fell slightly from 70.5 to 66.8 per cent of world GDP. In terms of population they dropped a good deal more, from 71.7 to 54.9 per cent. As a group they experienced faster per capita growth than the rest of the world, and slower demographic growth.

Table 1-8. **The Ten Leading Economies in 1820 and 1992**

	GDP (million 1990 $)	GDP as Per Cent of World Total %	Population (000s)	Population as Share of World Total %
		1820		
1. China	199 212	28.7	381 000	35.5
2. India	110 982	16.0	209 000	19.6
3. France	37 397	5.4	30 698	2.9
4. UK	36 164	5.2	21 240	2.0
5. Russia	33 779	4.9	45 005	4.2
6. Japan	21 831	3.1	31 000	2.9
7. Austria	13 460	1.9	14 268	1.3
8. Spain	12 975	1.9	12 203	1.1
9. USA	12 432	1.8	9 656	0.9
10. Prussia	11 864	1.7	11 214	1.1
Top Ten Total	490 096	70.5	765 284	71.7
World	694 772	100.0	1 067 894	100.0
		1992		
1. USA	5 675 617	20.3	255 610	4.7
2. China	3 615 603	12.9	1 167 000	20.9
3. Japan	2 417 603	8.6	124 336	2.3
4. Germany	1 359 696	4.9	80 576	1.5
5. India	1 188 096	4.2	881 2001	6.2
6. France	1 030 356	3.7	57 372	1.1
7. Italy	939 685	3.4	57 900	1.1
8. UK	927 772	3.3	57 848	1.1
9. Russia	801 837	2.9	149 400	2.7
10. Brazil	756 014	2.7	156 012	2.9
Top Ten Total	18 712 219	66.8	2 987 254	54.9
World	28 000 037	100.0	5 440 983	100.0

Source: As these estimates refer to countries within the boundaries of the years specified, they are taken from Tables H2 and H3 for France, Germany, India, Russia and the UK. Otherwise from Appendices A and C. "Austria" refers to the Austrian half of the Austro-Hungarian Empire. The Polish and Finnish provinces are not included in the 1820 figure for Russia.

Notes

1. Simon Kuznets (1966) put the turning point for "modern economic growth" at 1750, but in the light of recent evidence suggesting that growth in the eighteenth century was slower than previously thought (Crafts, 1985), I prefer to use 1820 as a starting point. Recent evidence has also falsified the earlier view, espoused most strongly by Rostow (1960) and Gerschenkron (1962), that there was a long drawn-out sequence of staggered "takeoffs" in West European countries throughout the nineteenth century. It now seems clear that growth was generally much faster after 1820 than it was in the "protocapitalist" period from 1500 to 1820, when Western Europe was slowly pulling ahead of the rest of the world.
2. Paul Bairoch (1981) published estimates showing a much narrower gap between his "developed" and "third world" groups at the beginning of the nineteenth century, but it is not clear how he derived his estimate for the "third" world. See Maddison (1983) for a comment.

Chapter 2

Causal Influences on Growth Performance

Over the long run there have been four main causal influences which go a long way to explain why such large increases in per capita output have been feasible. These are: (a) technological progress; (b) accumulation of physical capital in which technical progress usually needs to be embodied; (c) improvement in human skills, education, organising ability; and (d) closer integration of individual national economies through trade in goods and services, investment, intellectual and entrepreneurial interaction. In the literature on economic growth, there are also three other elements considered to have had an important causal role. These are economies of scale, structural change, and the relative scarcity or abundance of natural resources. All of these causal influences have been interactive so it is not easy to separate the specific role of each.

Technical Progress

Technological progress has been the most fundamental element of change. It is also the most difficult to measure in a summarising statistic, though it is easy to illustrate its long-term impact. This has probably been greatest in transport and communications. In 1820, the carriage of goods was mainly in vehicles drawn by horses or other pack animals, by canal barge or by sailing vessels. In the nineteenth century railways and steam ships were very important substitutes. In the twentieth, motor and air transport developed on a large scale. Speedier movement and lower costs raised productivity, increased interspatial specialisation, and reduced interregional price spreads. The development of passenger transport transformed people's lives. In 1820, the journey from Paris to Lyon took five days by public transport. Most people could not afford a carriage and did not have a horse, so they travelled mainly on foot, and the distances which could be covered were limited. Now, the train to Lyon takes two hours. In the advanced capitalist countries, most families have at least one car, and in other parts of the world, public transport by bus or railway is usually available. Similarly with communications. In 1820, hand-written letters were an important means of communication for government and a small educated class. Carrier pigeons provided a quick source of information over limited distances. But an exchange of letters between Europe and America took several weeks and between Europe and Asia several months. Now there are worldwide telephone networks, faxes, computer links and E-mail. In 1820, British newspaper sales amounted to 29 million, i.e. about 1.4 newspapers per year per head of population. Now most families throughout the world have daily access to news and entertainment on radio and television.

The spread of electricity and the use of power have also helped to transform production processes. Household stocks of electrical and transport equipment are complementary to the capital of producers in many ways. Thus the mobility of households and widespread use of refrigerators have had a major impact on the nature and location of capital invested in retailing.

Technological innovation at the beginning of the nineteenth century was largely done by individual inventors or small-scale entrepreneurs, but now the great bulk of it is carried out by large-scale firms with substantial budgets for R and D, as well as by governments.

The processes of innovation and adaptation of known techniques to local conditions are carried out on a world-wide basis, but a special role has been played by the "lead" countries. The UK was the country with the highest level of productivity in the nineteenth century[1], and bore a major responsibility for pushing out the frontiers of technology. The process of diffusion and transfer was helped substantially by the migration of British capital. The technological activity of other, "follower" countries involved a considerable effort of mimicry and adaptation, and a lesser degree of innovation. Some innovation did take place in follower countries, e.g. German developments in the chemical industry, but the British economy operated, on average, nearest to "best practice" technology. However, average British practice was well below "best practice" because the economy (like all others) operated with a capital stock of many vintages. It is usually only the operations with the newest capital which represent "best practice".

Throughout the nineteenth century and until 1913, UK productivity levels were above those of all the other European countries, so although they were closer followers than most of the world, their average technical distance from the UK was substantial.

In the twentieth century the American margin of leadership over the other advanced countries became bigger than that of the UK in the nineteenth, and its rate of progress (as measured by labour and total factor productivity performance) between 1913 and 1973 was much faster than the UK ever achieved. This is a major reason why the world economy was able to grow faster in the twentieth century than in the nineteenth. The frontiers of technology were being pushed out faster than before.

In the period 1950 to 1992 the margin of US productivity leadership has been substantially eroded. The advanced capitalist countries of Europe have drawn much closer to US levels of productivity. This is also true of the most dynamic sectors of the Japanese economy, but its level of performance is very uneven, and its average productivity is significantly lower than that of Europe.

One would have expected some acceleration in the rate of technical progress as more countries operate near to the frontier, but in fact it seems to have slowed down significantly in the past twenty years (a point developed further below).

In the analysis of technical progress, the leader-follower dichotomy is, in my view, fundamental. The two successive lead countries had a substantial lead over the advanced follower countries of Western Europe from 1820 until quite recently. Their lead over most countries of Latin America, Asia, and Africa was, and is, very much bigger. We can therefore get some idea of the changing pace of technical advance only by close inspection of performance in the lead country. Follower countries can draw upon the lead country's fund of technology by building up their stocks of physical and human capital, opening their economies to facilitate trade, and by possessing institutions which nurture absorptive capacity. Effective access to lead-country technology is certainly not a free good. If the follower countries do the right things, they may have an easier ride than the leaders had. But one should not interpret the rapid growth that catch-up situations may involve as an acceleration of technical progress.

Japan is the archetypal case of a successful "follower". In order to narrow the gap between itself and the leader, it changed its political, social and economic institutions in 1867, took several decades to create a huge stock of physical and human capital, and mounted a very substantial private and governmental effort to promote technical transfer and adaptation. The process of gap-narrowing and accelerated capital accumulation was concentrated on the period after 1950, both in Japan and in the West European follower countries. As a result they recorded very large increases in labour and total factor productivity at this time. This is often interpreted as an acceleration of technical progress. In fact it was mainly a process of technological catch-up. As long as there is a distinguishable lead country, it is its performance which provides the real clue of the pace of technical progress.

Although it is very difficult to assess the pace of technical progress directly, some rough indication can be derived from the growth accounting for the two successive lead countries (see Table 2-6 below).

The Accumulation of Physical Capital

If there had been no technical progress, the accumulation of physical capital since 1820 would have been relatively modest. Investment would largely have been devoted to replacing worn out machinery and buildings with new and identical replicas, and increasing the stock to accommodate the needs of an expanding work force. The major incentive to accumulate has arisen because new technology brings new products and better ways of producing older products. Figure 2-1 illustrates the huge increases in capital stock which have accompanied capitalist development in the UK, USA and Japan. Table 2-2 also shows the situation in France, Germany and the Netherlands.

Figure 2.1. **Growth of capital stock and GDP since 1820**
(million 1990 Geary-Khamis dollars)

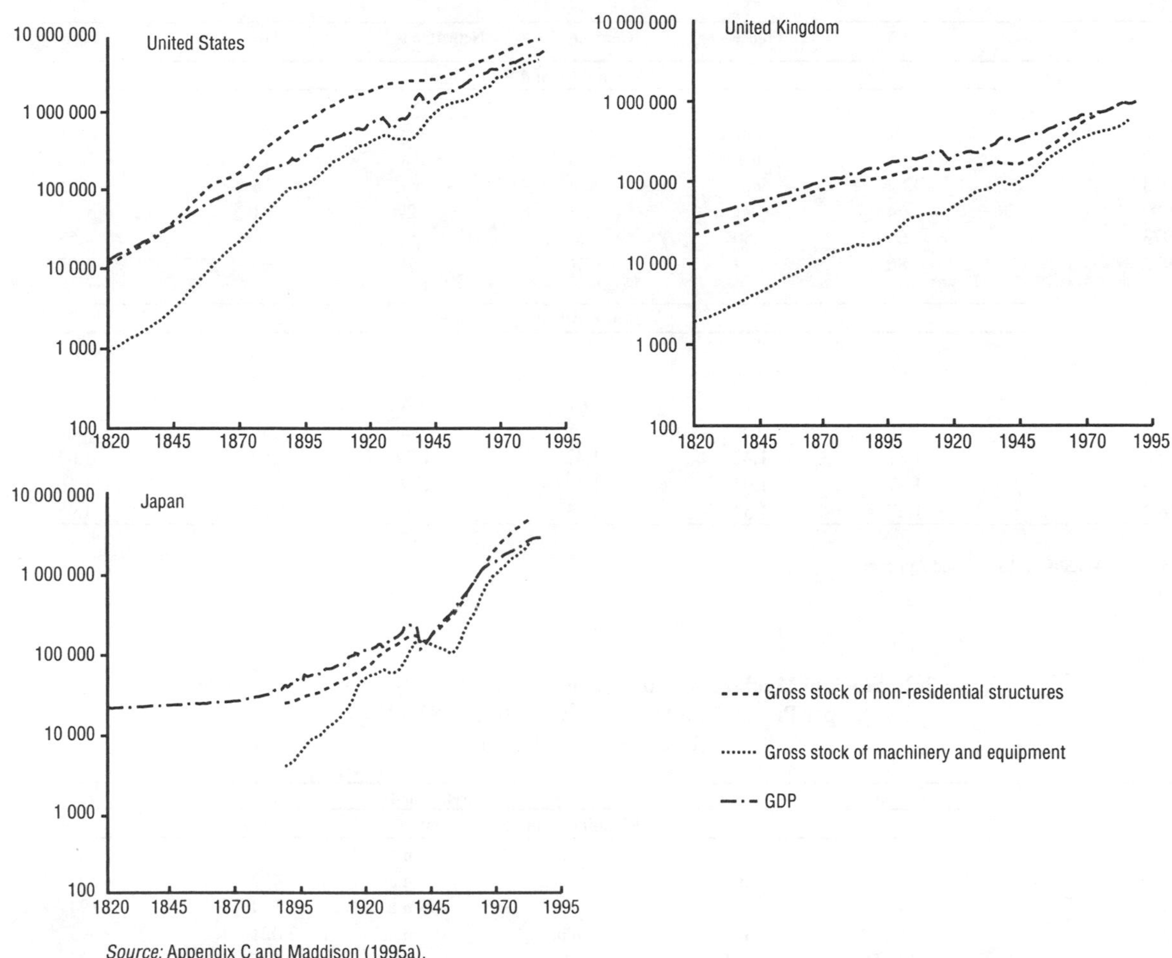

Source: Appendix C and Maddison (1995a).

Estimates of capital stock over the whole period since 1820 are available only for the UK and the USA. It is possible to build up estimates of reasonable quality by the perpetual inventory method, i.e. by cumulating new investment of different kinds, deducting old assets which are scrapped, with standard assumptions on asset lives and adjustment for war damage if necessary. This way one arrives at estimates of gross stock (which I prefer). Net stock can be calculated by deducting depreciation rather than scrapping. For the UK, Feinstein's (1988) investment estimates go back to the eighteenth century. For the USA, investment series start later, so the capital stock estimates for 1820-40 are based on Gallman's (1986) wealth survey material.

Over the period 1820-1992, the US stock of non-residential structures increased nearly 800-fold. A good deal of this was capital "widening", i.e. provision for the needs of a work force that increased 38-fold, but there was also a very substantial capital "deepening". Non-residential structures increased 21-fold per person employed. The increase in the stock of machinery and equipment was much larger. The 1992 stock was about 5,400 times as big as that of 1820; per worker, there was a 141-fold increase. In 1820 machinery was important in only a few parts of the economy, in 1992 it was found in large quantities in factory, field and office. In 1820 only 7 per cent of non-residential capital was machinery and equipment, in 1992, the ratio was 35 per cent.

In the UK, the capital stock grew much more slowly than in the United States. This was mainly because the employment increase was much smaller. Nevertheless, the increase in structures per worker was 15-fold, and in machinery and equipment 97-fold.

Table 2-1. **Ratio of Gross Non-Residential Capital Stock to GDP, 1820-1992**

	USA	France	Germany	Netherlands	UK	Japan
	Machinery and Equipment					
1820	.07	n.a.	n.a.	n.a.	.05	n.a.
1890	.46	n.a.	n.a.	n.a.	.11	.10
1913	.52	n.a.	n.a.	n.a.	.18	.25
1950	.64	.21	.39	.27	.31	.74
1973	.65	.50	.62	.61	.52	.58
1992	.86	.74	.70	.78	.65	1.07
	Non-residential Structures					
1820	.88	n.a.	n.a.	n.a.	.63	n.a.
1890	2.59	n.a.	n.a.	n.a.	.72	.61
1913	2.78	n.a.	n.a.	n.a.	.66	.64
1950	1.81	1.42	1.42	1.79	.50	1.03
1973	1.47	1.05	1.32	1.36	.80	1.16
1992	1.57	1.52	1.63	1.53	1.17	1.95

Source: Maddison (1995a) and Appendix K.

Table 2-2. **Stock of Machinery and Equipment and Non-Residential Structures per Person Employed, Six Countries, 1820-1992**

(1990 international dollars)

	USA	France	Germany	Netherlands	UK	Japan
	Machinery and Equipment					
1820	281	n.a.	n.a.	n.a.	238	n.a.
1870	1 367	n.a.	n.a.	n.a.	857	n.a.
1890	4 115	n.a.	n.a.	n.a.	1 114	194
1913	6 932	n.a.	n.a.	n.a.	2 021	695
1950	15 150	2 325	3 948	3 878	4 699	3 234
1973	26 259	15 778	18 513	20 394	13 893	13 287
1992	39 636	33 930	31 736	30 044	23 095	40 243
	Non-residential Structures					
1820	3 503	n.a.	n.a.	n.a.	2 973	n.a.
1870	10 294	n.a.	n.a.	n.a.	6 254	n.a.
1890	23 270	n.a.	n.a.	n.a.	7 014	1 171
1913	37 905	n.a.	n.a.	n.a.	7 404	1 709
1950	42 673	15 795	14 364	25 686	7 556	4 518
1973	59 461	33 037	39 697	45 393	21 464	26 402
1992	72 625	69 232	70 119	57 918	41 797	73 135

Source: A. Maddison, "Standardised Estimates of Fixed Capital Stock: A Six Country Comparison", in Maddison (1995a), and Appendix J.

For Japan, our estimates of capital stock start only in 1890 when the country had a much lower income level than the USA, and only a tiny fraction of its levels of capital per worker. In the process of catching-up with the USA, the Japanese stock of machinery and equipment per worker increased 207-fold and of non-residential structures 62-fold from 1890 to 1992. By the latter year the Japanese capital stock per worker was bigger than in the USA.

There seems no doubt that high rates of capital accumulation, and high and increasing levels of capital per worker were a necessary condition for the productivity increases achieved in the capitalist epoch.

It is clear from Figure 2-1 that the US accession to productivity leadership involved a much bigger effort of domestic investment and creation of a much higher level of capital per worker than the UK had ever achieved[2]. Since 1950, in the effort to catch up with US productivity levels, European countries, and the dynamic economies of Asia have also had to increase the capital intensity of their economic activity very substantially.

Improvements in "Human Capital"

Another striking feature which has characterised the period since 1820, is the enormous increase in the average level of education. In 1820, the majority of the population in all countries was illiterate. In the advanced capitalist countries universal enrolment in primary education became obligatory in the nineteenth century and the proportion receiving secondary and higher education has risen steadily in the twentieth. The total stock of education in the age group 15-64 is illustrated in Table 2-3, with primary education given a weight of 1, secondary 1.4 and higher education 2, to provide a rough correction for the remuneration which these different levels attract. In Japan and the USA the average person's "human capital" by this yardstick, increased ten-fold from 1820 to 1992. The expansion of education took place for a diversity of reasons, cultural and recreational, as well as economic, but the economic impact has been very substantial. It was first stressed by Schultz (1961), incorporated in Denison's growth accounts in 1962, and been rediscovered more recently by the "new" growth theorists. The increase in educational levels helped to "embody" technical progress, because the content of education changed over time to accommodate to the growing stock of knowledge. There has been a proliferation of specialised intellectual disciplines to facilitate the absorption of knowledge and to promote its development through research.

The education stock is, of course, only a rough measure of changes in human capital. It is better than enrolment ratios which are often used as a crude proxy in the new growth literature, but it should be adjusted for differences of efficiency of education systems in transmitting cognitive skills, and supplemented with information on less formal types of skill acquisition.

Table 2-3. **Years of Education Per Person Aged 15-64, Six Countries, 1820-1992**
(average for both sexes)

	USA	France	Germany	Netherlands	UK	Japan
1820	1.75	n.a.	n.a.	n.a.	2.00	1.50
1870	3.92	n.a.	n.a.	n.a.	4.44	1.50
1913	7.86	6.99	8.37	6.42	8.82	5.36
1950	11.27	9.58	10.40	8.12	10.60	9.11
1973	14.58	11.69	11.55	10.27	11.66	12.09
1992	18.04	15.96	12.17	13.34	14.09	14.87

Source: Appendix K and Maddison, (1991) p. 64, updated. See Table 3-14 below for estimates for nine other countries. Primary education was given a weight of 1, secondary 1.4 and higher 2 in line with evidence on the relative earnings associated with different levels of education in these countries in Psacharopoulos (1975), p. 165.

Interaction Between Economies

The degree of integration of different parts of the world has grown dramatically since 1820 and the increased openness has had an important impact on growth potential. In 1820 exports were only 1 per cent of world product. By 1913, the ratio had risen to 8.7 per cent. By then it was meaningful to speak of an interactive "world" economy, rather than an aggregate of countries, many of which had little knowledge or contact with foreign technology. There was a very bad patch from 1913 to 1950, a period of neomercantilism, when the trade ratio declined, but after 1950, it moved sharply upward. By 1992, it had risen to 13.5 per cent (see Table 2-4).

This growth in international trade has been important in enabling countries to specialise in the types of product at which they are most efficient. It has also eliminated the handicap of countries with limited natural resources. The attractiveness of such international exchange has been greatly facilitated by improvements of technology in transport which have reduced costs and made distance less relevant. Trade has also been important in diffusing new products and new technologies. Its role in this respect has been strengthened by international investment flows which have done even more to diffuse technology and organisational improvements.

The proportionate importance of foreign trade depends on the size of an economy. It is very much bigger in the Netherlands than in the United States, and has enabled the Netherlands to specialise on what it does best and raise its productivity to the same level as the USA. Small countries can therefore get proportionately bigger benefits from international trade than large countries. It is also clear that the opening of economies has been strongly associated with rapid economic growth. This has been the case with the accelerated post-war growth of the most dynamic European and Asian countries, whereas the inward-looking Latin American economies performed much worse.

Table 2-4. **Merchandise Exports as Per Cent of GDP in Sample Countries**
(exports and GDP at 1990 prices)

	1820	1870	1913	1929	1950	1973	1992
France	1.3	4.9	8.2	8.6	7.7	15.4	22.9
Germany	n.a.	9.5	15.6	12.8	6.2	23.8	32.6
Netherlands	n.a.	17.5	17.8	17.2	12.5	41.7	55.3
UK	3.1	12.0	17.7	13.3	11.4	14.0	21.4
Total Western Europe	n.a.	10.0	16.3	13.3	9.4	20.9	29.7
Spain	1.1	3.8	8.1	5.0	1.6	5.0	13.4
USSR/Russia	n.a.	n.a.	2.9	1.6	1.3	3.8	5.1
Australia	n.a.	7.4	12.8	11.2	9.1	11.2	16.9
Canada	n.a.	12.0	12.2	15.8	13.0	19.9	27.2
USA	2.0	2.5	3.7	3.6	3.0	5.0	8.2
Argentina	n.a.	9.4	6.8	6.1	2.4	2.1	4.3
Brazil	n.a.	11.8	9.5	7.1	4.0	2.6	4.7
Mexico	n.a.	3.7	10.8	14.8	3.5	2.2	6.4
Total Latin America	n.a.	9.0	9.5	9.7	6.2	4.6	6.2
China	n.a.	0.7	1.4	1.7	1.9	1.1	2.3
India	n.a.	2.5	4.7	3.7	2.6	2.0	1.7
Indonesia	n.a.	0.9	2.2	3.6	3.3	5.0	7.4
Japan	n.a.	0.2	2.4	3.5	2.3	7.9	12.4
Korea	0.0	0.0	1.0	4.5	1.0	8.2	17.8
Taiwan	-	-	2.5	5.2	2.5	10.2	34.4
Thailand	n.a.	2.1	6.7	6.6	7.0	4.5	11.4
Total Asia	n.a.	1.3	2.6	2.8	2.3	4.4	7.2
World	1.0	5.0	8.7	9.0	7.0	11.2	13.5

Source: Appendices C, E and I. As the export figures refer to the customs territory of the year cited, the GDP denominator refers to the same area and is taken from Appendix H; in the case of Korea in 1913 and 1929 the denominator was adjusted to include the whole country (see country note in Appendix B).

Economies of Scale

There is a very wide range (440:1) in the size of our 56 sample countries, but there is no significant relationship between size and productivity performance. Some small economies like Norway and Ireland have much higher per capita incomes than very large economies like India, China or Russia. Most of the benefits of specialisation and scale can be obtained by small countries through international trade.

The average size of productive establishments in advanced capitalist countries is much smaller than is often imagined. In the private sector of the US economy there are about 6 million establishments, and on average they employ 14 people. Manufacturing has the largest establishments, with an average employment of 51 people in 1990 (down from an average of 66 in 1980). The median US manufacturing establishment is five times as big as the average, but it is no bigger than the median in the Netherlands. Thus there is little evidence that big countries have much of a scale advantage, and again, small countries can get most of the benefits of specialisation between firms through international trade.

However, it does seem likely that in the six decades 1913-73 when US labour and total factor productivity accelerated, economies of scale did play a significant role in augmenting American performance. It also seems likely that, since 1950, West European and some Asian economies benefited similarly when they replicated patterns of consumption in standardised items which the USA had earlier pioneered (see the discussion in Chapter 3 on the acceleration of US total factor productivity after 1913).

Structural Change

Over time, economic growth has brought major changes in the structure of employment and output, in response to changes in demand, technology and international specialisation. These structural changes are illustrated, in terms of employment, for seven countries in Table 2-5.

Structural changes are usually considered to be an important independent source of growth, and politicians often tend to assume that some sectors are more noble or better for growth than others. Thus in the eighteenth century, French economists thought of agriculture as the font of prosperity, and this antiquated idea has still some resonance in the highly protectionist stance of the European Union's policy for this sector. Other analysts, e.g. Kaldor, Mahalanobis, and many contemporary governments who provide industrial subsidies, consider industry to be the noble sector. More recently, governments have targeted parts of the service sector for such favoured treatment, particularly national-flag airlines.

Table 2-5. **Proportion of Employment by Major Economic Sector, 1820-1992**

	USA	France	Germany	Netherlands	UK	Japan	China	Russia
	Agriculture, Forestry and Fisheries							
1820	70.0	n.a.	n.a.	n.a.	37.6	n.a.	n.a.	n.a.
1870	50.0	49.2	49.5	37.0	22.7	70.1	n.a.	n.a.
1913	27.5	41.1	34.6	26.5	11.7	60.1	n.a.	70.0
1950	12.9	28.3	22.2	13.9	5.1	48.3	77.0	46.0
1992	2.8	5.1	3.1	3.9	2.2	6.4	58.6	17.0
	Mining, Manufacturing, Construction & Utilities							
1820	15.0	n.a.	n.a.	n.a.	32.9	n.a.	n.a.	n.a.
1870	24.4	27.8	28.7	29.0	42.3	n.a.	n.a.	n.a.
1913	29.7	32.3	41.1	33.8	44.1	17.5	n.a.	n.a.
1950	33.6	34.9	43.0	40.2	44.9	22.6	7.0	29.0
1992	23.3	28.1	37.8	24.3	26.2	34.6	22.0	36.0
	Services							
1820	15.0	n.a.	n.a.	n.a.	29.5	n.a.	n.a.	n.a.
1870	25.6	23.0	21.8	34.0	35.0	n.a.	n.a.	n.a.
1913	42.8	26.6	24.3	39.7	44.2	22.4	n.a.	n.a.
1950	53.5	36.8	34.8	45.9	50.0	29.1	16.0	25.0
1992	74.0	66.8	59.1	71.8	71.6	59.0	20.0	47.0

Source: Appendix K, Maddison (1991), Bairoch and Associates (1968), OECD, *Labour Force Statistics 1972-92*, Paris, 1994, and national sources.

In the short term, structural shifts can be important for growth. Thus the post-war acceleration of growth in continental Europe and Japan started with large resources of underemployed labour in agriculture, and there were significant possibilities for quickening growth by moving this labour into more productive activity. However, shifts from low- to high-productivity sectors are nearly always accompanied by increases in the physical capital stock; improvements in skill, education, or organisation; or greater openness in international trade. One must therefore be careful to avoid double counting in measuring the impact of structural shifts.

Natural Resources

A factor of production which once figured prominently in economic theory, is natural resources, for which land is the most convenient proxy. There are very large differences between countries in the ratio of natural resources to population. The United States had 48 hectares per head of population in 1820, and 3.7 hectares in 1992, whereas Japan had only 1.2 hectares in 1820 and 0.3 hectares in 1992. The difference in resource endowment made it easier for the USA to grow, and was a handicap for Japan. It also affected the pattern of American and Japanese technology in agriculture (see Hayami and Ruttan, 1985). But in the long run, the inevitable decline in per capita natural resource availability, and the handicap of countries with low resource endowment has been more than made good by advances in technology, and possibilities for international trade. Early pessimists like Malthus and Ricardo were wrong about the role of scarce natural resources as retardant of growth. In spite of the huge increase in world population, and unchanged human biological needs for food, the proportion of employment in agriculture has dropped enormously. In the advanced capitalist countries, agriculture now accounts for less than 5 per cent of employment. In agriculture and mining, technological development and geological prospection have increased the yield from an essentially fixed stock of resources in a way which Malthus would never have thought feasible.

Productivity and Growth Accounts

Over the past sixty years, economists have developed methods for assembling quantitative evidence to measure the impact on growth of labour input and most of the other causal influences mentioned above. These techniques help considerably to illuminate the dynamic forces in capitalist development, though technical progress, the most elusive, is not measured directly, but generally left as a residual.

Table 2-6 sets out successive steps in the effort to "explain" growth in the six advanced countries which are best documented. We are trying to explain differences in intercountry and intertemporal growth rates of GDP. In the first panel of Table 2-6, GDP, like all the other items, is shown in terms of compound growth rates. Appendix B shows in detail how the estimates of GDP were constructed. Appendix C shows how they can be converted into a common numeraire (1990 Geary-Khamis dollars).

The next step is to estimate labour input and labour productivity. Great importance was attached to this measure when it was developed in the USA in the 1930s by the Works Project Administration, the Bureau of Labor Statistics and the National Bureau of Economic Research. At that time, when there was massive unemployment, such measures were needed to analyse what potential the economy might have if unemployment were reduced to more normal levels. Colin Clark (1940) made extensive use of sectoral labour productivity measures in his pioneering comparative study of "economic progress", and Rostas (1948) used them in his pathbreaking comparison of British and American performance levels, which was the most conclusive documentary evidence of the extent of the lead which the USA had developed over the UK. It is still a very useful device for measuring performance, because it is feasible to push the measure further back in time than some of the other items in the accounts. It is clear from Table 2-6 that labour input has grown unevenly over time and between countries. It has been very different from the movement of population. Over the long term, working hours of the average person fell by half; labour input increased less than population; and labour productivity rose a good deal faster than GDP per capita. From 1820 to 1992 Japanese labour productivity rose 46-fold compared with a 28-fold increase in per capita GDP.

The measure of labour input is subject to a significant margin of error the further back one goes in time, and there is still room for improvement in the measurement of working hours in the advanced countries, even for recent years. For lower income countries, measurement of labour input is necessarily rough, partly because of the smaller statistical effort they have been able to mount, and also because it is inherently more difficult to define employment when a large proportion of the population is engaged in activities where the production unit is the family. Appendix J provides estimates of labour input and productivity for 40 of our sample countries. Maddison (1980) provides a more elaborate analysis of the possibilities for refining labour market accounts.

Economists who developed labour productivity measures were aware of the need to use more complex concepts which would take account of capital inputs as well as labour. Early post-war analysts laid great stress on the role of capital in economic growth, though for lack of accurate information, some of them assumed that the capital-output ratio was stable. In the 1950s and early 1960s, others, in lieu of capital measures, used (ICORs) incremental investment output ratios (Maddison 1964, and ECE 1964). The new growth theorists have now reverted to using investment as a proxy for capital stock estimates for the large number of countries for which the latter are not available.

A major breakthrough in capital stock measurement came in 1951, when Raymond Goldsmith pioneered the "perpetual inventory" method in which stock estimates were derived from long-term investment series at constant prices. John Kendrick used such measures in 1961 in a major study of US economic growth from 1869 to 1953 which took account of both capital and labour inputs. In the course of the 1970s and 1980s, several OECD countries developed official capital stock estimates on a perpetual inventory basis, as they had a long enough run of investment data to permit their construction. Academic researchers such as Feinstein and Gallmann pushed these capital stock estimates much further back in time.

The different national capital estimates are similar conceptually but not easily comparable because of substantially different assumptions about asset lives, differences in coverage, and the difficulty of deriving suitable purchasing power parity coefficients to convert them into a common currency. Standardised estimates adjusted to deal with these problems for France, Germany, Japan, the Netherlands, UK and USA

Table 2-6. **Successive Steps in Growth Accounting, 1820-1992**

(annual average compound growth rates)

	USA	France	Germany	Netherlands	UK	Japan
			GDP			
1820-70	4.22	1.27	2.00	1.93	2.04	.31
1870-1913	3.94	1.63	2.81	2.20	1.90	2.34
1913-50	2.84	1.15	1.06	2.43	1.19	2.24
1950-73	3.92	5.02	5.99	4.74	2.96	9.25
1973-92	2.39	2.26	2.30	2.14	1.59	3.76
			Total Hours Worked			
1820-70	3.09	n.a.	n.a.	n.a.	.86	.21
1870-1913	2.02	-.10	.92	.92	.76	.45
1913-50	.35	-.75	.45	1.10	-.46	.40
1950-73	1.15	.01	.00	-.04	-.15	1.44
1973-92	1.27	-.46	-.38	-.07	-.57	.61
			Labour Productivity (GDP per hour worked)			
1820-70	1.10	n.a.	n.a.	n.a.	1.16	.09
1870-1913	1.88	1.74	1.87	1.27	1.13	1.89
1913-50	2.48	1.87	.60	1.31	1.66	1.85
1950-73	2.74	5.11	5.99	4.78	3.12	7.69
1973-92	1.11	2.73	2.69	2.21	2.18	3.13
			Total Non-Residential Capital Stock			
1820-70	5.46	n.a.	n.a.	n.a.	2.61	n.a.
1870-1913	5.53	n.a.	n.a.	n.a.	1.73	3.49[a]
1913-50	2.01	n.a.	n.a.	n.a.	1.09	4.17
1950-73	3.27	4.80	5.93	4.55	5.17	9.18
1973-92	3.13	4.30	3.37	3.07	3.32	6.81
			Capital Productivity (GDP per unit of non-residential capital)			
1820-70	-1.18	n.a.	n.a.	n.a.	-.55	n.a.
1870-1913	-1.51	n.a.	n.a.	n.a.	.16	-.95[a]
1913-50	.81	n.a.	n.a.	n.a.	.10	-1.85
1950-73	.63	.22	.05	.18	-2.10	.06
1973-92	-.72	-1.96	-1.04	-.90	-1.67	-2.85

Table 2-6. (continued) **Successive Steps in Growth Accounting, 1820-1992**
(annual average compound growth rates)

	USA	France	Germany	Netherlands	UK	Japan
			Total Factor Productivity			
1820-70	-.15	n.a.	n.a.	n.a.	.15	n.a.
1870-1913	.33	n.a.	n.a.	n.a.	.31	-.31
1913-50	1.50	n.a.	n.a.	n.a.	.81	.36
1950-73	1.72	3.22	4.05	2.71	1.48	5.08
1973-92	.18	.73	1.54	.77	.69	1.04
			Foreign Trade Effect			
1913-50	.03	.02	-.09	.10	.01	.03
1950-73	.11	.37	.48	1.32	.32	.53
1973-92	.05	.12	.15	.32	.15	.09
			Structural and Labour Hoarding (Dishoarding) Effects			
1913-50	.29	.04	.00	n.a.	-.04	-.15
1950-73	.10	.36	.68	-.07	.10	2.10
1973-92	-.17	.15	.17	-.12	-.09	.09
			Scale Effect			
1913-50	.09	.03	.04	.07	.04	.07
1950-73	.12	.15	.18	.14	.09	.28
1973-92	.07	.07	.07	.06	.05	.11
			Unexplained Residual			
1913-50	1.09	n.a.	n.a.	n.a.	.80	.39
1950-73	1.39	2.34	2.71	1.32	.97	2.17
1973-92	.23	.39	1.15	.51	.58	.75

a) 1890-1913

Source: Panels 1 to 6 from Appendix K for Japan, UK and USA. For France, Germany and the Netherlands, labour inputs and labour productivity from Appendix J, capital inputs from Maddison (1995a). Other elements from Maddison (1995b). Total factor productivity is the ratio of GDP growth to the weighted average of associated inputs (labour, human capital, non-residential gross fixed capital, and land); with weights for all six countries as in Appendix K.

from Maddison (1991 and 1995a) are used in panels 4 and 5 of Table 2-6. These capital stock estimates are also broken down into non-residential structures, and machinery. This is a very pertinent distinction, as the rate of growth of the latter component has been much faster than the former (see Figure 2-1 and Tables 2-1 and 2-2), and technical progress is probably more rapidly embodied in machinery investment than in structures.

From the fourth and fifth panels of Table 2-6 one can readily see that capital input did not move in parallel with output as had often been assumed. Table 2-6 shows that US capital inputs rose much faster than output from 1820 to 1913, and slower in 1913-73. Capital productivity was negative in the first period, and positive in the latter. The US capital-output ratios first rose and then fell (Table 2-1).

Once measures of capital stock were available, the next step was to develop measures of joint factor productivity, i.e. the ratio of output to combined inputs of capital and labour. Jan Tinbergen made the first international comparisons of this kind in 1942 with very rough measures of capital. Kendrick (1961) was a much more sophisticated exercise by sector of the economy.

In 1961 Theodore Schultz suggested that inputs of "human capital" should also be regarded as a factor of production. The main component he had in mind was the increase in the educational levels, but improvements in skill through working with sophisticated equipment, and improvements in health were also relevant. The idea proved attractive and measures of joint factor productivity were soon constructed in which education was treated as part of factor input. In growth accounts, the normal procedure is to treat increases in education as an improvement in labour quality, rather than as an independent factor of production analogous with physical capital. In the sixth panel of Table 2-6, total factor productivity was calculated by relating changes in output to the combined input of quality adjusted labour, non-residential physical capital and land (which is taken as a proxy for natural resources).

A climate propitious for the development of even more ambitious growth accounts was created by the ferment of discussion on US growth performance in the 1950s and early 1960s. This was partly due to the political situation of competitive coexistence in which Nikita Krushchev was threatening to overtake the United States, but the theorists were also encouraged by the likelihood that their ideas could probably be tested empirically. The key writings in this first wave of modern growth theory were by Moses Abramovitz (1956) and Robert Solow (1956, 1960, 1962 and 1963).

Abramovitz produced a brilliant recapitulation of what was then known about the quantifiable causes of US growth. He stressed the degree of ignorance in these matters and put forward the idea of including education and research in the growth accounts. Solow's 1956 article was of major importance and by far the most influential. He broke with the Harrod-Domar models which had dominated the post-war literature, and had included the notion of constant capital-output ratios. He constructed a model with two inputs, labour and the productive services derived from the capital stock. He assumed constant returns to scale, diminishing returns to each input, and exogenous technical progress. In his 1960 and 1962 articles and his 1963 book he stressed the likelihood that a substantial part of technical progress was embodied in successive vintages of the capital stock and he put forward some tentative guesses as to how big this impact might have been. Salter (1960) stressed the same point. Unfortunately this important idea has so far been subject to much less empirical testing than what is generally considered to be his "standard" model.

Edward Denison (1962) adopted the key ideas of Solow (1956) and Schultz (1961) in creating "growth accounts" to explain twentieth-century American economic performance. In 1967 he applied the technique to explain differences in growth rates and levels of achievement in eight West European countries and the USA for 1950-64. In 1976, he incorporated Japan into his sample. Denison used an augmented version of joint factor productivity similar to that in Table 2-6. He adopted the basic neo-classic features one finds in the 1956 Solow model, i.e. the use of income shares as factor weights, and the assumption of exogenous technical progress, but his procedures were eclectic and he also allowed for economies of scale. He rejected Solow's (1960, 1962 and 1963) suggestions for embodying technical progress in successive vintages of the capital stock. He wanted it to be the major item in his final performance measure, the "residual". This, as he acknowledged, was not confined to measuring technical progress but also reflected the effect of unmeasured influences and possible mismeasurement.

In addition to the augmented factor inputs, Denison included other, supplementary, elements of explanation. These included foreign trade effects, the impact of structural change, economies of scale in domestic markets, as well as some other influences like government regulation and crime, changes in capacity use, labour hoarding etc.

Panels 7, 8 and 9 of Table 2-6 show the impact of four major supplementary influences on economic growth. Panel 7 shows the foreign trade effect. I assumed that foreign trade (export plus import) expansion produced 10 per cent economies of scale in 1913-50 and 1973-92 and 20 per cent in 1950-73. This effect is weighted by the share of exports plus imports in GDP in the initial year of the period. The trade effect was biggest in the golden age (1950-73), small or negative in 1913-50, and fairly modest in 1973-92. The reason for giving trade a bigger bonus effect in 1950-73 is that this was a period of massive reduction of tariffs, elimination of most non-agricultural quantitative restrictions on goods and removal of the most important exchange controls. The impact of this liberalisation in improving resource allocation and facilitating transfers of technology was bigger than in 1913-50 when there were increases in tariffs, quantitative restrictions and exchange controls, and in 1973-92 when progress in tariff reduction was (by 1950-73 standards) relatively modest.

Panel 8 shows the combined effect of structural change and labour hoarding (dishoarding). The latter is related to the structural change effect and only applies to Germany and Japan, where the proportion of self-employed people and family workers was higher than in the other economies. The structural effect was measured as the difference between actual output growth in each of three sectors (agriculture, industry and services) and the change in output which would have occurred if the structure of employment had not changed (whilst assuming the labour productivity growth within each of the three sectors had remained as actually experienced). The impact of this augmented structural effect is significant in size and there can be substantial changes in direction. These economies now have the bulk of their activity in services where productivity grows most slowly, and the average level of service productivity is now lower than in industry. Thus there is now a significant structural drag in some economies, whereas in the golden age, when growth was very vigorous, structural change had a large positive impact by propelling labour rapidly into more productive employment. The changes between different phases were most marked in the case of Japan.

Panel 9 shows the impact of economies of scale at the national level. These are not included in strict neo-classic analysis like that of Jorgenson, but Denison always included a significant scale bonus as national economies increased in size. I have always assumed a smaller scale bonus than Denison, equivalent to 3 per cent of the GDP change, and I think it is likely to have been less important than analogous gains arising from the increased openness of the economies via foreign trade.

The tenth panel shows the residual in the growth accounts, i.e. the unexplained residue after taking account of total factor productivity and the supplementary influences on growth. I have not been able to measure the supplementary influences and the residual for the whole period covered by the accounts, but the difference between the residual and total factor productivity is likely to have been far more important in the golden age than in earlier periods.

In this growth accounting exercise, no attempt is made to measure the effect of technical progress directly. The residual in the lead country can provisionally be taken as a measure of technical progress. For the follower countries, the residual was bigger than in the USA from 1950 to 1992, and smaller in 1913-50. For the followers, the residual includes the impact of technological catch-up (or falling behind) as well as technical progress.

Denison presented the derivation of his estimates transparently, so that readers could reproduce or modify them in case of disagreement. He also was careful to point out possible errors, and to distinguish harder evidence from softer conjectures. The accounting approach is a very flexible device for organising evidence on causal influences affecting the growth process. It is possible to modify the accounts by changing the weights of different items, by adding new items or dropping old ones. I have myself used a Denisonian framework with very substantial modifications, dropping his assumption that work intensity increases as hours decline, using a different concept of output, bigger weights for capital and foreign trade effects, lower weights for domestic economies of scale, and embodying part of technical progress in successive vintages of capital[3]. The growth accounting approach can also be used to test the findings of econometricians who use the regression approach to causal analysis. They experiment with new ideas about what is important in the growth process, and may come up with exciting results. Often the most exciting ones come from simple regressions. If some elements are left out, those which remain may take over a large part of their "explanatory" power, because of the close interactions of most elements in the growth process. It is then useful to cross-check the explanatory items discovered by econometricians in the stodgier but more transparent framework of growth accounts. When a new or more heavily weighted item is added to the accounts, one may find that growth is overexplained, and then there is reason to rework the regression.

There have now been a large number of studies in the growth accounting tradition. I covered 34 countries in various studies for the post-war period (Maddison 1970, 1972, 1989; Maddison and Associates, 1992). For six of the advanced capitalist countries I have made more ambitious and systematic attempts to improve the quality of the measures and push the analysis further back in time (Maddison 1987, 1991, 1995b and Appendix K of the present volume). Kendrick (1976 and 1994) has developed very ambitious estimates to measure the "total" stock of capital in the United States, adding the stock of R and D to that of physical capital, human capital, and inventories. He has also made several successive attempts to provide international comparisons of growth accounts for the business sector of the economy using the OECD's database. Abramovitz has played a very creative role as a consumer, interpreter, and critical commentator on international growth accounts. He and Paul David have atoned for the non-publication of their splendid 1965 manuscript by publishing a large number of articles over the past 30 years interpreting the causal factors in US growth. There have been individual country studies in the growth accounting tradition for Brazil, Canada, France, India, Japan, Korea, Mexico, the UK and the USA, as well as regional comparisons for different parts of the world[4].

Parallel with the growth accounting literature there was a steady flow of articles after 1966 by Dale Jorgenson and his associates. These were mainly on the US economy but also covered several other advanced capitalist countries. Jorgenson's approach was more rigorously neo-classic than Denison's in excluding economies of scale. He defined output and capital somewhat differently, included intermediate inputs in the analysis, concentrated on the private sector of the economy and disaggregated in much finer detail by branch and sector. He was more ambitious in trying to squeeze the residual in the growth accounts to zero, whereas Denison was willing to live with the fact that his growth accounts left a substantial part of growth unexplained. There was a useful interaction between the two approaches in 1969-72 with three articles by Jorgenson and Griliches, and two lengthy comments by Denison, which led Jorgenson and Griliches to concede that they had exaggerated their initial degree of explanation. The great virtue of Jorgenson's approach is that it helps to identify the locus of technical progress by showing in detail how productivity has changed in different sectors and branches of the economy.

After a hiatus of almost 25 years, there was a revival of interest by economic theorists and econometricians in the characteristics and causes of economic growth in the late 1980s. To some extent this new interest was stirred by the availability of new comparative evidence of growth rates and levels in advanced capitalist countries in Maddison (1982 and 1991) and the comprehensive data set on income levels, growth rates and associated information for 130 countries for 1960 onwards in the Penn World Tables (PWT) of Summers and Heston (1988 and 1991).

The three seminal articles in this new wave were Baumol (1986), Romer (1986) and Lucas (1988). Baumol was concerned more with the characteristics of long-term growth experience than with causes. He focused on convergence in productivity and per capita income levels. For sixteen advanced capitalist countries, he concentrated on movements between two points; the initial year 1870 and the end year 1979. He suggested that post-war convergence within this group was a reinforcement of an earlier tendency which had existed since 1870. In support of this view he cited Abramovitz (1986) who had shown a long-term reduction in the coefficients of variation of labour productivity levels within the 16 country sample at successive benchmarks from 1870 to 1979. Baumol concluded that the sixteen countries formed a convergence club, and found further evidence (in Summers and Heston) of post-war intraregional convergence in centrally planned economies and middle income countries.

Baumol's emphasis on convergence and his use of the Summers Heston database to test hypotheses by regression had a very powerful influence on the research agenda of the new growth literature.

There were two weaknesses in Baumol's analysis:

a) his sample was limited mainly to high income countries and biased in favour of the convergence hypothesis. The new growth theorists seized on this weakness and tried to remedy it by maximalist coverage. In the Summers-Heston database they had access to information for 130 countries and could test the hypothesis on a global basis. These data were available for only 25 of the 172 years we have covered, but it was sufficient for them to conclude that Baumol's convergence thesis applied only to a limited group of countries.

b) The second problem with Baumol's analysis was that by concentrating on convergence he fudged the leader-follower dichotomy and obscured a very important aspect of the historical performance of nations. There was in fact a big difference between comparative growth performance before and after 1950. From 1870 to 1950, 13 of the advanced capitalist countries which Baumol examined were falling behind US productivity levels, whereas 15 of them were catching up on the USA after 1950 (see Tables 2-7, 2-8 and Figure 2-2). This phenomenon of falling behind and then catching up can also be seen for GDP per capita for a longer period and a wider range of countries in Table 1-4 and Figure 1-2. The contrast between this long-run feature and the post-war situation has not been sufficiently recognised in the new growth literature, and hence it tends to exaggerate the generality of findings which are valid only for a truncated time period.

Romer and Lucas were more interested than Baumol in theoretical issues and in modifying the analysis of growth causality which Solow had developed in his 1956 article. Romer stressed the interrelation between technical progress and the growth of physical capital, Lucas gave greater stress to the interaction of technical progress and human capital. Solow's (1956) approach implied that diminishing returns would set in if investment were pushed hard, whereas Romer stressed the likelihood of spillovers or externalities which would produce constant or increasing returns. Thus he spoke of growth being "unbounded". He did not test his hypothesis, but illustrated its plausibility by citing long-term evidence of accelerating labour productivity growth from the nineteenth century to the 1970s (from Maddison 1982). He did not consider evidence of the long-run relation between capital stock and output growth, and he might have felt less sure of the empirical support for his position if he had been able to see the evidence of Table 2-6. This shows a sharp fall in labour productivity, capital productivity and total factor productivity after 1973.

Romer was interested in developing an approach which would explain why all countries had not converged to the same level of income. In doing this he did not pay much attention to interaction between countries. For him technical progress and economic growth are mainly endogenous processes, without much possibility for follower countries to borrow from the technological leader. He did not acknowledge the specificity of the nation-state as the basic unit of analysis, and assimilated the problem of explaining differential country performance to that of explaining the behaviour of individuals or firms within a single economy. It is quite plausible that technical progress has been to a large degree endogenous in the Romer sense for the United States, but this is unlikely to have been the general situation. Large and fairly

Figure 2.2. **Labour Productivity (GDP per hour) levels, 1820-1992**

a. 1990 Geary-Khamis dollars

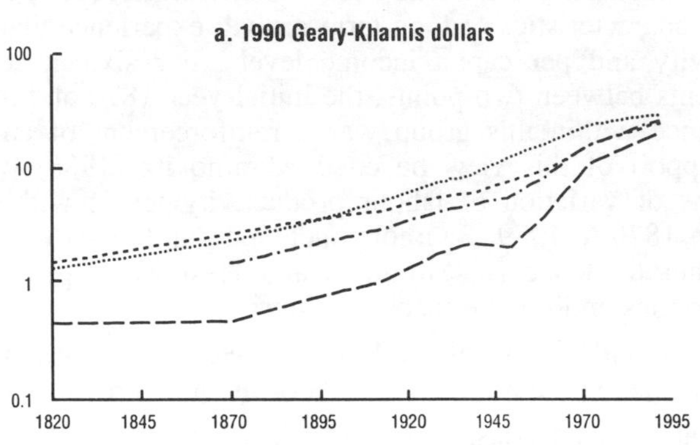

b. United States = 100

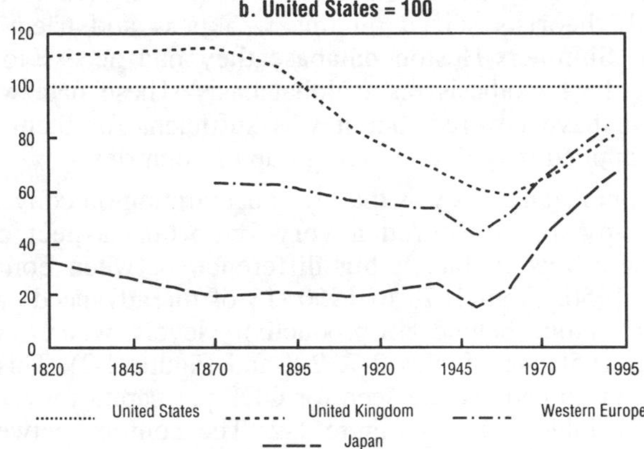

United States United Kingdom Western Europe Japan

Source: Appendix J, "Western Europe" in these two figures excludes the United Kingdom.

advanced follower countries like France, Germany, the UK or Japan have had elements of endogeneity in their technological development, but for the rest of the world technological progress is likely to have been exogenous.

Lucas (1988) was interested in modifying what he considered to be the "standard neoclassical" model in a way which would give better explanations of why the income levels of different nations had not converged. He did this by adding human capital which he assumed to interact with technical progress and to produce spillovers or externalities. He talks of the "Solow-Denison framework" in referring to the "standard neoclassical" model, but Denison had already augmented the Solow (1956) model back in 1961, and Lucas was not an innovator in adding human capital. However, he attached greater importance to human capital as an engine of growth, and his linkage between human capital and technical progress was not present in the growth accounting approach. The new growth theorists who have followed Lucas in incorporating human capital have treated it differently from growth accountants who treat education as an augmentation of labour quality, using relative earnings of people with a given level of education as weights. Disciples of Lucas treat human capital as a separate factor of production analogous to physical capital. Using this approach one might expect them to use costs of education at different levels as weights, rather than earnings. In fact they generally use school enrolment rates as crude proxy measures for human capital.

Table 2-7(a). **Labour Productivity Level (GDP per Hour Worked) in Advanced Capitalist Countries, 1870-1992**

(US level = 100)

	1870	1913	1929	1938	1950	1973	1992
Austria	62	57	44	39	32	65	83
Belgium	94	70	64	61	48	70	98
Denmark	67	66	68	61	46	68	75
Finland	37	35	34	36	32	57	70
France	60	56	55	62	45	76	102
Germany	70	68	58	56	35	71	95[a]
Italy	46	41	38	44	34	66	85
Netherlands	103	78	84	72	51	81	99
Norway	48	43	45	50	43	60	88
Sweden	54	50	44	49	56	77	79
Switzerland	77	63	72	68	69	78	87
UK	115	86	74	69	62	68	82
Arith. Average	69	59	57	56	46	70	87
Australia	147	103	86	83	69	72	78
Canada	71	82	69	61	77	81	87
USA	100	100	100	100	100	100	100
Japan	20	20	24	25	16	48	69

a Figure refers to West Germany; including East Germany it would be 85.

Source: Table J-4.

Table 2-7(b). **Labour Productivity Level (GDP Per Hour Worked) in Medium and Low Income Countries, 1950-92**

(US level = 100)

	1950	1973	1992		1950	1973	1992
Greece	20	46	59[a]	Argentina	49	47	41
Ireland	30	43	71[a]	Brazil	19	24	23
Portugal	20	42	48	Chile	37	38	37
Spain	21	46	69	Colombia	22	25	27
				Mexico	24	33	29
Arith. Average	23	44	62	Peru	23	27	15
				Venezuela	71	82	58
Czechoslovakia	29	34	28				
Hungary	21	28	25	Arith. Average	35	39	33
Poland	19	24	21				
USSR	24	28	19	Bangladesh	6	3	4
				China	7	6	10
Arith. Average	23	29	23	India	5	4	5
				Indonesia	8	8	12
				Pakistan	6	6	9
				Philippines	11	11	10
				South Korea	10	14	29
				Taiwan	9	18	38
				Thailand	6	7	15
				Arith. Average	8	9	15

a) 1991.

Source: Table J-4.

Table 2-8. **Falling Behind and Catching-up: Rates of Divergence from or Convergence Towards the US Labour Productivity Level (GDP Per Hour Worked), 1870-1992**

(annual average compound growth rates)

	1870-1950	1950-73	1973-92
Austria	-0.81	3.12	1.30
Belgium	-0.84	1.70	1.76
Denmark	-0.46	1.69	0.52
Finland	-0.20	2.62	1.09
France	-0.37	2.33	1.57
Germany	-0.88	3.18	1.53
Italy	-0.37	2.98	1.27
Netherlands	-0.87	2.01	1.05
Norway	-0.15	1.48	2.04
Sweden	0.04	1.39	0.17
Switzerland	-0.14	0.52	0.59
UK	-0.77	0.39	1.03
Arithmetic Average	-0.49	1.96	1.16
Australia	-0.95	0.21	0.39
Canada	0.10	0.23	0.35
Japan	-0.30	4.84	1.96
Greece		3.60	1.29[a]
Ireland		1.56	2.87[a]
Portugal		3.20	0.73
Spain		3.60	2.16
Arithmetic Average		2.99	1.76
Czechoslovakia		0.68	-1.06
Hungary		1.12	-0.49
Poland		1.03	-0.78
USSR		0.64	-1.92
Arithmetic Average		0.87	-1.06
Argentina		-0.19	-0.70
Brazil		1.02	-0.25
Chile		0.14	-0.20
Colombia		0.56	0.35
Mexico		1.25	-0.62
Peru		0.69	-2.87
Venezuela		0.63	-1.87
Arithmetic Average		0.59	-0.88
Bangladesh		-2.33	0.77
China		-0.65	2.88
India		-0.59	1.46
Indonesia		-0.11	2.00
Pakistan		0.08	1.77
Philippines		0.00	-0.56
South Korea		1.33	4.04
Taiwan		2.84	4.13
Thailand		0.94	3.90
Arithmetic Average		0.17	2.27

a) 1973-91.

Source: Derived from Table J-5.

Romer and Lucas were mainly concerned with theoretical issues, but there have been a great many attempts to test their ideas and Baumol's hypothesis by applying econometric techniques to the database of Summers and Heston. It is worth considering three influential contributions to this literature.

Barro (1991) reached rather circumspect conclusions in applying the new approaches to the evidence of the Summers and Heston material. He found human capital to be an important contributor to growth, but his regression analysis left a good deal of the weak performance of sub-Saharan Africa and Latin America unexplained. He and Sala-i-Martin (1992) found convergence of levels of income between US states for the period since 1840, and suggested that the convergence implications of the augmented Solow model were likely to be fulfilled when the institutional, political and policy setting of countries was similar. This they characterised as "conditional" convergence.

Mankiw, Romer and Weil (1992) considered that the new growth theory had been too cavalier in dismissing the Solow (1956) model. They augmented it to include human capital and tested it with the Summers and Heston material. They used it selectively, dropping oil-producing countries from their first sample of 98 countries, then using a 75-country sample from which they had dropped countries where the data were shaky or idiosyncratic. Finally they concentrated on 22 OECD countries for which they did find convergence. They concluded that their augmented Solow model was robust if one allowed for the institutional and policy differences between countries, which prevent convergence from occurring.

The new growth theory has been useful in re-emphasising a number of fundamental issues concerning the interrelation of technical progress, economies of scale and formation of physical and human capital. The distinction between the "conditional" convergence of countries where the institutional policy mix is similar and repudiation of the idea of "unconditional" convergence (on a global scale) is useful and is one way of bringing attention to the interaction of "proximate" and "ultimate" causal influences. It is a fundamental point which has been strongly emphasised by Abramovitz (1989) and it is central to North's (1990) attempt to develop a broader view of growth causality.

The concern of the new growth school to build models where greater explanatory power is allocated to technical progress is a topic of fundamental importance, touched upon by many other analysts, and not tackled very seriously by the growth accountants. Non-neoclassic authors like Kaldor (1957) or Maurice Scott (1989) have also stressed the strength of the link between investment and technical progress. The evolutionary school (Verspagen 1992 and Fagerberg 1994) has hopes of finding better explanations of technical progress by improvement and closer scrutiny of R and D statistics.

In my view, the most promising route towards better explanations of technical progress is to develop and test the ideas of Solow (1960, 1962 and 1963) and Salter (1960) who emphasised the impact of technical progress in raising the quality of successive vintages of capital. With the perpetual inventory technique it is relatively easy to see the age-structure of the capital stock, and, as better capital estimates become available for more countries, longer periods, and disaggregated by type of asset and industry, these relationships can be explored more seriously. Such work would reinforce the analysis already done by Jorgenson and his associates in locating the parts of the economy where progress in labour and total factor productivity has been most rapid. If countries could be persuaded to provide the type of census information on interfirm spreads of productivity performance which have in the past been available for the USA, our depth of vision would be significantly improved (see Klotz, Madoo and Hansen, 1980).

The new wave has succeeded in reviving causal analysis of economic growth as a central field of concern in economic theory. It has also done a great service in globalising the perspectives of empirical research. It is clearly useful to improve the quality of the database, and to extend it much further back in time. The present study is intended to facilitate this by assessing the quality of the information we already have, and enlarging the intertemporal and interspatial field of vision.

The Institutional Context

Thus far we have discussed proximate elements of growth causality which are more or less measurable and can be embedded in a growth accounting framework or fitted into an econometric model. It is not too difficult to deploy this evidence to explain why the West European countries which are institutionally similar to the USA were able to mount such a successful catch-up effort in the past half century, or indeed, to explain why Japan, after a deep institutional transformation around 1867 was able to catch-up with the West. The real puzzle is not so much the success of the West, but the backwardness of the rest.

If we are to explain why the economic growth experience of nations has been so diverse, and why income spreads are now so wide, it is necessary to go beyond proximate and measurable elements of causality and consider institutional, social or policy influences which may retard or encourage economic development. Economic "backwardness" is a topic which has concerned economic historians for decades. Gerschenkron (1962) drew attention to this problem and correctly stressed the need for historical perspective, but his spatial perspective was concentrated on European countries. North and Thomas (1973), North (1981 and 1990) and Abramovitz (1986) are other influential analysts who stress the importance of institutions or differential social capability, but they also deal with a limited range of backwardness, i.e. varieties of European experience.

As the variety of country situations is so varied, it is difficult to reach general conclusions about the influence of deeper layers of causality. For this we really need individual country studies. However, I do have some tentative judgements about the way institutional situations have helped condition the performance of the seven different groups of nations, and it is worth making them explicit.

West European Countries

The West European countries already had high levels of income by world standards in 1820, and historical evidence suggests that they gradually pulled ahead of the rest of the world from 1500 to the beginning of the nineteenth century. In this protocapitalist period their growth was much slower than it has been since, because technical progress then moved at a slower pace. Nevertheless their socio-institutional development prepared them to exploit the possibilities for faster growth and rapid technical progress which emerged in the nineteenth century. Thus the West European group provided leadership in productivity and technology for several centuries. Northern Italy and Flanders played this role from 1400 to 1600, the Netherlands from then until the end of the eighteenth century, and the UK in the nineteenth.

The main characteristics of Western Europe which have favoured its development are as follows:

The most fundamental was the recognition of human capacity to transform the forces of nature through rational investigation and experiment. Thanks to the Renaissance and the Enlightenment, Western elites gradually abandoned superstition, magic, and submission to religious authority. The Western scientific tradition that underlies the modern approach to technical change and innovation had clearly emerged by the seventeenth century and began to impregnate the educational system. Circumscribed horizons were abandoned, and the quest for change and improvement was unleashed.

The ending of feudal constraints on the free purchase and sale of property was followed by a whole series of developments which gave scope for successful entrepreneurship. Nondiscretionary legal systems protected property rights. The development of accountancy helped further in making contracts enforceable. State fiscal levies became more predictable and less arbitrary. The growth of trustworthy financial institutions and instruments provided access to credit and insurance, which made it easier to assess risk and to organise business rationally on a large scale over a wide area. Techniques of organisation, management and labour discipline were also improved.

A third distinctive feature of Western Europe was the emergence of a system of nation-states in close propinquity, which had significant trading relations and relatively easy intellectual interchange in spite of their linguistic and cultural differences. This stimulated competition and innovation. Migration to or refuge in a different culture and environment were options open to adventurous minds; printing and universities added to the ease of interchange.

The Western family system was different from that in other parts of the world. It involved controls over fertility and limited obligations to more distant kin. This reinforced the possibilities for accumulation. It also had a lasting impact on their demography. Their population growth was much more modest than the subsequent experience of Africa, Asia and Latin America.

Since 1820, the institutional arrangements of Western Europe have not stood still. The degree of democratic participation and the socioeconomic role of government have changed a good deal in ways that have generally been positive for growth. The welfare state has made capitalist property relations and the operation of market forces more legitimate by removing most of the grievances which motivated proponents of a socialist alternative.

In the post-war period, interrelations between these countries have involved articulate co-operation and some rudiments of a managed international order. This, too, has been favourable to economic growth.

Western Offshoots

The four Western Offshoots (Australia, Canada, New Zealand and the USA) inherited and adapted institutional arrangements, societal habits and language from the most economically advanced of the Western European nations, and they sloughed off some badges of status and inherited privilege which enhanced the modernity of their capitalist institutions. This modernity was most marked in the USA, whose institutions were created in a revolutionary break from the old world which was inspired partly by ideas of the French enlightenment. However, the United States condoned slavery as an institution for nearly the first century of its history, which slowed its growth and marred the quality of life. It also had fragile financial institutions which plunged it into economic collapse in the 1930s. The circumstances of the Western Offshoots differed importantly from those of Western Europe. They had huge natural resources and were distant from European wars. Their population grew much faster than in Western Europe through higher fertility and large-scale immigration. Over the long run, Canada's propinquity to the USA helped to give it the most rapid per capita growth of the group. Remoteness from the most dynamic parts of the world economy was a significant handicap for Australia and New Zealand who were the worst performers in the group.

"Southern" Europe

This is a miscellany of medium income countries whose institutional heritage has been different from Western Europe but they have been closely integrated with the West since 1948 as members of OEEC, OECD and the European Union. Most of them benefited from US Marshall Plan aid and latterly from very substantial EU transfers. Large parts of Greece were still part of the Ottoman Empire until 1913, and many of the most dynamic Greek entrepreneurs have operated in the diaspora rather than within the country itself. Ireland was in effect a British colony until 1920 and domestic conditions were depressing enough to create massive emigration. Spain and Portugal were once the most important colonial powers of Europe. Their brand of conquest imperialism brought substantial fiscal tribute from colonies, but led to irresponsible domestic fiscal policy and sapped the vigour of the forces for growth. They were less influenced than Western Europe by the Renaissance and Enlightenment, the content of their education system was adversely affected by clerical power, and large sections of the population were illiterate for much longer than in Western Europe. Turkish institutions were clearly very different from Western Europe's in the nineteenth century, but the Kemalist reforms of the 1920s were very significant and intended to assimilate it to European norms. However, Turkey is clearly the outlier in terms of demography and income level, and it might well have been included in the Asian group.

Eastern Europe

The institutional background of these seven countries is quite varied. What gives them homogeneity is not geography but the fact that they switched from capitalist institutions to those of a dirigiste command economy for a substantial period. Tsarist Russia's economic, social and political institutions were different from those in the West, and the country was further differentiated from 1917 onwards by the advent of communism. Czechoslovakia and Hungary were fairly prosperous members of the Habsburg Empire until 1918, and were more advanced than Poland, most of which was a Russian colony until 1918, or than Bulgaria, Romania and Yugoslavia which were parts of the Ottoman Empire for a good part of the nineteenth century.

Table 2-9. **Inequality of Pre-Tax Income of Households, 19 Countries**

(top decile per capita income as a multiple of that in bottom two deciles)

France (1970)	14.4	Argentina (1961)	11.2
Germany (1973)	10.5	Brazil (1970)	20.0
Netherlands (1967)	10.5	Chile (1968)	21.2
Sweden (1972)	8.1	Colombia (1974)	21.8
UK (1973)	9.1	Mexico (1969)	25.5
		Venezuela (1962)	25.0
Australia (1966-7)	7.2	India (1964-5)	12.4
Canada (1969)	12.6	Japan (1969)	7.5
USA (1972)	14.9	Korea (1970)	7.6
		South Africa (1965)	41.5
		Tanzania (1968)	16.4

Sources: Sawyer (1976) p. 14 for OECD countries; Lecaillon, Paukert, Morrisson and Germidis (1984), pp. 26-7 for other countries. Figures for South Africa refer to individual and not household income.

Latin America

Although most of Latin America became politically independent in the 1820s, and like North America has very large natural resources, it is very different in its institutional background. In the Western Offshoots, the indigenous populations were marginalised; in Latin America they were assimilated, but became an underclass. Peonage and slavery led to very wide disparities in income, wealth, education and economic opportunity (see Table 2-9). There has been continuing neglect of popular education, heavy-handed regulatory tendencies in government, a long history of debt default and fiscal irresponsibility. The last characteristic has led to chronic inflation, and long-standing political instability. These characteristics were important in keeping Latin American growth and levels of income well below those in North America [see Maddison 1992 for an analysis of twentieth century constraints on performance in Brazil and Mexico, and Maddison (1995a) for a much longer-term assessment of Mexico's institutional heritage].

Asia

The Asian countries were the biggest part of the world economy in 1820 with 69 per cent of world population and 57 per cent of world GDP. By 1992, they had regained a good deal of their old predominance, with 58 per cent of world population and 37 per cent of world GDP. In 1820 they were a rather homogeneous group in terms of per capita income, but by 1992 they had the widest intra-regional income spread: 27:1 between Japan and Bangladesh. This is huge compared with the spreads within the five regions previously discussed and one must therefore be circumspect in generalising about Asian characteristics, though their extreme heterogeneity is a phenomenon that developed only after 1950.

Three countries — China, India and Japan — accounted for 84 per cent of Asian population and 82 per cent of GDP in 1820. It is useful to examine their institutional characteristics in some detail to see in what way they might have hindered economic growth.

By Western standards, the most comprehensible case is Japan[5]. When challenged by the West, it reformed its institutions drastically, did what was necessary to promote growth, and eventually caught up. The other two countries were held back by indigenous institutions or attitudes, and not helped by their experience of Western colonialism.

Traditional Japan was very isolated. Travel and study abroad were prohibited. Japanese were not permitted to build ships with a carrying capacity above 75 tons. The only trade contact was with the Dutch, whose East India Company had established a small depot in Nagasaki to which they could send a ship once a year from Indonesia.

In 1853, the American navy forced a gunboat entry to Tokyo bay and extorted extraterritorial, legal and commercial privileges. These concessions were extended to France, the Netherlands, Russia and the

UK. The treaties restricted Japanese commercial and fiscal autonomy, opened the economy to foreign trade, and required tariffs to be no more than 5 per cent. This experience was not too different from that of China in the 1840s, but the intrusion was more sudden, and the Japanese reaction was very different.

In China, the foreigners appeared on the fringes of a huge country. The ruling elite regarded it as the locus of civilisation, and considered the "barbarian" intruders as an irritating nuisance. In Japan, they struck in the biggest city, humiliated the Shogun and destroyed his legitimacy as a ruler. The Japanese had already borrowed important elements of Chinese civilisation and saw no shame in copying a Western model which had demonstrated its superior technology so dramatically.

In 1867, the Tokugawa shogunate was overthrown, and the new Meiji regime carried out sweeping reforms. These provided Japan with an up-to-date version of Western capitalist institutions. The Emperor became the head of a centralised state with 46 prefectures. These replaced the previous territorial division between 270 feudal lords (the *daimyo*). Legal inequalities were abolished, and old distinctions in the dress and rights of *samurai* (the military), peasants, artisans and merchants disappeared. People obtained freedom to choose their trade or occupation, free of guild restrictions, and could produce any crop or commodity. Land could be bought and sold freely. Feudal property rights and rice stipends of the *daimyo* and *samurai* were commuted into state pensions and government bonds. State taxes replaced old feudal levies in kind, and their incidence was equalised throughout the realm. Primary education became compulsory. New textbooks were written with a Western content. Large numbers of studens were sent abroad for technical and higher education. A national monetary and banking system was created. Agricultural research and industrial development were promoted by government. The armed forces were reorganised and rearmed on Western lines.

The government set out on a programme of economic development and military aggrandizement which had no parallel in other Asian countries. The old Tokugawa society had operated with an unusually large elite group — a fossil emperor and his court in Kyoto, the Shogun and his government in Edo, 270 *daimyo* in their castle towns, and 420 000 *samurai*. Together with their households these people had been nearly 6 per cent of the population (about three times the proportion of the Chinese elite). There was an economic "surplus" which was redirected to more productive uses as these people were transformed into a modernising military-bureaucratic and business elite.

Finally, one must note that Japanese reproductive and family planning habits were such that demographic expansion was very modest by Asian standards.

The Chinese experience is more enigmatic[6]. 2000 years ago, its level of economic performance was probably similar to that of the Roman Empire, and above European levels from around 500 to 1400 AD. But Chinese per capita income stagnated from 1400 to 1950 whilst the West forged ahead. For a century after the 1840s China was a quasi-colony of the West, ceding extra-territorial rights in treaty ports to 20 foreign countries, its customs revenue controlled by foreigners, surrendering territory to French, British and Japanese colonialists.

Several aspects of Chinese society and culture make this increasing economic backwardness difficult to explain. The mainstream Chinese religion, Confucianism, was concerned with pragmatic prescriptions for behaviour in this world, rather than with problems of immortality, the soul, the after-life, or God. China tackled the challenges of nature with an engineering approach. A third of the cultivated land was irrigated. Famines were mitigated by a public granary system. In Moghul India, the proportion of irrigated land was one-tenth of that in China, and the incidence of famine depended on vagaries of the monsoon.

In the last (Ch'ing) dynasty, China had remarkably modern property relations. There was no serfdom, about 30 per cent of farmers were tenants paying rent in money or kind, and the rest were small peasant proprietors, with a low proportion of landless labourers. Moneylenders were active and land changed hands freely. Commercial activity was not subject to usury restrictions and merchants could move freely. Paper money existed from the early ninth century and merchants could use bills of exchange for payments.

China showed precocity in major inventions compared to the West. Water mills, efficient harnesses for horses, paper and porcelain were in use in the Han dynasty (200 BC to 200 AD), i.e. 1 000 to 1 500 years before they arrived in the West. Printing, the crossbow, iron, gunpowder and paper money were introduced during the Tang dynasty (600-900 AD), and the abacus in the Sung dynasty (1000-1271 AD). Chinese farming was more like horticulture than agriculture, with advanced techniques of irrigation, drainage, double cropping, seed selection, transplanting and use of manuals of best practice. New crops like maize and potatoes were imported from the new world. From 1400 to 1950, by increasingly intensive use of land and labour, it managed to support a seven-fold increase in population with no noticeable fall in living standards.

All of these characteristics suggest that China should have been able to develop its technology and productivity as fast as the West. It is not clear what prevented this from happening, but it seems likely that Chinese success in forging the world's biggest and most enduring political unit may have been incompatible with successful capitalist development. Two important characteristics which made for continuity and consolidated the central power may have been inimical to economic progress.

China had a non-phonetic ideographic script, which was intelligible to people who spoke very different regional variants of Chinese. This had a tremendous consolidating power in facilitating centralised control over a vast area. It was attractive to foreign invaders who saw it as a ready-made vehicle to enforce their rule. In the process of using the language, these barbarians assimilated Chinese cultural values. Mastery of written Chinese gave the literati and the bureaucracy a sophisticated and cultivated world view, but learning the 40 000 characters was a long and exhausting process which strengthened Chinese ethnocentrism, encouraged self-satisfaction, and inhibited intellectual deviance or curiosity. The difficulty of the language was a barrier to widespread literacy compared with Japan, which supplemented a much smaller number of characters with alphabetic scripts. The content of Chinese education was concentrated on calligraphy, ancient classics and conventional wisdom. It acted as an instrument of thought control, serving to inhibit unorthodox thinking and to preserve political stability. The Chinese were pragmatic inventors but did not develop the scientific approach which emerged in the West.

Another important Chinese characteristic was the strength and continuity of the bureaucracy, which emerged about 200 BC as an instrument of central power, an alternative to the previous elite of hereditary feudal lords. It was used in all later dynasties, even by the Yuan (Mongol) and Ch'ing (Manchu) who were initially warlords. Throughout most of subsequent Chinese history, military expenditure was modest by European, Indian or Japanese standards, because the bureaucracy was a more effective instrument of imperial control.

Bureaucrats achieved their status by passing competitive written examinations which tested their knowledge of Chinese classics. They were, in principle, a meritocracy, but the cost of prolonged education was a social barrier, and about a third of the licentiates obtained degree status by purchase rather than examination.

The bureaucracy was responsible for tax collection, policing, maintenance of order and arbitration of disputes. Confucian tradition and strong family discipline encouraged obedience to their decisions. These were not challengeable by lawyers, and often involved collective punishments for crimes and misdemeanours. Bureaucrats had large discretionary powers, and their judgement was influenced by the fact that their salaries were low. They augmented them by bribes and by siphoning off part of the tax revenue.

The top bureaucratic levels were closely enmeshed with the "gentry" class. The latter were usually landlords with rental incomes. They had legal privileges, were generally exempted from tax burdens, and like the bureaucracy, were differentiated from the masses by sartorial and other marks of distinction and deference. The context of the gentry's education was similar to that of the bureaucracy.

The bureaucracy supplied control functions which might otherwise have been provided by an aristocracy, priesthood or military. Their influence in promoting orthodox thinking and social stability helped keep the country together, but discouraged economic and social change.

Indian institutional arrangements were more complex and exploitative than those of China and Japan, and their inhibiting impact on economic development seems much clearer[7].

There were three main layers in the traditional Indian society when the British started to take over in the eighteenth century. The top fifth of the population were Muslims. Hindu village society was about 70 per cent of the population, and pagan tribal groups about a tenth.

The Moghul emperor's main instrument of social control was the warlord aristocracy. Its members provided military and administrative services and in return had a claim (*jagir*) on revenue from a given part of the village sector. Nobles were rotated from one *jagir* to another, and these estates were liable to royal forfeit on death. The *jagirdar* had an incentive to squeeze village society to minimal levels of subsistence, to spend as much as possible on consumption and to die in debt to the state. There was no motive to improve landed property. This elite, their families and those who provided for their needs were Muslims and mainly urban dwellers. There was also a smaller Hindu elite of nobles and princes who had thrown in their lot with the Moghuls. They had hereditary rights to village tax revenue in the areas they controlled.

Village society was ethnically and linguistically heterogeneous, but kept docile and exploitable by the sanctions of a hierarchical caste system. This segregated the rural population into mutually exclusive groups whose economic and social functions were rigidly hereditary. The requirements of ritual purity prevented social mobility and intermarriage, dictated food habits, and prevented most imaginable forms of social homogenisation.

The hereditary division of labour prevented people from raising their productivity by changing their economic activity. There was no allowance for aptitude, intelligence or new ideas in allocating jobs and little possibility of firing someone for inefficiency. At the top of village society were brahmins, and at the bottom were untouchables. In between the caste hierarchy varied in different parts of the country. In each village the dominant caste controlled the land, though their property rights were circumscribed. In general, land could not be transferred or sold to people outside the village, and tenants of the dominant caste could not be evicted. Artisan families within the village did not sell their products for money but had a hereditary patron-client relationship to a group of cultivating families who paid in kind.

Another characteristic of Indian society was the joint family system. All generations of the family lived together and pooled their income with little distinction between brothers or cousins. Women were completely subordinate to men, adult men were expected to do what their fathers told them.

These village arrangements were the base of economic life for more than 2 000 years. Villages were defensive self-contained units designed for survival in periods of war and alien domination. They paid taxes to whoever held state power, and were relatively indifferent to the passage of foreign invaders and rulers. Conquerors of India found a ready-made source of income, so they had no incentive to destroy the system. Instead they installed themselves as a new and separate caste. This was the choice of the Muslim conquerors and later of the British. Newcomers were not absorbed into a homogeneous culture as in China. They simply added another layer to a complex system of social segregation.

In addition to village society, India had a large number of tribal communities. Aboriginal tribes led an independent pagan existence as hunters and forest dwellers, completely outside Hindu society and paying no taxes to the Moghuls. In the Moghul period they probably accounted for 10 per cent of the population.

The top layer of this traditional structure was transformed by British rule, and the Muslims were the big losers. The warlord aristocracy was replaced by a new military-bureaucratic elite. The greater efficiency of government permitted a substantial reduction in the fiscal burden. The tax squeeze on village society was reduced. The incomes of the dominant castes in rural society were increased. Property rights became better defined in the village sector, to the detriment of the traditional rights of tenants and labourers. The British built 56 000 kilometres of railways, and irrigation was extended eight-fold during their rule. Consumption patterns changed to the detriment of urban artisans and village weavers. Some of the new elite's income and savings was siphoned out of India as remittances to the UK. There was little growth in per capita income during British rule, the caste system was not modified, the top official jobs were occupied by foreigners, the *de facto* privileges of British commercial interests were detrimental to Indian entrepreneurship. When the British left, 88 per cent of the population were illiterate.

Africa

In 1820, North Africa was part of the Ottoman Empire; Spain had toeholds in Morocco; Portugal in Angola and Mozambique; and the British had just taken over the Dutch settlement at the Cape. The rest of the continent was unknown and unexplored, occupied by hunter-gatherers, pastoralists or practitioners of subsistence agriculture. Levels of technology were primitive. The only territorial units which resembled those of today were Egypt, Ethiopia and Morocco. Slaves were the main export. Fifteen million of them left Africa between 1450 and 1870.

The European powers became seriously interested in grabbing Africa in the 1880s. France and Britain were the most successful. Twenty-two countries eventually emerged from French colonisation, twenty-one from British, five from Portuguese, three from Belgian, two from Spanish. Germany lost its colonies after the First World War, Italy after the Second.

The rush for Africa was a safety valve for European political rivalries. Territorial conquest was relatively cheap. None of the indigenous peoples (except Ethiopia) managed to repel European firepower for very long, and the risky face-offs between European powers were settled without serious conflict. The only cases where colonisation was motivated primarily by economic considerations were the Belgian Congo and Rhodesia, where Leopold II and Cecil Rhodes established personal fiefs.

The new rulers created boundaries to suit their mutual convenience, with little regard to local traditions or ethnicity. English, French and Portuguese became the official linguistic vehicles. Some notions of European law and property rights were introduced but colonists got the best land and African incomes were kept low by forced labour or apartheid practices. In economic and social matters the approach was generally minimalist. Little was done to build a transport infrastructure or to cater for popular education.

The postwar situation in Western Europe was one of rapid economic growth. It was clear that possession of colonies was not a means to economic prosperity, and all the European colonies were abandoned. The British colonial bond was broken in Egypt in 1956, in Ghana in 1957, Nigeria in 1960, Tanzania in 1961, and Kenya in 1963. White settler interests retarded the process in Zimbabwe and Namibia, and in South Africa the indigenous population did not get political rights until 1994. French decolonisation started with Morocco in 1956 and was more or less completed with the exodus from Algeria in 1962. Belgium abandoned Zaire in 1960. Portugal and Spain made their exit in 1975. In these years the cold war was at its height, and the continent again became the focus of international rivalry. China, the USSR, Cuba and East European countries supplied economic and military aid to countries viewed as proxies in a world wide conflict of interest. Western countries were strongly influenced by this competitive situation. They were less fastidious in allocating aid than they might otherwise have been. As a result Africa accumulated large foreign debts which had a meagre developmental pay-off.

Independence brought many serious challenges. One was the newness of the nation states. Their political leadership had to create elements of national solidarity and stability from scratch. Thirteen of the francophone countries had belonged to two large federations whose administrative and transport network had been centred on Dakar and Brazzaville. These networks had to be revamped. Zaire started independence with a civil war, Nigeria had one seven years later and Ethiopia suffered even more from this problem under its military dictatorship. In several cases, the new political elites sought to achieve political stability and reinforce their legitimacy by creating one-party states with the incumbent president keeping this position for life. This generally made matters worse by facilitating corruption and greatly reducing pressures to change mistaken policy. In some cases, this form of despotism was fairly enlightened, in others, well intentioned utopians led their countries into disastrous experiments, and in a few, venal and repressive rulers produced even worse results.

There was a great scarcity of people with education or administrative experience. Suddenly, these countries had to create a political elite, staff a national bureaucracy, establish a judiciary, create a police force and armed forces, send out dozens of diplomats, find school teachers and build up health services. The first big wave of job opportunities strengthened the role of patronage and rent-seeking, and reduced the attractions of entrepreneurship. The existing stock of graduates was too thin to meet the new demands and there was heavy dependence on foreign personnel.

Many countries overburdened their weak state apparatus with new economic tasks. "Planning" was *à la mode*. It was encouraged by many foreign advisers and appealed to the social engineering aspirations of some of the new leaders. The late colonial practice of rigging prices and exchange rates was reinforced rather than weakened. Dependence on foreign aid was taken to be axiomatic.

In fact, African countries achieved quite respectable rates of GDP growth, but their welfare impact was eaten away by explosive population increases. Demographic expansion was faster than in other regions, and shows little sign of deceleration (see Table A-2). African governments were slow to recognise the need for birth control and many aid donors were reluctant to help in this field.

* * *

In this chapter we first surveyed the "proximate" and measurable causes of growth. In this domain it is rather clear what the driving forces of successful capitalist development have been, but over the long haul, proximate analysis does not explain why the communist experiment failed, why Latin American performance has been worse than North American, why the ancient civilisations of Asia were so tardy in exploiting possibilities for growth, or why Africa is stuck at the income level that Western Europe had in 1820. We have offered some provisional explanations at the "institutional" level, but they are less precise and more difficult to test than proximate explanations. It is also difficult to generalise or prescribe, as "institutional" barriers vary a good deal between different countries and regions.

Another level at which one can attempt to explain differences in performance is to look at the impact of alternative economic policies. It is difficult to draw a fine line between institutions and policy, but it is true that countries with very different income levels, social structure and "institutional" constraints can contemplate a similar range of domestic fiscal or monetary policy options, different degrees of openness of their economy, and different kinds of incentive to foreign investors. The conventional wisdom about the effectiveness of policy options has varied over the long period we cover, and the "international economic order" has taken different configurations which have constrained or reinforced domestic policy options. These policy developments are covered in the next chapter on phases of capitalist development.

Notes

1. In defining productivity leadership, I have ignored the special case of Australia, whose impressive achievements in the nineteenth century were due largely to its natural resource advantages rather than to its technical achievements and stock of man-made capital.
2. There seems to be a widely held view that the United States had a lower capital intensity than the UK in the nineteenth century. This flatly contradicts the evidence of my standardised estimates. Field (1983) has been influential in spreading the erroneous perception. He asserts that the US ratio of tangible assets (excluding land) to output was one third of that of the UK in the mid-nineteenth century. He compares an early (1952) Goldsmith estimate of the net stock of US tangible assets in 1850 derived from survey data, with the gross stock of wealth in Great Britain in 1860 (at 1851-60) prices, which Feinstein derived by the perpetual inventory method using very long asset lives. Field adds an unexplained 400 million pounds to Feinstein's estimate and converts it into dollars by the exchange rate. This shaky assemblage was later described by James and Skinner (1985) as "strong historical evidence". Broadberry (1993) seems to have been convinced by Field. Engerman (in Gallman and Wallis 1992) also suggests that "the United States had a considerably lower capital-output ratio than did Great Britain (and the rest of the world) in the nineteenth century". He cites Goldsmith's balance sheets (including land, tangible and financial assets held at home and abroad) as evidence. However, Goldsmith valued British land at 60 times the US price.
3. See Maddison (1972) for a detailed review of Denison's methodology, and a confrontation of his results for nine countries with mine, using alternative assumptions within the same analytical framework. Maddison (1987) is a survey of the growth accounting literature, and presents my own detailed growth accounts for six advanced capitalist countries for 1913-84.
4. See Denison (1993) for a survey of most of this literature.
5. See Maddison (1969) for a discussion of Japan's Tokugawa background and the Meiji reaction to the West.
6. There are several major studies of China which are relevant to the topics I raise. Perkins (1969) analyses China's quantitative economic performance from 1368 to 1968; Elvin (1973) deals with China's early technical precocity and its failure to keep pace with the West after 1400; Chang (1962) deals with the bureaucracy and gentry and their sources of income; Weber (1964) deals with Chinese religion and its socio-economic impact.
7. See Maddison (1971) and Lal (1988) for an extensive analysis of India's institutional heritage.

Chapter 3

Phases of Development

Economic growth has not been steady since 1820. There have been five distinctive "phases": 1820-70; 1870-1913; 1913-50; 1950-73; and 1973-92 (1973-94 for regions where data availability permits). These were recognisable segments of the growth process, whose momentum differed from those which preceded and followed. The chronology of the five phases serves as an organising framework for summarising most of the quantitative evidence in our tables.

Phases are identified, in the first instance, by inductive analysis and iterative inspection of empirically measurable characteristics. Each must have a different and distinctive momentum, in dimensions which are analytically significant; these changes must extend to a substantial majority of countries under examination, and be sustained longer than a business cycle. They are not conceived as an analytical sequence of progressively interrelated "stages" such as one finds with Rostow, nor are they derived from a theoretical model of business cycle rhythm or Kondratieff-style long waves — which is one reason why their length is uneven[1].

Successive phases have not been initiated by collective planning decisions, innovative ideas, or changes in the ideology of domestic and international economic policy. Transitions from one phase to another have usually been determined by some kind of historical accident or system shock. However, the need to devise policies appropriate for new circumstances, or to suit the needs of new political elites (as in postcolonial Asia), has meant that each new phase has tended to be characterised by new "establishment" views about the efficacy of different kinds of policy instruments. These policy views (and the institutions in which they were incorporated) have had at least as much influence on performance as the autonomous play of market forces, or the atomised decision processes of individual economic agents. Thus performance in different phases has not had an ineluctable quality of the kind assumed in Schumpeterian long-wave analysis, but is the outcome of processes which may underexploit growth potential or push it to its limits.

Phase I (1820-70)

Our analysis begins with the nineteenth century, because it is clear that there was a very sharp increase in growth momentum compared with the eighteenth and earlier centuries. Any year in the period 1789-1815 would be an unsuitable starting point because these were years of revolution, war and economic blockade which affected the whole of Europe. There were strong repercussions in the Americas, and some echo of these events in Asia. 1820 was chosen as the initial point because it seemed likely that recovery from wartime disturbances was likely to have been more or less complete by then, though there is not really sufficient evidence to test this.

1870 was chosen as a terminal point for Phase 1, mainly because inspection of the quantitative evidence suggests very strongly that growth accelerated in all parts of the world economy thereafter. There were also important political changes around 1870 — the abandonment of the slave economy in the USA and the emergence of Italy and Germany as modern nation-states.

It is clear from Table 3-1 that per capita GDP growth was slower in 1820-70 in all seven major regions of the world economy than in 1870-1913. Most of the 1820-70 expansion occurred in Europe and its offshoots. In the "Western Offshoots" GDP grew faster in this period than in any other. They had the most rapid demographic expansion as well as the most rapid per capita growth.

Between 1820 and 1870, 63 per cent of the growth in world output took place in Europe. Belgium, Germany, the Netherlands and the UK did best but significant upward movement appears to have been a universal characteristic. The evidence falsifies the earlier view that there was a sequence of staggered "take-offs" in Western Europe in the nineteenth century. The propinquity of these countries, their substantial trade with each other, the ease of intellectual and entrepreneurial interaction, and institutional similarities ensured transmission of technical progress.

Table 3-1. **Phases of Growth by Major Region, 1820-1992**

(annual average compound growth rate)

	1820-70	1870-1913	1913-50	1950-73	1973-92	1820-1992
			GDP			
Western Europe	1.7	2.1	1.4	4.7	2.2	2.2
Western Offshoots	4.3	3.9	2.8	4.0	2.4	3.6
Southern Europe	1.0	1.5	1.3	6.3	3.1	2.1
Eastern Europe	1.6	2.4	1.6	4.7	- 0.4	2.0
Latin America	1.5	3.3	3.4	5.3	2.8	3.0
Asia[a]	0.2	1.1	1.0	6.0	5.1	1.9
Africa	0.4	1.1	3.0	4.4	2.8	1.9
World	1.0	2.1	1.9	4.9	3.0	2.2
			Population			
Western Europe	0.7	0.7	0.5	0.8	0.3	0.6
Western Offshoots	2.8	2.1	1.2	1.5	1.0	1.9
Southern Europe	0.3	0.4	0.9	1.4	1.4	0.8
Eastern Europe	0.9	1.3	0.4	1.2	0.7	0.9
Latin America	1.3	1.8	1.9	2.7	2.3	1.8
Asia[a]	0.1	0.6	0.9	2.1	1.9	0.9
Africa	0.3	0.7	1.9	2.4	2.9	1.3
World	0.3	0.8	0.9	1.9	1.8	1.0
			GDP per Capita			
Western Europe	1.0	1.3	0.9	3.9	1.8	1.5
Western Offshoots	1.4	1.8	1.6	2.4	1.4	1.7
Southern Europe	0.6	1.1	0.4	4.9	1.7	1.4
Eastern Europe	0.7	1.0	1.2	3.5	- 1.1	1.1
Latin America	0.2	1.5	1.5	2.5	0.5	1.1
Asia[a]	0.1	0.6	0.1	3.8	3.2	1.0
Africa	0.1	0.4	1.0	2.0	- 0.1	0.6
World	0.6	1.3	0.9	2.9	1.2	1.2

a) includes Oceania.

Source: Derived from Appendix G.

Outside Europe and the Western Offshoots, per capita income growth was meagre. Asia and Africa showed only exiguous progress. Demographic momentum was substantial in Latin America, but per capita growth was slow. Most of Brazil was still a relatively backward slave economy, Mexico was plagued by political instability (71 rulers and 200 ministers of finance between 1821 and 1876) and two foreign invasions. Argentina's main economic activity was sheep rearing and wool exporting; government efforts to open the country to settlement were concentrated on wars to exterminate the Indian population; by 1870 there were only 732 kilometres of railway lines.

The technological leader in this period was the UK. British productivity growth was slower than that of the USA when the latter became the world leader, but Britain did a great deal to diffuse the fruits of technical change by its policy of free trade. It absorbed about a quarter of world imports. They were mainly food and raw materials, its exports mainly manufactured goods. It was the largest provider of trade-related services such as shipping, short-term trade finance and insurance. Its growth performance was favoured by increased efficiency of resource allocation. By 1870, its farm sector employed less than a quarter of its working population. Its joint factor productivity growth was better than that of the US economy, and GNP rose faster than GDP because of increased earnings from foreign investment.

By 1870, commercial policy had become very liberal throughout the world compared to the eighteenth century when use of foreign shipping was tightly restricted, colonial produce had to be brought to the ports of the metropole before re-export, and internal trade was subject to numerous transit levies. As a result of such restrictions, a substantial fraction of world trade was done by smugglers. During the Napoleonic wars these restrictions were worsened by economic blockade.

In 1820-70, these mercantilist barriers were largely eliminated. The UK removed all tariff barriers and trade restrictions between 1846 and 1860. Free trade policy was enforced in British colonies, and in quasi-colonies such as China, Thailand and Turkey. In Germany, the customs union (Zollverein) of 1834 ended barriers between the German states and the external Zollverein tariff was lowered after 1850. In 1860 the Cobden-Chevalier Treaty removed French quantitative restrictions and reduced tariff barriers to a modest level. This was followed by French commercial treaties with Belgium, the Zollverein, Italy, Switzerland, Spain and other countries. These treaties had most-favoured-nation clauses which meant that bilateral liberalisation applied equally to all countries.

The progress of transport technology, railways, steamships and the construction of the Suez Canal also contributed to reducing costs and increasing the benefits of trade[2].

As a result of these changes, foreign trade rose four times as fast as world output in this period. This led to economies of specialisation of the type which Adam Smith and Ricardo had emphasised as sources of economic progress. There was technical progress, but this was slower than in later phases, judging by the slow pace at which total factor productivity increased in the UK, and the actual decline in total factor productivity in the USA (see Chapter 2).

Phase II (1870-1913)

This was a relatively peaceful and prosperous era which was brought to an end by the outbreak of the First World War.

We can see from Tables 3-1 and 3-2 that per capita growth accelerated in all regions and in most countries. Population growth also quickened outside Western Europe and its offshoots, so that world GDP increased more than twice as fast as in 1820-70. The acceleration was greatest in Latin America (particularly in Argentina and Mexico), in Asia (particularly Japan), and Africa (where Ghana and South Africa did best). For the world as a whole, the per capita GDP growth record of this period was second only to that in the golden age (1950-73).

It was an era of improved communications and substantial factor mobility. There was a massive flow of foreign capital, particularly from the UK which directed about half its savings abroad. French and German investment were also very substantial, and there were significant flows from the USA and other countries. Table 3-3 shows the amount of capital invested abroad in 1914 and its distribution by investors and recipient region. British foreign assets were equivalent to one and a half times its GDP, French assets about fifteen percent more than GDP, German assets about 40 per cent, and US assets 10 per cent[3]. A good deal of this foreign investment went into railway construction. Table 3-4 shows the increase in length of railway lines for 36 countries from 1870 to 1913. The total rose from 191 thousand kilometres in 1870 to nearly a million in 1913, and undoubtedly played a significant role in the acceleration of economic growth in this era[4].

From 1870 to 1913 there was large-scale international migration with an outflow of 17.5 million people from Europe to the Western Offshoots. A large number of Chinese and Indians moved to Burma, Ceylon, Malaya, Indonesia, Singapore and Thailand.

International trade continued to grow faster than output, but its role as an engine of growth was less spectacular than in 1820-70. There was some increase in tariff levels. Germany adopted a more protectionist tariff in 1879 which provoked French retaliation in 1881 and 1892. France also applied a system of imperial preference within its colonial empire. Most highly protected were the Latin American countries, Russia and the USA.

Colonialism was at its apogee in 1913, by which time the European countries had parcelled out Africa. The USA, Japan and Russia had joined them in colonising and staking out spheres of influence in Asia.

Table 3-2. **Phases of Per Capita Real GDP Growth in the 56 Sample Countries, 1820-1992**

(annual average compound growth rates)

	1820-70	1870-1913	1913-50	1950-73	1973-92
12 West European Countries					
Austria	0.7	1.5	0.2	4.9	2.2
Belgium	1.4	1.0	0.7	3.5	1.9
Denmark	0.9	1.6	1.6	3.1	1.6
Finland	0.8	1.4	1.9	4.3	1.6
France	0.8	1.5	1.1	4.0	1.7
Germany	1.1	1.6	0.3	5.0	2.1
Italy	0.6	1.3	0.8	5.0	2.4
Netherlands	1.1	0.9	1.1	3.4	1.4
Norway	0.5	1.3	2.1	3.2	2.9
Sweden	0.7	1.5	2.1	3.1	1.2
Switzerland	n.a.	1.5	2.1	3.1	0.8
UK	1.2	1.0	0.8	2.5	1.4
Arithmetic Average	0.9	1.3	1.2	3.8	1.8
4 Western Offshoots					
Australia	1.8	0.9	0.7	2.4	1.4
Canada	1.2	2.2	1.4	2.9	1.5
New Zealand	n.a.	1.2	1.3	1.7	0.5
USA	1.3	1.8	1.6	2.4	1.4
Arithmetic Average	1.4	1.5	1.3	2.4	1.2
5 South European Countries					
Greece	n.a.	n.a.	0.5	6.2	1.5
Ireland	1.2	1.0	0.7	3.1	2.7
Portugal	n.a.	0.5	1.2	5.7	2.1
Spain	0.5	1.2	0.2	5.8	1.9
Turkey	n.a.	n.a.	0.8	3.3	2.6
Arithmetic Average	n.a.	0.9	0.7	4.8	2.2
7 East European Countries					
Bulgaria	n.a.	n.a.	0.3	5.2	- 1.4
Czechoslovakia	0.6	1.4	1.4	3.1	- 0.1
Hungary	n.a.	1.2	0.5	3.6	0.0
Poland	n.a.	n.a.	n.a.	3.4	- 0.6
Romania	n.a.	n.a.	n.a.	4.8	- 1.6
USSR	0.6	0.9	1.8	3.4	- 1.4
Yugoslavia	n.a.	n.a.	1.0	4.4	- 0.5
Arithmetic Average	n.a.	1.2	1.0	4.0	- 0.8

Table 3-2 (continued). **Phases of Per Capita Real GDP Growth in the 56 Sample Countries, 1820-1992**

(annual average compound growth rates)

	1820-70	1870-1913	1913-50	1950-73	1973-92
7 Latin American Countries					
Argentina	n.a.	2.5	0.7	2.1	-0.2
Brazil	0.2	0.3	1.9	3.8	0.9
Chile	n.a.	n.a.	1.0	1.2	1.9
Colombia	n.a.	n.a.	1.4	2.3	1.9
Mexico	-0.1	1.7	1.0	3.1	1.1
Peru	n.a.	n.a.	2.1	2.5	-1.7
Venezuela	n.a.	n.a.	5.3	1.6	-0.8
Arithmetic Average	n.a.	1.5	1.9	2.4	0.4
11 Asian Countries					
Bangladesh	n.a.	n.a.	-0.3	-0.6	2.2
Burma	n.a.	n.a.	-1.3	1.8	1.3
China	0.0	0.6	-0.3	2.9	5.2
India	0.1	0.4	-0.3	1.6	2.4
Indonesia	0.1	0.8	-0.1	2.5	3.1
Japan	0.1	1.4	0.9	8.0	3.0
Pakistan	n.a.	n.a.	-0.3	1.8	2.7
Philippines	n.a.	n.a.	-0.2	1.8	0.7
South Korea	n.a.	n.a.	-0.2	5.2	6.9
Taiwan	n.a.	n.a.	0.4	6.2	6.2
Thailand	n.a.	0.4	0.0	3.2	5.3
Arithmetic Average	0.1	0.7	0.2	3.1	3.5
10 African Countries					
Côte d'Ivoire	n.a.	n.a.	n.a.	3.1	-2.2
Egypt	n.a.	n.a.	0.0	2.7	3.8
Ethiopia	n.a.	n.a.	n.a.	1.7	-1.7
Ghana	n.a.	n.a.	1.7	0.2	-1.2
Kenya	n.a.	n.a.	n.a.	1.9	0.6
Morocco	n.a.	n.a.	n.a.	0.1	1.8
Nigeria	n.a.	n.a.	n.a.	3.2	0.1
South Africa	n.a.	n.a.	1.2	2.4	-0.6
Tanzania	n.a.	n.a.	n.a.	1.9	-0.5
Zaire	n.a.	n.a.	n.a.	0.8	-3.9
Arithmetic Average	n.a.	n.a.	1.0	1.8	-0.4

Source: Derived from Appendix D.

Table 3-3. **Gross Nominal Value of Capital Invested Abroad in 1914**

($ million at current exchange rates)

	Western Europe	Western Offshoots	Southern Europe	Eastern Europe	Latin America	Asia	Africa	Total
UK	263	8 254	248	618	3 682	2 873	2 373	18 311
France	1 255	386	1 332	2 663	1 158	830	1 023	8 647
Germany	1 310	1 000	835	834	905	238	476	5 598
USA	674	900	3	29	1 649	246	13	3 514
Belgium, Netherlands and Switzerland	990	535	837	1 350	796	413	579	5 500
Japan, Russia, Portugal & Sweden	100	100	0	100	200	1 500	200	2 200
Total	4 592	11 175	3 255	5 594	8 390	6 100	4 664	43 770

Source: UK, France and Germany from Feis (1965), pp. 23, 51 and 74. USA from Lewis (1938) pp. 606 and 654-5. Other countries from UN (1949) p. 2. This source gives a total of $5.5 billion for Belgium, the Netherlands and Switzerland with no breakdown. I assumed that the distribution of these countries` investment was the same as that of France and Germany combined. The UN gives a figure of $2.2 billion for Japan, Portugal, Russia and Sweden combined. My allocation of the investments of these 4 countries is based on rough guesses of their geographic interests, and reference to the breakdown in 1938.

Table 3-4. **Length of Railway Lines in Service, 1870-1950**
(kilometres)

	1870	1913	1950		1870	1913	1950
Belgium	2 897	4 676	4 046	Argentina	732	33 478	42 864
Denmark	770	3 868	4 815	Brazil	745	24 614	36 681
Finland	483	3 560	4 726	Chile	732	8 070	8 503
France	15 544	40 770	41 300	Colombia	0	1 061	3 526
Germany	18 876	63 378	36 924	Mexico	349	20 447[a]	23 332
Italy	6 429	18 873	21 550	Peru	669	3 276	3 097
Netherlands	1 419	3 305	3 204	Venezuela	13	858	997
Norway	359	3 085	4 469				
Sweden	1 727	14 377	16 516	China	0	9 854	22 238
Switzerland	1 421	4 832	5 152	India	7 678	55 822	54 845
UK	21 500	32 623	31 352	Indonesia	80	4 967	6 616[b]
				Japan	0	10 570	27 401
Australia	1 529	31 453	44 579	Thailand	0	956	1 796
Canada	4 211	47 160	69 167				
USA	85 170	401 977	360 137	Côte d'Ivoire	0	316	834
				Egypt	1 184	4 358	5 625
Portugal	714	2 958	3 590	Ethiopia	0	311	784
Spain	5 295	15 088	18 098	Ghana	0	337	862
Turkey	180	5 438	7 671	Kenya	0	855	4 917
				Morocco	0	427	1 695
Russia/USSR	10 731	70 156	116 900	Nigeria	0	1 506	3 063
				South Africa	0	14 149	20 175
				Tanzania	0	1 435	2 147[c]
				Zaire	0	1 507	4 764

a) 1912; b) 1951; c) 1947
Source: Mitchell (1982, 1983 and 1992).

Colonies received some benefits from world expansion, but a substantial part was siphoned off to the metropolitan powers.

The British Empire, which was run on a free trade basis, had substantial hangovers from mercantilism. In Asian colonies, British shipping, banking and insurance interests enjoyed a *de facto* monopoly. Administration was efficient and free of corruption, but it was by white men, living in white cantonments, with British clubs, so there was an automatic *de facto* discrimination against local enterprise, which was reinforced by neglect of education amongst the native population, and some direct discrimination in government purchasing policies. In Indonesia, the Dutch system of royal monopoly in trade, forced deliveries and forced labour was abolished in 1870, but metropolitan interests were very strong and the profitability of empire was greater than in the British case.

Japan and the USA were colonial latecomers. Both created their own trade zones with commercial preferences. They pushed public investment and infrastructure development in Taiwan, Korea and the Philippines much more forcefully than other colonial powers did in the lands they controlled.

China and Thailand were not colonies, but their sovereignty had been limited in tariff matters and by extraterritorial rights ceded to foreigners. As a result, both countries were very reluctant to borrow to finance development.

The only country which provides some sort of test of what might have happened in Asia if power had been vested in a westernising national bourgeoisie is Japan, which achieved faster growth that the other Asian countries by colossal investment in education, by westernising its institutions, and by government activism in fostering industry. But the growth performance of Japan was not spectacular in this period, because a good deal of its energy and resources went into military modernisation and imperial conquest.

With limited exceptions in Germany and Japan, this was not a period when governments felt the need of activist policies to promote growth. They assumed that the free operation of market forces in conditions of monetary and financial stability would automatically lead to something like an optimal allocation of resources. Low taxes and free labour markets were felt to be the best stimulus to investment. Domestic policy was generally inspired by principles of fiscal responsibility and sound money. Taxes and

Table 3.5. **Total Government Expenditure as a Percentage of GDP at Current Prices, 1880-1992**

	1880	1913	1938	1950	1973	1992
France	11.2	8.9	23.2	27.6	38.8	51.0[d]
Germany	10.0[a]	17.7	42.4	30.4	42.0	46.1[d]
Japan	9.0[b]	14.2	30.3	19.8	22.9	33.5
Netherlands	n.a.	8.2[c]	21.7	26.8	45.5	54.1
UK	9.9	13.3	28.8	34.2	41.5	51.2
USA	n.a.	8.0	19.8	21.4	31.1	38.5
Average	10.0	11.7	27.7	26.7	37.0	45.7

a) 1881; b) 1885; c) 1910; d) 1990.
Source: Maddison (1984 and 1991) to 1973; 1992 from OECD *National Accounts, 1980-1992*, Paris, 1994.

government expenditure were low and generally in balance; spending was mainly confined to provision for domestic order and national defence. Social spending was small, generally covering only elementary education and preventive health measures, though Bismarck began to provide pensions and welfare payments in Germany in the 1880s, and Lloyd George introduced similar measures in the UK in 1909. Table 3-5 provides an idea of the growth of government expenditure since 1880. It is clear that it was generally rather modest in 1913 by later standards.

Stable institutions and market freedom also characterised international transactions. Most of the world moved to fixed exchange rates by adopting the gold standard which the UK had practiced since 1821. Germany adopted the gold mark in 1871-3; Belgium, France, Italy and Switzerland created the Latin Monetary Union in 1873-4 based on the gold franc. The Scandinavian Union of Denmark, Norway and Sweden was created in 1875-6. The Netherlands adopted the gold standard at the same time and Egypt in 1885. The USA adopted a fixed gold parity in 1879, Austria in 1892, Japan in 1895, Russia in 1897, Argentina and Mexico in 1905. The colonial empires of these countries were also included in these decisions.

It was a world which relied on simple rules and protection of property rights. There were no international organisations like the OECD, IMF, BIS and GATT to "manage" a world "system", and no equivalent of the World Bank, UN agencies, or bilateral aid donors to direct capital flows in the light of "developmentalist" objectives.

Phase III (1913-50)

This was an era deeply disturbed by war, depression, and beggar-your-neighbour policies. It was a bleak age, whose potential for accelerated growth was frustrated by a series of disasters[5]. It was also an age in which the conceptions of capitalism were changing, particularly in Europe where the role of government spending increased very substantially, as did government intervention in the form of subsidies, controls and trade restrictions. In Italy, Portugal and Spain fascist regimes were established. European fascist ideas had substantial echoes in Argentina and Brazil. Russia departed the capitalist world to experiment with an autarkic command economy. By the end of the period, the European fascist experiments had been destroyed or discredited, but the USSR succeeded in incorporating the whole of Eastern Europe in its camp of command economies.

As the events of these years were very complex, it is useful to look at the evidence separately for four sub-periods; 1913-29, 1929-38, 1938-44 and 1944-9. Figure 3-1 shows how feeble GDP growth was in 1913-50 as a whole compared with the rapid growth that followed in the golden age from 1950 to 1973.

a) 1913-29

Table 3.6 shows the evidence available on annual GDP movements for major regions. It is complete for Western Europe and the Western Offshoots, involves a modicum of "guesstimation" for Latin America, and a substantial degree of interpolation for Asia. The picture for Southern Europe, Eastern Europe and Africa is incomplete, but we know enough to see what happened to a relatively large part of the world economy.

Table 3-6. **Annual Growth Performance of Major Regions, 1913-50**
(aggregate GDP of regions in billion 1990 $)

	Western Europe	Western Offshoots	Southern Europe	Eastern Europe	Latin America	Asia	Africa	Total for 56 Sample Countries
1913	732.3	583.4	83.8	365.8	94.2	657.7	36.9	2554.1
1914	696.6	539.9			89.0	667.9		
1915	714.4	553.5			89.8	684.0		
1916	742.6	626.2			92.5	710.9		
1917	717.1	614.1			92.9	730.3		
1918	687.8	661.0			96.9	698.6		
1919	654.2	663.9			97.8	742.9		
1920	667.5	660.4			104.5	718.3		
1921	659.5	645.7			104.1	752.0		
1922	718.3	682.0			110.6	762.1		
1923	720.1	765.8			121.7	764.1		
1924	774.8	790.1			126.2	779.5		
1925	813.8	812.0			128.8	791.9		
1926	813.1	860.9			135.5	807.8		
1927	857.6	872.5			141.7	818.9		
1928	892.9	885.6			153.1	841.9		
1929	922.3	934.2	116.2	403.4	158.3	858.3	57.5	3450.1
1930	899.1	855.5		414.3	152.1	853.8		
1931	850.2	787.0		413.8	142.1	854.5		
1932	824.4	691.3	114.8	402.4	138.0	879.6	62.5	3112.5
1933	859.1	677.9		413.0	151.4	899.3		
1934	887.6	729.8		438.5	162.8	862.7		
1935	925.7	784.4		483.6	170.6	903.3		
1936	969.4	889.2		519.8	180.0	956.2		
1937	1 017.6	930.1		549.4	189.7	965.1		
1938	1 040.7	899.2	115.6	586.5	194.0	959.0	73.8	3868.9
1939	1 099.8	966.1			202.7	986.9		
1940	1 079.6	1 042.5			205.2	999.1		
1941	1 084.3	1 224.5			216.0	997.3		
1942	1 074.4	1 463.1			214.8	982.3		
1943	1 070.9	1 731.4			220.7	982.7		
1944	1 015.4	1 865.3			239.4	944.5		
1945	898.4	1 791.5			247.9	819.1		
1946	916.6	1 450.0			271.2	813.9		
1947	977.1	1 436.7			288.3	824.2		
1948	1 047.1	1 488.7	132.1	576.5	307.2	833.4	97.5	4 482.4
1949	1 132.4	1 500.6	132.6	636.3	318.1	843.0	100.3	4 663.3
1950	1 220.4	1 629.7	137.2	694.0	332.4	898.5	103.1	5 015.2

Source: This table refers only to the 56 sample countries. The regional totals are derived from the individual country estimates in Appendix C. For Western Europe and Western Offshoots, there were no gaps in the country estimates. For Southern Europe, Eastern Europe and Africa there were too many gaps to make annual estimates feasible. For Latin America, there was a gap for Mexico for 1914-20, where this was a period of revolution and civil war: I assumed the Mexican 1913 level to prevail in 1914-20. For Colombia, there was a gap for 1914-24. Here I assumed that the annual GDP movement for the missing years was parallel to that in the other six countries. For Asia the estimates were complete for India (including what later became Bangladesh and Pakistan 1913-46), for Indonesia, Korea and Taiwan. For China I interpolated the years 1914-28 and 1939-46, and took the 1947-49 movement from Rawski (1989). For Burma, Philippines and Thailand I interpolated the years 1914-28, 1930-37, and 1939-49.

The region which fared worst was Eastern Europe. There were 3.3 million military deaths from the war. Another 10 million died in the course of the Russian revolution, civil war and foreign intervention. The forced collectivisation of agriculture and political repression that went with the switch from capitalism to collectivism caused massive suffering in Russia and the Ukraine in the 1920s and 1930s.

Many frontiers were redrawn in Eastern Europe as Germany was truncated and the Austrian, Hungarian and Turkish empires disappeared. Estonia, Finland, Latvia, Lithuania, Czechoslovakia, Poland and Yugoslavia emerged as new national entities. The new Austria had only a third of the income and a quarter of the population of its pre-war share of the Habsburg Dual Monarchy. Imperial Hungary was also cut to a third of its former size. The division of the old area led to new tariff barriers, upset traditional transport routes, and created massive problems of adjustment to new market situations. Poland had to forge a national economy out of three different currency and fiscal areas.

The war caused a drop in GDP in most West European countries, with the biggest damage to living standards in Belgium, France and Austria. Western Europe's 1913 GDP level was not regained until 1924;

Figure 3.1. **A confrontation of GDP growth by major region, 1913-50 and 1950-92**

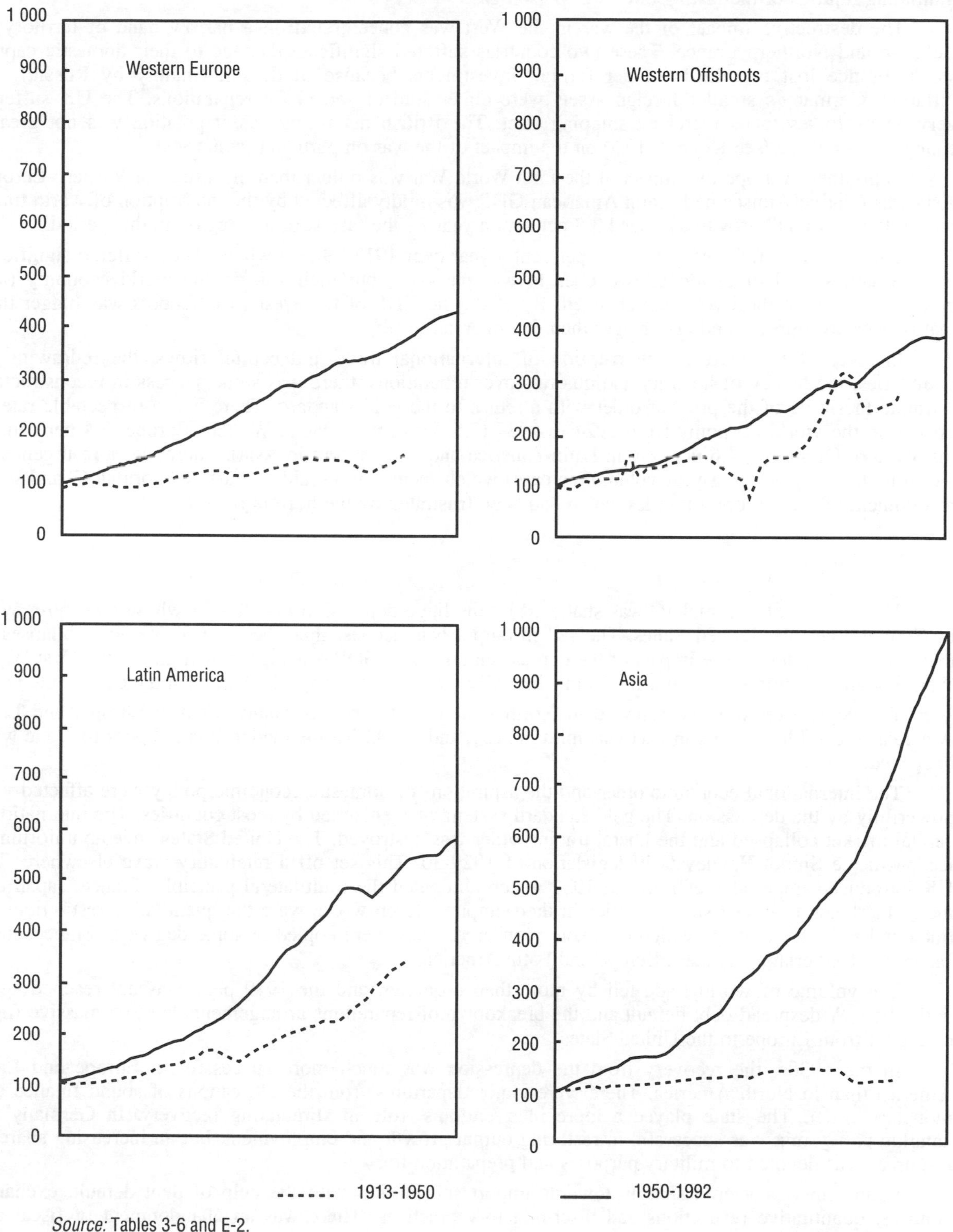

Source: Tables 3-6 and E-2.

for a decade, per capita product was well below pre-war levels. A large proportion of resources was diverted from consumption and investment to war purposes. There were 5.4 million deaths amongst the armed forces (including 2 million in Germany, 1.3 million in France, and three-quarters of a million in the UK). Apart from the grief inflicted on the families of these victims, many of the survivors were left with mutilating injuries or the lasting effects of poison gas.

The destructive impact of the war in the West was concentrated on a narrow band of territory in Belgium and Northern France. These two countries suffered significant damage to their domestic capital stock. France lost two-thirds of her foreign investments because of default (mainly by Russia) and inflation. Germany's smaller foreign assets were either sold or seized for reparations. The UK suffered very heavy losses to its merchant shipping fleet. The British net foreign asset position was not greatly changed by the war (see Keynes, 1920 on the impact of the war on particular countries).

In Southern Europe the impact of the First World War was milder than in Eastern or Western Europe. Asia was relatively unscathed. Latin American GDP was mildly affected by the interruption of world trade, but its 1913-29 GDP growth averaged 3.3 per cent a year — the fastest of any region in this period.

The Western Offshoots grew by 3 per cent a year over 1913-29 as a whole. They suffered significant war casualties, and diversion of resources to war purposes, but their role in the world economy (and particularly that of the USA) had changed. By 1929, the GDP of the Western Offshoots was bigger than that of Western Europe, and also bigger than that of Asia.

In spite of the wartime interruption of international trade and capital flows, the redrawing of boundaries, the legacy of hostility and quarrels over reparations, there was some success in reconstructing a fragile facsimile of the pre-war order with a return to the gold standard. There was a respectable rate of growth in the world economy from 1924 to 1929 (3.5 per cent a year in Western Europe, 3.4 per cent in the Western Offshoots, 4.6 per cent in Latin America and 1.9 per cent in Asia). There was a resurgence of world trade (5.7 per cent a year volume increase) which seemed to herald a return to "normalcy" and some recoupment of growth opportunities which had been frustrated by the horrors of war.

b) 1929-38

The illusion of "normalcy" was shattered by the huge depression of 1929-33 whose epicentres were in Germany and the United States. The fall in output was deepest there because of massive collapses of their financial systems. The impact of the depression on world GDP was bigger than that of the First World War, though consumption did not fall as much as GDP, whereas the opposite had been the case in the war.

The depression was most severe in North America, Austria, Germany, Central Europe, and Latin America (see Table 3-7). Its impact was mild in Asia, and for Africa the evidence is too poor to judge what happened.

The international economic order and the aspirations of domestic economic policy were affected very powerfully by the depression. The gold standard system was jettisoned by most countries. The international capital market collapsed and the liberal trading order was destroyed. The United States gave an unfortunate lead with the Smoot-Hawley tariff legislation of 1929-30. This set off a retaliatory wave elsewhere. The UK introduced imperial preference in 1932 which abrogated the multilateral principle. France, Japan and the Netherlands followed similar tactics in their empires. Even worse were the quantitative restrictions on trade and foreign exchange which Germany pioneered. They were copied in some degree in France, Italy, Japan, the Netherlands, Eastern Europe and Latin America.

The volume of world trade fell by more than a quarter, and the 1929 peak was not reached again until 1950. Widespread debt default and the breakdown of reparations arrangements led to a massive flight of capital from Europe to the United States.

In the 1930s, the recovery from the depression was much more successful in Europe and Latin America than in North America. There were major departures from the old canons of sound finance and monetary order. The state played a more interventionist role in stimulating recovery. In Germany the autarkic policy mix was successful in restoring output growth and employment, but an increasing share of resources was devoted to military purposes and preparation for war.

Latin America veered sharply towards import substitution with the help of debt default, exchange controls, quantitative restrictions and discriminatory practices. There was an abandonment of fiscal and monetary orthodoxy, and moves towards government intervention and state ownership.

Table 3-7. **Biggest Cyclical (Peak to Trough) GDP Movement Within the Years 1928-1935**

Austria	-22.5	Bulgaria	-12.7
Belgium	-7.9	Czechoslovakia	-18.2
Denmark	-3.6	Hungary	-9.4
Finland	-4.0	Poland	-20.7
France	-14.7	Romania	-5.6
Germany	-24.5	USSR	-1.1
Italy	-5.5	Yugoslavia	-11.9
Netherlands	-7.8	Arith. Average	-9.6
Norway	-7.8		
Sweden	-6.2	Argentina	-13.7
Switzerland	-8.0	Brazil	-4.4
UK	-5.8	Chile	-30.0
Arith. Average	-9.9	Colombia	-1.5
		Mexico	-20.8
Australia	-9.2	Peru	-25.8
Canada	-29.6	Venezuela	-22.6
New Zealand	-14.6	Arith. Average	-17.0
USA	-28.5		
Arith. Average	-20.5	Bangladesh	-0.9
		Burma	n.a.
Greece	-6.5	China	-8.7
Ireland	n.a.	India	-0.9
Portugal	n.a.	Indonesia	-9.3
Spain	-6.1	Japan	-7.3
Arith. Average	n.a.	Korea	-1.5
		Pakistan	-0.9
		Philippines	n.a.
		Taiwan	-6.2
		Thailand	n.a.
		Arith. Average	-4.4

Source: Appendix C.

In the USA, where the financial collapse and its deeply depressive consequences were a predominant concern of policy, the government created a significant amount of employment through public works policies, but great emphasis was placed on reflating prices, so that the burden of debt would be reduced. Prices were boosted by farm support legislation, trade union power was bolstered in an effort to raise wages, the dollar was revalued against gold and silver for the same reasons and early New Deal legislation tried to strengthen cartels (until the moves were declared unconstitutional). This mix, which owed more to Irving Fisher than to Keynes, was not successful in pushing America back on a path which exploited its production potential. It took the Second World War to achieve this.

c) 1938-44

Judging by the aggregate regional evidence of Table 3-6, the world economy fared better in 1938-44 than would have been thought possible in years of such widespread and violent conflict. In the Western Offshoots, output more than doubled (a growth rate of nearly 13 per cent a year) as the large slack in the economy was mobilised for war production. Latin American output increased by nearly a quarter, and output was reasonably well sustained in Asia and Western Europe.

The impact of war was very uneven by country. Within Western Europe, the worst affected countries were Belgium, France, the Netherlands and Norway, and there is little doubt of the immense costs of war for Greece, Poland, the USSR, and Yugoslavia for which sharp evidence is poor.

During the war, German economic power increased dramatically and was used to impose a "New Order" on Europe. By 1940, German population was around 93 million, as Austria, the Sudetengau of Czechoslovakia, the Saar, Memel, Danzig, a large part of Poland, Eupen and Malmedy, Alsace and

Table 3-8. **Movement in GDP, 1938-44**

Austria	+18.0	Spain	+30.5
Belgium	-15.7	Bulgaria	-8.8
Denmark	+1.8		
Finland	+4.9	Argentina	+24.0
France	-49.7	Brazil	+19.4
Germany	+24.2	Chile	+20.0
Netherlands	-46.7	Colombia	+18.4
Norway	-12.7	Mexico	+38.9
Sweden	+20.9	Peru	+16.3
Switzerland	-0.8	Venezuela	+18.1
UK	+22.0		
		India	+17.1
Australia	+32.4	Indonesia	-42.2
Canada	+75.4	Japan	+16.6
New Zealand	+9.6	Korea	-1.7
USA	+114.4	Taiwan	-39.7

Source: Appendix C.

Lorraine and parts of Yugoslavia had been incorporated in the Reich. As a result of its successful *Blitzkrieg*, Germany controlled a large part of the European economy. Belgium, the occupied zone of France and the rump of Poland were under German military government, Norway and the Netherlands were under German commissars. The protectorate of Bohemia and Moravia — a fief of the SS — was a German colony with German currency. Slovakia was a puppet State. Germany had 3 million allied prisoners of war and imported foreign workers on a large scale (7.5 million at the peak). Occupation levies and enforced credits from occupied countries added a further 14 per cent to German disposable income. Bulgaria, Finland, Hungary, Italy and Romania were allies; Spain a highly cooperative neutral; Sweden provided a steady supply of iron ore; Albania, Greece and Yugoslavia were under occupation.

When Germany attacked the USSR in 1941, she controlled a compact area with better armed forces and a collective GDP much bigger than that of the 197 million people in Stalin's newly enlarged Soviet empire. At that time the Wehrmacht had lost only 200 000 men, and it must have seemed that the Russian campaign would be another cheap victory. In fact, it was the beginning of the most destructive phase of a war in which there were 16 million military deaths (including 10 million Soviet and 3.8 million German) as well as a loss of 26 million civilians (of whom 20 million were deliberately murdered in concentration camps or exterminated by *Einsatzgruppen* in Poland and the USSR).

Wartime living standards in Western Europe fell much more relatively than they had in the First World War. In France, the level of output during the occupation averaged less than two-thirds of that in 1938 and occupation levies (for troop support, military construction and transfers to Germany) took a third of this, so French wartime consumption levels were only about 45 per cent of those in 1938.

Belgian and Dutch experience was similar to that in France. Norway was fortunate in that output fell only 13 per cent, but with half a million occupation troops added to its small population, occupation costs took a third of Norwegian income, so wartime standards were less than two-thirds of those in pre-war years. Denmark probably fared best amongst the occupied countries. Experience was worst in Greece, Poland, the USSR and Yugoslavia, because their inhabitants were regarded by the Nazis as subhuman. In these countries wartime living standards fell below subsistence levels and large numbers died from malnutrition. In Germany itself the wartime reduction in living standards was small, because of heavy levies on the rest of Europe and the use of foreign workers to maintain domestic food output. In the UK, per capita consumption levels fell on average by less than 10 per cent, distribution of supplies was more equitable than anywhere else and health standards actually rose during the war. The UK was able to use resources (about $50 billion) 20 per cent above its GDP by running down foreign assets, accumulating debt and receiving US and Canadian aid. This permitted a very high degree of mobilisation and cushioned the fall in living standards.

Damage to the European capital stock was much more extensive than in the First World War. There was fighting in France, Germany, Greece, Italy, the Netherlands, Poland, the USSR and Yugoslavia which did extensive damage. The USSR followed a scorched-earth policy to deny resources to Germany. The Allies dropped 2 million tons of bombs on the Continent (mostly on Germany) and the Germans attacked the UK with bombs and rockets. Submarines sank a great deal of merchant shipping, and livestock was destroyed on a large scale. Wartime levels of investment were low, though in both the UK and Germany wartime investment in armaments production turned out later to be useful for civilian production. The biggest losses to capital stock were probably in Poland and Yugoslavia. The second largest were probably in the USSR and UK.

The UK accumulated very large war debts to Commonwealth countries and sold foreign investments during the war. Then in 1946, before Marshall Plan aid started, it borrowed about $4.6 billion from the USA and another $1.3 billion from Canada. As a result its net foreign asset position declined from a positive balance of $21 billion in 1938 to a negative one of $2 billion in 1947. Unlike the situation after the First World War these debts were honoured in full and were a very heavy burden for the UK. By 1947 France's pre-war net asset position of $3.9 billion had been reduced to zero. The Netherlands had lost about half of its pre-war $4.8 billion assets by 1947 and lost more later. The net foreign assets of Belgium declined only slightly. In 1938 Germany had been a net debtor by about $2 billion. She acquired asserts illegally and accumulated more debt during the war. No service payments were made on pre-war debt until 1953, and in that year German pre-war and post-war debts were scaled down. Germany was therefore a net gainer on foreign account because of the war.

d) 1944-49 (The Aftermath of War)

1950 is a useful starting point for measuring post-war achievements. By then, recovery from war was certainly complete if one uses the level of world GDP as a criterion. One might argue for 1948 as a post-war benchmark because world output was then already higher than in 1938. However, this was not the case for the world outside the Americas, and even in 1950, recovery of pre-war levels was not complete in all countries (Japan and Hungary recovered pre-war levels in 1951, China and Taiwan in 1952, Poland in 1953, Indonesia in 1954, Greece and Korea in 1955, and Burma in 1961).

It seems more legitimate to treat the years 1945 to 1949 as the aftermath of the war rather than the beginning of the post-war golden age. These years were very disturbed in Europe, with frontiers redrawn, millions of displaced persons and refugees in camps, desperate balance-of-payments problems, reallocation of labour from war to peacetime occupations, and a capital stock which had suffered badly from wartime damage and neglect. The future was also overshadowed by the cold war, which led to the incorporation of the East European economies in the Soviet bloc. The shape of the post-war order did not emerge until the Marshall Plan started functioning in 1948.

In Asia, these years saw the collapse of the Japanese empire, civil war in China, the disintegration of the British, Dutch and French Empires. There was a very troubled transition to independence in Indonesia and the different parts of French Indochina and a messy partition of India.

In the USA, the problems of transition from war to peace were of a completely different order, but GDP dropped by a quarter from 1944 to 1947 as the war economy and the troops were demobilised and resources were shifted to more peaceful activity. In 1948, this was followed by military recommitment overseas, and the establishment of Marshall Plan aid to Europe.

The Acceleration of Technical Progress in Phase III

The fact that the major disasters of the twentieth century were concentrated in the period 1913-50 tends to obscure a significant improvement in the pace of technical progress.

Table 2-6 above shows clearly the impressive technical dynamism of the US economy in this period. Labour productivity grew by 2.5 per cent a year, accelerating substantially over the 1.9 per cent of 1870-1913. The new growth rate was more than twice as fast as that of the UK in the century following 1820. Furthermore this acceleration occurred with much more modest growth in the physical capital stock than in the nineteenth century.

In 1913-50, US total factor productivity grew at 1.6 per cent a year, almost 5 times as fast as in 1870-1913. The rate of progress accelerated further in 1950-73. Thus there was a 60-year boom in technical potential which was to be of tremendous significance for the performance of the world economy in the twentieth century.

The influence of the lead country in diffusing technical progress depends partly on its size, and partly on its degree of integration in the world economy. The American economy was already bigger than that of

Table 3-9. **Stock of Passenger Cars in Use, 44 Countries, 1913-73**

(000s)

	1913	1950	1973		1913	1950	1973
Austria	12	49	1 541	Bangladesh	-	3	23
Belgium	10	274	2 390	Burma	-	8	32
Denmark	3	118	1 245	India	-	154	690
Finland	-	27	894	Indonesia	-	31	483
France	91	1 500	14 500	Japan	-	48	14 473
Germany	61	516	17 023	Korea	-	2	78
Italy	22	342	13 424	Pakistan	-	16	177
Netherlands	4	139	2 957	Philippines	-	45	319
Norway	1	60	838	Taiwan	-	3	95
Sweden	3	252	2 503	Thailand	-	10	215
Switzerland	5	147	1 652				
UK	106	2 258	13 497	Côte d'Ivoire	-	3a	45
				Egypt	-	60	167
Portugal	-	61	770	Ethiopia	-	5	46
Spain	-	89	3 804	Ghana	-	7	55
				Kenya	-	17	81
Australia	n.a.	768	4 520	Morocco	-	38	281
Canada	29	1 913	7 866	Nigeria	-	7	150
USA	1 190	40 339	101 986	South Africa	-	471	1 737
				Tanzania	-	7	40
Argentina	-	318	1 914	Zaire	-	11	78
Brazil	-	200	3 386				
Chile	-	40	225				
Colombia	-	31	327				
Mexico	-	173	1 767				
Peru	-	32	247				
Venezuela	-	70	820				

a) 1954.
Source: Mitchell (1982, 1983 and 1992 with revisions kindly supplied by Brian Mitchell).

Britain and Germany combined in 1913. By 1950 it was larger than that of Western Europe as a whole. However, the US role as a diffusionist was very limited during most of Phase III, because of the disturbances in the world economy, the limited American role in international trade and investment, the disastrous collapse of its economy and its international economic policy in the 1930s.

The improvement in US productivity performance in 1913-50 occurred for four main reasons:

a) from 1820 to 1913 the US had made a massive investment in the infrastructure which was needed to exploit its prodigal natural resource endowment and provide its booming population with urban facilities. By 1913, its stock of non-residential structures was already five times as high per person employed and more than four times as high relative to GDP as in the UK (which had devoted a large part of its savings to foreign investment in railways and other infrastructure development in Latin America, Europe and Australasia). Between 1913 and 1950, a much smaller proportionate expansion of American capital was necessary to sustain a growth less dependent on exploiting the US natural resource advantage. The capital-output ratio for structures fell quite dramatically as one can see in Table 2-1 above;

b) a much bigger proportion of new investment went into machinery and equipment in 1913-50 than in 1820-1913. This kind of investment embodied technical change more rapidly than did structures. One strong indicator of this is the fact that machinery and equipment is scrapped much earlier because of technical obsolescence. In 1950 the average age of the machinery and equipment in the capital stock was 6.4 years, whereas the average age for structures was 19.3 years;

c) the research and development effort was greatly intensified. The driving forces of innovation changed from the nineteenth century, with less emphasis on individual action and more on corporate and government efforts. Anti-trust legislation drove US firms to invest in research for survival, whereas European cartels, and governmental tolerance or encouragement of collusive business practices made for a less dynamic situation. Around 1913, there were about 370 research units in US manufacturing employing around 3 500 people. By 1946, there were 2 303 research units employing nearly 118 000 people. In 1946 there were 4 scientific workers in US manufacturing per 1 000 wage earners, 5 times the ratio in the UK. US government-sponsored research played a much more important role in agriculture and mining than in the UK. The link between business firms and universities was closer[6];

d) there were substantial economies of scale of a new kind. It was not only that US economy had grown so large relative to Europe, nor was it only the growth in the average size of plants. The most striking feature was the increased role of very large enterprises which played an active role in standardising and enlarging markets. Giant firms played a strategic role by controlling large numbers of plants at different stages of production and distribution [see Chandler (1977 and 1990)]. They required a new form of business management, whose professional education was pioneered in the USA. Multiunit enterprises coordinated advertising, packaging, transport, sales, and marketing. They handled the allocation of large amounts of capital, spread risks and increased productivity over a very large range of new industries, such as breakfast cereals, canned soup, cigarettes, sewing machines, photographic equipment, refrigerators, washing machines, vacuum cleaners, cinemas and automobiles. In the case of cars, Rostas (1948) showed that US production in 1935 was above 4 million, well over ten times that of the UK. The number of American engine types was much smaller, the number of assembly plants only little higher and labour productivity was five times as high. In the same year US automobile output was 16 times that of Germany and 23 times that of France. Table 3.9 gives some idea of the extent to which US car ownership had moved ahead of that in other countries by 1950. By that time the USA had 80 per cent of the car stock in the 44 countries. By 1973 the share had dropped to 46 per cent and fell further thereafter.

Phase IV (1950-73)

The years 1950 to 1973 were a golden age of unparalleled prosperity. World per capita GDP grew by 2.9 per cent a year — more than three times as fast as in Phase III. World GDP rose 4.9 per cent a year, and world exports 7 per cent. This dynamism could be observed in all regions. In all of them, GDP per capita grew faster than in any other phase. The acceleration was greatest in Europe and Asia.

There were several reasons for unusually favourable performance in the golden age[7]. In the first place, the Western economies created a functioning international order with explicit and rational codes of behaviour, and strong and flexible institutions for cooperation (OEEC, OECD, IMF, World Bank) which had not existed before. There was a very serious East-West split from 1948 onwards and the area covered by communist rule was much bigger than before, but the split reinforced the harmony of interest between capitalist economies, so the quarrels and beggar-your-neighbour behaviour of pre-war years did not recur. The US played its leadership role in a responsible and generous fashion, providing a substantial flow of aid for Europe when it was most needed, fostering procedures for articulate cooperation and liberal trading policies. Until the 1970s it also provided the world with a strong anchor for international monetary stability. North-South relations were transformed from the colonial tutelage of pre-war years to a situation where much more emphasis was placed on action to stimulate development by providing trade opportunities and financial aid. Here again, East-West rivalry reinforced the Western commitment. There was a huge expansion of trade in the advanced capitalist economies which transmitted a dynamic influence throughout the world economy.

The second new element of strength was the character of domestic policies which were self-consciously devoted to promotion of high levels of demand and employment in the advanced countries. The growth path was not only faster than ever before, but the business cycle virtually disappeared. Investment rose to unprecedented levels and expectations became euphoric. Until the 1970s, there was also much milder inflationary pressure than could have been expected in conditions of secular boom.

The third element in this virtuous circle situation was the potential for growth on the supply side. Throughout Europe and Asia there was still substantial scope for "normal" elements of "recovery" from the years of depression and war. Additionally and more importantly, was the continued acceleration of technical progress in the lead country. Furthermore, the USA played a very active diffusionist role in the

Table 3-10. **Variations in Volume of Merchandise Exports, 47 Countries, 1820-1992**

(annual average compound growth rate in export volume)

	1820-70	1870-1913	1913-1950	1950-73	1973-92
Austria	4.5	3.5	-3.0	10.7	6.5
Belgium	5.4[a]	4.2	0.3	9.2	3.7
Denmark	1.9[b]	3.3	2.4	6.9	4.7
Finland	n.a.	3.9	1.9	7.2	2.8
France	4.0	2.8	1.1	8.2	4.4
Germany	4.8[c]	4.1	-2.8	12.4	4.0
Italy	3.4	2.2	0.6	11.6	4.8
Netherlands	n.a.	2.3[d]	1.5	10.4	3.7
Norway	n.a.	3.2	2.7	7.3	6.7
Sweden	7.0[e]	3.1	2.8	6.9	2.7
Switzerland	4.1	3.9	0.3	8.1	2.7
UK	4.9	2.8	0.0	3.9	3.9
Arith. Average	4.4	3.2	0.7	8.6	4.2
Australia	n.a.	4.8	1.3	5.6	5.0
Canada	n.a.	4.1	3.1	7.0	4.6
USA	4.7	4.9	2.2	6.3	5.1
Arith. Average	n.a.	4.6	2.2	6.3	4.9
Greece	n.a.	n.a.	n.a.	11.9	6.2
Ireland	n.a.	n.a.	n.a.	6.8	8.8
Portugal	n.a.	n.a.	n.a.	5.7	8.5
Spain	3.7[f]	3.5	-1.6	9.2	8.0
Turkey	n.a.	n.a.	n.a.	4.3	7.9
Arith. Average	n.a.	n.a.	n.a.	7.6	7.9
Argentina	n.a.	5.2[g]	1.6	3.1	5.8
Brazil	n.a.	1.9	1.7	4.7	7.1
Chile	n.a.	3.4[h]	1.4	2.4	9.2
Colombia	n.a.	2.0	3.9	3.8	6.1
Mexico	n.a.	5.4[i]	-0.5	4.3	9.7
Peru	n.a.	5.3	2.7	5.8	-1.1
Venezuela	n.a.	n.a.	5.4	4.0	-1.3
Arith. Average	n.a.	3.9	2.3	4.0	5.1
Bangladesh	n.a.	2.4	-1.5	2.0	8.6
China	n.a.	2.6	1.1	2.7	11.0
India	n.a.	2.4	-1.5	2.5	3.9
Indonesia	n.a.	4.2	2.3	6.5	7.5
Japan	n.a.	8.5	2.0	15.4	6.2
Pakistan	n.a.	2.4	-1.5	3.6	8.7
Philippines	n.a.	2.8[j]	3.7	5.9	7.0
Korea	n.a.	-	-1.1	20.3	12.8
Taiwan	n.a.	-	2.6	16.3	10.8
Thailand	n.a.	4.1	2.3	4.4	12.9
Arith. Average	n.a.	3.7	0.8	8.0	8.9
Côte d'Ivoire	n.a.	n.a.	n.a.	n.a.	8.2
Egypt	n.a.	2.7	1.2	2.1	1.6
Ethiopia	n.a.	n.a.	n.a.	7.0	-4.3
Ghana	n.a.	6.7	3.1	2.1	2.5
Kenya	n.a.	n.a.	n.a.	6.8[l] [k]	4.0
Morocco	n.a.	n.a.	n.a.	n.a.	4.3
Nigeria	n.a.	6.0	n.a.	7.9 [k]	-2.4
South Africa	n.a.	8.1	n.a.	6.2	7.0
Tanzania	n.a.	n.a.	n.a.	7.1 [k]	-2.2
Zaire	n.a.	n.a.	n.a.	2.7	-5.2
Arith. Average	n.a.	5.9	2.2	5.2	1.4
World	4.2	3.4	1.3	7.0	3.7

a) 1831-70; b) 1844-70; c) 1840-70; d) 1872-1913; e) 1851-70; f) 1826-70; g) 1877-1912; h) 1888-1913; i) 1877/8 to 1910/11; j) 1882-1912; k) goods and services.

Source: Appendix I, except for African countries, which were derived from 1950 onwards from World Bank, *World Tables*, 1983 and 1994 editions, supplemented by UN trade statistics. 1870-1950 from national sources and Lewis (1981). 1870-1913 volume movement for Egypt, Ghana, Nigeria and South Africa derived by deflating export values by UK import unit value index.

golden age. For this reason, the supply response to improved international and domestic policy was much more positive than could have been anticipated.

Table 3-10 shows the great acceleration in international trade which went with the creation of the new liberal order. The biggest benefits accrued to Western Europe, Southern Europe and Asia, where growth averaged 8.6, 7.6 and 8 per cent a year respectively. Latin America was rather strongly resistant to trade liberalisation, so it benefitted only mildly from the new order. For Africa the expansion was not as buoyant as in Europe and Asia, but better on average than in Latin America.

Ultimately, there was also a restoration of private international capital flows, but until the 1960s, the major item sustaining development was official aid.

During the golden age, there was a very marked upsurge in rates of domestic investment in European countries and in Asia (see Figure 3-2). This was a response to opportunities offered by technical progress. As the Asian and European countries were starting from a lower level, and recovering from productivity levels depressed by long years of adversity, they could push their rates of investment well above those in the USA, without running into diminishing returns. As a result Europe and Japan were able to bring their capital stock much closer to American levels. In many respects, these follower countries were replicating the consumption patterns, technology, and organisational methods which had been developed in the United States when it built up standardised markets for new consumer goods such as cars and household durables.

Another important condition for successful catch-up was the fact that most of Western Europe and Japan already had relatively high levels of skill and education (see Table 3-12). Their endowment in human capital was just as close to US levels in 1950 as it is today, even though their physical capital stocks were much lower. These reserves of skill were very important in permitting the vast accumulation of capital to take place efficiently.

The productivity gains in this process of catch up are shown in Tables 3-13a and 3-13b. Between 1950 and 1973, all the West European countries had much faster labour productivity growth than the USA. In 1950, after eight decades of falling further behind, their average productivity was less than half the US level, but by 1973 they had moved much closer to the frontiers of technology, and were to continue further on this virtuous path after 1973. The proportional gains in Japan were even more spectacular, though Japanese labour productivity levels still remained below those of Europe (see Figure 2-2).

In Southern Europe, growth performance in 1950-73 was even better than in Western Europe in all significant respects (growth of GDP, GDP per capita and labour productivity). The new international order offered particularly favourable opportunities for these countries to be reintegrated in the flow of international trade, investment, tourist earnings and emigrants' remittances. They were greatly helped by their close propinquity to markets which were growing fast.

In terms of total factor productivity the performance of the European follower countries *vis-à-vis* the USA was less spectacular, because they were increasing their capital stock a good deal faster. Nevertheless they did a good deal better than ever before. In Japan, the 1950-73 total factor productivity performance was extraordinarily favourable, because of the much lower starting point, the huge reserves of skill, education and organisational experience, and the improvements in resource allocation in moving from what had been a highly militarised economy to one which could devote all its energies and resources to economic growth.

In the Western Offshoots, there was significant improvement in performance in the golden age. Per capita GDP grew faster than ever before and productivity growth also accelerated, but the pace of advance was more modest than in Europe.

In Eastern Europe, the years 1950-73 also saw growth rates very much faster than in the past. As indicated in Appendix B, the measures we have used probably exaggerate performance in Bulgaria and Romania, but for the other countries and for Eastern Europe as a whole, there is no doubt that there was substantial growth acceleration. The costs were higher than in the West, because investment rates and labour inputs were proportionately higher and resource allocation was less efficient in the command economies. Military commitments were also proportionately higher than in the West, so that consumption grew a good deal more slowly than GDP.

Latin America had done better than any other part of the world economy in Phase III, and was operating much nearer to its potential in 1950 than Europe or Asia. Partly as a consequence of this, its performance in the golden age improved rather modestly. In per capita terms, it was similar to that of the Western Offshoots. It could probably have done somewhat better by adopting more open trade policies, less dirigisme in resource allocation, and a greater commitment to social change and improvement in its

Figure 3.2. **Gross domestic investment as percentage of GDP at current prices (11 countries), 1870-1989**

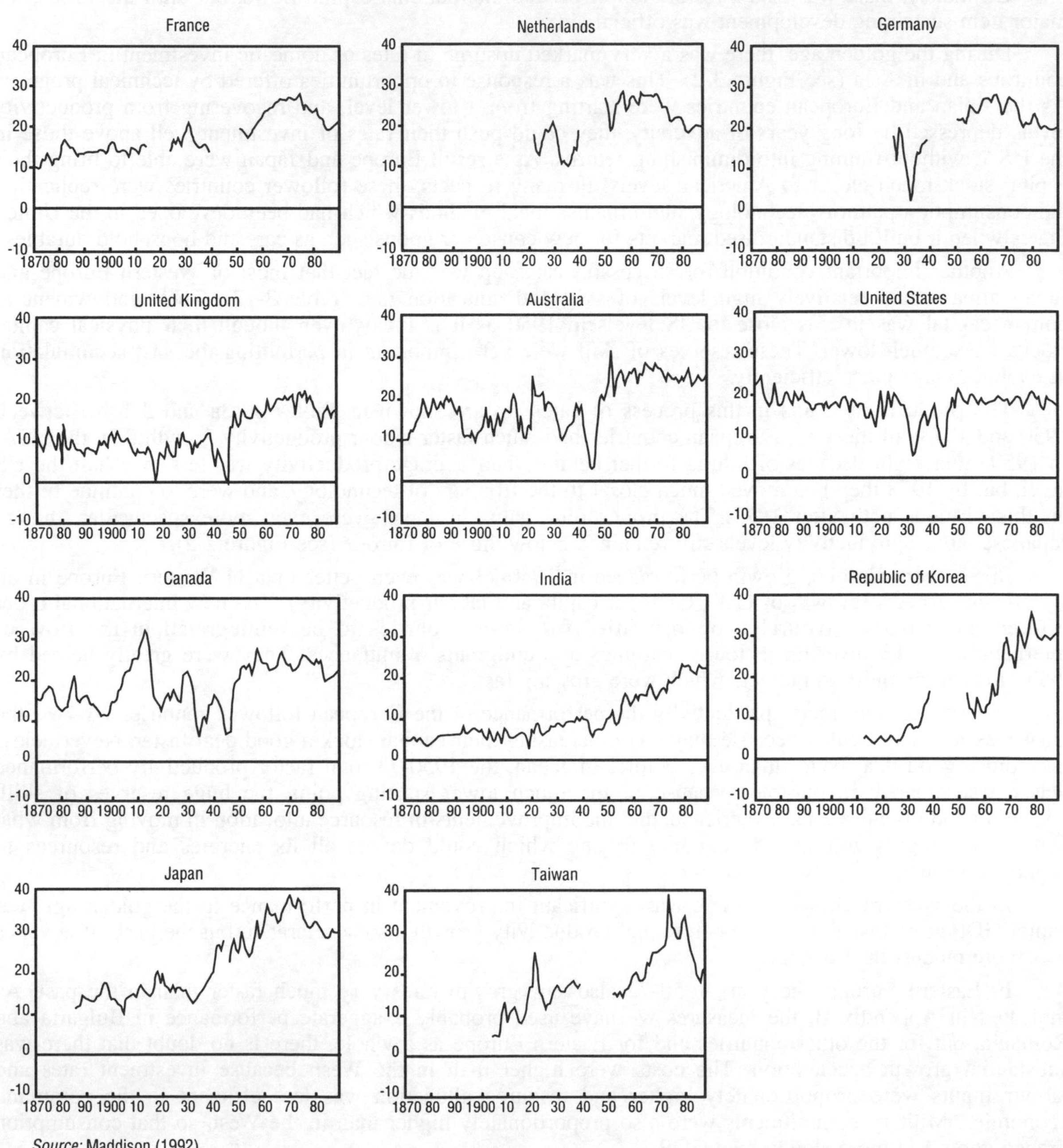

Source: Maddison (1992).

Table 3-11. **Gross Non-Residential Capital Stock Per Person Employed, 1950-92**

	1950	1973	1992	1950	1973	1992
	(in 1990 international dollars)			(USA = 100)		
France	18 120	48 815	103 162	31	57	92
Germany	18 312	58 210	101 855	32	68	91
Netherlands	29 564	65 787	87 962	51	77	78
UK	12 444	35 399	64 892	22	42	58
Japan	7 752	34 777	113 376	13	41	101
USA	57 600	85 178	112 261	100	100	100

Source: Maddison (1995a).

Table 3-12. **Years of Education Per Person Aged 15-64, 20 Countries, 1950-92**

(average for both sexes)

	1950	1973	1992	1950	1973	1992
	(equivalent years of primary education)			(USA = 100)		
Belgium	9.83	11.99	15.24	87	82	84
France	9.58	11.69	15.96	85	80	88
Germany	10.40	11.55	12.17	92	79	67
Italy	5.49	7.62	11.20	49	52	62
Netherlands	8.12	10.27	13.34	72	70	74
Sweden	9.50	10.44	14.24	84	72	79
UK	10.84	11.66	14.09	96	80	78
Portugal	2.53	4.62	9.11	22	32	50
Spain	5.13	6.29	11.51	46	43	64
USA	11.27	14.58	18.04	100	100	100
Argentina	4.80	7.04	10.70	43	48	59
Brazil	2.05	3.77	6.41	18	26	36
Chile	5.47	7.98	10.93	49	55	61
Colombia	2.66	4.91	9.14	24	34	51
Mexico	2.60	5.22	8.22	23	36	46
Venezuela	2.21	4.41	10.18	20	30	56
India	1.35	2.60	5.55	12	18	31
Japan	9.11	12.09	14.86	81	83	82
Korea	3.36	6.82	13.55	30	47	75
Taiwan	3.62	7.35	13.83	32	50	77

Source: Updated from Maddison (1989 and 1995b) and from estimates supplied by André Hofman. Primary education was given a weight of 1, secondary 1.4, and higher 2, in line with evidence on the relative earnings associated with the different levels of education.

human capital, but Latin America did not have the same incentives to change its policy mix, which European countries got from Marshall Plan aid.

In all Asian countries in our sample, except Bangladesh, the most notable feature was the general acceleration of growth. Japan had the best performance, but South Korea and Taiwan also did extremely well. In the other Asian countries, the rate of progress in the golden age was more modest than in Europe.

Because of the variety of Asian experience it is difficult to summarise the characteristics of the Asian "model". However, one can discern the following elements making for the great acceleration in post-war growth in countries which had been colonies or virtual colonies before the Second World War:

a) the end of colonial rule and the advent to power of new national elites capable of mounting a very large increase in capital formation, and increasing the educational levels of their populations;

b) the absence of the extreme inequalities in income and wealth which characterise Latin America. This made for greater socio-political coherence, and probably helped to ensure that Asian countries were less subject to short-term vagaries in policy of a populist kind;

c) the colonial drain was replaced by a net inflow of foreign capital and foreign aid. Generally speaking, Asian countries were cautious in their foreign borrowing and fiscal policies, and did not suffer from the domestic capital flight that plagued Latin America;

d) the period after 1950 was one of buoyant world trade, thanks to the acceleration of growth in the capitalist core, and the reduction of trade barriers. A good many Asian countries, and in particular those with super-growth, took advantage of these new trade outlets by remaining competitive and aggressively seeking new markets. The opening up of their economies improved their efficiency and facilitated their growth;

e) many Asian countries have high labour inputs, with much longer working hours than in other parts of the world;

f) Asian countries were able to get a large catch-up bonus because their post-war starting levels of productivity were so low, and they were so far from the productivity frontier.

The African countries started in 1950 with an average per capita GDP somewhat higher than in Asia. Africa was the last area to emerge from colonialism. Education, health and infrastructure were very poor, and many countries continued to have a heavy reliance on foreign cadres. Their population growth was extremely rapid but per capita GDP increased less than any other region. Their newness as nation-states led many of their rulers to try to forge national unity by creating one-party regimes. This reinforced a tendency towards dirigisme that led to market distortions, artificial exchange rates and policies harmful to agriculture. Nevertheless, in the golden age, African per capita income grew by an average of 1.8 per cent a year.

Phase V (1973-94)

In the early 1970s, the world economy was overheating. Governments had to cope with strong inflationary pressure, a breakdown in the Bretton Woods fixed exchange rate system and the OPEC oil shock. There was a sharp reduction in the pace of economic growth throughout the world in 1974-5, and the momentum of the golden age has never been regained except in Asia. To some extent the slowdown is due to a retardation of technical progress, but 1973-94 has been an era of chequered performance, in which most of the world economy has operated below potential.

The biggest setback occurred in Eastern Europe, where total output is now well below 1973 levels, and per capita GDP has fallen by a third after faltering for a decade. The economic system is in a messy process of transition to capitalism. National frontiers have changed drastically, with the former USSR split into 15 countries, Yugoslavia into six, Czechoslovakia into two. East Germany has been incorporated into the Federal Republic. The COMECOM trade and payments system disintegrated, and it was necessary to change the direction, price and commodity structure of international trade.

In African countries, total GDP has been better sustained than in Eastern Europe, but population growth was eight times greater, so average per capita GDP fell about 8 per cent from 1973 to 1992, and virtually the whole period since 1973 has been marked by faltering per capita performance.

Latin American performance since 1973 has also been poor. All the sample countries reacted with insouciance to the OPEC oil shock of 1973 and the world-wide explosion of prices. Governments felt they could accommodate to high rates of inflation, and were able to borrow on a large scale at negative real interest rates to cover external deficits incurred as a result of expansionary policies. After the Mexican debt moratorium in 1982, their supply of private foreign funds dried up and the service costs of existing debt soared because of rising interest rates. Most countries were then forced into desperate measures to curtail domestic demand, in the attempt to achieve internal financial equilibrium and external balance. Latin American per capita income peaked in 1980. In 1994, it was still about 3 per cent below what it had been fourteen years earlier.

After a number of experiments with unsuccessful heterodox approaches, most Latin American governments eventually adopted the neoliberal policy mix pioneered by Chile, which involved a return to orthodox fiscal and monetary restraint, more modest levels of demand, privatisation and a reopening of the economies to international trade. This switch in the conventional policy wisdom involved painful

Table 3-13a. **Rate of Growth of Labour Productivity (GDP per Hour Worked), Advanced Capitalist Countries, 1870-1992**

(annual average compound growth rate)

	1870-1913	1913-50	1950-73	1973-92
Austria	1.7	0.9	5.9	2.5
Belgium	1.2	1.4	4.5	2.9
Denmark	1.9	1.5	4.5	1.7
Finland	1.8	2.2	5.4	2.2
France	1.7	1.9	5.1	2.7
Germany	1.9	0.6	6.0	2.7
Italy	1.7	2.0	5.8	2.4
Netherlands	1.3	1.3	4.8	2.2
Norway	1.6	2.5	4.2	3.2
Sweden	1.8	2.8	4.1	1.3
Switzerland	1.5	2.7	3.3	1.7
UK	1.2	1.6	3.1	2.2
Arith. Average	1.6	1.8	4.7	2.3
Australia	1.1	1.4	2.9	1.5
Canada	2.3	2.3	3.0	1.5
USA	1.9	2.5	2.7	1.1
Japan	1.9	1.9	7.7	3.1

a) 1973-91.
Source: Table J-4.

Table 3-13b. **Rate of Growth of Labour Productivity (GDP per Hour Worked) in Medium- and Low-Income Countries, 1950-92**

(annual average compound growth rate)

	1950-73	1973-92		1950-73	1973-92
Greece	6.4	2.5[a]	Argentina	2.4	0.5
Ireland	4.3	4.1[a]	Brazil	3.7	0.9
Portugal	6.0	1.9	Chile	2.9	1.0
Spain	6.4	3.3	Colombia	3.3	1.5
Arithmetic Average	5.8	3.0	Mexico	4.0	0.5
			Peru	3.4	-1.8
Czechoslovakia	3.4	0.1	Venezuela	3.4	-0.8
Hungary	3.9	0.6	Arithmetic Average	3.3	0.3
Poland	3.8	0.4			
USSR	3.4	-0.8	Bangladesh	0.3	1.9
Arithmetic Average	3.6	0.1	China	2.1	4.1
			India	2.0	2.8
			Indonesia	2.6	3.1
			Pakistan	2.8	2.9
			Philippines	2.7	0.6
			South Korea	4.1	5.2
			Taiwan	5.6	5.3
			Thailand	3.6	5.1
			Arithmetic Average	2.9	3.4

a) 1973-91.
Source: Table J-4.

Table 3-14. **East European Economic Performance in Phases IV and V**

	GDP Growth		Per Capita GDP Growth		GDP Per Hour Worked		Number of Years in which GDP below Previous Peak	
	1950-73	1973-92	1950-73	1973-92	1950-73	1973-92	1950-73	1973-92
	annual average compound growth rates							
Bulgaria	6.0	-1.5	5.2	-1.4	6.1	n.a.	2	12
Czechoslovakia	3.8	0.2	3.1	-0.1	3.4	0.1	2	4
Hungary	4.1	-0.0	3.6	0.0	3.9	0.6	2	7
Poland	4.8	0.1	3.4	-0.6	3.8	0.4	2	12
Romania	5.9	-1.1	4.8	-1.6	6.2	n.a.	n.a.	10
USSR	4.8	-0.5	3.4	-1.4	3.4	-0.8	2	5
Yugoslavia	5.6	0.2	4.4	-0.5	n.a.	n.a.	2	6
Average	5.0	-0.4	4.0	-0.8	4.5	0.1	2	8

Source: Appendices C, D and J.

Table 3-15. **African Economic Performance in Phases IV and V**

	GDP Growth		Per Capita GDP Growth		Population Growth		GDP Deflator	
	1950-73	1973-92	1950-73	1973-92	1950-73	1973-92	1950-73	1973-92
	annual average compound growth rates							
Côte d'Ivoire	6.3	1.6	3.1	-2.2	3.1	3.9	3.4[a]	6.7
Egypt	5.1	6.3	2.7	3.8	2.3	2.4	1.9	12.7
Ethiopia	4.1	1.3	1.7	-1.7	2.3	3.0	1.4[a]	4.1
Ghana	3.6	1.6	0.2	-1.2	3.4	2.8	5.7	40.5
Kenya	5.0	4.3	1.9	0.6	3.0	3.7	2.2	10.6
Morocco	2.7	4.3	0.1	1.8	2.6	2.5	3.7[b]	7.8
Nigeria	5.2	2.7	3.2	0.1	2.0	2.6	5.4	19.0
South Africa	4.9	1.8	2.4	-0.6	2.4	2.4	4.0	14.0
Tanzania	4.4	2.7	1.9	-0.5	2.5	3.1	3.3[b]	20.5
Zaire	4.1	-0.9	0.8	-3.9	3.3	3.2	25.6[b]	52.0[c]
Average	4.5	2.6	1.8	-0.4	2.7	3.0	5.7	18.8

a. 1960-73; b. 1955-73; c. 1973-89.

Source: Appendices A, C and D. GDP deflators from World Bank, *World Tables*, various issues. South Africa from national sources.

Table 3-16. **Latin American Performance in Phases IV and V**

	GDP Growth		Per Capita GDP Growth		GDP Per Hour Worked		GDP Deflator	
	1950-73	1973-94	1950-73	1973-94	1950-73	1973-92	1950-73	1973-94
	annual average compound growth rates							
Argentina	3.8	1.6	2.1	0.2	2.4	0.5	26.8	258.4
Brazil	6.8	3.4	3.8	1.0	3.7	0.9	28.4	268.5
Chile	3.4	3.7	1.2	2.1	2.9	1.0	48.1	71.8
Colombia	5.2	4.0	2.3	2.0	3.3	1.5	10.4	24.6
Mexico	6.4	3.4	3.1	0.9	4.0	0.5	5.6	37.6
Peru	5.3	1.4	2.5	-1.0	3.4	-1.8	8.6	125.2
Venezuela	5.4	1.7	1.6	-1.2	3.4	-0.8	2.3	21.5
Average	5.2	2.7	2.4	0.6	3.3	0.3	18.6	115.4

Source: Appendices C, D and J. GDP deflators from Maddison (1989) and ECLAC sources.

Figure 3.3. **A confrontation of the growth of GDP per capita by region, 1950-73 and 1973-92**

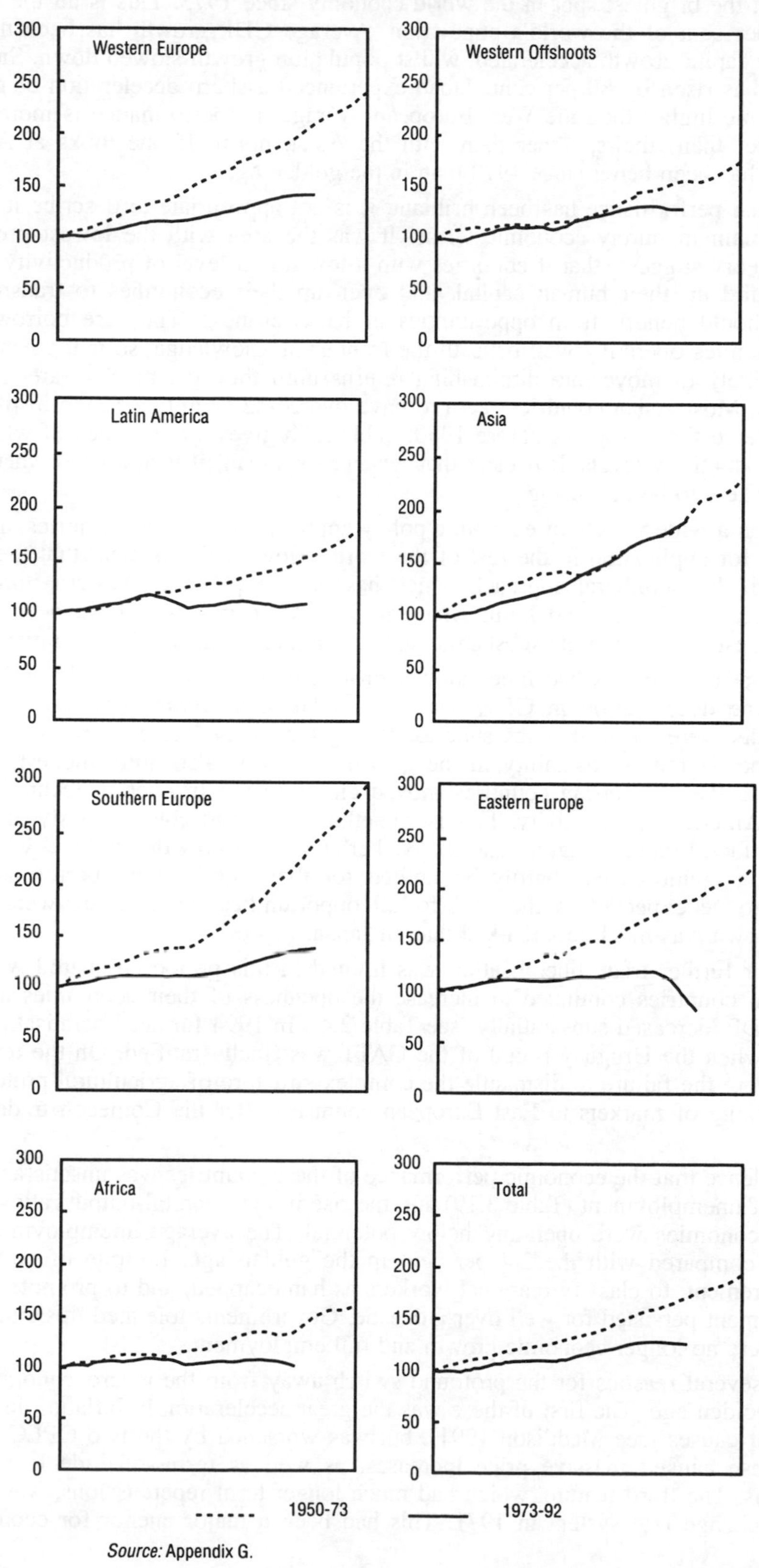

Source: Appendix G.

transitions and some disappointing setbacks, of which the most spectacular was that in Mexico at the end of 1994.

Asia has been the brightest spot in the world economy since 1973. This is all the more encouraging as it contains 58 per cent of the world's population. Average GDP growth has been the same as in the golden age, but per capita growth accelerated, whilst population growth slowed down. Since 1973, average per capita product has risen by 80 per cent. Japan experienced a sharp deceleration of growth. As it now has a level of income higher than the West European average, its performance is more comparable with (though rather better than) theirs, rather than with the Asian norm. If one looks at Asian performance excluding Japan, it has been better since 1973 than in the golden age.

Although Asian performance has been brilliant, it is not appropriate to describe it as a miracle. It is not difficult to explain in purely economic terms. It was the area with the lowest productivity level in 1950. Economic theory suggests that if countries with a low initial level of productivity can increase their investment rate, build up their human capital, and open up their economies to transmission of foreign technology, they should benefit from opportunities of backwardness. They are borrowing and adapting technology to economies operating well beneath the frontier of knowledge, so that when they mount a big push, they are unlikely to move into diminishing returns until they get much nearer to the level of the advanced countries. Most Asian countries seem to have overcome or mitigated the institutional barriers to growth which hindered their progress before 1950. Table 2.7b gives a crude idea of where Asia stands in the hierarchy of productivity levels. It is clear that (except for Japan) it is at a level where opportunities of backwardness are likely to be promising.

There has been a wide variety of economic policy approaches in Asian countries, and it is difficult to distil clear lessons for application in the rest of the world. However, it is clear that the Asian model has been different from the neoliberal approach which has been popular in Western Europe and has been recommended to Eastern Europe and Latin America. The Asian countries have been more significantly influenced by Japanese policy with its substantial and continuing elements of corporatism and dirigisme.[8]

Western European countries had much slower growth in 1973-94 than in the golden age. In all the twelve countries the deceleration in GDP, per capita GDP and labour productivity was quite sharp. However, the results were in most cases superior to anything they had experienced before the postwar golden age, and the degree of instability in the growth path was also quite modest by such standards. Furthermore, all the West European countries moved closer to the frontier of technology by continuing their catch-up on American productivity. This is something they had conspicuously failed to do between 1870 and 1950. In fact, France, Belgium and the Netherlands have now drawn level with US productivity. The West European countries can hardly be faulted for their productivity performance. A substantial deceleration was to be expected as the once-for-all opportunities for catch-up were eroded, and their productivity slowdown was much less marked than in Japan.

The scope for further trade liberalisation was limited in this period compared with the golden age, but West European countries continued to increase the openness of their economies after 1973, and the ratio of trade to GDP increased substantially (see Table 2.4). In 1994 further liberalisation was agreed on a world-wide basis when the Uruguay round of the GATT was finally ratified. On the trade front, the main disappointments were the failure to dismantle the complex structure of agricultural protection, and the less than generous opening of markets to East European countries after the Comecon trade bloc collapsed in the 1990s.

The real evidence that the economic performance of these countries was unsatisfactory can be seen in their rising rates of unemployment (Table 3.19) and the rise in their capital-output ratios (Table 2.1). These suggest that the economies were operating below potential. The average unemployment rate in 1984-93 was 6.8 per cent compared with the 2.4 per cent in the golden age. In spite of costly programmes to promote early retirement, to classify marginal workers as handicapped, and to promote work sharing, high rates of unemployment persisted for well over a decade. Governments tolerated this situation because their main objectives were no longer economic growth and full employment.

There were several reasons for the profound switch away from the macroeconomic goals and policy weaponry of the golden age. The first of these was the great acceleration in inflation in 1973-83. This was due to a variety of causes (see Maddison 1991), but was worsened by the two OPEC oil shocks of 1973 and 1979-80. These caused massive price increases, as well as terms-of-trade losses and balance-of-payments problems. The third feature, which had much longer term repercussions, was the collapse of the post-war fixed exchange rate system in 1971. This had been a major anchor for economic policy in the golden age.

Table 3-17. **Asian Performance in Phases IV and V**

	GDP Growth		Per Capita GDP Growth		GDP Per Hour Worked		GDP Deflator	
	1950-73	1973-92	1950-73	1973-92	1950-73	1973-92	1950-73	1973-92
	annual average compound growth rates							
Bangladesh	1.7	4.5	-0.6	2.2	0.3	1.9	5.0	11.9
Burma	3.8	3.3	1.8	1.3	n.a.	n.a.	1.4	13.2
China	5.1	6.7	2.9	5.2	2.1	4.1	n.a.	n.a.
India	3.7	4.7	1.6	2.4	2.0	2.8	4.4	8.5
Indonesia	4.5	5.3	2.5	3.1	2.6	3.1	77.5	13.6
Japan	9.2	3.8	8.0	3.0	7.7	3.1	5.2	3.9
Pakistan	4.4	5.9	1.8	2.7	2.8	2.9	3.4	9.6
Philippines	5.0	3.1	1.8	0.7	2.7	0.6	4.6	13.7
South Korea	7.6	8.3	5.2	6.9	4.1	5.2	30.1	12.3
Taiwan	9.3	7.8	6.2	6.2	5.6	5.3	7.2	6.1
Thailand	6.4	7.5	3.2	5.3	3.6	5.1	2.6	6.2
Average	5.5	5.5	3.1	3.5	3.4	3.4	14.1	9.9
Average (ex Japan)	5.2	5.7	2.6	3.6	2.9	3.4	15.1	10.6

Source: Appendices C, D and J. GDP Defllators from Maddison (1989) p. 70, World Bank, *World Tables*, various issues, and national sources for Taiwan.

Table 3-18. **Performance of OECD Economies in Phases IV and V**

	GDP Growth		Per Capita GDP Growth		GDP Per Hour Worked		Number of Years in which GDP below Previous Peak	
	1950-73	1973-94	1950-73	1973-94	1950-73	1973-92	1950-73	1973-94
	annual average compound growth rates							
Austria	5.3	2.3	4.9	2.0	5.9	2.5	0	3
Belgium	4.1	1.9	3.5	1.8	4.5	2.9	2	3
Denmark	3.8	1.9	3.1	1.7	4.5	1.7	0	3
Finland	4.9	1.9	4.3	1.5	5.4	2.2	0	4
France	5.0	2.1	4.0	1.6	5.1	2.7	0	2
Germany	6.0	2.2	5.0	1.8	6.0	2.7	1	3
Italy	5.6	2.5	5.0	2.2	5.8	2.4	0	2
Netherlands	4.7	2.1	3.4	1.4	4.8	2.2	1	4
Norway	4.1	3.3	3.2	2.8	4.2	3.2	1	1
Sweden	3.7	1.4	3.1	1.0	4.1	1.3	0	7
Switzerland	4.5	1.1	3.1	0.7	3.3	1.7	1	9
UK	3.0	1.7	2.5	1.5	3.1	2.2	1	8
Average	4.6	2.0	3.8	1.7	4.7	2.3	0.6	4.1
Greece	7.0	2.1	6.2	1.3	6.4	2.5[a]	1	4
Ireland	3.2	3.6	3.1	2.8	4.3	4.1[a]	3	1
Portugal	5.7	2.5	5.7	1.8	6.0	1.9	0	5
Spain	6.8	2.3	5.8	1.7	6.4	3.3	1	3
Turkey	6.1	4.5	3.3	2.1	5.2[b]	3.0[b]	1	2
Average	5.8	3.0	4.8	1.9	5.7	3.0	1.2	3
Australia	4.7	2.9	2.4	1.5	2.9	1.5	1	1
Canada	5.1	2.9	2.9	1.4	3.0	1.5	1	5
New Zealand	3.7	1.6	1.7	0.9	n.a.	n.a.	6	9
USA	3.9	2.5	2.4	1.5	2.7	1.1	2	4
Average	4.4	2.5	2.4	1.3	2.9	1.4	2.5	4.8

a) 1973-91; b) refers to GDP per person employed with no adjustment for changes in working hours.

Source: Appendices C, D and J.

Table 3.19 **Experience of Unemployment and Inflation, OECD Countries, 1950-93**

	Unemployment as per cent of Labour Force			Change in Consumer Price Index (average annual compound growth rate)		
	1950-73	1974-83	1984-93	1950-73	1973-83	1983-93
Austria	2.6	2.3	3.5[a]	4.6	6.0	3.1
Belgium	3.0	8.2	9.6	2.9	8.1	3.0
Denmark	2.6	7.6	7.8[a]	4.8	10.7	3.7
Finland	1.7	4.7	7.0	5.6	10.5	4.7
France	2.0	5.7	10.0	5.0	11.2	3.6
Germany	2.5	4.1	6.2	2.7	4.9	2.3
Italy	5.5	7.2	11.1	3.9	16.7	6.4
Netherlands	2.2	7.3	8.9	4.1	6.5	1.8
Norway	1.9	2.1	4.1	4.8	9.7	5.1
Sweden	1.8	2.3	3.2	4.7	10.2	6.3
Switzerland	0.0	0.4	1.0a	3.0	4.3	3.2
UK	2.8	7.0	9.6	4.6	13.5	5.2
Average	2.4	4.9	6.8	4.2	9.4	4.0
Greece	4.6[b]	3.2	7.6[c]	3.7	18.8	17.5
Ireland	5.2[b]	8.8	16.1	4.3	15.7	3.8
Portugal	2.4[b]	6.5	6.1	3.2	22.6	13.2
Spain	2.9[b]	9.1	19.0	4.6	16.4	6.9
Average	3.6[b]	6.9	12.2	4.0	18.4	10.4
Australia	2.1	5.9	8.4	4.6	11.3	5.6
Canada	4.7	8.1	9.6	2.8	9.4	4.0
New Zealand	0.2[b]	1.9	6.8	4.4	13.9	7.4
USA	4.6	7.4	6.4	2.7	8.2	3.8
Average	2.9	5.8	7.8	3.6	10.7	5.2
Japan	1.6	2.1	2.5	5.2	7.6	1.7

a. 1984-92; b. 1960-73; c. 1984-91.

Source: Unemployment rates from Maddison (1991), OECD *Labour Force Statistics,* various issues and OECD *Economic Outlook*, December 1994. Consumer price indices from Maddison (1991), OECD *Economic Outlook*, various issues, and IMF *International Financial Statistics*.

On any reasonable accounting, the most sophisticated governments could have been expected to lose output in dealing with the threefold interactive shocks that occurred in the 1973-83 period. The new challenges were unavoidable, and it was widely felt that the threat of hyperinflation required policy to concentrate on the restoration of price stability. Economic growth and full employment became secondary considerations.

After 1983, there was a change in the situation these countries faced. They had squeezed the abnormal inflationary pressures out of their economies. The rate of price increase was pushed below that which had obtained in the golden age, and below that in most other parts of the world. The power of the OPEC cartel was broken by energy economy and development of new oil resources. In 1992 oil prices were one third lower than in 1983, whereas 1983 prices had been nine times as high as in 1973. A more or less workable set of monetary arrangements had emerged by 1983. The continental European countries had created a new zone of monetary stability with fixed but adjustable pegs in the European Monetary System. Japan, the USA, and the UK (except in 1990-2) had opted for floating rates. These arrangements were not as convenient as the Bretton Woods system, but they were not a serious menace to economic growth. However, the European Commission pushed its Member countries to maintain very narrow exchange rate margins and to aim at exchange rate fixity, as a prelude to monetary union. This required countries to bring their rates of inflation down towards those prevailing in Germany (as the D-mark was the effective monetary anchor), rather than being content to return to the golden age norm. Pursuit of this new policy objective meant that economic policy had to be more deflationary than it would otherwise have been. The goal was all the more difficult to achieve because of the concurrent deregulation of financial markets and abandonment of remaining exchange controls. Official reserves were now small in relation to the potential for private speculation. There were very serious setbacks to these ambitious policy aspirations. In 1992 Italy and the UK went back to floating rates. In 1993 the currency margins had to be widened from 2.25 to 15 per cent, and in 1995 the Portuguese and Spanish currencies dropped below the 15 per cent margin and had to be devalued.

The other reason for the persistence of high unemployment was the fact that West European countries had developed advanced welfare states and job security systems in the golden age when the economic climate was different. When large scale unemployment emerged, these arrangements mitigated the social impact of recession and sustained demand, but they proved an obstacle to reemployment. Social charges add about 85 per cent to wage costs on average for manufacturing workers in Belgium, France, Germany, Italy and the Netherlands, and social legislation provides job security on such an extensive scale that employers are reluctant to take on new people, particularly if their skills have been eroded by long-term unemployment.

In the Southern European countries, experience since 1973 has had a strong resemblance to that in Western Europe to which they have become very closely linked through trade and capital movements, the operation of European Community transfers and fashions in economic policy. They also experienced a sharp deceleration in the growth of GDP, per capita GDP and labour productivity, compared to the golden age but they substantially reduced the gap between their productivity levels and those of the United States (see Table 2.7b). Ireland was the most remarkable performer in this respect, and Portugal made the slowest progress. The growth of trade was more rapid than in Western Europe, and was also faster than it had been in the golden age.

The unemployment and inflation experience of Southern Europe has been the most disappointing feature of the situation since 1973. It has been much worse than that of Western Europe. Inflation averaged 18.4 per cent a year in 1973-83. It fell in 1983-93, but was very much higher than in the golden age or in Western Europe. Unemployment averaged 12.2 per cent in 1983-93, more than three times its level in the golden age (see Table 3.19).

Within the Western offshoots, there was also a slowdown in growth after 1973, an acceleration in inflation and a rise in unemployment rates. The US situation was the most markedly different from that in the West European countries.

In the golden age, when the dollar was the world's monetary anchor, the American rate of inflation was lower than that in all other OECD countries except Germany. Inflation accelerated in 1973-83, and dropped back thereafter, but the United States did not try so hard as Europe to squeeze inflation back to or below the levels of the golden age. For most of the time it treated the exchange rate with benign neglect. From 1950 to 1973, the United States had operated with unemployment rates about twice the West European level, partly because its labour market had higher turnover rates with much better opportunities for part-time or casual work. Since 1973, there has been some increase, but proportionately much less than in European countries. In 1984-93, unemployment was actually below the European average. The labour market has continued to be flexible with a very much smaller proportion of long-term unemployed than in Europe. As a result, the deceleration in the growth of US per capita income in 1973-94 was smaller than in European countries.

The most striking change in the USA after 1973, was the marked slowdown in the rate of growth of labour and total factor productivity. Performance in these respects has been worse than at any time since 1870. This is all the more surprising as the European countries are now also operating near the productivity frontier. One might have expected some acceleration of technical progress, as the collective R and D effort of the advanced capitalist countries is much bigger than when most of the burden was borne by the USA.

Although the evidence is not very firm, it is worth considering what could have caused the slowdown in US productivity, because of its long-term world-wide implications.

The first possibility is that US output growth has been mismeasured. There have been suspicious falls in US construction productivity, and the US output measure may be misleading for this activity. There have also been problems with measuring output in computers. However, the measure of US output I have used incorporates a new weighting procedure and new deflators for computers, and it does not seem likely that future measurement revisions are likely to be large.

A second consideration is the erosion of the American natural resource advantage. This is reflected in the substantial fall in US mining productivity since 1973.

A third factor is the changing structure of the economy. There has been a very significant movement towards service sectors, where measured productivity growth is slow. This move has obviously played a role in the slowdown, and is characteristic of all Western economies.

A fourth consideration which seems to have some validity, is that this has been a period when the fruits of investment could only be plucked with some delay, which was also true of the huge US investment in railways before 1913. Paul David (1991) has argued that computers and information technology have been hard to digest, and once digested will lead the United States to a productivity rebound. Although one need not agree with the precise historical parallel with electric motors which David draws, he has provided some grounds for hoping that the US total factor productivity slowdown since 1973 may turn out to be temporary. If the pay-off on investment has simply been retarded, then there may ultimately be some rebound in productivity growth.

The most gloomy possibility is the one which Julius Wolf evoked in 1912, and which Kuznets reiterated in the 1930s and 1940s (Kuznets, 1953), i.e. we may have reached a point where technical progress is slower because we have exploited the easier inventions, there is less left to discover and the unknown has been harder to penetrate. One can be sceptical about this proposition, but it certainly cannot be ignored.

Notes

1. See Rostow (1960), Schumpeter (1939) and Maddison (1991), for a discussion of the stage and long-wave approaches.
2. See Douglass North (1968).
3. Maddison (1992) for the denominator (included in an unpublished appendix available from the author).
4. See Fogel (1964) and Coatsworth (1981) for differing assessments of the importance of railways in the USA and Mexico.
5. See Maddison (1989) for a more detailed survey of policy developments in this period; Maddison (1976) for an analysis of the impact of the two world wars; and Maddison (1985) for experience in 1929-38.
6. See Mowery and Rosenberg (1989) for an excellent and detailed survey of the British and American research effort.
7. See Maddison (1989 and 1991) for a more detailed policy analysis and growth accounts for different regions. See Maddison (1985) for a detailed narrative of developments in 1973-83 in Latin America and Asia.
8. See World Bank (1993). for an analysis of Asian policy approaches.

Bibliography

ABRAMOVITZ, M. (1956), "Resource and Output Trends in the United States Since 1870", *American Economic Review*, May.

ABRAMOVITZ, M. (1986), "Catching up, Forging Ahead, and Falling Behind", *Journal of Economic History*, June.

ABRAMOVITZ, M. (1989), *Thinking About Growth*, Cambridge University Press.

ABRAMOVITZ, M. (1993), "The Search for Sources of Economic Growth: Areas of Ignorance, Old and New", *Journal of Economic History*, June.

BAIROCH, P. (1981), "The Main Trends in National Economic Disparities since the Industrial Revolution", in BAIROCH, P. and M. LEVY-LEBOYER, eds., *Disparities in Economic Development since the Industrial Revolution*, Macmillan, London.

BAIROCH, P. and ASSOCIATES (1968), *The Growth of Population and its Structure*, Université Libre de Bruxelles.

BARRO, R.J. (1991), "Economic Growth in a Cross Section of Countries", *Quarterly Journal of Economics*, May.

BARRO, R.J. and X. SALA-I-MARTIN (1992), "Convergence", *Journal of Political Economy*, (100).

BAUMOL, W.J. (1986), "Productivity Growth, Convergence and Welfare: What the Long Run Data Show", *American Economic Review*, December.

BENNETT, M.K. (1954), *The World's Food*, Harper, New York.

BOLOTIN, B.M. (1992), "The Former Soviet Union as Reflected in National Accounts Statistics", in HIRSCH, S., ed., *Memo 3: In Search of Answers in the Post-Soviet Era*, Bureau of National Affairs, Washington, D.C.

BROADBERRY, S.N. (1993), "Manufacturing and the Convergence Hypothesis: What the Long Run Data Show", *Journal of Economic History*, December.

COATSWORTH, J.H. (1981), *Growth Against Development: The Economic Impact of Railroads in Porfirian Mexico*, Northern Illinois University Press, De Kalb.

CHANDLER, A.D., Jr. (1977), *The Visible Hand: The Managerial Revolution in American Business*, Harvard.

CHANDLER, A.D., Jr. (1990), *Scale and Scope: The Dynamics of Industrial Capitalism*, Harvard.

CHANG, CHUNG-LI (1962), *The Income of the Chinese Gentry*, Greenwood, Westport.

CLARK, C. (1940), *The Conditions of Economic Progress*, Macmillan, London.

CRAFTS, N.F.R. (1985), *British Economic Growth During the Industrial Revolution*, Oxford University Press.

DAVID, P.A. (1991), "Computer and Dynamo: The Modern Productivity Paradox in a Not Distant Mirror", in OECD, Paris, *Technology and Productivity: The Challenge for Economic Policy*, pp. 315-48.

DE LONG, J.B. and L. SUMMERS (1991), "Equipment Investment and Economic Growth", *Quarterly Journal of Economics*, May.

DENISON, E.F. (1962), *The Sources of Economic Growth in the United States and the Alternatives Before Us*, Committee on Economic Development, New York.

DENISON, E.F. (1967), *Why Growth Rates Differ*, Brookings, Washington, D.C.

DENISON, E.F. (1991), "Scott's A New View of Economic Growth: A Review Article", *Oxford Economic Papers*, (43).

DENISON, E.F. (1993), "The Growth Accounting Tradition and Proximate Sources of Economic Growth", in SZIRMAI, VAN ARK, and PILAT.

DENISON, E.F. and W.K. CHUNG (1976), *How Japan's Economy Grew So Fast*, Brookings, Washington, D.C.

DOUGLAS, P.H. (1948), "Are There Laws of Production?", *American Economic Review*, March.

E.C.E. (1964), *Some Factors in Economic Growth in Europe During the 1950s*, United Nations, Geneva.

ELVIN, M, (1973), *The Pattern of the Chinese Past*, Methuen, London.

FAGERBERG, J. (1994), "Technology and International Differences in Growth Rates", *Journal of Economic Literature*, September.

FEIS, H. (1965), *Europe: The World's Banker 1870-1914*, Norton, New York (originally published in 1930).

FEINSTEIN, C.H. and S. POLLARD, eds. (1988), *Studies in Capital Formation in the United Kingdom 1750-1920*, Oxford University Press.

FIELD, A.J. (1983), "Land Abundance, Interest/Profit Ratios, and Ninetheenth Century American and British Technology", *Journal of Economic History*, June.

FOGEL, R.W. (1964), *Railroads and American Economic Growth*, Johns Hopkins, Baltimore.

GALLMAN, R.E. (1986), "The United States Capital Stock in the Nineteenth Century", in ENGERMAN, S.L. and R.E. GALLMAN, eds., *Long Term Factors in American Economic Growth*, University of Chicago.

GALLMAN, R.E. (1987), "Investment Flows and Capital Stocks: US Experience in the Nineteenth Century", in KILBY, P., ed., *Quantity and Quiddity: Essays in US Economic History*, Wesleyan University Press, Middletown.

GALLMAN, R.E. and J.J. WALLIS (1992), *American Economic Growth and Standards of Living Before the Civil War*, University of Chicago Press.

GERSCHENKRON, A. (1965), *Economic Backwardness in Historical Perspective*, Praeger, New York.

GOLDSMITH, R.W. (1951), "A Perpetual Inventory of National Wealth", in GAINSBURGH, M.R., *Studies in Income and Wealth*, Vol. 14, Princeton.

HAYAMI, Y. and V.W. RUTTAN (1985), *Agricultural Development*, second edition, Johns Hopkins, Baltimore.

HOFMAN, A. (1993) "Economic Development in Latin America", in SZIRMAI, VAN ARK and PILAT.

JAMES, J.A. and J.S. SKINNER (1985), "The Resolution of the Labour Scarcity Paradox", *Journal of Economic History*, September.

JORGENSON, D.W. and Z. GRILICHES (1964), "The Explanation of Productivity Change", *Review of Economic Studies*, May. The subsequent interchange with Denison is in *Survey of Current Business* (Pt. 11), May 1972.

KALDOR, N. (1957), "A Model of Economic Growth", *Economic Journal*, December.

KENDRICK, J.W. (1961), *Productivity Trends in the United States*, Princeton.

KENDRICK, J.W. (1976), *The Formation and Stocks of Total Capital*, Columbia University Press, New York.

KENDRICK, J.W. (1994), "Total Capital and Economic Growth", *Atlantic Economic Journal*, March.

KENDRICK, J.W. and B.N. VACCARA (1980), *New Developments in Productivity Measurement and Analysis*, University of Chicago.

KEYNES, J.M. (1920), *The Economic Consequences of the Peace*, Macmillan, London.

KLOTZ, B., R. MADOO and R. HANSEN (1980), "A Study of High and Low Labor Productivity Establishments in US Manufacturing", in Kendrick and Vaccara (1980).

KUZNETS, S. (1953), *Economic Change: Selected Essays*, Norton, New York.

KUZNETS, S. (1966), *Modern Economic Growth*, Yale.

KUZNETS, S. (1973), *Population, Capital and Growth: Selected Essays*, Norton, New York.

LAL, D. (1988), *Cultural Stability and Economic Stagnation*, Clarendon Press, Oxford.

LECAILLON, J., F. PAUKERT, C. MORRISSON and D. GERMIDIS (1984), *Income Distribution and Economic Development*, ILO, Geneva.

LEWIS, C. (1938), *America's Stake in International Investment*, Brookings, Washington, D.C.

LEWIS, W.A. (1981), "The Rate of Growth of World Trade, 1830-1973", in GRASSMAN, S. and E. LUNDBERG, eds., *The World Economic Order: Past and Prospects*, Macmillan, London.

LUCAS, R.E. (1988) "On the Mechanics of Economic Development", *Journal of Monetary Economics* (22).

MADDISON, A. (1960), "Growth and Fluctuation in the World Economy 1870-1960", *Banca Nazionale del Lavoro Quarterly Review*, June, pp. 100-48.

MADDISON, A. (1964), *Economic Growth in the West*, Allen and Unwin, London, and Norton, New York.

MADDISON, A. (1969) *Economic Growth in Japan and the USSR*, Allen and Unwin, London and Norton, New York.

MADDISON, A. (1970), *Economic Progress and Policy in Developing Countries*, Allen and Unwin, London.

MADDISON, A. (1971), *Class Structure and Economic Growth: India and Pakistan Since the Moghuls*, Allen and Unwin, London and Norton, New York.

MADDISON, A. (1972), "Explaining Economic Growth", *Banca Nazionale Del Lavoro Quarterly Review*, September.

MADDISON, A. (1976), "Economic Policy and Performance in Europe 1913-1970", in CIPOLLA, C.M. ed., *Fontana Economic History of Europe*, Vol.5:2, Collins, London.

MADDISON, A. (1980), "Monitoring the Labour Market", *Review of Income and Wealth*, June.

MADDISON, A. (1982), *Phases of Capitalist Development*, Oxford University Press.

MADDISON, A. (1983a), "A Comparison of Levels of GDP per Capita in Developed and Developing Countries, 1700-1980", *Journal of Economic History*, March.

MADDISON, A. (1983b), "Economic Stagnation since 1973, its Nature and Causes: A Six Country Survey", *De Economist,* 131, Nr. 4.

MADDISON, A. (1984), "Origins and Impact of the Welfare State, 1883-1983", *Banca Nazionale del Lavoro Quarterly Review*, March.

MADDISON, A. (1985), *Two Crises: Latin America and Asia, 1929-38 and 1973-83*, OECD Development Centre, Paris.

MADDISON, A. (1987), "Growth and Slowdown in Advanced Capitalist Economies: Techniques of Quantitative Assessment", *Journal of Economic Literature*, June.

MADDISON, A. (1988), "Ultimate and Proximate Growth Causality", *Scandinavian Economic History Review*, (2).

MADDISON, A. (1989), *The World Economy in the 20th Century*, OECD Development Centre, Paris.

MADDISON, A. (1990), "The Colonial Burden: A Comparative Perspective", in SCOTT, M.Fg. and D. LAL, eds., *Public Policy and Economic Development*, Oxford University Press.

MADDISON, A. (1991), *Dynamic Forces in Capitalist Development*, Oxford University Press.

MADDISON, A. (1992), "A Long-Run Perspective on Saving", *Scandinavian Journal of Economics*, June, pp. 181-213.

MADDISON, A. (1994), "Explaining the Economic Performance of Nations, 1820-1989", in BAUMOL, W.J., R.R. NELSON and E.N. WOLFF, eds., *Convergence of Productivity: Cross National Studies and Historical Evidence*, Oxford University Press, New York.

MADDISON, A. (1995a), *Explaining the Economic Performance of Nations: Essays in Time and Space*, Elgar, Aldershot.

MADDISON, A. (1995b), "Macroeconomic Accounts for European Countries", in VAN ARK, B. and N.F.R. CRAFTS, eds., *Quantitative Aspects of Postwar European Growth*, Cambridge University Press.

MADDISON, A. (1995c), "Wirtschaftswachstum und Lebensstandard im 20 Jahrhundert", in FISCHER, W., ed., *Wirtschaftssystem und Lebensstandard*, Deutsche Genossenschaftsbank, Berlin.

MADDISON, A. and ASSOCIATES (1992), *The Political Economy of Poverty, Equity and Growth: Brazil and Mexico*, Oxford University Press, New York.

MADDISON, A. and G. PRINCE, eds. (1989), *Economic Growth in Indonesia, 1820-1940*, Foris, Dordrecht.

MADDISON, A. and H. van der WEE, eds. (1994), *Economic Growth and Structural Change: Comparative Approaches over the Long Run*, Proceedings of the Eleventh International Economic History Congress, Milan, September.

MANKIW, N.G., D. ROMER and D.N. WEIL (1992), "A Contribution to the Empirics of Economic Growth", *Quarterly Journal of Economics*, (107).

MARER, P. and ASSOCIATES (1992), *Historically Planned Economies: A Guide to the Data*, World Bank, Washington D.C.

MILWARD, A.S. (1977), *War, Economy and Society, 1939-1945*, Allen Lane, London.

MITCHELL, B.R. (1982), *International Historical Statistics: Africa and Asia*, Macmillan, London.

MITCHELL, B.R. (1983), *International Historical Statistics, The Americas and Australasia*, Macmillan, London.

MITCHELL, B.R. (1992), *European Historical Statistics 1750-1988*, Macmillan, London.

MOWERY, D.C. and N. ROSENBERG (1989), *Technology and the Pursuit of Economic Growth*, Cambridge University Press.

NORTH, D.C. (1968), "Sources of Productivity Change in Ocean Shipping, 1600-1850", *Journal of Political Economy*, September-October.

NORTH, D.C. (1981), *Structure and Change in Economic History*, Norton, New York.

NORTH, D.C. (1990), *Institutions, Institutional Change and Economic Performance*, Cambridge University Press.

NORTH, D.C. and R.P. THOMAS (1973), *The Rise of the Western World*, Cambridge University Press.

PERKINS, D.W. (1969), *Agricultural Development in China, 1368-1968*, Aldine, Chicago.

PILAT, D. (1994), *The Economics of Rapid Growth: The Experience of Japan and Korea*, Elgar, Aldershot.

PSACHAROPOULOS, G. (1975), *Earnings and Education in OECD Countries*, OECD, Paris.

RAWSKI, T.G. (1989), *Economic Growth in Prewar China*, University of California Press, Berkeley.

ROMER, P.M. (1986), "Increasing Returns and Long Run Growth", *Journal of Political Economy*, 94, No. 5.

ROSENBLAT, A. (1945), *La Poblacion Indigena de América desde 1492 hasta la Actualidad*, I.C.E., Buenos Aires.

ROSTAS, L. (1948), *Comparative Productivity in British and American Industry*, Cambridge University Press.

ROSTOW, W.W. (1960), *The Stages of Economic Growth*, Cambridge University Press.

SALTER, W.E.G. (1960), *Productivity and Technical Change*, Cambridge University Press.

SAWYER, M. (1976), "Income Distribution in OECD Countries", *OECD Economic Outlook, Occasional Studies*, Paris, July.

SCHULTZ, T.W. (1961), "Investment in Human Capital", *American Economic Review*, March.

SCHUMPETER, J.A. (1939), *Business Cycles*, McGraw Hill, New York.

SCOTT, M.F. (1989), *A New View of Economic Growth*, Clarendon Press, Oxford.

SOLOW, R.M. (1956), "A Contribution to the Theory of Economic Growth", *Quarterly Journal of Economics*, February.

SOLOW, R.M. (1960), "Investment and Technical Progress", in ARROW, K.J., S. KARLIN and P. SUPPES, eds., *Mathematical Methods in the Social Sciences*, Stamford University Press.

SOLOW, R.M. (1962), "Technical Progress, Capital Formation and Economic Growth", *American Economic Review*, May.

SOLOW, R.M. (1963), *Capital Theory and the Rate of Return*, North Holland, Amsterdam.

SUMMERS, R. and A. HESTON (1988), "A New Set of International Comparisons of Real Product and Prices: Estimates for 130 Countries, 1950-1985", *Review of Income and Wealth*, March.

SUMMERS, R. and A. HESTON (1991), "The Penn World Table (Mark 5): An Expanded Set of International Comparisons, 1950-1988", *Quarterly Journal of Economics*, May.

SZIRMAI, A., B. VAN ARK and D. PILAT (1993), *Explaining Economic Growth: Essays in Honour of Angus Maddison*, North Holland, Amsterdam.

TINBERGEN, J. (1942), "Zur Theorie der langfristigen Wirtschaftsentwicklung", *Weltwirtschaftliches Archiv*, (55).

UN (1949), *International Capital Markets during the Inter-war Period*, Lake Success.

UN (1973), *The Determinants and Consequences of Population Trends*, Vol. 1, New York.

VERSPAGEN, B. (1992), *Uneven Growth Between Interdependent Economies*, Ph.D. Thesis, University of Limburg, Maastricht.

WEBER, M. (1964), *The Religion of China*, Collier Macmillan, London.

WOLF, J. (1912), *Die Volkswirtschaft der Gegenwart und Zukunft*, Deichert, Leipzig, 1912.

WORLD BANK (1993), *The East Asian Miracle: Economic Growth and Public Policy*, Oxford University Press.

WRIGHT, G. (1990), "The Origins of American Industrial Success 1870-1940", *American Economic Review*, September.

Appendix A

Population in 56 Sample Countries

Source Notes on Population Estimates

All figures are adjusted to refer throughout to population within 1990 frontiers. Except for Bangladesh, India and Pakistan all figures are on a mid-year basis.

Advanced Capitalist Countries

For 1950-1992, unless otherwise specified, the figures are from OECD, *Labour Force Statistics*. Figures for 1993 and 1994 are my extrapolations. In six of the countries there were no frontier changes. In Finland the territorial change in 1940 did not affect population as the people in the area ceded to the USSR were moved to other parts of Finland. For the other ten countries, the adjustments to the actual population figures are given below. In Austria and Italy, the figures for population within present frontiers were available annually from official sources. For other countries, I generally applied the adjustment coefficient for the year of merger or separation uniformly for all earlier years (except for Japan).

Australia: Bureau of Census and Statistics, *Demography Bulletin Yearbooks* to 1957. The population figures for 1820 and 1850 refer only to the settler population. The indigenous aboriginal population is excluded. The conventional estimate of the aboriginal population in 1820 is 300 000, falling to about 200 000 in 1850, but Noel Butlin thought the figures were a good deal higher. See his "Contours of the Australian Economy 1788-1860", *Australian Economic History Review*, September 1986.

Austria: Up to 1960 from *Statistisches Handbuch für die Republik Österreich*, 1975, p. 9; *Statistisches Handbuch für den Bundesstaat Österreich*, Vienna, 1936, p. 21; and A. Kausel, *Österreichs Volkseinkommen 1830 bis 1913*, Statistical Office, Vienna, 1979. The figures refer throughout to the present territory of Austria.

Belgium: Interpolated from *Annuaire statistique de la Belgique et du Congo Belge*, 1955. I raised the 1820-1924 figures by 0.8 per cent to include Eupen and Malmedy, acquired in 1925.

Canada: The population figures for 1820 refer only to the white population and are derived from *Seventh Census of Canada*, 1931, vol. 1, *Summary*, Dominion Bureau of Statistics, Ottawa, 1936. From the estimates of Rosenblat (cited below for the USA), it would seem that the population of Indians and Eskimos was probably around 75 000 in 1820. 1850-1930 from M.C. Urquhart and K.A.H. Buckley, *Historical Statistics of Canada*, Cambridge, 1965, p. 14. 1820-1948 increased by 2.6 per cent to include Newfoundland, acquired in 1949.

Denmark: S.A. Hansen, *Økonomisk vækst i Danmark*, vol. ii, Institute of Economic History, Copenhagen, 1974, pp. 201-4. 1820-1920 increased by 5.3 per cent to include North Slesvig.

Finland: O. Turpeinen, *Ikaryhmittainen Kuolleisuus Suomessa vv. 1751-1970*, Helsinki, 1973.

France: 1820-1860 from L. Henry and Y. Blayo, "La Population de la France de 1740 à 1860", *Population*, November 1975, pp. 97-9; 1861-1950, from *Annuaire statistique de la France*, 1966, pp. 66-72. Figures include Savoy, Nice and Alsace-Lorraine throughout.

Germany: 1820-1960 derived from estimates of the actual population within the borders of the epoch in A. Maddison, *Dynamic Forces in Capitalist Development*, Oxford University Press, 1991. Here they are adjusted to refer throughout to the territory of the Federal Republic (1989 boundaries). 1960 onwards from OECD, *Labour Force Statistics*. 1820-1944 figures are benchmarked on the proportion of population within the Federal Republic territory in 1936. See notes on GDP coverage in Appendix B below.

Italy: 1820 derived from K.J. Beloch, *Bevölkerungsgeschichte Italiens*, de Gruyter, Berlin, 1961, pp. 351-4. 1870-1950 resident population from *Sommario di statistiche storiche dell Italia, 1861-1975*, ISTAT, Rome, 1976, adjusted to mid-year.

Japan: Estimates for 1820-1860 supplied by Akira Hayami; 1870-1950, from *Japan Statistical Yearbook 1975*, pp. 9, 10 and 13, adjusted to mid-year. Figures for 1935-46 include armed forces overseas. Data on armed forces and geographic change taken from I.B. Taeuber, *The Population of Japan*, Princeton, 1958, chapter XVI. It was assumed that in 1946 only half of the overseas forces had been repatriated to Japan. I adjusted for the temporary loss of Okinawa, i.e. an upward adjustment of 0.78 per cent for 1946 rising gradually to 0.92 per cent in 1972.

Netherlands: 1900-50, from *Zeventig jaren statistiek in tijdreeksen*, CBS, The Hague, 1970, p. 14, adjusted to a mid-year basis. 1870-1900, interpolated from census results from *Jaarcijfers voor Nederland*

1939, The Hague, 1940, p. 4. Earlier years from J.A. Faber *et al.*, "Population Changes and Economic Development in the Netherlands: A Historical Survey", *A.A.G. Bijdragen*, vol. 12, 1965, p. 110, and C.A. Oomens, *De loop van de bevolking van Nederland in de negentiende eeuw, Statistische onderzoekingen*, M35, CBS, The Hague, 1989, p. 16.

New Zealand: 1870-1919 non Maori population from K. Rankin, "New Zealand's Gross National Product: 1859-1939", *Review of Income and Wealth*, March 1992. Maori population 1870-1919 interpolated from figures for benchmark years in G.R. Hawke, *The Making of New Zealand*, Cambridge University Press, 1985, p. 20. Hawke does not give figures for 1820 and 1850, but his graph on p. 10 suggests that the indigenous Maori population was about 100 000 in 1820, and white settler population negligible. For 1850 his graph suggests the Maori population had declined to about 65 000 and whites numbered 25 000. 1920-49 from UN, *Demographic Yearbook*, 1960, pp. 148-50. 1950 onwards from OECD sources.

Norway: *Historical Statistics 1968*, CBS, Oslo, pp. 44-6.

Sweden: Figures for 1820 onwards supplied by Olle Krantz.

Switzerland: *Annuaire statistique de la Suisse*, 1952, pp. 42-3, and K.B. Mayer, *The Population* of Switzerland, Columbia, 1952, pp. 19 and 29.

UK: 1871-1949 from C.H. Feinstein, *National Income Expenditure and Output of the United Kingdom 1855-1965*, Cambridge, 1972, pp. T120-1, home population except 1915-20 and 1939 onwards when armed forces overseas are included. 1820-1871, England (excluding Monmouth) from E.A. Wrigley and R.S. Schofield, *The Population of England 1541-1871*, Arnold, London, 1981, pp. 533-5. Ireland 1821 derived from D. Dickson, C. O Gráda, and S. Daultrey, "Hearth Tax, Household Size, and Irish Population Change 1672-1821", *Proceedings of the Royal Irish Academy*, vol. 82, C, No. 6, Dublin, 1982; and 1821-41 from J. Lee, "On the Accuracy of the Pre-Famine Irish Censuses", in J.M. Goldstrom and I.A. Clarkson, *Irish Population, Economy, and Society*, Oxford, 1981. Other parts of UK from B.R. Mitchell, *Abstract of British Historical Statistics*, Cambridge, 1962, and P. Deane and W.A. Cole, *British Economic Growth 1688-1959*, Cambridge, 1964. 1820-1919 reduced by 6.63 per cent to exclude Southern Ireland, lost in 1920.

My population adjustment for the years 1820-1919 was made in such a way as to ensure congruence with the GDP estimates available for these years. In most cases, retropolation of a fixed adjustment coefficient which refers to the year in which frontiers changed can be expected to provide a reasonable approximation to the situation one would find if one could recalculate the annual figures for each area separately. In the British case we do have separate information on the population of Ireland as a whole and for the rest of the UK before 1920, and we know that the movements in the two parts of the country were quite disparate. Unfortunately, there are, as yet, no separate estimates of population or GDP for Southern Ireland before 1926. Our counterfactual constant frontier population is therefore somewhat anomalous, but it is the best option available if we are to preserve consistency with the GDP series. Table A-1 illustrates the problem.

USA: *Historical Statistics of the United States, Colonial Times to 1970*, US Department of Commerce, 1975, pp. 8 and 1168, resident population except for 1917-19, and 1930 onwards when armed forces overseas are included. 1820-1949 increased by 0.39 per cent to include Alaska and Hawaii, incorporated in 1950. The figures for 1820 and 1850 in Table 1(a) exclude the indigenous population. In 1820 the territory of the USA was a little less than one half of what it is today. The increase was due to the acquisition of Texas, California and other Western lands from Mexico between 1845 and 1853. The settlement of the border with Canada brought in the territory which is now Idaho, Oregon and Washington in 1846. These territories were very sparsely settled, but consisted very largely of the indigenous Indian population. Indians were not separately specified in US censuses before 1860; and before 1890 those living in Indian territory or reservations, were excluded. For this reason it is difficult to find estimates of the Indian population in 1820 or 1850. The most plausible figure I could find for a year near to 1820 was that of Angel Rosenblat, *La Población Indígena de America desde 1492 hasta la Actualidad*, I.C.E., Buenos Aires, 1945, p. 36, who estimates a total of 400 000 for the US and Canada combined in 1825. The bulk of these, probably about 325 000, were in the area of the USA. I have not included the Indian population in the estimates for 1820 and 1850 because indigenous economic activity is not included in the measure of GDP I have used.

Table A-1. **Population of the UK and the Irish Component, 1820-1920**

	Actual Population in Year Cited (000s)				Irish Proportion (%)	Southern Irish Proportion (%)	My Counterfactual Estimate of UK Population Adjusted to Exclude Impact of Frontier Change (%)
	Actual UK	Non-Ireland	Ireland	Southern Ireland			
1820	21 240	14 156	7 084	n.a.	33.4	n.a.	19 832
1840	26 758	18 403	8 355	n.a.	31.2	n.a.	24 985
1870	31 393	25 974	5 419	n.a.	17.3	n.a.	29 312
1900	41 155	36 686	4 469	n.a.	10.9	n.a.	38 426
1913	45 649	41 303	4 346	n.a.	9.5	n.a.	42 622
1920	46 821	42 460	4 361	3 103	9.3	6.63	43 718

"South European" Countries

Greece: 1900-40 derived (with some interpolation between 1900 and 1920) from I. Svennilson, *Growth and Stagnation in the European Economy*, ECE, Geneva, 1954, pp. 236-7. 1941-9 from UN, *Demographic Yearbook 1951*, New York, 1952, pp. 124-5. 1950 onwards from OECD sources. Estimates are adjusted throughout to refer to present territory.

Ireland: 1820-1870 from J.M. Goldstrom and L.A. Clarkson, *Irish Population, Economy and Society*, Oxford University Press, 1981; 1870-1920 from Feinstein (1972), table 55; 1920-50 from UN, *Demographic Yearbook*, New York, 1960. 1950 onwards from OECD sources. The estimates are adjusted to refer to the present territory of the Irish Republic.

Portugal: 1820-1969 from A.B. Nunes, E. Mata and N. Valerio, "Portuguese Economic Growth, 1833-1985", *Journal of European Economic History*, Fall 1989; 1970 onwards from OECD, *Labour Force Statistics*, Paris.

Spain: 1820-1955 from A. Carreras, ed., *Estadisticas Historicas de España: Siglos XIX-XX*, Fundacion Banco Exterior, Madrid, 1989, pp. 68-72; 1956-9 interpolated; 1960-90 from OECD, *National Accounts 1960-91*, vol. I, Paris, 1993.

Turkey: 1900-1913 derived from E. Kirsten, E.W. Buchholtz, and W. Köllmann, *Raum und Bevölkerung in der Weltgeschichte*, Ploetz, 1956, vol. II, p. 247; 1927-49 from UN, *Demographic Yearbook*, 1960; 1950 onwards from OECD sources. Estimates are adjusted throughout to refer to present boundaries.

East European Countries

Bulgaria: 1870-1940 derived from I. Svennilson, *Growth and Stagnation in the European Economy*, ECE, Geneva, 1954, p. 237 (adjusted to post-war frontiers); 1941-9 from UN, *Demographic Yearbook*, New York, 1960; 1950s and 60s from Joint Economic Committee, US Congress, *Economic Developments in Eastern Europe*, Washington, D.C. 1970, p. 125; 1970-85 from World Bank, *Historically Planned Economies: A Guide to the Data*, Washington, D.C., 1992. Thereafter from World Bank, *World Tables 1994*. Figures are adjusted to refer to present territory.

Czechoslovakia: 1820-1913 derived from the movement of population in Bohemia, Moravia and Silesia as given by H. Helczmanovszki, "Die Bevölkerung Österreich-Ungarns", in *Geschichte und Ergebnisse der Zentralen Amtlichen Statistik in Österreich 1829-1979*, OSZ, Vienna, 1974, pp. 376 and 379; 1920-49 from UN, *Demographic Yearbook*, New York, 1960; thereafter as for Bulgaria.

Hungary: as for Czechoslovakia.

Poland: as for Bulgaria.

Romania: same sources as for Bulgaria; 1870-1913 derived from Svennilson (1954), 1920-49 from UN (1960).

USSR: 1820-1897 from B.R. Mitchell, *European Historical Statistics 1750-1970*, Macmillan, London, 1975, p. 65; 1897-1940 from F. Lorimer, *The Population of the Soviet Union: History and Prospects*, League of Nations, Geneva, 1946; 1946-49 movement from G.W. Nutter, *The Growth of Industrial Production in the Soviet Union*, NBER, Princeton, 1962, p. 519; 1950-69 from *Narodnoe Khoziastvo SSSR*, Moscow, various issues (adjusted to mid year); 1970-89 from World Bank, *Historically Planned Economies: A Guide to the Data*, Washington, D.C., 1992. 1990 and 1991 from B.M. Bolotin, "The Former Soviet Union as Reflected in National Accounts Statistics", *In Search of Answers in the Post Soviet Era*, IMEMO, Moscow, 1992. 1991-2 movement derived from World Bank, *World Tables 1994*, estimates for the 15 successor countries. Figures refer throughout to territory of USSR in 1990, with adjustment of pre 1940 figures by 1940 ratio of expanded Soviet territory to population within previous boundaries (1.118).

Yugoslavia: 1890-1949 derived from I. Svennilson, *Growth and Stagnation in the European Economy*, ECE, Geneva, 1954, p. 237. 1950 onwards from OECD Development Centre. Figures refer to post 1954 boundaries throughout.

Latin America

Argentina: 1820-1890 from L. Bethell, ed., *The Cambridge History of Latin America*, vol. III, 1985, p. 626 and vol. IV, 1986, p. 122; 1900-69 from André Hofman, "International Estimates of Capital: A 1950-1989 Comparison of Latin America and the USA", *Research Memorandum 509*, Institute of Economic Research, University of Groningen, October 1992; 1970-92 from World Bank, *World Tables*. 1993 and 1994 are my extrapolations.

Brazil: 1820 from N.H. Leff, *Underdevelopment and Development in Brazil*, vol. 1, Allen and Unwin, London, 1982, p. 241; 1851-1949 from IBGE, *O Brasil em Numeros*, Rio, 1960, p. 5; 1950-88 from A. Maddison and Associates, *The Political Economy of Poverty, Equity and Growth: Brazil and Mexico*, Oxford University Press, New York, 1992; 1989-92 from World Bank sources. 1993 and 1994 are my extrapolations.

Chile: 1820-1900 from B.R. Mitchell, *International Historical Statistics: The Americas and Australasia*, Macmillan, London, 1983, p. 51. 1900-92 from André Hofman. 1993 and 1994 are my extrapolations.

Colombia: 1820-1994 as for Chile.

Mexico: 1820-90 derived from A. Rosenblat, *La Población Indígena de América desde 1492 hasta la Actualidad*, ICE, Buenos Aires, 1945, and F. Rosenzweig, ed., *Fuerza de Trabajo y Actividad Económica Por Sectores, Estadistícas Económicas del Porfiriato*, Colegio de México, no date (1960?). 1895-1909 and 1921-49 from INEGI, *Estadísticas Históricas de México*, vol. I, Mexico DF, 1985, p. 311; 1910-21 from R.G. Greer, "The Demographic Impact of the Mexican Revolution 1910-21", Master's thesis, University of Texas, 1966. 1950-84 from Maddison and Associates (1992); 1985-92 from World Bank, *World Tables*. 1993 and 1994 are my extrapolations.

Peru: 1820-1900 derived from B.R. Mitchell (1983), p. 52 and L. Bethell, ed. vol. IV (1986), p. 122; 1920-50 movement backcast from UN, *Demographic Yearbook 1960*, New York, 1960, pp. 136-8; 1950-85 from R. Webb, *The Political Economy of Poverty, Equity and Growth: Peru*, 1987, processed. 1986-92 from World Bank, *World Tables*. 1993 and 1994 are my extrapolations. 1901-19 figures are interpolations.

Venezuela: 1820-1969 derived from A. Baptista, *Bases cuantitativas de la economía venezolana 1820-1989*, Comunicaciones Corporativas D, Caracas, 1991, p. 21. 1970-92 from World Bank, *World Tables*. 1993 and 1994 are my extrapolations.

Asia

Bangladesh: Prepartition (1941) population estimated at 41 966 thousand by K. Davis, *Population of India and Pakistan*, Princeton, 1951, p. 198 from 1941 census. For earlier years population assumed to move (with intercensal interpolation) as in prepartition Bengal (plus native States and agencies) as given in the censuses from 1891 to 1941 (see M.W.M. Yeatts, *Census of India 1941*, vol. I, *India*, Part I *Tables*, Delhi, 1943, pp. 62-6); 1950-60 from OECD Development Centre, 1970 onwards from World Bank, *World Tables*; 1960-70 movement interpolated between these two sources.

Burma: Census results for 1891-1941 are given in Aye Hlaing, "Trends of Economic Growth and Income Distribution in Burma 1870-1940", *Journal of the Burma Research Society*, 1964, p. 96. I interpolated these and estimated 1870 from the movement he shows for Lower Burma. 1950 onwards from OECD Development Centre.

China: 1820-1930 derived (with interpolation) from P.K.C. Liu and Kuo-shu Hwang, "Population Change and Economic Development in Mainland China since 1400", in Chi-ming Hou and Tzong-shian Yu, eds., *Modern Chinese Economic History*, Academia Sinica, Taipei, 1979, p. 82, and 1933-53 (with interpolation) from D.H. Perkins, *Agricultural Development in China, 1368-1968*, Aldine, Chicago, 1969, p. 16. 1950-69 from *Statistical Yearbook of China*, State Statistical Bureau, People's Republic of China, Hong Kong, 1984, adjusted to a mid-year basis; 1970-90 from World Bank, *Historically Planned Economies: A Guide to the Data*, Washington, D.C., 1992. 1991 onwards from World Bank.

India: 1820 derived by interpolation of Irfan Habib's estimate of 200 million in 1800 (see "Population" in T. Raychaudhuri and I. Habib, *The Cambridge Economic History of India*, Cambridge, 1982, p. 167 and Moni Mukherjee's estimate of 227 million for 1856. 1856-1946 from A. Maddison, *Class Structure and Economic Growth*, Norton, New York, 1971, pp. 164-5. The 1820-1946 movement is taken here to be parallel to that for undivided India (all figures multiplied by .823367 — the 1946 ratio). 1950-90 supplied by the Central Statistical Organisation, New Delhi in May 1992. 1991 onwards from World Bank. Indian figures are for fiscal years beginning 1st April.

Indonesia: 1820-70 from A. Maddison, "Dutch Income in and from Indonesia", *Modern Asian Studies*, 1989. 1870-1990 supplied by Pierre van der Eng. 1991 onwards from World Bank. Irian Jaya is included in the population figures throughout. East Timor is included from 1980 onwards.

Pakistan: Prepartition (1941) population estimated at 28 169 thousand by K. Davis, *op. cit.*, p. 198. For earlier years, population assumed to move (with intercensal interpolation) as in prepartition total for Punjab (province, states, etc.). Sind and North West Frontier Province as given for census years by M.W.M. Yeatts, *op. cit.* 1950 onwards as for Bangladesh.

Philippines: 1820-1913 from E. Kirsten, E.W. Buchholtz and W. Köllmann, *Raum und Bevölkerung in der Weltgeschichte*, Ploetz, Wurzburg, 1956 (1901-12 and 1914-25 figures are my interpolations); 1926-50 movement from UN, *Demographic Yearbook*, New York, 1960; 1950 onwards as for Bangladesh.

South Korea: 1900-1913 assumed to grow at same pace as Japan. 1913-40 growth for Korea as a whole from Sang-Chul Suh, *Growth and Structural Change in Korean Economy, 1910-1940*, Harvard, 1978, p. 41. 1940 level in South Korea from K.S. Kim and M. Roemer, *Growth and Structural Transformation*, Harvard, 1979, p. 35. 1940-49 from UN *Demographic Yearbook 1960*, p. 142. 1950-60 from OECD Development Centre, 1970 onwards from World Bank, *World Tables*, Washington, D.C. 1961-9 interpolated.

Taiwan: 1900-49 derived from S.P.S. Ho, *Economic Development of Taiwan, 1860-1970*, Yale, 1978, pp. 313-4 adjusted to a mid-year basis. 1950-68 from national accounts, and 1969 onwards from *Taiwan Statistical Data Book*, Taipei, 1992.

Thailand: 1820-1949 interpolated from figures for 18 benchmark years given in Sompop Manarungsan, "Economic Development of Thailand, 1850-1950", Ph.D. thesis, University of Groningen, 1989, p. 32. 1950-92 as for South Korea.

Africa

1900 and 1913 estimates for Kenya, Morocco, Nigeria and Tanzania were derived from Statistisches Reichsamt, *Statistisches Handbuch der Weltwirtschaft*, Berlin, 1935. For Côte d'Ivoire the proportionate movement for 1900-50 assumed to be the same as in Ghana, for Ethiopia and Zaire it was assumed to be like that for the other countries combined. Except as otherwise specified the 1950-60 figures are from the OECD Development Centre, and the figures for 1970 onwards are from World Bank sources. The 1960-70 movement was interpolated.

Egypt: 1900 and 1913 derived from D.C. Meade, *Growth and Structural Change in the Egyptian Economy*, Irwin, Illinois, 1967, p. 295. 1950-69 from Summers and Heston (1991). 1970 onwards from World Bank sources. 1951-4, 1956-59, 1961-4, and 1965-9 are interpolations.

Ethiopia: 1950 onwards derived from World Bank, *World Tables*, various issues. Figures for 1951-4, 1956-9, 1961-4 are interpolations.

Ghana: 1900 and 1913 derived from A. Szereszewski, *Structural Changes in the Economy of Ghana, 1891-1911*, Weidenfeld and Nicolson, London, 1965, p. 126.

Nigeria: 1950-92 annual estimates are interpolations from benchmark years as given (in the light of the 1992 census results) in "Le recensement du Nigeria", *Population et Sociétés*, INED, Paris, October 1992.

South Africa: 1900 and 1913 derived from B.R. Mitchell, *International Historical Statistics: Africa and Asia*, Macmillan, London, 1982, p. 41. 1920-49 movement from UN, *Demographic Yearbook*, New York, 1960; 1950-60 from OECD Development Centre; 1960-70 interpolated; 1970 onwards from World Bank, *World Tables*, Washington, D.C.

Zaire: 1950 onwards from OECD Development Centre.

Table A-2. **Rates of Population Growth, 1820-1992**

(annual average compound growth rates)

	1820-70	1870-1913	1913-50	1950-73	1973-92
12 West European Countries					
Austria	0.7	0.9	0.1	0.4	0.2
Belgium	0.8	1.0	0.3	0.5	0.2
Denmark	1.0	1.1	1.0	0.7	0.2
Finland	0.8	1.3	0.8	0.7	0.4
France	0.4	0.2	0.0	1.0	0.5
Germany	0.9	1.2	0.8	0.9	0.2
Italy	0.6	0.7	0.6	0.7	0.3
Netherlands	0.9	1.2	1.3	1.2	0.6
Norway	1.2	0.8	0.8	0.8	0.4
Sweden	1.0	0.7	0.6	0.6	0.3
Switzerland	0.8	0.9	0.5	1.4	0.4
UK	0.8	0.9	0.5	0.5	0.2
Arithmetic Average	0.8	0.9	0.6	0.8	0.3
4 Western Offshoots					
Australia	8.1	2.6	1.4	2.2	1.4
Canada	3.3	1.7	1.5	2.1	1.1
New Zealand	n.a.	3.2	1.4	1.9	0.7
USA	2.9	2.1	1.2	1.4	1.0
Arithmetic Average	4.8	2.4	1.4	1.9	1.1
5 South European Countries					
Greece	n.a.	n.a.	0.9	0.7	0.8
Ireland	-0.5	-0.5	-0.1	0.1	0.8
Portugal	0.6	0.8	0.9	0.1	0.7
Spain	0.6	0.5	0.9	1.0	0.6
Turkey	n.a.	n.a.	1.3	2.7	2.3
Arithmetic Average	0.2	0.3	0.8	0.9	1.0
7 East European Countries					
Bulgaria	n.a.	1.4	1.1	0.8	- 0.1
Czechoslovakia	0.6	0.7	-0.2	0.7	0.4
Hungary	0.4	0.7	0.5	0.5	- 0.1
Poland	n.a.	n.a.	-0.2	1.3	0.7
Romania	n.a.	1.5	0.7	1.1	0.5
USSR	1.0	1.4	0.4	1.4	0.8
Yugoslavia	n.a.	n.a.	0.5	1.1	0.7
Arithmetic Average	0.7	1.1	0.4	1.0	0.4

Table A-2 (continued). **Rates of Population Growth 1820-1992**
(annual average compound growth rates)

	1820-70	1870-1913	1913-50	1950-73	1973-92
7 Latin American Countries					
Argentina	2.5	3.4	2.2	1.7	1.4
Brazil	1.6	2.1	2.1	2.9	2.4
Chile	1.6	1.4	1.5	2.2	1.6
Colombia	1.4	1.8	2.3	2.9	2.0
Mexico	0.7	1.1	1.6	3.2	2.5
Peru	1.4	1.2	1.5	2.8	2.4
Venezuela	1.7	1.3	1.5	3.8	3.0
Arithmetic Average	1.6	1.8	1.8	2.8	2.2
11 Asian Countries					
Bangladesh	n.a.	n.a.	0.8	2.3	2.3
Burma	n.a.	2.5	1.1	2.0	2.0
China	-0.1	0.5	0.6	2.1	1.5
India	0.4	0.4	1.0	2.1	2.2
Indonesia	1.0	1.3	1.2	2.0	2.1
Japan	0.2	0.9	1.3	1.1	0.7
Pakistan	n.a.	n.a.	1.7	2.5	3.1
Philippines	1.7	1.4	2.1	3.1	2.4
South Korea	n.a.	n.a.	1.9	2.2	1.3
Taiwan	n.a.	n.a.	2.2	3.0	1.5
Thailand	0.4	1.0	2.2	3.1	2.1
Arithmetic Average	0.6	1.0	1.5	2.3	1.9
10 African Countries					
Côte d'Ivoire	n.a.	n.a.	2.1	3.1	3.9
Egypt	n.a.	n.a.	1.4	2.3	2.4
Ethiopia	n.a.	n.a.	1.9	2.3	3.0
Ghana	n.a.	n.a.	2.1	3.4	2.8
Kenya	n.a.	n.a.	2.7	3.0	3.7
Morocco	n.a.	n.a.	1.9	2.6	2.5
Nigeria	n.a.	n.a.	2.0	2.0	2.6
South Africa	n.a.	n.a.	2.2	2.4	2.4
Tanzania	n.a.	n.a.	2.0	2.5	3.1
Zaire	n.a.	n.a.	1.9	3.3	3.2
Arithmetic Average	n.a.	n.a.	2.0	2.7	3.0

Table A-3a. **Population of 17 Advanced Capitalist Countries, 1820-1994**

(thousands at mid-year)

	Australia	Austria	Belgium	Canada	Denmark	Finland	France	Germany	Italy
1820	33	3 189	3 434	741	1 155	1 169	31 250	14 747	20 176
1850	389	3 950	4 449	2 430	1 499	1 628	36 350	19 952	25 571
1870	1 620	4 520	5 096	3 736	1 888	1 754	38 440	23 055	27 888
1871	1 675	4 562	5 137	3 801	1 903	1 786	37 731	23 164	28 063
1872	1 722	4 604	5 178	3 870	1 918	1 819	37 679	23 295	28 233
1873	1 769	4 646	5 219	3 943	1 935	1 847	37 887	23 484	28 387
1874	1 822	4 688	5 261	4 012	1 954	1 873	38 044	23 733	28 505
1875	1 874	4 730	5 303	4 071	1 973	1 899	38 221	24 023	28 630
1876	1 929	4 772	5 345	4 128	1 994	1 928	38 398	24 329	28 837
1877	1 995	4 815	5 394	4 184	2 019	1 957	38 576	24 640	29 067
1878	2 062	4 857	5 442	4 244	2 043	1 983	38 763	24 933	29 252
1879	2 127	4 899	5 492	4 312	2 064	2 014	38 909	25 222	29 425
1880	2 197	4 941	5 541	4 384	2 081	2 047	39 045	25 479	29 534
1881	2 269	4 985	5 606	4 451	2 101	2 072	39 191	25 667	29 672
1882	2 348	5 030	5 673	4 503	2 120	2 098	39 337	25 832	29 898
1883	2 447	5 075	5 740	4 560	2 137	2 130	39 472	25 999	30 113
1884	2 556	5 121	5 807	4 617	2 160	2 164	39 629	26 214	30 366
1885	2 650	5 166	5 876	4 666	2 186	2 195	39 733	26 390	30 644
1886	2 741	5 212	5 919	4 711	2 213	2 224	39 858	26 631	30 857
1887	2 835	5 257	5 962	4 760	2 237	2 259	39 889	26 911	31 049
1888	2 932	5 303	6 007	4 813	2 257	2 296	39 920	27 215	31 243
1889	3 022	5 348	6 051	4 865	2 276	2 331	40 004	27 525	31 468
1890	3 107	5 394	6 096	4 918	2 294	2 364	40 014	27 822	31 702
1891	3 196	5 446	6 164	4 972	2 311	2 394	39 983	28 116	31 892
1892	3 274	5 504	6 231	5 022	2 327	2 451	39 993	28 401	32 091
1893	3 334	5 563	6 300	5 072	2 344	2 430	40 014	28 678	32 303
1894	3 395	5 622	6 370	5 121	2 367	2 511	40 056	29 007	32 513
1895	3 460	5 680	6 439	5 169	2 397	2 483	40 098	29 381	32 689
1896	3 523	5 739	6 494	5 218	2 428	2 515	40 192	29 806	32 863
1897	3 586	5 798	6 548	5 269	2 462	2 549	40 348	30 267	33 078
1898	3 642	5 856	6 604	5 325	2 497	2 589	40 473	30 740	33 285
1899	3 691	5 915	6 662	5 383	2 530	2 624	40 546	31 216	33 487
1900	3 741	5 973	6 719	5 457	2 561	2 646	40 598	31 666	33 672
1901	3 795	6 035	6 801	5 536	2 594	2 667	40 640	32 134	33 877
1902	3 850	6 099	6 903	5 650	2 623	2 686	40 713	32 639	34 166
1903	3 896	6 164	6 997	5 813	2 653	2 706	40 786	33 126	34 436
1904	3 946	6 228	7 086	5 994	2 681	2 735	40 859	33 604	34 715
1905	4 004	6 292	7 175	6 166	2 710	2 762	40 890	34 078	35 011
1906	4 062	6 357	7 258	6 282	2 741	2 788	40 942	34 552	35 297
1907	4 127	6 421	7 338	6 596	2 775	2 821	40 942	35 038	35 594
1908	4 197	6 485	7 411	6 813	2 809	2 861	41 046	35 518	35 899
1909	4 278	6 550	7 478	6 993	2 845	2 899	41 109	36 001	36 213
1910	4 375	6 614	7 498	7 188	2 882	2 929	41 224	36 481	36 572
1911	4 500	6 669	7 517	7 410	2 917	2 962	41 307	36 928	36 917
1912	4 661	6 724	7 590	7 602	2 951	2 998	41 359	37 373	37 150
1913	4 821	6 767	7 666	7 852	2 983	3 027	41 463	37 843	37 248
1914	4 933	6 806	7 723	8 093	3 018	3 053	41 476	38 301	37 526
1915	4 971	6 843	7 759	8 191	3 055	3 083	40 481	38 637	37 982
1916	4 955	6 825	7 762	8 214	3 092	3 105	39 884	38 260	38 142
1917	4 950	6 785	7 729	8 277	3 130	3 124	39 288	38 063	37 981
1918	5 032	6 727	7 660	8 374	3 165	3 125	38 542	37 749	37 520
1919	5 193	6 420	7 628	8 548	3 202	3 117	38 700	37 966	37 250
1920	5 358	6 455	7 552	8 798	3 242	3 133	39 000	38 184	37 398
1921	5 461	6 504	7 504	9 028	3 285	3 170	39 240	38 610	37 691
1922	5 574	6 528	7 571	9 159	3 322	3 210	39 420	38 815	38 086
1923	5 697	6 543	7 635	9 256	3 356	3 243	39 880	39 070	38 460
1924	5 819	6 562	7 707	9 394	3 389	3 272	40 310	39 314	38 810
1925	5 943	6 582	7 779	9 549	3 425	3 304	40 610	39 608	39 165
1926	6 064	6 603	7 844	9 713	3 452	3 339	40 870	39 899	39 502
1927	6 188	6 623	7 904	9 905	3 475	3 368	40 940	40 146	39 848
1928	6 304	6 643	7 968	10 107	3 497	3 396	41 050	40 378	40 186
1929	6 396	6 664	8 032	10 305	3 518	3 424	41 230	40 595	40 469
1930	6 469	6 684	8 076	10 488	3 542	3 449	41 610	40 811	40 791
1931	6 527	6 705	8 126	10 657	3 569	3 476	41 860	41 024	41 132
1932	6 579	6 725	8 186	10 794	3 603	3 503	41 860	41 207	41 431
1933	6 631	6 746	8 231	10 919	3 633	3 526	41 890	41 402	41 753

Table A-3a (cont. 2)

	Australia	Austria	Belgium	Canada	Denmark	Finland	France	Germany	Italy
1934	6 682	6 760	8 262	11 030	3 666	3 549	41 950	41 642	42 093
1935	6 732	6 761	8 288	11 136	3 695	3 576	41 940	41 932	42 429
1936	6 783	6 758	8 315	11 243	3 722	3 601	41 910	42 208	42 750
1937	6 841	6 755	8 346	11 341	3 749	3 626	41 930	42 534	43 068
1938	6 904	6 753	8 374	11 452	3 777	3 656	41 960	42 990	43 419
1939	6 971	6 653	8 392	11 570	3 805	3 686	41 900	43 446	43 865
1940	7 042	6 705	8 346	11 688	3 832	3 698	41 000	43 792	44 341
1941	7 111	6 745	8 276	11 818	3 863	3 702	39 600	44 047	44 734
1942	7 173	6 783	8 247	11 969	3 903	3 708	39 400	44 417	45 004
1943	7 236	6 808	8 242	12 115	3 949	3 721	39 000	44 151	45 177
1944	7 309	6 834	8 291	12 268	3 998	3 735	38 900	43 809	45 290
1945	7 389	6 799	8 339	12 404	4 045	3 758	39 700	45 000	45 442
1946	7 474	7 000	8 367	12 634	4 101	3 806	40 290	46 190	45 725
1947	7 578	6 971	8 450	12 901	4 146	3 859	40 680	46 992	46 040
1948	7 715	6 956	8 557	13 180	4 190	3 912	41 110	48 251	46 381
1949	7 919	6 943	8 614	13 469	4 230	3 963	41 480	49 198	46 733
1950	8 177	6 935	8 640	13 737	4 269	4 009	41 836	49 983	47 105
1951	8 418	6 936	8 679	14 047	4 304	4 047	42 156	50 528	47 418
1952	8 634	6 928	8 731	14 491	4 334	4 091	42 460	50 859	47 666
1953	8 821	6 933	8 778	14 882	4 369	4 139	42 752	51 350	47 957
1954	8 996	6 940	8 820	15 321	4 406	4 187	43 057	51 880	48 299
1955	9 201	6 947	8 869	15 730	4 439	4 235	43 428	52 382	48 633
1956	9 421	6 952	8 924	16 123	4 466	4 282	43 843	53 008	48 921
1957	9 640	6 966	8 989	16 677	4 488	4 324	44 311	53 656	49 182
1958	9 842	6 987	9 053	17 120	4 515	4 360	44 789	54 292	49 476
1959	10 056	7 014	9 104	17 522	4 587	4 395	45 240	54 876	49 832
1960	10 275	7 048	9 154	17 909	4 581	4 430	45 684	55 433	50 198
1961	10 508	7 087	9 184	16 269	4 612	4 461	46 163	56 175	50 524
1962	10 700	7 130	9 218	18 615	4 647	4 491	46 998	56 837	50 844
1963	10 907	7 175	9 283	18 965	4 684	4 523	47 816	57 389	51 199
1964	11 122	7 224	9 367	19 325	4 720	4 549	48 310	57 971	51 601
1965	11 341	7 271	9 448	19 678	4 757	4 564	48 758	58 619	51 988
1966	11 599	7 322	9 508	20 048	4 797	4 581	49 164	59 148	52 332
1967	11 799	7 377	9 557	20 412	4 839	4 606	49 548	59 286	52 667
1968	12 009	7 415	9 590	20 729	4 867	4 626	49 915	59 500	52 787
1969	12 263	7 441	9 613	21 028	4 893	4 624	50 315	60 067	53 317
1970	12 507	7 467	9 638	21 324	4 929	4 606	50 772	60 651	53 661
1971	13 067	7 501	9 673	21 595	4 963	4 612	51 251	61 302	54 015
1972	13 304	7 544	9 711	21 848	4 992	4 640	51 701	61 672	54 400
1973	13 505	7 586	9 742	22 125	5 022	4 666	52 118	61 976	54 779
1974	13 723	7 599	9 772	22 479	5 045	4 691	52 460	62 054	55 130
1975	13 893	7 579	9 801	22 831	5 060	4 712	52 699	61 829	55 441
1976	14 033	7 566	9 818	23 025	5 073	4 726	52 909	61 531	55 701
1977	14 192	7 568	9 845	23 316	5 089	4 739	53 145	61 400	55 730
1978	14 359	7 562	9 872	23 647	5 106	4 753	53 376	61 327	56 127
1979	14 516	7 549	9 837	23 768	5 117	4 765	53 606	61 359	56 292
1980	14 695	7 549	9 847	24 070	5 125	4 780	53 880	61 566	56 416
1981	14 923	7 565	9 853	24 366	5 122	4 800	54 182	61 682	56 503
1982	15 184	7 571	9 856	24 604	5 119	4 827	54 480	61 638	56 639
1983	15 393	7 552	9 855	24 803	5 114	4 856	54 729	61 423	56 825
1984	15 579	7 553	9 855	24 995	5 112	4 882	54 947	61 175	56 983
1985	15 788	7 558	9 858	25 181	5 114	4 902	55 170	61 024	57 128
1986	16 018	7 565	9 862	25 374	5 121	4 918	55 394	61 066	57 221
1987	16 264	7 575	9 870	25 644	5 127	4 932	55 630	61 077	57 331
1988	16 518	7 595	9 921	25 939	5 130	4 946	55 884	61 451	57 441
1989	16 803	7 624	9 938	26 254	5 133	4 964	56 423	62 063	57 525
1990	17 045	7 718	9 967	26 610	5 141	4 986	56 735	63 254	57 647
1991	17 292	7 823	10 005	27 000	5 154	5 029	57 050	63 889	57 783
1992	17 529	7 884	10 025	28 436	5 170	5 042	57 372	64 846	57 900
1993	17 769	7 945	10 045	28 836	5 186	5 055	57 696	65 817	58 017
1994	18 012	8 006	10 045	29 936	5 201	5 068	58 022	66 802	58 134

Table A-3a (cont. 3)

	Japan	Netherlands	New Zealand	Norway	Sweden	Switzerland	UK	USA
1820	31 000	2 355		970	2 585	1 829	19 832	9 656
1850	32 000	3 095		1 392	3 483	2 379	25 601	23 352
1870	34 437	3 615	291	1 735	4 164	2 664	29 312	40 061
1871	34 648	3 650	306	1 745	4 186	2 680	29 464	41 098
1872	34 859	3 693	320	1 755	4 227	2 697	29 761	42 136
1873	35 070	3 735	335	1 767	4 274	2 715	30 044	43 174
1874	35 235	3 799	367	1 783	4 320	2 733	30 346	44 212
1875	35 436	3 822	406	1 803	4 362	2 750	30 662	45 245
1876	35 713	3 866	434	1 829	4 407	2 768	30 999	46 287
1877	36 018	3 910	450	1 852	4 457	2 786	31 350	47 325
1878	36 315	3 955	467	1 877	4 508	2 803	31 682	48 362
1879	36 557	4 000	494	1 902	4 555	2 821	32 030	49 400
1880	36 807	4 043	520	1 919	4 572	2 839	32 327	50 458
1881	37 112	4 091	539	1 923	4 569	2 853	32 619	51 743
1882	37 414	4 140	555	1 920	4 576	2 863	32 872	53 027
1883	37 766	4 189	574	1 919	4 591	2 874	33 100	54 311
1884	38 138	4 239	598	1 929	4 624	2 885	33 355	55 595
1885	38 427	4 289	614	1 944	4 664	2 896	33 627	56 879
1886	38 622	4 340	626	1 958	4 700	2 907	33 905	58 164
1887	38 866	4 392	640	1 970	4 726	2 918	34 172	59 448
1888	39 251	4 444	649	1 977	4 742	2 929	34 436	60 732
1889	39 688	4 497	656	1 984	4 761	2 940	34 713	62 016
1890	40 077	4 545	665	1 997	4 780	2 951	35 000	63 302
1891	40 380	4 601	674	2 013	4 794	2 965	35 296	64 612
1892	40 684	4 658	686	2 026	4 805	3 002	35 606	65 922
1893	41 001	4 716	705	2 038	4 816	3 040	35 938	67 231
1894	41 350	4 774	722	2 057	4 849	3 077	36 283	68 541
1895	41 775	4 883	735	2 083	4 896	3 114	36 621	69 851
1896	42 196	4 893	748	2 112	4 941	3 151	36 974	71 161
1897	42 643	4 954	764	2 142	4 986	3 188	37 336	72 471
1898	43 145	5 015	779	2 174	5 036	3 226	37 704	73 781
1899	43 626	5 077	794	2 204	5 080	3 263	38 070	75 091
1900	44 103	5 142	807	2 230	5 117	3 300	38 426	76 391
1901	44 662	5 221	824	2 255	5 156	3 341	38 784	77 888
1902	45 255	5 305	844	2 275	5 187	3 384	39 115	79 469
1903	45 841	5 389	867	2 288	5 210	3 428	39 445	80 946
1904	46 378	5 471	893	2 297	5 241	3 472	39 786	82 485
1905	46 829	5 551	919	2 309	5 278	3 461	40 131	84 147
1906	47 227	5 632	946	2 319	5 316	3 560	40 486	85 770
1907	47 691	5 710	969	2 329	5 357	3 604	40 837	87 339
1908	48 260	5 786	996	2 346	5 404	3 647	41 199	89 055
1909	48 869	5 842	1 024	2 367	5 453	3 691	41 568	90 845
1910	49 518	5 902	1 045	2 384	5 449	3 735	41 938	92 767
1911	50 215	5 984	1 067	2 401	5 542	3 776	42 267	94 234
1912	50 941	6 068	1 092	2 423	5 583	3 819	42 424	95 703
1913	51 672	6 164	1 122	2 447	5 621	3 864	42 622	97 606
1914	52 396	6 277	1 143	2 472	5 659	3 897	42 996	99 505
1915	53 124	6 395	1 152	2 498	5 696	3 883	43 268	100 941
1916	53 815	6 516	1 155	2 522	5 735	3 883	43 430	102 364
1917	54 437	6 654	1 152	2 551	5 779	3 888	43 523	103 817
1918	54 886	6 752	1 156	2 578	5 807	3 880	43 487	104 958
1919	55 253	6 805	1 195	2 603	5 830	3 869	43 449	105 473
1920	55 818	6 848	1 241	2 635	5 876	3 877	43 718	106 881
1921	56 490	6 921	1 275	2 668	5 929	3 876	44 072	108 964
1922	57 209	7 032	1 304	2 695	5 971	3 874	44 372	110 484
1923	57 937	7 150	1 326	2 713	5 997	3 883	44 596	112 387
1924	58 686	7 264	1 350	2 729	6 021	3 896	44 915	114 558
1925	59 522	7 366	1 382	2 747	6 045	3 910	45 059	116 284
1926	60 490	7 471	1 412	2 763	6 064	3 932	45 232	117 857
1927	61 430	7 576	1 437	2 775	6 081	3 956	45 389	119 502
1928	62 361	7 679	1 454	2 785	6 097	3 988	45 578	120 971
1929	63 244	7 782	1 471	2 795	6 113	4 022	45 672	122 245
1930	64 203	7 884	1 493	2 807	6 131	4 051	45 866	123 668
1931	65 205	7 999	1 514	2 824	6 152	4 080	46 074	124 633
1932	66 189	8 123	1 527	2 842	6 176	4 102	46 335	125 436
1933	67 182	8 237	1 540	2 858	6 201	4 122	46 520	126 180

Table A-3a (cont. 4)

	Japan	Netherlands	New Zealand	Norway	Sweden	Switzerland	UK	USA
1934	68 090	8 341	1 552	2 874	6 222	4 140	46 666	126 978
1935	69 238	8 434	1 562	2 889	6 242	4 155	46 868	127 859
1936	70 171	8 516	1 573	2 904	6 259	4 168	47 081	128 681
1937	71 278	8 599	1 587	2 919	6 276	4 180	47 289	129 464
1938	71 879	8 685	1 604	2 936	6 298	4 192	47 494	130 476
1939	72 364	8 782	1 627	2 954	6 326	4 206	47 991	131 539
1940	72 967	8 879	1 636	2 973	6 356	4 226	48 226	132 637
1941	74 005	8 966	1 629	2 990	6 389	4 254	48 216	133 922
1942	75 029	9 042	1 639	3 009	6 432	4 286	48 400	135 386
1943	76 005	9 103	1 633	3 032	6 491	4 323	48 789	137 272
1944	77 178	9 175	1 654	3 060	6 560	4 364	49 016	138 937
1945	76 224	9 262	1 688	3 091	6 636	4 412	49 182	140 474
1946	77 199	9 424	1 759	3 127	6 719	4 467	49 217	141 940
1947	78 119	9 630	1 797	3 165	6 803	4 524	49 519	144 688
1948	80 155	9 800	1 833	3 201	6 884	4 582	50 014	147 203
1949	81 971	9 956	1 871	3 234	6 956	4 640	50 312	149 770
1950	83 563	10 114	1 909	3 265	7 015	4 694	50 363	152 271
1951	84 974	10 264	1 948	3 296	7 071	4 749	50 574	154 878
1952	86 293	10 382	1 996	3 328	7 125	4 815	50 737	157 553
1953	87 463	10 494	2 049	3 362	7 171	4 877	50 880	160 184
1954	88 752	10 616	2 095	3 395	7 213	4 929	51 066	163 026
1955	89 790	10 751	2 139	3 429	7 262	4 980	51 221	165 931
1956	90 727	10 888	2 183	3 462	7 315	5 045	51 430	168 903
1957	91 513	11 026	2 233	3 494	7 367	5 126	51 657	171 984
1958	92 349	11 187	2 286	3 525	7 415	5 199	51 870	174 882
1959	93 237	11 348	2 335	3 556	7 454	5 259	52 157	177 830
1960	94 053	11 486	2 377	3 585	7 480	5 362	52 373	180 671
1961	94 890	11 639	2 427	3 615	7 520	5 512	52 807	183 691
1962	95 797	11 806	2 485	3 639	7 562	5 666	53 292	186 538
1963	96 765	11 966	2 537	3 667	7 604	5 789	53 625	189 242
1964	97 793	12 127	2 589	3 694	7 662	5 887	53 991	191 889
1965	98 883	12 292	2 635	3 723	7 734	5 943	54 350	194 303
1966	99 790	12 455	2 683	3 753	7 807	5 996	54 643	196 560
1967	100 850	12 597	2 728	3 785	7 869	6 063	54 959	198 712
1968	102 050	12 730	2 754	3 819	7 912	6 132	55 214	200 706
1969	103 231	12 878	2 780	3 851	7 968	6 212	55 461	202 677
1970	104 334	13 039	2 820	3 879	8 043	6 267	55 632	205 052
1971	105 677	13 194	2 864	3 903	8 098	6 343	55 907	207 661
1972	107 179	13 329	2 913	3 933	8 122	6 401	56 079	209 896
1973	108 660	13 439	2 971	3 961	8 137	6 441	56 210	211 909
1974	110 160	13 545	3 032	3 985	8 160	6 460	56 224	213 854
1975	111 520	13 666	3 087	4 007	8 192	6 404	56 215	215 973
1976	112 770	13 774	3 116	4 026	8 222	6 333	56 206	218 035
1977	113 880	13 856	3 128	4 043	8 251	6 316	56 179	220 239
1978	114 920	13 942	3 129	4 060	8 275	6 333	56 167	222 585
1979	115 880	14 038	3 138	4 073	8 294	6 351	56 227	225 055
1980	116 800	14 150	3 144	4 087	8 311	6 385	56 314	227 757
1981	117 650	14 247	3 157	4 100	8 324	6 429	56 379	230 138
1982	118 450	14 313	3 183	4 116	8 327	6 467	56 335	232 520
1983	119 260	14 367	3 226	4 128	8 329	6 482	56 377	234 799
1984	120 020	14 424	3 258	4 141	8 337	6 505	56 488	237 011
1985	120 750	14 491	3 272	4 153	8 350	6 533	56 618	239 279
1986	121 490	14 572	3 277	4 169	8 370	6 573	56 763	241 625
1987	122 090	14 665	3 304	4 187	8 398	6 619	56 930	243 942
1988	122 610	14 760	3 317	4 209	8 436	6 672	57 065	246 307
1989	123 120	14 849	3 330	4 227	8 493	6 647	57 236	248 781
1990	123 540	14 951	3 363	4 241	8 559	6 712	57 411	249 924
1991	123 920	15 070	3 406	4 262	8 617	6 792	57 649	252 688
1992	124 336	15 178	3 414	4 286	8 678	6 905	57 848	255 610
1993	124 753	15 286	3 422	4 310	8 739	7 020	58 349	258 566
1994	125 188	15 389	3 460	4 333	8 804	7 028	58 702	261 558

Table A-3b. **Population in 5 "South European Countries", 1820-1994**

(thousands at mid-year)

	Greece	Ireland	Portugal	Spain	Turkey
1820		5 041	3 297	12 203	
1850		4 894	3 811	14 779	
1870		3 856	4 353	16 201	
1890		3 357	5 100	17 757	
1900	4 962	3 180	5 450	18 566	11 900
1901	4 997	3 164	5 497	18 659	11 981
1902	5 032	3 156	5 552	18 788	12 063
1903	5 067	3 144	5 613	18 919	12 145
1904	5 102	3 136	5 670	19 050	12 228
1905	5 138	3 130	5 720	19 133	12 311
1906	5 174	3 129	5 758	19 316	12 395
1907	5 210	3 122	5 800	19 450	12 480
1908	5 246	3 120	5 840	19 585	12 565
1909	5 283	3 121	5 883	19 721	12 651
1910	5 320	3 120	5 937	19 858	12 737
1911	5 355	3 117	6 004	19 994	12 824
1912	5 390	3 108	6 008	20 128	12 912
1913	5 425	3 092	6 004	20 263	13 000
1914	5 463	3 084	6 053	20 398	13 085
1915	5 502	3 044	6 107	20 535	13 171
1916	5 541	3 040	6 147	20 673	13 257
1917	5 580	3 040	6 187	20 811	13 344
1918	5 620	3 045	6 104	20 950	13 431
1919	5 660	3 097	6 082	21 091	13 519
1920	5 700	3 103	6 084	21 232	13 608
1921	5 837	3 096	6 148	21 411	13 697
1922	5 890	3 002	6 216	21 628	13 787
1923	6 010	3 014	6 271	21 847	13 877
1924	6 000	3 005	6 344	22 069	13 968
1925	5 958	2 985	6 429	22 292	14 059
1926	6 042	2 971	6 507	22 518	14 151
1927	6 127	2 957	6 580	22 747	14 250
1928	6 205	2 944	6 658	22 977	14 476
1929	6 275	2 937	6 729	23 210	14 705
1930	6 351	2 927	6 812	23 445	14 928
1931	6 440	2 933	6 908	23 675	15 174
1932	6 516	2 949	7 003	23 897	15 414
1933	6 591	2 962	7 096	24 122	15 658
1934	6 688	2 971	7 189	24 349	15 906
1935	6 793	2 971	7 279	24 579	16 158
1936	6 886	2 967	7 379	23 810	16 434
1937	6 973	2 948	7 476	25 043	16 725
1938	7 061	2 937	7 575	25 279	17 016
1939	7 156	2 934	7 677	25 517	17 517
1940	7 280	2 958	7 758	25 757	17 821
1941	7 362	2 993	7 800	25 979	18 011
1942	7 339	2 963	7 859	26 182	18 203
1943	7 297	2 946	7 934	26 387	18 396
1944	7 284	2 944	8 013	26 594	18 592
1945	7 322	2 952	8 101	26 802	18 790
1946	7 418	2 957	8 182	27 012	19 203

Table A-3b (cont. 2)

	Greece	Ireland	Portugal	Spain	Turkey
1947	7 529	2 974	8 258	29 223	19 625
1948	7 749	2 985	8 358	27 437	20 056
1949	7 856	2 981	8 434	27 651	20 497
1950	7 566	2 969	8 512	27 868	20 809
1951	7 659	2 961	8 547	28 086	21 634
1952	7 733	2 953	8 563	28 332	22 219
1953	7 817	2 949	8 587	28 571	22 818
1954	7 893	2 941	8 607	28 812	23 433
1955	7 966	2 921	8 657	29 056	24 065
1956	8 031	2 898	8 698	29 355	24 771
1957	8 096	2 885	8 737	29 657	25 498
1958	8 173	2 853	8 789	29 962	26 246
1959	8 258	2 846	8 837	30 271	27 017
1960	8 327	2 834	8 891	30 583	27 755
1961	8 398	2 819	8 944	30 904	28 447
1962	8 448	2 830	9 002	31 158	29 156
1963	8 480	2 850	9 040	31 430	29 883
1964	8 510	2 864	9 053	31 741	30 628
1965	8 551	2 876	8 996	32 085	31 391
1966	8 614	2 884	8 871	32 453	32 192
1967	8 716	2 900	8 798	32 850	33 013
1968	8 741	2 913	8 743	33 240	33 855
1969	8 773	2 926	8 696	33 566	34 719
1970	8 793	2 950	8 663	33 876	35 605
1971	8 831	2 978	8 624	34 190	36 554
1972	8 889	3 024	8 637	34 498	37 502
1973	8 929	3 073	8 630	34 810	38 451
1974	8 962	3 124	8 879	35 147	39 399
1975	9 046	3 177	9 308	35 515	40 348
1976	9 167	3 228	9 403	35 937	40 925
1977	9 309	3 272	9 508	36 367	41 835
1978	9 430	3 314	9 609	36 778	42 774
1979	9 548	3 368	9 714	37 108	43 741
1980	9 642	3 401	9 819	37 386	44 737
1981	9 730	3 443	9 851	37 751	45 864
1982	9 790	3 480	9 877	37 961	47 020
1983	9 847	3 505	9 892	38 180	48 205
1984	9 900	3 529	9 904	38 342	49 420
1985	9 934	3 540	9 905	38 505	50 664
1986	9 964	3 541	9 903	38 668	51 630
1987	9 984	3 542	9 898	38 716	52 747
1988	10 005	3 538	9 889	38 809	53 970
1989	10 038	3 515	9 795	38 888	55 255
1990	10 140	3 503	9 908	38 959	56 473
1991	10 269	3 524	9 814	39 025	57 693
1992	10 300	3 547	9 820	39 085	58 775
1993	10 401	3 570	9 854	39 145	60 604
1994	10 503	3 593	9 850	39 205	62 007

Table A-3c. **Population in 7 East European Countries, 1820-1992**

(thousands at mid-year)

	Bulgaria	Czechoslovakia	Hungary	Poland	Romania	USSR	Yugoslavia
1820		7 190	4 571			50 398	
1850		8 698	5 228			62 408	
1870	2 586	9 876	5 717		6 621	81 747	
1890	3 445	11 320	6 622	22 854	9 060	108 465	9 690
1900	3 961	12 120	7 127	24 750	10 299	126 444	11 174
1913	4 794	13 245	7 840	26 710	12 527	156 192	13 590
1920	5 072	12 979	7 950	23 968	12 340	154 607	12 422
1921	5 148	13 008	8 029	24 330	12 479	152 836	12 607
1922	5 255	13 159	8 103	24 935	12 666	152 403	12 796
1923	5 365	13 293	8 173	25 569	12 843	153 055	12 987
1924	5 476	13 413	8 232	25 992	13 020	155 581	13 180
1925	5 590	13 537	8 299	26 425	13 209	158 983	13 378
1926	5 705	13 644	8 383	26 815	13 399	162 621	13 578
1927	5 798	13 728	8 454	27 148	13 574	166 117	13 780
1928	5 873	13 807	8 520	27 509	13 760	169 269	13 986
1929	5 950	13 884	8 583	27 856	13 952	172 017	14 194
1930	6 027	13 964	8 649	28 204	14 141	174 212	14 407
1931	6 106	14 052	8 723	28 615	14 355	175 987	14 618
1932	6 186	14 138	8 785	29 022	14 554	176 807	14 819
1933	6 267	14 216	8 848	29 421	14 730	177 401	15 022
1934	6 349	14 282	8 919	29 771	14 924	178 453	15 228
1935	6 415	14 339	8 985	30 129	15 069	179 636	15 439
1936	6 469	14 387	9 046	30 471	15 256	181 502	15 651
1937	6 514	14 429	9 107	30 791	15 434	184 626	15 860
1938	6 564	14 603	9 167	31 062	15 601	188 498	16 084
1939	6 614	14 683	9 227	31 365	15 751	192 379	16 305
1940	6 666	14 713	9 287	30 021	15 907	195 970	
1941	6 715	14 671	9 344		15 774		
1942	6 771	14 577	9 396		15 839		
1943	6 828	14 538	9 442		15 840		
1944	6 885	14 593	9 497		15 946		
1945	6 942	14 152	9 024		15 929		
1946	7 000	12 916	9 042	23 959	15 971	173 900	
1947	7 064	12 164	9 079	23 734	15 849	174 000	15 596
1948	7 130	12 339	9 158	23 980	15 893	175 100	15 817
1949	7 195	12 339	9 250	24 410	16 084	177 500	16 040
1950	7 251	12 389	9 338	24 824	16 311	180 050	16 346
1951	7 258	12 532	9 423	25 271	16 464	183 200	16 588
1952	7 275	12 683	9 504	25 753	16 630	186 400	16 798
1953	7 346	12 820	9 595	26 255	16 847	189 500	17 048
1954	7 423	12 952	9 706	26 761	17 040	192 700	17 284
1955	7 499	13 093	9 825	27 281	17 325	196 150	17 519
1956	7 576	13 229	9 911	27 815	17 583	199 650	17 685

Table A-3c (cont. 2)

	Bulgaria	Czechoslovakia	Hungary	Poland	Romania	USSR	Yugoslavia
1957	7 651	13 358	9 839	28 310	17 829	203 150	17 859
1958	7 728	13 474	9 882	28 770	18 056	206 700	18 018
1959	7 798	13 565	9 937	29 240	18 226	210 450	18 214
1960	7 867	13 654	9 984	29 561	18 403	214 350	18 402
1961	7 943	13 780	10 028	29 965	18 567	218 150	18 612
1962	8 013	13 860	10 061	30 324	18 681	221 750	18 819
1963	8 078	13 952	10 088	30 691	18 813	225 100	19 029
1964	8 144	14 058	10 120	31 161	18 927	228 150	19 222
1965	8 201	14 159	10 153	31 496	19 027	230 900	19 434
1966	8 258	14 240	10 185	31 698	19 141	233 500	19 644
1967	8 310	14 305	10 224	31 944	19 285	236 000	19 840
1968	8 370	14 361	10 264	32 305	19 721	238 350	20 029
1969	8 434	14 416	10 303	32 555	20 000	240 600	20 209
1970	8 490	14 334	10 337	32 526	20 253	242 757	20 371
1971	8 536	14 390	10 365	32 805	20 470	245 083	20 572
1972	8 576	14 465	10 394	33 068	20 663	247 459	20 775
1973	8 621	14 560	10 426	33 363	20 828	249 747	20 963
1974	8 679	14 686	10 471	33 691	21 029	252 131	21 164
1975	8 721	14 802	10 532	34 022	21 245	254 469	21 365
1976	8 759	14 918	10 589	34 362	21 446	256 760	21 573
1977	8 804	15 031	10 637	34 698	21 658	259 029	21 780
1978	8 814	15 138	10 673	35 010	21 855	261 253	21 970
1979	8 826	15 211	10 698	35 225	22 048	263 425	22 166
1980	8 862	15 262	10 710	35 578	22 201	265 542	22 304
1981	8 878	15 314	10 713	35 902	22 353	267 722	22 471
1982	8 894	15 366	10 711	36 227	22 478	270 042	22 630
1983	8 909	15 415	10 700	36 571	22 553	272 540	22 800
1984	8 925	15 459	10 679	36 914	22 625	275 066	22 960
1985	8 941	15 500	10 657	37 203	22 725	277 537	23 120
1986	8 957	15 532	10 640	37 456	22 824	280 236	23 270
1987	8 971	15 565	10 621	37 664	22 940	283 100	23 420
1988	8 981	15 597	10 596	37 862	23 054	285 463	23 560
1989	8 989	15 629	10 576	37 963	23 152	287 845	23 690
1990	8 636	15 662	10 553	38 119	23 200	289 350	23 810
1991	8 570	15 694	10 344	38 245	22 974	291 200	23 930
1992	8 505	15 615	10 313	38 365	22 748	292 375	23 931

Table A-3d. **Population in 7 Latin American Countries, 1820-1994**

(thousands at mid-year)

	Argentina	Brazil	Chile	Colombia	Mexico	Peru	Venezuela
1820	534	4 507	885	1 206	6 587	1 317	718
1850	1 100	7 234	1 443	2 065	7 662	2 001	1 324
1870	1 796	9 797	1 943	2 392	9 219	2 606	1 653
1890	3 376	14 199	2 651	3 369	11 729	3 346	2 224
1900	4 693	17 984	2 974	3 998	13 607	3 791	2 542
1901	4 873	18 392	3 011	4 079	13 755	3 831	2 576
1902	5 060	18 782	3 048	4 162	13 904	3 871	2 609
1903	5 254	19 180	3 086	4 247	14 055	3 911	2 643
1904	5 455	19 587	3 124	4 334	14 208	3 952	2 690
1905	5 664	20 003	3 163	4 422	14 363	3 993	2 706
1906	5 881	20 427	3 202	4 512	14 519	4 035	2 720
1907	6 107	20 860	3 242	4 604	14 676	4 077	2 741
1908	6 341	21 303	3 282	4 697	14 836	4 119	2 761
1909	6 584	21 754	3 323	4 793	14 997	4 162	2 780
1910	6 836	22 216	3 364	4 890	15 000	4 206	2 805
1911	7 098	22 687	3 406	4 990	14 990	4 250	2 834
1912	7 370	23 168	3 448	5 091	14 980	4 294	2 856
1913	7 653	23 660	3 491	5 195	14 970	4 339	2 874
1914	7 885	24 161	3 537	5 330	14 960	4 384	2 899
1915	8 072	24 674	3 584	5 468	14 950	4 430	2 918
1916	8 226	25 197	3 631	5 609	14 940	4 477	2 929
1917	8 374	25 732	3 679	5 754	14 930	4 523	2 944
1918	8 518	26 277	3 728	5 903	14 920	4 571	2 958
1919	8 672	26 835	3 777	6 056	14 910	4 619	2 973
1920	8 861	27 404	3 827	6 213	14 900	4 667	2 992
1921	9 092	27 969	3 877	6 374	14 895	4 730	3 008
1922	9 368	28 542	3 928	6 539	15 129	4 793	3 025
1923	9 707	29 126	3 980	6 709	15 367	4 859	3 049
1924	10 054	29 723	4 033	6 882	15 609	4 927	3 077
1925	10 358	30 332	4 086	7 061	15 854	4 996	3 114
1926	10 652	30 953	4 140	7 243	16 103	5 067	3 152
1927	10 965	31 587	4 195	7 431	16 356	5 141	3 185
1928	11 282	32 234	4 250	7 624	16 613	5 216	3 221
1929	11 592	32 894	4 306	7 821	16 875	5 294	3 259
1930	11 896	33 568	4 370	7 914	17 175	5 374	3 300
1931	12 167	34 256	4 434	8 009	17 480	5 456	3 336
1932	12 402	34 957	4 500	8 104	17 790	5 540	3 368
1933	12 623	35 673	4 567	8 201	18 115	5 626	3 401
1934	12 834	36 404	4 634	8 299	18 445	5 715	3 431
1935	13 044	37 150	4 703	8 398	18 781	5 806	3 465
1936	13 260	37 911	4 773	8 498	20 933	5 899	3 510
1937	13 490	38 687	4 843	8 599	21 315	5 995	3 565
1938	13 724	39 480	4 915	8 702	21 704	6 093	3 623
1939	13 984	40 289	5 003	8 935	22 100	6 194	3 699
1940	14 169	41 114	5 093	9 174	20 558	6 298	3 784
1941	14 402	42 069	5 184	9 419	21 155	6 415	3 858
1942	14 638	43 069	5 277	9 671	21 770	6 537	3 934
1943	14 877	44 093	5 371	9 930	22 403	6 661	4 020
1944	15 130	45 141	5 467	10 196	23 054	6 787	4 114

Table A-3d (cont. 2)

	Argentina	Brazil	Chile	Colombia	Mexico	Peru	Venezuela
1945	15 390	46 215	5 565	10 469	23 724	6 919	4 223
1946	15 654	47 313	5 665	10 749	24 413	7 053	4 347
1947	15 942	48 438	5 767	11 036	25 122	7 192	4 486
1948	16 307	49 590	5 870	11 332	25 852	7 335	4 656
1949	16 737	50 769	5 975	11 635	26 603	7 480	4 843
1950	17 150	51 941	6 082	11 946	27 376	7 630	5 035
1951	17 492	53 494	6 215	12 288	28 140	7 830	5 229
1952	17 840	55 093	6 351	12 641	28 954	8 020	5 427
1953	18 196	56 739	6 489	13 003	29 814	8 230	5 647
1954	18 558	58 435	6 631	13 376	30 720	8 450	5 892
1955	18 928	60 181	6 776	13 759	31 669	8 670	6 153
1956	19 254	61 980	6 936	14 170	32 662	8 900	6 420
1957	19 586	63 832	7 100	14 593	33 701	9 150	6 686
1958	19 923	65 740	7 267	15 028	34 784	9 400	6 945
1959	20 267	67 704	7 438	15 477	35 909	9 660	7 210
1960	20 616	69 739	7 614	15 939	37 073	9 930	7 494
1961	20 939	71 752	7 798	16 422	38 273	10 220	7 786
1962	21 267	73 823	7 986	16 920	39 510	10 520	8 086
1963	21 601	75 955	8 179	17 433	40 790	10 820	8 390
1964	21 939	78 147	8 377	17 961	42 118	11 140	8 704
1965	22 283	80 403	8 579	18 506	43 500	11 470	9 026
1966	22 609	82 724	8 757	19 045	44 935	11 800	9 351
1967	22 940	85 112	8 938	19 599	46 418	12 130	9 696
1968	23 276	87 569	9 123	20 169	47 952	12 480	10 044
1969	23 616	90 097	9 311	20 756	49 538	12 830	10 383
1970	23 962	92 759	9 504	21 360	51 176	13 193	10 604
1971	24 348	95 061	9 680	21 871	52 884	13 568	10 981
1972	24 757	97 419	9 853	22 350	54 661	13 952	11 377
1973	25 183	99 836	10 023	22 812	56 481	14 347	11 791
1974	25 617	102 312	10 189	23 282	58 320	14 750	12 221
1975	26 052	104 851	10 350	23 776	60 153	15 161	12 665
1976	26 489	107 452	10 508	24 291	61 979	15 580	13 122
1977	26 928	110 117	10 661	24 828	63 813	16 008	13 594
1978	27 367	112 849	10 815	25 384	65 658	16 440	14 074
1979	27 803	115 649	10 975	25 951	67 518	16 871	14 553
1980	28 237	118 518	11 145	26 525	69 655	17 295	15 024
1981	28 666	121 458	11 325	27 107	71 305	17 714	15 488
1982	29 090	124 471	11 515	27 699	72 968	18 127	15 943
1983	29 508	127 559	11 713	28 295	74 633	18 538	16 394
1984	29 922	130 723	11 916	28 891	76 293	18 955	16 850
1985	30 331	133 966	12 121	29 481	78 524	19 383	17 317
1986	30 735	137 288	12 329	30 066	80 063	19 820	17 791
1987	31 133	140 692	12 538	30 646	81 584	20 267	18 272
1988	31 526	143 661	12 748	31 219	83 098	20 723	18 757
1989	31 913	147 000	12 961	31 785	84 617	21 189	19 246
1990	32 293	150 368	13 173	32 345	86 154	21 663	19 738
1991	32 646	153 164	13 360	32 873	87 821	22 135	20 191
1992	33 003	156 012	13 550	33 410	89 520	22 617	20 654
1993	33 364	158 913	13 743	33 956	91 252	23 110	21 128
1994	33 729	161 868	13 939	34 511	93 018	23 614	21 613

Table A-3e. **Population in 10 Asian Countries, 1820-1992**

(thousands at mid-year)

	Bangladesh	Burma	China	India	Indonesia	Pakistan	Philippines	South Korea	Taiwan	Thailand
1820	20 000		381 000	175 349	17 927	13 651	2 176			4 665
1850			412 000	187 657	22 977		3 612			5 230
1870		4 245	358 000	212 189	28 922		5 063			5 775
1890	26 908	7 489	380 000	234 336	37 579	18 382	6 476			6 670
1900	29 012	10 174	400 000	235 729	42 746	19 759	7 324	8 772	2 864	7 320
1901	29 231	10 490	402 243	237 067	43 275	19 902	7 465	8 870	2 903	7 413
1902	29 461	10 642	404 498	238 645	43 810	19 898	7 609	8 968	2 942	7 507
1903	29 693	10 796	406 766	240 113	44 352	19 894	7 755	9 068	2 982	7 602
1904	29 926	10 953	409 047	241 684	44 901	19 890	7 904	9 169	3 022	7 699
1905	30 161	11 112	411 340	243 253	45 457	19 886	8 056	9 271	3 085	7 797
1906	30 398	11 273	413 646	244 820	45 993	19 882	8 211	9 375	3 140	7 896
1907	30 637	11 437	415 965	246 385	46 535	19 878	8 369	9 479	3 172	7 996
1908	30 878	11 603	418 297	247 948	47 085	19 874	8 530	9 584	3 200	8 098
1909	31 121	11 771	420 642	249 509	47 642	19 870	8 694	9 691	3 232	8 201
1910	31 366	11 942	423 000	250 868	48 206	19 866	8 861	9 799	3 275	8 305
1911	31 612	12 115	427 662	251 626	48 778	19 862	9 032	9 956	3 334	8 431
1912	31 699	12 220	432 375	251 766	49 358	19 935	9 206	10 115	3 402	8 559
1913	31 786	12 326	437 140	251 906	49 934	20 008	9 384	10 277	3 469	8 689
1914	31 874	12 433	441 958	252 045	50 517	20 081	9 565	10 448	3 528	8 822
1915	31 962	12 541	446 829	252 084	51 108	20 154	9 749	10 590	3 562	8 957
1916	32 050	12 650	451 753	252 222	51 705	20 228	9 937	10 760	3 583	9 094
1917	32 138	12 760	456 732	252 360	52 083	20 302	10 128	10 931	3 621	9 232
1918	32 227	12 871	461 766	252 497	52 334	20 376	10 323	11 107	3 658	9 418
1919	32 316	12 983	466 855	252 608	53 027	20 450	10 522	11 285	3 692	9 608
1920	32 405	13 096	472 000	252 670	53 723	20 525	10 725	11 457	3 736	9 802
1921	32 494	13 212	473 673	254 206	54 367	20 600	10 932	11 686	3 797	10 000
1922	32 730	13 351	475 352	256 806	55 020	20 864	11 143	11 920	3 870	10 202
1923	32 967	13 491	477 037	259 501	55 683	21 132	11 358	12 158	3 940	10 435
1924	33 206	13 633	478 728	262 091	56 354	21 403	11 577	12 401	4 009	10 673
1925	33 447	13 776	480 425	264 775	57 036	21 678	11 800	12 622	4 095	10 916
1926	33 689	13 921	482 128	267 555	57 727	21 956	12 026	12 812	4 195	11 165
1927	33 933	14 067	483 837	270 229	58 429	22 238	12 305	13 004	4 289	11 419
1928	34 179	14 215	485 552	272 998	59 140	22 523	12 543	13 199	4 388	11 734
1929	34 427	14 364	487 273	275 861	59 863	22 812	12 890	13 397	4 493	12 058
1930	34 677	14 515	489 000	278 618	60 596	23 105	13 194	13 563	4 614	12 392
1931	34 928	14 667	492 640	282 670	61 496	23 402	13 507	13 794	4 742	12 735
1932	35 575	14 870	496 307	286 385	62 400	23 840	13 829	14 028	4 867	13 087
1933	36 234	15 075	500 000	290 180	63 314	24 286	14 158	14 266	4 995	13 399
1934	36 905	15 283	502 639	293 955	64 246	24 740	14 497	14 508	5 128	13 718
1935	37 589	15 494	505 292	297 808	65 192	25 203	14 843	14 738	5 255	14 045
1936	38 285	15 708	507 959	301 740	66 154	25 675	15 199	14 915	5 384	14 379
1937	38 994	15 925	510 640	305 751	67 136	26 155	15 563	15 094	5 530	14 721
1938	39 716	16 145	513 336	309 740	68 131	26 644	15 934	15 275	5 678	14 980
1939	40 452	16 368	516 046	313 805	69 145	27 143	16 275	15 458	5 821	15 244
1940	41 201	16 594	518 770	317 948	70 175	27 651	16 585	15 627	5 987	15 513
1941	41 966	16 824	521 508	321 565	71 316	28 169	16 902	15 552	6 163	15 787
1942		16 727	524 261	325 341	72 475		17 169	15 934	6 339	16 060
1943		16 908	527 028	328 625	73 314		17 552	16 092	6 507	16 462
1944		17 090	529 810	332 976	73 565		17 887	16 670	6 520	16 868

Table A-3e (cont. 2)

	Bangladesh	Burma	China	India	Indonesia	Pakistan	Philippines	South Korea	Taiwan	Thailand
1945		17 272	532 607	336 917	73 332		18 228	18 020	6 533	17 284
1946		17 454	535 418	340 857	74 132		18 574	19 369	6 546	17 710
1947		17 636	538 244	344 367	75 146		18 905	19 886	6 346	18 148
1948	41 539	17 818	541 085	347 913	76 289	35 911	19 283	20 027	6 697	18 569
1949	42 327	18 000	543 941	353 333	77 654	36 767	19 669	20 208	7 280	19 000
1950	43 135	18 182	546 815	359 000	79 043	37 646	20 062	20 557	7 882	19 442
1951	45 100	18 458	557 480	365 000	80 525	38 532	20 675	20 571	8 255	20 025
1952	45 962	18 773	568 910	372 000	82 052	39 440	21 307	20 682	8 541	20 626
1953	46 840	19 093	581 390	379 000	83 611	40 369	21 958	20 874	8 822	21 245
1954	47 734	19 420	595 310	386 000	85 196	41 319	22 629	21 207	9 134	21 882
1955	48 646	19 752	608 655	393 000	86 807	42 293	23 321	21 636	9 480	22 538
1956	49 575	20 088	621 465	401 000	88 456	43 288	24 033	22 260	9 823	23 214
1957	50 521	20 470	637 408	409 000	90 124	44 308	24 767	22 901	10 133	23 910
1958	51 487	20 859	653 235	418 000	91 821	45 351	25 524	23 560	10 460	24 628
1959	52 470	21 255	666 005	426 000	93 565	46 419	26 305	24 240	10 806	25 367
1960	53 491	21 722	667 070	434 000	95 254	47 626	27 101	24 943	11 155	26 372
1961	54 682	22 200	660 330	444 000	97 085	48 788	27 999	25 566	11 510	27 186
1962	55 900	22 688	665 770	454 000	99 028	49 978	28 926	26 025	11 857	28 025
1963	57 145	23 187	682 335	464 000	101 009	51 197	29 884	26 860	12 210	28 890
1964	58 418	23 697	698 355	474 000	103 031	52 446	30 874	27 531	12 570	29 782
1965	59 719	24 218	715 185	485 000	105 093	53 725	31 897	28 219	12 928	30 702
1966	61 049	24 751	735 400	495 000	107 197	55 036	32 953	28 924	13 283	31 650
1967	62 409	25 303	754 550	506 000	109 343	56 379	34 044	29 647	13 617	32 627
1968	63 799	25 867	774 510	518 000	111 532	57 754	35 172	30 388	13 945	33 634
1969	65 220	26 444	796 025	529 000	113 765	59 163	36 337	31 147	14 264	34 673
1970	66 671	27 034	818 315	541 000	116 044	60 607	37 540	31 923	14 565	35 745
1971	68 598	27 637	841 105	554 000	118 368	62 573	38 655	32 596	14 865	36 884
1972	70 629	28 262	862 030	567 000	121 282	64 610	39 778	33 266	15 142	38 017
1973	72 699	28 886	881 940	580 000	124 271	66 706	40 900	33 935	15 427	39 142
1974	74 704	29 521	900 350	593 000	127 338	68 849	42 012	34 606	15 709	40 257
1975	76 582	30 170	916 395	607 000	130 485	71 033	43 103	35 281	16 001	41 359
1976	78 323	30 834	930 685	620 000	133 713	73 251	44 143	35 849	16 329	42 450
1977	79 969	31 512	943 455	634 000	137 026	75 494	45 153	36 412	16 661	43 532
1978	81 582	32 206	956 165	649 000	140 425	77 779	46 164	36 969	16 974	44 602
1979	83 225	32 910	969 005	664 000	143 912	80 135	47 209	37 534	17 308	45 659
1980	84 969	33 511	981 235	679 000	147 490	82 581	48 323	38 124	17 642	46 700
1981	86 879	34 171	993 861	694 000	150 657	85 114	49 540	38 723	17 970	47 727
1982	88 920	34 844	1 008 281	709 000	153 894	87 736	50 800	39 326	18 297	48 740
1983	91 064	35 530	1 023 288	724 000	157 204	90 452	52 055	39 910	18 596	49 739
1984	93 254	36 230	1 036 803	739 000	160 588	93 265	53 351	40 406	18 873	50 720
1985	95 456	36 943	1 051 013	755 000	164 047	96 180	54 700	40 806	19 136	51 683
1986	97 676	37 874	1 066 758	770 000	166 990	99 199	56 004	41 184	19 357	52 654
1987	99 915	38 828	1 083 998	785 000	169 987	102 324	57 356	41 575	19 564	53 605
1988	102 163	39 807	1 101 596	801 000	173 041	105 558	58 721	41 975	19 788	54 536
1989	104 412	40 810	1 118 619	816 000	176 152	108 900	60 097	42 380	20 006	55 448
1990	106 656	41 670	1 133 680	848 000	179 322	112 351	61 480	42 793	20 230	55 801
1991	108 756	41 870	1 150 090	863 478	182 487	115 588	62 687	43 176	20 441	56 679
1992	111 400	42 070	1 167 000	881 200	185 900	119 200	64 300	43 600	20 600	57 600

Table A-3f. **Population in 10 African Countries, 1900-1992**

(thousands at mid-year)

	Cote d'Ivoire	Egypt	Ethiopia	Ghana	Kenya	Morocco	Nigeria	South Africa	Tanzania	Zaire
1900	1 263	10 162	7 837	1 784	2 228	3 800	15 589	4 768	3 968	4 246
1913	1 446	12 144	9 025	2 043	2 436	4 500	17 390	6 153	4 054	4 890
1950	3 091	20 460	18 344	4 368	6 534	9 157	36 147	13 863	8 341	9 938
1951	3 156	20 965	18 725	4 571	6 691	9 399	36 834	14 252	8 496	10 169
1952	3 223	21 471	19 114	4 783	6 847	9 641	37 530	14 652	8 654	10 371
1953	3 361	21 977	19 510	5 237	7 164	10 123	38 970	15 486	8 979	10 563
1954	3 361	22 483	19 916	5 237	7 164	10 123	38 970	15 486	8 979	10 798
1955	3 432	22 988	20 329	5 480	7 315	10 363	39 711	15 920	9 146	11 035
1956	3 505	23 577	20 779	5 744	7 521	10 673	40 466	16 367	9 316	11 269
1957	3 579	24 165	21 239	6 007	7 726	10 980	41 235	16 826	9 489	11 540
1958	3 655	24 753	21 709	6 272	7 930	11 290	42 019	17 298	9 665	11 850
1959	3 733	25 342	22 190	6 535	8 135	11 597	42 818	17 783	9 845	12 155
1960	3 813	25 831	22 681	6 827	8 249	11 891	43 636	18 281	10 027	12 569
1961	3 956	26 578	23 210	7 010	8 341	12 220	44 509	18 661	10 329	12 582
1962	4 104	27 255	23 752	7 198	8 643	12 557	45 399	19 049	10 643	13 700
1963	4 258	27 946	24 307	7 392	8 958	12 905	46 307	19 445	10 966	14 302
1964	4 418	28 660	24 874	7 591	9 283	13 262	47 233	19 849	11 297	14 932
1965	4 583	29 387	25 455	7 794	9 620	13 627	48 178	20 262	11 640	15 589
1966	4 755	30 204	26 078	7 958	9 970	13 949	49 142	20 683	11 993	16 275
1967	4 931	30 891	26 765	8 123	10 331	14 277	50 125	21 113	12 355	16 990
1968	5 119	31 595	27 471	8 294	10 707	14 613	51 128	21 552	12 729	17 739
1969	5 311	32 316	28 190	8 467	11 094	14 958	52 151	22 000	13 116	18 519
1970	5 510	33 053	28 937	8 614	11 498	15 310	53 193	22 458	13 513	19 239
1971	5 742	33 648	29 646	8 877	11 902	15 712	54 257	23 011	13 877	19 778
1972	5 982	34 253	30 412	9 138	12 327	16 113	55 343	23 575	14 223	20 327
1973	6 231	34 886	31 224	9 388	12 773	16 511	56 450	24 147	14 572	20 902
1974	6 489	35 561	32 074	9 621	13 244	16 908	57 878	24 723	14 951	21 486
1975	6 755	36 289	32 954	9 835	13 741	17 305	59 342	25 301	15 379	22 090
1976	7 037	37 080	33 860	10 023	14 258	17 702	60 843	25 886	15 877	22 785
1977	7 323	37 942	34 790	10 177	14 805	18 097	62 383	26 474	16 403	23 500
1978	7 612	38 869	35 741	10 322	15 383	18 501	63 961	27 066	17 000	24 350
1979	7 902	39 850	36 716	10 501	15 992	18 926	65 580	27 664	17 517	25 500
1980	8 194	40 875	37 717	10 740	16 632	19 382	67 239	28 270	18 098	26 380
1981	8 487	41 943	38 740	11 030	17 305	19 867	68 940	28 884	18 691	27 230
1982	8 778	43 048	39 776	11 366	18 012	20 378	70 715	29 503	19 295	28 120
1983	9 078	44 185	40 859	11 747	18 745	20 916	72 536	30 143	19 907	29 040
1984	9 400	45 342	42 040	12 168	19 490	21 478	74 404	30 827	20 529	29 990
1985	9 755	46 511	43 350	12 620	20 241	22 061	76 320	31 569	21 161	30 980
1986	10 138	47 664	44 769	13 073	20 999	22 706	78 228	32 362	21 806	31 500
1987	10 548	48 798	46 280	13 526	21 768	23 376	80 184	33 200	22 464	32 460
1988	10 980	49 910	47 868	13 977	22 549	23 960	82 188	34 078	23 135	33 460
1989	11 433	50 999	49 510	14 425	23 345	24 520	84 243	34 988	23 819	34 490
1990	11 902	52 061	51 180	14 870	24 160	25 091	86 351	35 919	24 517	35 560
1991	12 330	53 571	52 954	15 336	25 016	25 732	88 510	36 762	25 235	36 670
1992	12 800	54 679	54 790	15 800	25 500	26 300	91 300	37 600	26 100	37 815

Appendix B

Intertemporal Measures of Real Gross Domestic Product

Estimates of national income started 300 years ago. The first big step was taken by practitioners of the "political arithmetic" which William Petty pioneered in the seventeenth century. In 1696, Gregory King estimated English national income, using a variety of evidence on income, expenditure and production. He made rougher estimates for France and Holland as well, to compare capacity to tax, save, and mobilise for war. Davenant and Temple had a similar interest in such exercises in England as did Vauban and Boisguilbert in France. But King was the most distinguished of these pioneers.

In the course of the eighteenth and nineteenth centuries, there were several significant attempts to estimate GDP for particular years for different countries. Michael Mulhall was the first to produce a significant array of estimates for purposes of international comparison. In 1896, he published income levels for 19 countries (in his *Industries and Wealth of Nations*). Like King, he converted their incomes to a large extent by exchange rates. He followed a more or less standardised technique, calculating national income by industry of origin for 9 sectors. His estimates were better documented than those of King.

In 1940 Colin Clark took a major step forward, with estimates of real income levels for 30 countries in "international units", i.e. he made the first crude corrections for differences in the purchasing power parity of currencies. He also presented estimates of the growth of real income over time for 14 countries. In many cases his time series were weak because he was willing to make crude links between different and not always comparable "spot" estimates, and to make use of some dubious deflators, but he made an exhaustive survey of the work of virtually all the economists and statisticians who had published in his field in the nineteenth and twentieth centuries and had extensive correspondence with the statisticians of his day who were engaged in such work. Clark never hesitated to adjust these estimates to conform to his own ideas about the appropriate coverage of the accounts or methods of treatment of particular items. He also used the estimates analytically. Systematic comparative confrontation is a particularly good way of testing the plausibility and consistency of estimates and may well induce careful scrutiny of "outlier countries". In 1940, however, there was no agreement on the coverage and methodology of national accounts, and the comparability of the different estimates was therefore restricted.

The move towards modern standardised concepts of national accounts arose from developments in the USA in the 1930s and in the UK in the 1940s. Simon Kuznets was involved in the first presentation of official estimates to the US Senate in 1934 and with longer run estimates in the National Bureau of Economic Research. From 1941 to 1948, Milton Gilbert was responsible for the official US estimates, and developed conventions wider in coverage than Kuznets preferred, because they treated some items of government and private expenditure as final rather than intermediate product.

In the UK, the official commitment to national accounts started in wartime under pressure from Keynes. The first official accounts were prepared by James Meade and Richard Stone. In 1944 there were consultations between British, Canadian and US statisticians with a view to standardisation of concepts and procedures. In the post-war years, comparable accounts were felt to be a political necessity to facilitate assessment of needs for Marshall Aid and burden-sharing in NATO. Richard Stone was the main person involved in developing the standardised approach, and he and Milton Gilbert were very active in the 1950s in seeing that it was implemented in OEEC countries. Shortly after, the OEEC system was merged with the standardised UN system which was applied by official statisticians in most countries in the post-war years, except in communist countries.

Thanks to these efforts, there are now official estimates of GDP growth in nominal and real terms for the years since 1950 for about 150 countries. These are, in principle, reasonably comparable in scope, though many still have substantial shortcomings. The standardised system provides a coherent macroeconomic framework covering the whole economy, which can be crosschecked in three ways. From the production side, it is the sum of value added in different sectors, e.g. agriculture, industry and services, net of duplication. It is also the sum of final expenditures, e.g. by consumers, investors and government. From the income side, it is the total of wages, rents and profits. When fully elaborated, it can provide an integrated view of development over time in volume, value, relative and absolute prices and changes in economic structure. In some cases, the framework has been expanded to provide a fuller set of growth accounts, including measures of labour input and capital stock.

For some countries, there have been retrospective official or quasi-official estimates for pre-war years, back to 1830 for Austria, 1860 for Finland, 1865 for Norway, 1900 for the Netherlands, 1925 for Germany, 1926 for Canada and 1929 for the USA. However, the work on retrospective national accounts has largely been undertaken outside government by scholars who have generally followed UN/OECD guidelines, and made explicit links of their series with the official post-war estimates. Many of these were influenced or stimulated by Simon Kuznets who organised international cooperation in this domain in the International Association for Research in Income and Wealth, founded in 1947.

The most satisfactory of the scholarly exercises were those carried out in the UK by Charles Feinstein, and by Noel Butlin in Australia. Other countries where there has been a major effort are Japan where Kazushi Ohkawa inaugurated the 14 volume study of Hitotsubashi University; Sweden, where Olle Krantz is completing the fifth round of estimates (which go back to 1800); Finland, where Riitta Hjerppe supervised the 13 volume study financed by the Bank of Finland; the USA, where we have the studies of Gallman, Kendrick and Kuznets; and France, for which we have the studies of Toutain and Levy-Leboyer. Canada, Denmark, Italy and Germany have all had major scholarly studies which still leave room for improvement. For Austria and Norway we have official studies which are not fully documented in their published form. In Belgium, Ireland and the Netherlands there are major research groups working to improve the long-term picture which is still a bit shaky. Amongst OECD countries, the weakest long-term estimates are for Greece, Ireland, New Zealand, Portugal, Switzerland and Turkey.

For most other parts of the world, the quality of the estimates is poorer than for our first group, but for Argentina, Brazil, India, Indonesia, Korea, Mexico, Spain and Taiwan the estimates are at about the same level as we presently have for Belgium and the Netherlands.

Table B-1 summarises the type of indicator available for the advanced capitalist countries for pre-war years. For 11 of them I used the estimates by industry of origin. For the UK I used Feinstein's compromise estimate which is an average for the movements he found for production, expenditure and real income. For Norway and the USA, the long-run indicators refer to real expenditure and this is also the case for the Netherlands for the interwar period. For New Zealand the estimate relies on proxy indicators and for Switzerland on deflated income. For most of the other countries where estimates for pre-war are available, the predominant method for measuring real product is by industry of origin.

The reliability of the growth measure will depend on the quality of the source material and the sophistication and ingenuity of those preparing the estimates. The likelihood of avoiding obvious errors is much greater if there have been several rounds of estimation or if growth performance has been measured by more than one method. However, there are some significant problems which affect the comparability of the growth measures.

Sensitivity of Recorded Growth Rates to Weighting Procedures

One of these is the sensitivity of the estimates to bias introduced by the choice of benchmark weights. Obviously, if one were faced with massive disparities of approach to this question, comparative analysis would be gravely compromised because, over time, technological change leads to the emergence of new products, and with rising income the pattern of consumer expenditure and the structure of investment change. Relative and absolute prices change and so do the patterns of output and employment. For this reason it is necessary to build up the long-term growth estimates in separate time segments which cover a span of years in which such changes are not overwhelming. Thus it would be absurd to compare growth for 1820-1992 in country A using 1820 weights throughout, and in country B using 1992 weights throughout. Ideally it would be desirable to have synchronous changes in weighting in all the countries under comparison. For historical comparisons, this is not feasible, but in recent years, OECD countries have been moving towards this objective.

In fact, most studies are linked segments with weights that are periodically changed even where the constant price (volume estimates) may be expressed for convenience in numeraire prices of a single year. Thus for France, Toutain gives constant price estimates using a 1905-13 numeraire, and, for Finland, Hjerppe gives the figures in 1926 or 1985 Finnish marks, but their underlying procedure involves 20-year linked segments using prices and value added weights characteristic for each sub-period. For Sweden, Krantz used 20- to 25-year sub-periods with Laspeyres volume indices and Paasche deflators. For the other countries, changes in weights are at less regular intervals. The country notes specify what these are. In the case of Italy I broke up the estimates of Fua and Associates which were originally in 1938 weights for a ninety year period.

In some cases, the weights appear to be fixed for excessively long periods, or it is not easy to see what procedures were used. The Hoffmann indices for Germany are presented in 1913 prices and the Hansen figures for Denmark in 1929 prices. In practice, there was probably some degree of variance in the

Table B-1. **Summary Confrontation of Methods Used in Constructing Historical National Accounts for 16 Advanced Capitalist Countries**

Main Authors	Value Added Approach	Expenditure Approach	Income Approach
	AUSTRALIA		
N.G. Butlin, 1986	1788-1827, VA, 1828-1860, VAVOP		
N.G. Butlin, 1962	1861-1939, 13 sectors,VAVOP	1861-1939, 4 categories of investment, VAVOP	
N.G. Butlin, 1977		1900-74, 9 categories, VAVOP	
	AUSTRIA		
A. Kausel, 1979	1830-1913, 5 sectors, VAVOP		
A. Kausel, 1965	1913, 1920, 1937 and 1946-1950, 11 branches, VAVOP	1913, 1924, 1937 and 1948-1950, 6 categories, VAVOP	1913, 1924 and 1948-1950, 8 categories, VA
	BELGIUM		
J. Gadisseur, 1973	1846-1913, 2 sectors (ag. and ind.), VO. I made a crude service proxy for 1846-1913, even cruder proxies for 1830-1846 using Gadisseur for industry and Goossens for agriculture		
C. Carbonnelle, 1959	1920-1938, 6 branches, VO. I made a crude service interpolation		
	CANADA		
O.J. Firestone, 1957	1851-70, 8 sectors, VAVOP		
O.J. Firestone, 1958	1867-1953, 8 sectors, VAVOP. Detailed analysis for benchmark years at decade intervals. Rougher annual estimates	1867-1953, substantial detail by category, VAVOP	
M.C. Urquhart, 1986 and 1993	1870-1926, 18 sectors on an annual basis and benchmark estimates for 2 distributive sectors. Substantial branch details for agriculture and manufacturing, VA. Deflation only for GNP aggregate	1870-1926 partial: investment for 7 sectors, government expenditure and exports, VA	
Statistics Canada	1926 onwards, 15 sectors, VA	1926 onwards, 14 categories VAVOP	1926 onwards, 11 categories, VA

Main Authors	Value Added Approach	Expenditure Approach	Income Approach
	DENMARK		
S.A. Hansen, 1974	1818-1950, 23 branches, VAVOP	1844-1950, 3 categories, VAVOP	
	FINLAND		
R. Hjerppe, 1989	1860-1985, 13 branches, VAVOP	1860-1985 5 categories VAVOP	1860-1985, 5 categories of wages and salaries.VA. Cost of living and wholesale price index
	FRANCE		
M. Levy-Leboyer & F. Bourguignon, 1985	1820-1913, 5 sectors, VAVOP. I used only the industry measure for 1820-70	1820-1913, 13 categories, VA	1820-1913 wages, VA
J.C. Toutain, 1987	1815-1913, 1920-1938 and 1950. 14 branches, VAVOP. For 1820-70 I used his indicators for agriculture and services. For 1870-1960 I used his GDP estimates.		
	GERMANY		
R.H. Tilly, 1978	2 branches (ag. 1831-1849 and ind. 1831-1846/7) for Prussia for 3 benchmark years, VO. I made a crude service sector proxy, adjusted to cover all Germany using demographic ratios, and linked to Hoffmann in 1850		
W.G. Hoffmann, 1965	1850-1913, 1924-1938, 9 branches (with detail for 147 industries), VO. Weighting system not clear.	1850-1913, 1924-1938 1950, 5 categories VAVOP	1850-1913, 1925-1938, 9 categories, VA
	ITALY		
R. Ercolani & O. Vitali (Fua Group), 1975	1861-1952, 11 branches, VAVOP	1861-1952, 18 categories, VAVOP	1861-1971, 2 categories of wages and salaries, VA
Maddison, 1991	Reweighted version of the above supplemented with production estimates of Fenoaltea		
	JAPAN		
K. Ohkawa and M. Shinohara, 1979	1885-1940, 5 sectors, VAVOP. I used this source for 1885-1940 and their expenditure estimate for 1940-50	1885-1940, 1930-44 and 1946-70, 6 categories, VAVOP	1906-40, 1953-70, 4 categories, VA

Main Authors	Value Added Approach	Expenditure Approach	Income Approach
NETHERLANDS			
J.L. van Zanden, 1987	Four benchmarks (1820, 1850, 1880 and 1910). 8 sectors, VO		Four benchmarks (1820, 1850, 1880 and 1910) wage and three types of property income, VA
C. van Bochove & T.A. Huitker, CBS,1987	1921-39, 21 sectors. VA (not yet published)	1921-1939, 1946-1986. 7 categories, VAVOP. I used this for 1921-60, and deflated income for 1900-21	1900-1921. 1 category, deflated by cost of living index, 1921-39, 1946-86, 9 categories, VA
NORWAY			
Central Bureau of Statistics, 1970	1930-1939, 1946-1950. 11 branches, VAVOP	1865-1939, 1936-1950. 7 categories, VAVOP. I filled the 1939-1946 gap from another CBS source and adjusted from the Norwegian to the OECD concept of GDP	1930-1939, 1940-1950. 149 items, VA
SWEDEN			
O. Krantz and C.A. Nilsson, 1975	1861-1970, 7 sector breakdown, VAVOP	1861-1970, 7 category breakdown	
O. Krantz and Associates, 1986-91. 7 background vols. 2 (on agriculture and foreign trade) pending	1800-1980, industry of origin, VAVOP		
SWITZERLAND			
C. Clark, 1957			1890, 1895, 1899, 1913, 1924-1951. VAVOP. 1 category crudely deflated
UK			
P. Deane, 1968		1830-1914, 5 categories, VAVOP. I used her 1830-1855 figures	
C.H. Feinstein, 1972	1855-1913, 1920-1960, 4 sectors, VAVOP. Plus VO for 15 branches	1870-1960 7 categories, VAVOP	1855-1960, 5 categories, VA

Main Authors	Value Added Approach	Expenditure Approach	Income Approach
		USA	
R.E. Gallman, 1966		1839, 1844, 1849, 1854, 1859 benchmarks and overlapping decade averages from 1834-43 to 1899-1908. Gallman replicates Kuznets' technique and methods of presentation. Uses a large amount of information on commodity output and rougher estimates for services to build up volume estimates of final flows to consumers (4 way breakdown) and to capital formation (3-way breakdown). Full details of estimates not published. I derived my 1840-69 estimates from Gallman.	
N.S. Balke and R.J. Gordon, 1989		1869-90. For this period Kuznets (1961) published only 5-year moving averages as he considered the annual information to be too weak. Balke and Gordon revamped the existing commodity flow estimates to incorporate extra information on construction, transport and communications. They provided annual estimates of nominal GDP, real GDP in 1982 prices and a GDP deflator. I used their estimates for 1869-90.	
J.W. Kendrick, 1961	Private Domestic Product: volume indices for 10 benchmark years from 1869 to 1953 with a 10-sector breakdown. His service estimate is a residual and his total is derived from the expenditure GDP. For most of the individual sectors he provides annual figures.	Decade averages of GDP for 1869-78 and 1879-88 and annual estimates for 1889-1953. Kendrick used Kuznets' (1961) commodity flow estimates with adjustments to put them on the basis used by the US Dept. of Commerce. VAVOP	
Dept. of Commerce		1929-onwards annual estimates, 14 categories. For 1959 onwards there are 3 weighting variants: 1987 weights, annual chain-weighting and quinquennially changing benchmarks. I used the latter. VAVOP	VA

VA means that the source cited shows current values. VO means that the source provides volume indices or constant price estimates. P means that the appropriate deflators are given or are implicitly available in the source cited. I have not included New Zealand in the Table as Rankin (1992) used proxy indicators.

structure of their component deflators or volume indices, if only because of the accidental character of data availability. Where a full set of estimates is presented for values (VA), volumes (VO) and prices (P) or unit values, one can reweight the published series to enhance international comparability. Usually the published detail is limited, so reweighting is possible only in less aggregated form than in the original.

For the post-war years, for most of the advanced capitalist group, the weights have been changed several times, and there is now a EUROSTAT recommendation that weights be changed every five years. The recommendation has been adopted in Belgium, Canada, Germany, Ireland, Sweden and the UK. Thus when Germany or the UK issue official estimates for a period of several decades in "1985" prices, this is simply a *numeraire*, and the underlying estimates are segments weighted by the price structure of successive base years. In most other OECD countries the weighting base is changed at longer intervals of ten years or so.

Two exceptions are the Netherlands, which since 1981 has changed its weights every year, and the USA where the official estimates have hitherto been revised every five years, but with a single set of price weights for the whole period back to 1929. For the Netherlands, den Bakker has published a number of alternative weighting systems. For the USA, the Dept. of Commerce has now produced three alternative weighting systems, i.e. the official estimates where the weights are the same for over 60 years;a chain-weighted system like that used in the Netherlands, and an index with shifting 5-year weights. For 1959-92, US GDP grew 2.88 per cent a year with the official measure, 3.16 with 5-year changes in weights, and 3.12 per cent with the Dutch technique. Here the US version with 5-year changing weights was used as it is closer methodologically to the procedures used in the other countries.

The Canadian and Danish statistical authorities now also provide chain-weighted estimates as alternatives to their official fixed weight measures (see Karen Wilson, "The Introduction of Chain Volume Indices in the Income and Expenditure Accounts", *Statistics Canada*, Ottawa, 1991).

Revisions to Correct for Inadequate Coverage

Another type of problem arises from revisions in the level of income to cover previously inadequate coverage of the accounts. The most extreme case is Italy where there have been several official benchmark revisions, each involving a substantial upward adjustment in the level of output. To a large extent these were necessary to improve coverage of the "underground" economy. The last revision in 1985 involved an upward adjustment of 18.7 per cent. The Italian authorities themselves have not made an explicit link with their earlier accounts. The easy solution is to raise all the previous estimates uniformly by 18.7 per cent, but this is unsatisfactory as the gap in coverage in fact occurred gradually. For this reason I used the available evidence to provide a more gradual phasing in this last large jump. Leandro Prados has made the same type of tapered adjustment for Spain. In the Netherlands there was an upward adjustment of 6.2 per cent for the year 1969, and the Dutch authorities have revised their estimates to account for this. It has recently been officially acknowledged in Greece and Portugal that the official GDP estimates for 1990 needed an upward adjustment of 25.2 per cent and 14.2 per cent respectively. The necessary corrections were made, but for lack of better information, the estimates for all earlier years were raised in the same proportion. In the case of Argentina the latest revision involved an upward adjustment of 36 per cent. The authorities have revised their estimates back to 1980, and for earlier years there was no alternative but to raise all the estimates in the same proportion. In the case of Peru, de Soto has argued that the official accounts made inadequate allowance for informal activity but there is not enough evidence to warrant an adjustment.

Intercountry Variations in Measurement Procedures and Source Material

Although great progress has been made in standardising the conceptual basis for national accounts, there are still significant differences in the way various items are actually measured. Thus the UK and the USA place major reliance on information on income flows which is derived from tax sources, whereas Germany relies more on output information from industrial surveys. It is not clear that there is a systematic bias in the overall measurement of growth because of such differences, but when the primary returns are from *enterprises*, the boundaries of sectors will not be identical with those in countries which rely on reports from *establishments*.

A more significant source of discrepancy arises in service sectors (including government activities) where output is difficult to measure. In some countries, employment indicators are used as a proxy. In others, there may be detailed weighting to allow for changes in the relative importance of personnel with differences in skill and qualification, or imputation for productivity growth.

Measurement of output in high-tech industries can also be tackled in different ways. When the USA introduced a *hedonic* price index for computers, which took much better account of characteristics such as memory capacity and speed of operation, the new price index fell much more sharply than its predecessor, and added 0.3 per cent a year to GDP growth for 1982-8 (see M.F. Foss, M.E. Manser and A.H. Young, eds., *Price Measurements and Their Uses*, University of Chicago, 1993, p. 2).

Special Problems of Former Communist Economies

The problems of measuring real GDP growth for communist countries are *sui generis* and are discussed separately below for East Germany, other East European countries, and for China. It seems likely that the figures for GDP growth shown below for Bulgaria, Romania and Yugoslavia for 1950 to the mid 1980s exaggerate the economic performance of these countries, even though they were prepared by analysts who were attempting to make measures of GDP with the same criteria as those used for Western countries. For the period since 1989, when the East European countries were undergoing major transition, their growth may be understated because the authorities have not found it easy to cover all the new private sector activity.

The Need for Caution and Cross-Checks

In spite of the fact that national accounts estimation is one of the oldest branches of economics — it has as long a history as the scholarly study of demography — it is clear from the above comments that there is still scope for much further work to improve the estimates we have.

The most promising procedure for filling gaps in knowledge is to proceed on the same lines as in the past: i.e. to follow the tradition of building up indexes of the volume of value added in sectors like agriculture, industry, transport, communications and housing services where indicators are likely to be most readily available, refining the already existing deflators and crosschecking the necessarily rougher estimates for services with techniques used in other countries. It is essential that the techniques and results of research should be described as transparently as possible, so that further work can build upon it. It is equally necessary when producing new estimates to replace those which already exist, and that any substantial differences from the old estimates be explained.

When estimates are presented transparently it is much simpler to modify them in the light of supplementary information, or to modify procedures which can be improved. Thus it was possible to adjust or augment (apart from adjustments for geographic coverage) the estimates for Belgium, Brazil, France, Germany, Ireland, Italy, Korea, Mexico, Portugal, the UK and USSR.

Where proxy procedures are used, it is desirable to test their validity against the historical estimates of GDP we already have and to do this for as many countries as possible.

It is useful to make plausibility checks, e.g. to see whether the apparent growth rates or levels of performance of the country in question make it an "outlier". If it appears to be growing much faster or more slowly than countries with a similar level of income, one needs to inquire into the reasons why this should be so. It is also useful to look at the year-to-year movements. If these are large and erratic the reasons need to be scrutinised. One is also likely to discover errors or problems in the estimates if they are used in an analytic framework of comparative growth accounts which will tend to highlight outlier characteristics.

Where annual changes are used for purposes of cyclical analysis, users should scrutinise the methodology used in the different national estimates, because some of the methods employed tend to smooth out cyclical fluctuations.

Advanced Capitalist Countries

The figures are adjusted to exclude the impact of territorial change. For Belgium and Japan the GDP correction coefficient for territorial change was identical with that for population. For the eight other countries, the GDP adjustment coefficient was different, because independent evidence was available for GDP within the old and new frontiers. In all cases, however, the territorial scope of the GDP estimates is compatible with those for population in Appendix A.

In order to enhance comparability in coverage and weighting procedures, the estimates for 1960 onwards are generally from OECD, *National Accounts*, various editions. There are, however, some exceptions as noted below. 1993 and 1994 are from OECD *Economic Outlook*, December 1994.

The sources for individual countries are as follows:

Australia: 1828-60 GDP by industry of origin at 1848-50 prices from N.G. Butlin, "Contours of the Australian Economy 1788-1860", *Australian Economic History Review*, Sept. 1986, pp. 112-13;1820-8 real GDP derived from the *GNE*/GDP ratio in Butlin, 1986, and real *GNE* per capita figures in N.G. Butlin, "Our 200 Years", *Queensland Calendar*, 1988. 1860-1 link derived by using the 1860-1 GDP deflator in W. Vamplew (ed.), *Australians: Historical Statistics*, Fairfax, Broadway, 1987, p. 219. 1861-1938/9, GDP by industry of origin in 1910/11 prices from N.G. Butlin, *Australian Domestic Product, Investment and Foreign Borrowing 1861-1938/39*, Cambridge, 1962, pp. 460-l; amended as indicated in N.G. Butlin, *Investment in Australian Economic Development 1861-1900*, Cambridge, l964, p. 453, and with revised deflator shown in M.W. Butlin, *A Preliminary Annual Database 1900/01 to 1973/74*, Discussion Paper 7701, Reserve Bank of Australia, May 1977, p. 4l. l938/9-l950 from expenditure aggregates in 1966/7 prices in M.W. Butlin, *op. cit.*, p. 85. 1950 onwards from OECD sources. I adjusted all figures to a calendar-year basis.

Austria: 1830-1913, GDP by industry of origin in 1913 prices from A. Kausel, "Österreichs Volkseinkommen 1830 bis 1913" in *Geschichte und Ergebnisse der zentralen amtlichen Statistik in Österreich 1829-1979, Beitrage zur österreichischen Statistik*, Heft 550, Vienna, 1979, pp. 692-3. 1820-30 per capita movement assumed to be the same as that for 1830-40 (see Kausel, p. 701). 1913-50 gross national product in 1937 prices by expenditure and industry of origin, from A. Kausel, N. Nemeth, and H. Seidel, "Österreichs Volkseinkommen, 1913-63", *Monatsberichte des Österreichischen Institutes für Wirtschaftsforschung*, 14th Sonderheft, Vienna, August 1965, p. 38 and 42;1937-45 from F. Butschek, *Die Österreichische Wirtschaft 1938 bis 1945*, Fischer, Stuttgart, 1979, p. 65. The figures are corrected for territorial change, which was large. (In 1911-13, present-day Austria represented only 37.4 per cent of the total output of the Austrian part of the Austro-Hungarian Empire.) The figures refer to the product generated within the present boundaries of Austria.

Belgium: 1820-46 movement in agricultural output from estimates supplied by Martine Goossens, 1831-46 industrial output estimates supplied by Jean Gadisseur (1820-31 assumed to increase at same pace as in 1831-42), service output 1820-46 assumed to move with population. 1846-1913 GDP derived from movements in agricultural and industrial output from J. Gadisseur, "Contribution à l'étude de la production agricole en Belgique de 1846 à 1913", *Revue belge d'histoire contemporaine*, vol. IV, 1-2, 1973, and service output which was assumed to move with employment in services (derived for census years from P. Bairoch, *La Population active et sa structure*, Université Libre de Bruxelles, Brussels, 1968, pp. 87-8). 1913 weights and 1913-50 GDP estimates derived from C. Carbonnelle, "Recherches sur l'évolution de la production en Belgique de 1900 à 1957", *Cahiers Économiques de Bruxelles*, no. 3, April 1959, p. 358. Carbonnelle gives GDP figures for only a few benchmark years but gives a commodity production series for many more years. Interpolations were made for the service sector to arrive at a figure for GDP for all the years for which Carbonnelle shows total commodity production. Figures corrected to exclude the effect of the cession by Germany of Eupen and Malmedy in 1925, which added 0.81 per cent to population and was assumed to have added the same proportion to output. The GDP figures for 1914-19 and 1939-47 are interpolations between the 1913 and 1920 estimates and 1938-48 respectively, assuming the same pattern of movement as in France.

Canada: 1851-70 GNP by industry of origin in 1935-39 prices from O.J. Firestone, "Canada's Changing Economy in the Second Half of the 19th Century", NBER, New York, 1957, processed. l870-l926 GDP (value added in 20 sectors) in current prices, with the aggregate deflator at 1900 prices from M.C. Urquhart and Associates, ed., *Gross National Product, Canada 1870-1926: The Derivation of* *the Estimates*, McGill Queen's University Press, Montreal, 1993, pp. 11-12 and 24-5, linked to the 1926-60 official constant price estimates. In the official series, 1926-60 was in three segments: 1926-47 (in 1935-9 prices), 1947-56 (in 1949 prices) and 1956-60 (in 1957 prices), see Statistics Canada, *National Income and Expenditure Accounts*, vol. 1, *The Annual Estimates 1926-1974*, Ottawa, 1975, p. 323. 1960 onwards from OECD, *National Accounts*. I adjusted the figures for 1949 onwards by .987 to offset the incorporation of Newfoundland in that year.

It should be noted that the growth of GDP shown by Urquhart for 1870-1926 is faster (3.5 per cent per annum) than the 3.3 per cent shown by O.J. Firestone, *Canada's Economic Development 1867-1953*, Income and Wealth Series VII, Bowes and Bowes, London, 1958. Urquhart and Associates have a significantly lower estimate of the value of total product in 1870 and a higher estimate in the 1920s than Firestone. Their deflator rises only slightly faster than Firestone's. Firestone estimated GDP by industry of origin, and by type of expenditure in current and constant (1935-9) prices. His basic effort was concentrated on benchmark years at decade intervals. The Urquhart study which is otherwise very fully documented and transparent, makes inadequate reference to Firestone, and it is not clear why the estimates differ, or why the Urquhart team could not estimate sectoral deflators as Firestone did. This is obviously worth further study as it is clear that Canada (together with Argentina) was an outlier in terms of per capita GDP growth from 1870 to 1913. For 1820-50, I assumed that per capita product in Canada grew at the same rate as in the USA.

Denmark: 1820-1947 GDP at 1929 factor cost by industry of origin from S.A. Hansen, *Økonomisk vaekst i Danmark*, vol. II, Institute of Economic History, Copenhagen, 1974, pp. 229-32 (figures from 1921 onwards adjusted to offset the acquisition of North Schleswig, which added 5.3 per cent to the population, and 4.5 per cent to GDP). The Hansen study was much more elaborate than that of K. Bjerke and N. Ussing, *Studier over Danmarks Nationalprodukt 1870-1950,* GADS, Copenhagen, 1958. Hansen published a 23-way breakdown of value added, compared with the 2-way breakdown of Bjerke and Ussing, and he covered a much longer period. 1947-60 GDP at 1955 factor cost from Søren Larsen, "Reviderede tidsserier for produktionsvaerdi og bruttofaktorindkomst for perioden 1947-65", CBS, Copenhagen, 1992, mimeographed. 1960 onwards from OECD, *National Accounts*.

Finland: 1820-60 per capita GDP assumed to increase by 22.5 per cent, as indicated in S. Keikkinen, R. Hjerppe, Y. Kaukiainen, E. Markkanen and I. Nummela, "Förändringar i levnadsstandarden i Finland, 1750-1913", in G. Karlsson, ed., *Levestandarden i Norden 1750-1914*, Reykjavik, 1987, p. 74. 1860-1960 GDP by industry of origin at market prices from R. Hjerppe, *The Finnish Economy 1860-1985: Growth and Structural Change*, Bank of Finland, Helsinki, 1989, pp. 198-200. She uses a Laspeyres-type volume index for about 20 years at a time, with the segments being chained.

France: There are two major studies of French economic growth which appeared in 1985 and 1987.

J.C. Toutain, *Le Produit intérieur de la France de 1789 à 1982*, Presses Universitaires de Grenoble, 1987, is the latest and most comprehensive of these. It is the fifteenth volume in a series on the quantitative history of the French economy. The project was conceived by François Perroux in his Institute of Applied Economics (ISEA, now ISMEA) in the early 1950s (see F. Perroux and others, "La croissance economique française", in M. Gilbert, ed., *Income and Wealth*, Series III, Bowes and Bowes, Cambridge, 1953, pp. 45-101 for a review of the long history of French national income estimation).

The detailed work of ISMEA was supervised by Jean Marczewski who laid down the methodological basis which the group subsequently followed. The group's work was started at the initiative of Simon Kuznets and received initial financial support from the American Social Science Research Council. Marczewski was influenced by Kuznets' early emphasis on decade averages (which he used mainly as a cautious presentational device, but which Marczewski turned into a method of index construction with a more complex system of weights for the constant price estimates). The methodology is laid out in J. Marczewski, "Histoire quantitative — Buts et méthodes", *Cahiers de l'ISEA*, July 1961 and in "Some Aspects of the Economic Growth of France 1660-1958", *Economic Development and Cultural Change*, April 1961.

Marczewski attached primary importance to getting decennial averages to establish broad trends in the growth of physical product. Each pair of successive decades was crossweighted, and the changes in volume between the averages for successive pairs of decades were then chained to produce estimates for benchmark years.

Toutain published studies on agriculture in 1961, population in 1963 and transport in 1967. T.J. Markovitch produced four volumes on industry in 1965-6. There were subsequent volumes on wages and salaries (1967), consumption (1971), and state expenditure (1976) which provided material for an income and expenditure approach to supplement the industry of origin approach.

It was not until 1987, 26 years after the start of the project that Toutain provided annual estimates and extended the research to cover the whole economy. Toutain (1987, pp. 191-2) explains how he derived annual indicators which he adjusted to fit the decennial benchmarks. The latter were based on much more complete information than the annual indicators. Toutain presents volume and value indices for the three main sectors (agriculture, industry and services) and for GDP. He provides indicators for 6 service branches (housing, liberal professions, domestic service, transport, commerce and public services) and 7 industrial branches (mining, metallurgy, metal processing, food products, bread, textiles and construction). Toutain covers the years 1815-1913 and 1920-38 and links these to the official series for 1949-82. For his constant price estimates he uses a 1905-1913 numeraire, but his underlying benchmark procedure is based on chains of 20-year segments where successive decades are crossweighted with price structures characteristic of each of the two decades.

The alternative estimates for 1820-1913 are those of Levy-Leboyer, "Les Series de base", in M. Levy-Leboyer and F. Bourguignon, *L'Economie française au XIX siecle*, Economica, Paris, 1985. Levy-Leboyer provides estimates of GDP broken down by expenditure category in current prices. He gives volume and value estimates for agriculture, industry and a composite "non-agriculture". There is no explicit volume estimate for GDP but one can derive this (and his estimate for the volume of services) from the information he gives.

There are significant differences between the estimates of Toutain and Levy-Leboyer but the 1870-1913 GDP movement is not very different (see Tables B-2 and B-3).

Table B-2. **Confrontation of Toutain and Levy-Leboyer Estimates of Value and Volume of French GDP, 1820-1913**

	Value Added in Million Francs at Current Prices				Volume Indices by Sector (1913 = 100.0)			
	Agriculture	Industry	Services	GDP	Agriculture	Industry	Services	GDP
		Toutain				Toutain		
1820	3 637	3 252	2 076	8 965	46.9	9.7	29.6	22.0
1870	9 442	8 411	6 016	23 959	81.1	35.0	50.5	52.1
1913	13 024	19 212	17 335	49 571	100.0	100.0	100.0	100.0
		Levy-Leboyer				Levy-Leboyer		
1820	4 117	3 391	1 503	9 011	41.4	18.0	(17.5)	(25.1)
1870	7 958	6 374	4 980	19 312	71.5	42.4	(42.7)	(51.4)
1913	11 907	16 143	10 792	38 842	100.0	100.0	(100.0)	(100.0)

Sources: Toutain (1987) and Levy-Leboyer (1985). The figures in brackets are not explicit in Levy-Leboyer but are easily derived from the information he gives. I arrived at the Levy-Leboyer GDP volume index by using 1913 weights. The figures in this table are not adjusted to eliminate the effect of territorial changes.

Table B-3. **Confrontation of Toutain and Levy-Leboyer Sectoral and Aggregate Deflators**
(1913 = 100)

	Agriculture	Industry	Services	GDP	Agriculture	Industry	Services	GDP
		Toutain				Levy-Leboyer		
1820	59.6	174.5	40.5	82.2	83.5	116.7	79.6	92.4
1870	89.4	125.1	68.7	92.7	93.5	93.1	108.1	96.6
1913	100.0	100.0	100.0	100.0	100.0	100.0	100.0	100.0

Source: As for Table B-2.

Levy-Leboyer (1985) discusses the results which the Marczewski team produced in the 1960s and complains that they depart from those of earlier authors such as Mulhall and Bairoch. He gives the impression that his own procedures were adapted to accommodate what he considers to be the accepted wisdom of earlier years, but it is not clear in what respects this may be so. His critical comments on the Marczewski team are mainly directed to discussion of the current value series, and he was not, of course, able to comment on the much more comprehensive estimates which Toutain published in 1987.

Levy-Leboyer published his first annual estimates for agriculture and industry in his "La croissance économique en France au XIX siècle: Resultats préliminaires", *Annales: Economies, Sociétés, Civilisations*, July-August 1968, where his sources and weighting procedures are indicated in greater detail. In 1978 he revised his estimates for the commodity sector and made estimates of investment for 1820-1913, in "Capital Investment and Economic Growth in France 1870-1930", in P. Mathias and M.M. Postan, eds., *The Cambridge Economic History of Europe*, vol. VII, Part I, Cambridge University Press, 1978. The latter source gives little detail on his procedures in measuring commodity output.

The studies of Toutain and Levy-Leboyer are more transparent in important respects than those for some other countries (e.g. Hoffmann's estimates for Germany). Toutain's work is based on a much bigger and better documented research input, and represents a more serious effort to cover the services sector. However, it would have been useful to have Toutain's critique of the Levy-Leboyer estimates and some analysis of the sensitivity of his own results (for growth and cyclical movements) to alternative weighting procedures. It would also be useful to have a better idea of why Toutain's industrial movement is different from that of Markovitch.

There have been several estimates of French industrial production since Markovitch's work in 1965-6 (see Table B-4). Later investigators have all made some use of his benchmark weights. Levy-Leboyer (1968) showed faster growth than Markovitch, Crouzet showed slower growth, and Levy-Leboyer (1978 and 1985) made new estimates with slower growth. Toutain's (1987) estimate shows faster growth than Markovitch and is closer to Levy-Leboyer (1968) than to any of the others.

Table B-4. **Alternative Indices of French Industrial Output, 1820-1913**

(1913 = 100)

	Markovitch (1965)	Levy-Leboyer (1968)	Crouzet (1970)	Levy-Leboyer (1978 and 1985)	Toutain (1987)
1820	15.7	10.2	20.7	18.0	9.7
1870	47.8	32.8	40.0	42.4	35.0
1913	100.0	100.0	100.0	100.0	100.0
	Annual Average Compound Growth Rates				
1820-70	2.3	2.3	1.3	1.7	2.6
1870-1913	1.7	2.8	2.2	2.0	2.5
1820-1913	2.0	2.6	1.7	1.9	2.5

Source: Col. 1 from J.J. Markovitch "L'industrie française de 1789 à 1964 — Sources et méthodes", *Cahiers de l'ISEA*, AF4, July 1965, Table 1, pp. 216-7. Markovitch gives figures for decades or quinquennia, and I had to interpolate to get figures for the years shown here. Second, fourth and fifth columns from works already cited, third column from F. Crouzet, "Essai de construction d'un indice annuel de la production industrielle française au XIX siècle", *Annales ESC*, January-February 1970. All series, except Crouzet, include construction.

I adopted the Toutain GDP movement for 1870-1913, but as he shows an 1820-70 per capita movement which is substantially faster than the European norm and his measure of industrial growth is an outlier, a compromise estimate was used for 1820-70 growth. This involved use of the agriculture and services indicators of Toutain (1987) and the industrial index of Levy-Leboyer, with Toutain's 1870 sector values as weights. For 1920-38 and 1949-60 GDP the source was Toutain (1987). Interpolation between 1913 and 1920 was based on figures for industrial and agricultural output shown by J. Dessirier, "Indices comparés de la production industrielle et production agricole en divers pays de 1870 à 1928", *Bulletin de la statistique générale de la France, Études speciales*, October-December 1928;service output was assumed stable in this period. Interpolation between 1938 and 1949 was based on A. Sauvy's report on national income in 1938 francs to the Conseil Économique, *Journal officiel*, 7 April 1954. The figures are adjusted to exclude the impact of frontier changes. Between 1871 and 1918 France lost Alsace and Lorraine. For this period, GDP and population were 95.92 per cent of what they would otherwise have been. In 1861 France acquired Savoie, Haute Savoie and part of the Alpes Maritimes. This raised population and GDP by 1.797 per cent.

Table B-5 summarises the implications of the various possible estimates of French GDP (in per capita terms). It can be seen that the Toutain and the Levy-Leboyer estimates show faster growth than the compromise estimate for 1820-70. All estimates are adjusted to exclude the impact of frontier changes.

Table B-5. **Alternative Estimates of French GDP per Capita, 1820-1913**

	1820	1870	1913
The compromise estimate	1 218	1 858	3 452
Toutain (1987)	983	1 858	3 452
Levy-Leboyer (1985)	1 123	1 836	3 452

Germany: 1820-50, GDP estimated from Prussian output data in R.H. Tilly, "Capital Formation in Germany in the Nineteenth Century", in P. Mathias and M.M. Postan (eds.), *Cambridge Economic History of Europe*, vol. VII, I, 1978, pp. 395, 420, and 441. Using 1850 weights for agriculture, industry, and services from W.G. Hoffmann, F. Grumbach and H. Hesse, *Das Wachstum der deutschen Wirtschaft seit der Mitte des 19. Jahrhunderts*, Springer, Berlin, 1965, p. 454, Prussian per capita output in agriculture and industry were multiplied by population in Germany as a whole. Output in services was assumed to move with population.

1850-1938 and link to 1950 derived from Hoffmann's net domestic product (value added by industry) at 1913 factor cost (adjusted to exclude the impact of the reincorporation of the Saar, which Hoffmann includes from 1934): see Hoffmann, Grumbach and Hesse, *op. cit.*, pp. 454-5. This source gives no figures for 1914-24, but starts again in 1925. The pattern of movement in individual years 1914-24 was derived from annual indices of industrial and agricultural output in Dessirier, *op. cit.*, using Hoffmann's weights for these sectors and adjusting them to fit his sectoral output benchmarks for 1913 and 1925. Service output was interpolated between Hoffmann's 1913 and 1925 figures for this sector.

Hoffmann provides two estimates of real expenditure as well as his real product estimates. Net national expenditure for which he has a continuous series (col. 5 of pp. 827-8) shows an annual growth rate of 2.35 per cent for 1850-1938 compared with 2.27 for the net domestic product indicator I used. His measure of net domestic expenditure (col. 7 on pp. 827-8) starts only in 1880 and is interrupted after 1935. For 1880-1935 it shows a growth rate of 1.99 per cent a year compared to 2.05 per cent for the measure I used.

For net domestic expenditure, Hoffmann provides both current (pp. 825-6) and constant price estimates, and also gives an estimate of national income at current prices (pp. 506-9). However, for net domestic product he gives only constant price estimates and provides no deflators. This detracts from the transparency of the estimates and renders them resistant to the sensitivity testing and adjustment which is possible, e.g. with the estimates for France and Italy. It is also a pity that Hoffmann does not discuss the interrelationship of his product, expenditure, and income estimates, nor does he provide estimates of depreciation.

The Hoffmann estimates have received a detailed critique from Rainer Fremdling, "German National Accounts for the 19th and Early 20th Century: A Critical Assessment", *Vierteljahrschrift für Sozial und Wirtschaftsgeschicht*e, Heft 3, 1988, and Albrecht Ritschl has criticised Hoffmann's treatment of industrial production for 1925-38, see "On the Origins of the Great Depression in Germany", paper presented to the International Economic History Congress, Milan, 1994. Nevertheless, there is, at present, no better alternative measure of Germany's long-term growth.

Alternative estimates of GDP for 1925-38 (derived largely from income statistics) at 1936 market prices are available in K.-H. Raabe, "Die langfristige Entwicklung des Sozialprodukts im Bundesgebiet", *Wirtschaft und Statistik*, June 1954 (later reproduced in *Bevölkerung und Wirtschaft 1872-1972*, Statistical Office, Wiesbaden, 1972, p. 260), but the cyclical movements presented by Hoffmann seem more plausible. 1938-44 GNP in 1939 prices (from the expenditure side) for the 1938 territory (including Austria and Sudetenland) from W.C. Haraldson and E.F. Denison, "The Gross National Product of Germany 1936-1944", *Special Paper 1* (mimeographed) in J.K. Galbraith (ed.), *The Effects of Strategic Bombing on the German War Economy*, US Strategic Bombing Survey, 1945. 1946 (linked to 1936) from *Wirtschaftsproblemen der Besatzungszonen*, D.I.W. Duncker and Humblot, Berlin, 1948, p. 135;1945 was assumed to lie midway between 1944 and 1946. 1947-50 (linked to the adjusted Hoffmann estimates for the change between 1936 and 1950) from *Statistics of National Product and Expenditure No. 2, 1938 and 1947 to 1955*, OEEC, Paris, 1957, p. 63.

1950-80 GDP at 1985 market prices from Statistisches Bundesamt, *Volkswirtschaftliche Gesamtrechnungen, Revidierte Ergebnisse 1950 bis 1990*, Wiesbaden. Thereafter from OECD National Accounts publications.

The estimates are corrected for territorial change, which was extremely complicated:

a) In 1870 Germany took Alsace and Lorraine from France. This increased its population and GDP by 4 per cent;

b) between 1918 and 1923 Germany lost Alsace-Lorraine, Memel, Danzig, Eupen and Malmedy, Saarland, North Schleswig and Eastern Upper Silesia. These territories had a population of 7 330 thousand in 1918 out of a total of 66 811 thousand within the 1918 Reich frontiers, i.e. the old Reich was 12.3 per cent bigger in terms of population. However, as 1913 per capita income in the truncated area was 2.4 per cent higher than in the former Reich, the total income loss due to these changes was 9.7 per cent (for the population changes see A. Maddison, *Dynamic Forces in Capitalist Development*, 1991, pp. 232-5; for the per capita income difference see F. Grünig, "Die Anfänge der volkswirtschaftlichen Gesamtrechnung in Deutschland", *Beitrage zur empirischen Konjunkturforschung*, Berlin, 1950, p. 76);

c) in 1935, Germany regained the Saarland which added 1.79 per cent to population and income;

d) in 1938 Germany incorporated Austria and the Sudetenland which added over 8 per cent to GDP and later took over Alsace-Lorraine and parts of Poland and Yugoslavia. In 1941 these areas added 22.4 per cent to the GDP generated with the 1937 frontiers (see Haraldson and Denison, *op. cit.*, p. 12).

On the basis of the geographic distribution of German product in 1936 (see *Statistisches Handbuch für Deutschland 1928-1944*, Länderrat des Amerikanischen Besatzungsgebiets, Ehrenwirth, Munich, 1949, pp. 600-1) one can see that GDP generated within the boundaries initially fixed for the Federal Republic (excluding Saarland and West Berlin) was only 56.9 per cent of that within the 1936 boundaries, or 64.3 per cent if we add the Saar and West Berlin (which were incorporated in the Federal Republic statistics in 1960). 10.7 per cent of 1936 GDP was generated in territories east of the Oder Neisse which went to Poland and the USSR, and the rest went to the Soviet zone and East Berlin which later became the DDR.

In the course of 1990, the territory of the DDR reverted to the Federal Republic. Table B-6 compares the situation in the second half of 1990 (immediately after reunification) with that in 1936.

Table B-6. **Area Breakdown of German GDP, Population and Per Capita GDP, 1936 and 1990**

	1936		
	National Income million RM	Population (000)	Per Capita Income in RM
Federal Republic Territory[a]	41 757	42 208	989
DDR Territory	16 159	15 614	1 035
East of Oder-Neisse	6 968	9 514	732
Total (1936 territory)	64 884	67 336	964
of which:			
Saar	629	821	766
West Berlin	4 175	2 685	1 555
	1990 (second half year)		
	GDP billion DM	Population (000)	Per Capita GDP in DM
Federal Republic[a]	1 216.9	63 527	19 864
Former DDR	97.7	16 111	6 064
Total	1 359.6	79 638	17 007

a) including Saar and West Berlin.

Source: 1936 from *Handbuch* (1949); second half of 1990 from Statistisches Bundesamt, *Erste Ergebnisse der Sozialproduktsberechnung 1992*, Fachserie 18, Reihe 1, Wiesbaden, January 1993, pp. 39 and 41.

Table B-7. **Previous Estimates of the Performance of the East German Economy**

	Population (000s)	Index of GNP at Constant Prices (1950 = 100)	Inferential Level of GDP per capita in 1990 Geary-Khamis $		Population (000s)	Index of GDP at Constant Prices	Inferential Level of GDP per capita in 1990 Geary-Khamis $
1936	15 614	129.9	4 783	1970	17 058	231.9	7 816
				1971	17 061	237.1	7 990
1946	18 488	n.a.	n.a.	1972	17 043	245.1	8 268
1947	19 102	n.a.	n.a.	1973	16 980	252.8	8 559[b]
1948	19 044	n.a.	n.a.	1974	16 925	264.9	8 998
1949	18 793	n.a.	n.a.	1975	16 850	274.7	9 373
1950	18 388	100.0	3 127	1976	16 786	280.2	9 597
1951	18 335	n.a.	n.a.	1977	16 765	288.8	9 904
1952	18 334	n.a.	n.a.	1978	16 756	293.7	10 077
1953	18 271	n.a.	n.a.	1979	16 745	301.9	10 365
1954	18 057	n.a.	n.a.	1980	16 737	308.3	10 590
1955	17 928	136.4	4 374	1981	16 736	314.6	10 806
1956	17 735	n.a.	n.a.	1982	16 732	313.5	10 772
1957	17 478	n.a.	n.a.	1983	16 700	319.5	10 999
1958	17 262	n.a.	n.a.	1984	16 671	328.6	11 332
1959	17 148	n.a.	n.a.	1985	16 644	338.8	11 703
1960	17 114	173.9	5 842	1986	16 625	343.7	11 886
1961	17 002	175.2	5 924	1987	16 642	349.5	12 074
1962	16 874	180.0	6 133	1988	16 667	353.3	12 187
1963	16 930	185.8	6 309	1989	16 399	357.4	12 530[b]
1964	16 972	190.9	6 467				
1965	17 020	198.6	6 708	1990[a]	16 111		5 704
1966	17 058	204.7	6 899	1991	15 910		6 042
1967	17 082	211.3	7 111	1992	15 730		6 589
1968	17 084	220.9	7 434	1993	15 648		7 003
1969	17 076	226.1	7 612				

a) second half of 1990;

b) in 1973 and 1989, Czech levels of per capita GDP were $7 036 and $8 729 respectively. In my view, East German levels in this period were probably nearer to these Czech levels than to the levels previously thought to prevail in the DDR.

Source: GDP index derived as follows: 1936-50 movement from E.M. Snell and M. Harper, "Postwar Economic Growth in East Germany: A Comparison with West Germany", in *Economic Developments in Countries of Eastern Europe*, Joint Economic Committee, US Congress, Washington, D.C., 1970, p. 561; 1950-65 from T.P. Alton, "Economic Structure and Growth in Eastern Europe", in the same (1970) volume, p. 46; 1965-75 from Alton, *op. cit.* (1985), pp. 109-10; 1975-89 from T.P. Alton, ed., "Economic Growth in Eastern Europe 1975-1989", *Occasional Paper* 110, Research Project on National Income in East Central Europe, New York, 1990, p. 26. Population estimates derived for 1936-93 from the same Joint Economic Committee volumes, and from publications of the Federal Statistical Office, Wiesbaden. GDP per capita is benchmarked on the 1936 estimate in Table B-6 and its movement is derived from the first two columns of this table. The 1990-93 real GDP movement in the "neue Länder" (ex-DDR) from Statistisches Bundesamt, *Volkswirtschaftliche Gesamtrechnungen*, Fachserie 18, Reihe 3, various issues. The official 1990 estimate in DM for East Germany was converted into dollars with the same PPP as was used for the Federal Republic.

The 1936 and 1990 per capita ratios derivable from Table B-6 can be used in conjunction with the estimates of the movement in GDP per capita in the territory of the Bundesrepublik (Table D-1a of Appendix D). Thus we have an estimate for the Bundesrepublik area of $4 571 (in 1990 international dollars) for 1936 rising to $18 685 in 1990 and we can infer that, in the area of the DDR, per capita GDP rose from $4 783 to $5 704, i.e. at .33 per cent a year compared with 2.64 in the area of the Federal Republic.

The situation in the East German economy which became apparent after reunification was very different from what had previously been estimated. Western estimates of East German per capita GDP levels had put them at about three-quarters of those in the Federal Republic and about two-thirds of those in the United States (see T.P. Alton, "East European GNPs, Origins of Product, Final Uses, Rates of Growth, and International Comparisons", in *East European Economies: Slow Growth in the 1980s*, vol. 1, p. 127, Joint Economic Committee, US Congress, 1985). Per capita GDP growth in East Germany was thought to have been faster between 1950 and 1989 than in any other of the East European economies (3.6 per cent per annum, compared with 3.5 per cent in Bulgaria and Yugoslavia, 3.1 per cent in Romania, 2.6 per cent in Hungary, 2.4 per cent in Czechoslovakia and the USSR and 2.1 per cent per annum in Poland). After German reunification, W. Merkel and S. Wahl, *Das geplünderte Deutschland*, IWG, Bonn, 1991, presented a rough estimate which implied 1950-89 East German per capita GDP growth of only 2.6 per cent a year. In retrospect, this seems more plausible than Alton's estimate but it is not properly documented.

Table B-7 presents previous Western estimates of East German performance. The statistical basis was rather flimsy, and much more so than for Czechoslovakia and Hungary. Furthermore, the East German authorities are known to have deliberately understated the degree of inflation in ways which affected some components of the Alton estimates, e.g. trade. It is not plausible to believe that East German per capita growth could have been much different from that of Czechoslovakia, which was closest to it in the proportion engaged in agriculture, the nature of its industrial output, the skills of its labour force, levels of pre-war economic development, 1950 levels of income, and size of the population. If East German per capita growth performance in 1950-89 had in fact been like that of Czechoslovakia, its 1989 level would have been less than two-thirds of what it was imagined to be. This would still imply a drop in per capita product levels by more than a quarter from 1989 to the second half of 1990, but this would not be surprising in an economy whose governmental, administrative, police and military structures had been jettisoned, and whose competitiveness had been ruined by monetary union at a grossly overvalued exchange rate.

Italy: For 1861-1951, estimates of GDP at factor cost within present frontiers are available in G. Fua (ed.), *Lo sviluppo economico in Italia*, vol. iii, Angeli, Milan, 1969, pp. 410-12, but their use of 1938 weights for a ninety year period was likely to understate growth and reduce comparability with other countries, so I reweighted 1861-1913 with 1870 weights, and 1913-38 with 1913 weights. This produced a slight increase in growth rates which rose from 1.39 per cent a year to 1.47 per cent for the 1861-1913 segment, and raised growth in 1913-38 by 0.06 per cent a year. However, there was a bigger change (a further rise of GDP growth) for 1861-1913 by 0.32 per cent a year which resulted from a change I made for the industrial sector where the estimates of Stefano Fenoaltea were used for the years 1861-1913. The Fenoaltea estimates for mining, utilities, and construction are from "The Extractive Industries in Italy, 1861-1913", Journal of European Economic History, Spring 1988, "The Growth of the Utilities Industries in Italy 1861-1913", *Journal of Economic History*, Sept. 1982, "Construction in Italy, 1861-1913", *Rivista di Storia Economica*, International Issue, 1987. For manufacturing I used Fenoaltea, "Public Policy and Italian Industrial Development 1861-1913", Harvard Ph.D. Thesis, 1967 (Tables 24, 25, and 27) excluding utilities, and adding silk from Fenoaltea, "The Growth of Italy's Silk Industry, 1861-1913", *Rivista di Storia Economica*, October 1988. For 1951-70 I used estimates of R. Golinelli and M.M. Monterastelli, *Un metodo per la ricostruzione di serie storiche compatabili con la nuova contabilità nazionale*, Prometeia, Bologna, 1990. The official ISTAT estimates I used for 1970 onwards have a more complete coverage of the underground economy than is the case in other countries (20.2 per cent of total GDP). In other countries, underground activities which escape the net of official national accounts statisticians are typically about 3 per cent of GDP (see D. Blades, "The Hidden Economy and the National Accounts", OECD, *Occasional Studies*, June 1982, p. 39). I therefore made a 3 per cent downward adjustment to the benchmark level of Italian GDP to enhance international comparability. This has no effect on our index of Italian GDP growth: it only affects the level comparisons. See A. Maddison, "A Revised Estimate of Italian Economic Growth 1861-1989", *Banca Nazionale del Lavoro Quarterly Review*, June 1991 for further details.

There have been a number of territorial changes since 1861 when Italy became a nation. In 1866, after the war with Austria, the Venetian territories became part of Italy, and after 1870 the Papal states were added. In 1919 South Tirol, the old Austrian Kustenland provinces and the port of Zara were acquired. Fiume was added in 1922. In 1945, Zara, Fiume and part of Venezia-Giulia were ceded to Yugoslavia. Until the settlement of 1954 Trieste was in dispute and under international occupation; thereafter the city and a strip of coast went to Italy and the hinterland to Yugoslavia. In 1947, Tenda and Briga were added to France. The impact of these changes can be seen in Table H-2.

Japan: 1885-1940 GDP at 1934-6 market prices by industry of origin from K. Ohkawa and M. Shinohara, eds., *Patterns of Japanese Development: A Quantitative Appraisal*, Yale 1979, pp. 278-80. 1940-50 expenditure on GNP at 1934-36 prices adjusted to a GDP basis using coefficients from *op. cit.* pp. 268-9. 1945 GDP taken to be two-thirds of the 1944 level (see Y. Kosai, *The Era of High Speed Growth*, University of Tokyo, 1986, p. 34 for partial indicators for 1945). 1946 GDP assumed to lie halfway between 1945 and 1947. 1950-2 from *National Income White Paper*, (in Japanese) 1963 ed., p. 178, adjusted to a calendar year basis. 1952 onwards from OECD *National Accounts*. An upward adjustment of 0.66 per cent was made for 1946 to offset the impact of territorial change (loss of Okinawa). It was assumed that the official figures published by OECD are adjusted to exclude the effect of the reacquisition of Okinawa in 1973 (which added 0.92 per cent to population and to GDP). The figures for 1820 and 1870 are rough conjectures. For 1870-90, I assumed that per capita product rose at the same rate as in 1890-1913 and for 1820-70 that GDP per capita rose by 0.1 per cent a year in line with the position of those who think that there was modest growth in the Tokugawa period. See T.C. Smith, "Pre-Modern Economic Growth: Japan and the West", *Past and Present*, August 1973, pp. 127-60, and S.B. Hanley and K. Yamamura, *Economic and Demographic Change in Preindustrial Japan, 1600-1868*, Princeton, 1977.

Netherlands: J.L. van Zanden, "Economische groei in Nederland in de negentiende eeuw. Enkele nieuwe resultaten", *Economisch en Sociaal-Historisch Jaarboek*, 1987, pp. 58-60 provides a GDP index by industry of origin (8 sectors) for 1820, 1850, 1880 and 1910. His weights are derived from the sectoral breakdown of employment weighted by productivity. He and his associates are reworking these estimates and kindly supplied their provisional (Smits/Van Zanden) real GDP index, which I used for 1850-1900. 1900-60 from C.A. van Bochove and T.A. Huitker, "Main National Accounting Series, 1900-1986", *CBS Occasional Paper*, No. 17, The Hague, 1987. This official retrospective series links several segments. 1900-20 current price estimates of net national income are deflated by a fixed base cost of living index, 1921-39 is an elaborate re-estimate by type of expenditure with annual chain weighting procedures to produce volume and price indexes, 1939-48 was bridged by direct comparison of the two years with rough estimates of the same type as for 1900-20. 1948-69 was measured by the commodity flow method with fixed weights. 1969 onwards is the outcome of a major revision which raised the level of GDP by 6.2 per cent in the link year 1969. The revised index is in 1980 prices for 1969-81 and is an annual chain index from 1981. For 1960 onwards the estimates are from OECD, *National Accounts* (this incorporates the official estimates). G.P. den Bakker, "The Choice of Index Number Formulae and Weights in National Accounts", CBS, Occasional Papers NA-044, The Hague, 1991 presents several alternative weights for 1921-39. The official chain-weighted index rises by 2.6 per cent per annum for this period whereas an index with 1921 weights would rise by 3.0 per cent a year.

New Zealand: for 1870-1939 the source was an index of GNP in 1910/11 prices from K. Rankin, "New Zealand's Gross National Product: 1859-1939, *Review of Income and Wealth*, March 1992, pp. 60-1. These are proxy estimates based on regressions involving assumptions about velocity of circulation, nominal money supply, a variety of price indices (wholesale, export, import, farm and non-farm) and population. Rankin tests his method by applying the same procedure to Australia to see whether it approximated to Butlin's independent estimates of GNP. He discusses the plausibility of his results in the light of previous spot estimates of aggregate output in New Zealand, but he does not check his procedure for years after 1939 for which there are official estimates of total output. He does not explain clearly why he excludes the Maori population from his estimating procedure for per capita estimates, though he does explain that they were excluded from some of the spot estimates he discusses. The Rankin index was linked to estimates for 1939-50 from C. Clark, *The Conditions of Economic Progress*, third edition, Macmillan, London, 1957, pp. 171-2 (which Clark derived by deflating official estimates in current prices). Figures for 1950 onwards are from OECD Development Centre, and OECD National Accounts estimates. The index is for calendar years to 1939 and fiscal years starting April 1st thereafter.

Norway: 1865-1930 GDP by category of expenditure at 1910 market prices 1930-9 at 1938 prices and 1946-50 at 1955 prices from *National Accounts 1865-1960*, Central Bureau of Statistics, Oslo, 1965, pp. 348-59 (I adjusted gross fixed investment downwards by a third to eliminate repairs and maintenance).

1939-44 movement in national income (excluding shipping and whaling operations carried out from Allied bases 1940-4) from O. Aukrust and P.J. Bjerve, *Hva krigen kostet Norge*, Dreyers, Oslo, 1945, p. 45. 1945 assumed to be midway between 1944 and 1946. For 1820-65 it was assumed that the per capita GDP movement was the same as in Sweden.

Sweden: There have been five major studies of Swedish growth experience. E. Lindahl, E. Dahlgren and K. Kock, *Wages, Cost of Living and National Income in Sweden 1860-1930*, 2 vols., King, London, 1937, was the pioneering study, followed by O. Lindahl, *Sveriges Nationalprodukt 1861-1951*, Konjunkturinstitutet, Stockholm, 1956, Ö. Johansson, *The Gross Domestic Product of Sweden and Its Composition 1861-1955*, Almqvist and Wiksell, Stockholm, 1967, and O. Krantz and C.-A. Nilsson, *Swedish National Product 1861-1970*, CWK Gleerup, 1975. The fifth study has been in preparation for several years and is the most ambitious. Seven volumes have appeared since 1986. They cover the period since 1800. The new estimates involve a downward revision in the growth rate in the nineteenth century. Preliminary 1820-1960 GDP estimates by industry of origin were kindly supplied by Olle Krantz, his procedures are explained in Olle Krantz, "New Estimates of Swedish Historical GDP Since the Beginning of the Nineteenth Century", *Review of Income and Wealth*, June 1988. Krantz divided the period into eight segments with an average length of 22 years. For each segment he used Paasche deflators and Laspeyres volume indices, and then linked the segments. Krantz has also produced a supplementary estimate of the volume of domestic work (not included in GDP). See O. Krantz, *Husligt arbete 1800-1980*, Lund, 1987.

Switzerland: The historical estimates are poor and weaker than for all other West European countries. 1899-1950 real product in international units was taken from C. Clark, *Conditions of Economic Progress* (3rd ed.), Macmillan, London, 1957, pp. 188-9. For 1870-99 it was assumed that per capita product moved as in Germany. There is a graphical indication of the growth of Swiss real product in F. Kneschaurek, "Problemen der langfristigen Marktprognose", *Aussenwirtschaft*, December 1959, p. 336. This shows faster growth than C. Clark to 1938. On the other hand, U. Zwingli and E. Ducret, "Das Sozialprodukt als Wertmesser des langfristigen Wirtschaftswachstums", *Schweizerische Zeitschrift für Volkswirtschaft und Statistik*, March-June 1964, show slower growth for 1910-38 than Clark. For a survey of past attempts to estimate Swiss GDP growth before 1950, see *Annuaire statistique de la Suisse 1993*, Office fédéral de la Statistique, Berne, pp. 131-4. The figures for 1900-12 and 1914-23 are interpolations.

UK: 1820-31 derived from N.F.R. Crafts, "British Economic Growth 1700-1831: A Review of the Evidence", *Economic History Review*, May 1983. For 1801-31 Crafts shows growth rates for 6 sectors by industry of origin and for total "real national product". He uses the 1821 national income weights of P. Deane and W.A. Cole, *British Economic Growth 1688-1959*, Cambridge, 1964, p. 166. 1801-31 growth shown by Crafts (p. 187) refers to Great Britain (i.e. England, Wales and Scotland). Here it was adjusted to a U.K. basis assuming Irish output per head of population in 1831 to have been half of that in Great Britain (hypothesis of P. Deane, "New Estimates of Gross National Product for the United Kingdom 1830-1914", *Review of Income and Wealth*, June 1968) and to have been stagnant from 1801 to 1831. Crafts has recently made a very minor adjustment to his earlier estimates which I have ignored — see N.F.R. Crafts and C.K. Harley, "Output Growth and the British Industrial Revolution: a Restatement of the Crafts-Harley View", *Economic History Review*, 1992, pp. 703-30. 1830-1855 gross national product by type of expenditure at factor cost from P. Deane (1968), p. 106. Deane expresses her results in a 1900 numeraire but the underlying procedure involves linkage of segments with different weights. Her estimates of volume movement were linked to 1855-1960 GDP at factor cost (compromise) estimate of C.H. Feinstein, *National Income Expenditure and Output of the United Kingdom 1855-1965*, Cambridge, 1972, pp. T18-20. Feinstein's "compromise" figures average the results of his real expenditure, output and income estimates which he calculated separately (though he used the expenditure deflator to arrive at real income). For 1870-1960, the compromise measure shows a compound growth rate of 1.73 per cent a year, the output estimate 1.68 per cent, income 1.72 per cent, and expenditure 1.80 per cent a year. He used 1900 prices for 1870-1913, 1938 prices for 1913-38, a Fisher geometric average of 1938 and 1948 prices for 1938-48 and 1958 prices for 1948-60. Figures from 1920 onwards are increased by 3.8 per cent (Feinstein's coefficient) to offset the exclusion of output in the area which became the Irish Republic.

USA: The hard core of modern estimation was carried out by Simon Kuznets. He took over the NBER research in this field around 1930, and also prepared the first official estimates, *National Income 1929-32*, which were transmitted to the Finance Committee of the US Senate by the Dept. of Commerce in January 1934. This showed the flows of different categories of income broken down by industry together with corresponding employment estimates prepared by Robert Nathan. A cost-of-living index was provided as a tentative deflator, together with very fully documented appendices with sources. This approach was further elaborated in S. Kuznets, *National Income and Its Composition 1919-38*, NBER, New York, 1941, which contained estimates (at current and 1929 prices) of the industrial distribution of different categories of income (wage, property, and entrepreneurial).

Kuznets also derived estimates by category of expenditure for 1919 onwards by the "commodity flow" method, i.e. he used census and other information on production, and determined what part represented the final flow to consumers and capital formation. These flows from producers were given distributive mark-ups to reflect final sales values. Rougher estimates were made for services. This work was sponsored by the Committee on Credit and Banking which was interested in commodity flows as a counterpart to its interest in flows of financial resources. The details of this approach are described in S. Kuznets, *Commodity Flow and Capital Formation*, NBER, New York, 1938. The expenditure estimates were extended back to 1869 in S. Kuznets, L. Epstein and E. Jenks, *National Product Since 1869*, NBER, New York, 1946 (but these referred to overlapping decades and were not annual). This extension back to 1869 relied very heavily on W.H. Shaw, *Value of Commodity Output Since 1869*, NBER, New York, 1947, who used the same procedure for making commodity flow estimates of values as Kuznets (1938) did. Shaw also supplied price deflators. Estimates in the same form can also be found (in an analytical context) in S. Kuznets, *Income and Wealth of the United States: Trends and Structure*, Income and Wealth Series II, Bowes and Bowes, Cambridge, 1952; this study contains an annex on the estimates for 1800 to 1870 by Martin and King. Kuznets had a poor opinion of these, and although he did not produce alternative estimates, he gave a clear indication of the direction in which they were biased, and some clues for constructing estimates with limited information.

The final version of Kuznets' massive work appeared in his *Capital in the American Economy*, NBER, Princeton, 1961. Here he published annual estimates of GNP by type of expenditure in current and in 1929 dollars (pp. 555-8) back to 1889. As the underlying census information was inadequate before 1889, he showed only 5-year moving averages back to 1871 (pp. 559-64). He had three variants of GNP with different assumptions about which products were intermediate.

The US Department of Commerce, which has prepared the official US national accounts since 1941, took over Kuznets' commodity flow method in measuring consumption, but included several items as final product, i.e. a substantial proportion of government services, and some items of personal consumption which Kuznets regarded as intermediate items. Kuznets explained his disagreement with their procedures in his "Discussion of the New Department of Commerce Income Series", *Review of Economics and Statistics*, August 1948. The official side was not convinced by his arguments, see M. Gilbert, G. Jaszi, E.F. Denison, and C.F. Schwartz, "Objectives of National Income Measurement: A Reply to Professor Kuznets" in the same publication.

This discussion is very important in the history of national accounting conventions for the decisions of the Dept. of Commerce have had a world-wide impact in establishing the boundaries used in the standardised national accounting system which takes a broader view of their scope than Kuznets would have liked. For a further discussion of the problems on a more theoretical level, see J.R. Hicks, "The Valuation of the Social Income", *Economica*, May 1940, and S. Kuznets, "On the Valuation of Social Income — Reflections on Professor Hicks' Article", *Economica*, February and May issues, 1948.

Apart from the intrinsic merit of their position, the Dept. of Commerce team greatly strengthened their bargaining power by wartime (1944) agreements with the Canadian and British statistical offices. Milton Gilbert and Richard Stone established a working partnership which they developed further in their later work for OEEC, see E.F. Denison, "Report on Tripartite Discussions of National Income Measurement", *Studies in Income and Wealth*, vol. 10, NBER, New York, 1972.

The Kuznets estimates were published in transparent form with the full scholarly apparatus characteristic of the NBER. It was therefore possible for John Kendrick (who in any case had access to the worksheets) to convert the Kuznets annual estimates of GNP (variant III) back to 1889 (with some minor adjustment) by type of expenditure to a Dept. of Commerce basis, see J.W. Kendrick, *Productivity Trends in the United States*, NBER, Princeton, 1961, pp. 298-9. Like Kuznets, Kendrick used fixed 1929 weights for his volume estimates, but he also gave a chain-weighted alternative, which for 1889-1929 shows a growth rate of 3.82 per cent a year compared with 3.68 for his fixed-weight index for the private domestic economy (p. 327). For 1869-1889 Kendrick presented only decade averages, as it seemed probable that they exaggerated growth. Kendrick (1961) augmented the NBER sectoral production studies (by Barger, Fabricant and others) to show movements in output or value added on an annual basis back to 1869 in many cases. However, he did not construct a complete estimate of GDP by industry of origin. His aggregate (pp. 302-3) covers 9 production sectors in combination with total private GDP by type of expenditure. The bulk of private service activity was derived as a residual. Even then his estimates were presented only for 10 benchmark years. Thus we have the paradox that the USA is one of the few countries where the construction of historical accounts by industry of origin has been neglected, though the statistical basis for such estimates is better than elsewhere.

Robert Gallman revised and extended the Kuznets estimates backwards (variant I) using the same commodity flow approach and techniques of presentation. He first estimated value added (in 1879 prices) for agriculture, mining, manufacturing and construction for benchmark years, see R.E. Gallman, "Commodity Output, 1839-1899", in W.N. Parker, *Trends in the American Economy in the Nineteenth Century*, NBER, Princeton, 1960, p. 43. He used these results, census, and other information to construct his estimates of GNP by type of expenditure (four-way breakdown of consumption and three-way breakdown of capital formation) in 1860 prices, see R.E. Gallman, "Gross National Product in the United States 1834-1909", in D.S. Brady, ed., *Output, Employment and Productivity in the United States after 1800*, NBER, New York, 1966, p. 26. Unfortunately he provided figures only for five benchmark years, 1839, 1844, 1849, 1854, and 1859 and for overlapping decades from 1834-43 to 1899-1908, and he has not yet published his annual estimates.

Estimates for 1840-69 were taken from Gallman, and for 1869-90 from N.S. Balke and R.J. Gordon, "The Estimation of Prewar Gross National Product: Methodology and New Evidence", *Journal of Political Economy*, February 1989, p. 84. They revamped the Gallman-Kendrick-Kuznets commodity flow estimates, using additional information on construction, transport and communications, to provide annual estimates of nominal GNP, real GNP and a GNP deflator. For 1869-90, their average annual estimate for real GNP growth was 4.16 per cent a year, which is lower than the unpublished Kendrick figure of 5.44 per cent, or the 5.55 per cent of Kuznets'. Both Kuznets and Kendrick thought their own estimates of the 1869 level were too low, and the Balke-Gordon estimates therefore seem preferable.

For 1820-40, the evidence is rather weak, and one must still rely on the kind of reasoning which Kuznets (1952) first applied, and which can be found in P.A. David, "The Growth of Real Product in the United States before 1840: New Evidence, Controlled Conjectures", *Journal of Economic History*, June 1967, and more recently in T. Weiss, "US Labor Force Estimates and Economic Growth, 1800-1860", in R.E. Gallman and J.J. Wallis, eds., *American Economic Growth and Standards of Living Before the Civil War*, University of Chicago Press, 1992, p. 27. I used a variant of the Kuznets-David inferential approach. I calculated agricultural productivity 1820-40, taking agricultural value added (output of crops and livestock products plus change in livestock inventories, minus intermediate products consumed) from M.W. Towne and W.D. Rasmussen, "Farm Gross Product and Gross Investment in the Nineteenth Century", in Parker, ed. (1960, p. 25), and agricultural employment from Weiss (1992, p. 51). Agricultural productivity (thus measured) grew by .62 per cent a year from 1820-40. Like Kuznets and David, I assumed that productivity growth in the rest of the economy was faster (1 per cent a year). Although service productivity growth is likely to have been modest, the assumption of faster growth in non-agriculture seems warranted as K.L. Sokoloff found manufacturing productivity to have grown by 2.2 per cent a year, see his "Productivity Growth in Manufacturing During Early Industrialisation: Evidence from the American Northeast, 1820-1860", in S.L. Engerman and R.E. Gallmann, *Long Term Factors in American Economic Growth*, Chicago, 1986, p. 695

For 1929 onwards the source was the official US Dept. of Commerce estimates of GDP by category of expenditure: 1929-58 at 1987 prices from *National Income and Product Accounts of the United States*, vol. 1, BEA, US Dept. of Commerce, Washington, D.C., February 1993. 1959-92 from A.H. Young, "Alternative Measures of Changes in Real Output and Prices, Quarterly Estimates for 1959-92", *Survey of Current Business*, March 1993. Young presents three alternative indices of real GDP volume. I used his index where benchmarks change every five years, because this is closer to the procedure used in other OECD countries for this period. The option I used produces faster growth than the officially preferred series where 1987 weights are used throughout. Unfortunately, for 1929-58, the correspondingly weighted series are not yet available. Figures for years before 1960 exclude Alaska and Hawaii, which added .294 per cent to 1960 GDP (see *Survey of Current Business*, December 1980, p. 17). I adjusted the figures to exclude the impact of this geographic change.

"South European" Countries

The term "South European" is used to refer to lower income OECD countries, whose institutional heritage was somewhat different from that of the advanced European capitalist countries. Irish economic characteristics make it fit neatly within this group, though some Irish eyes may smile at my aberrant geography. 1993 and 1994 are from OECD *Economic Outlook*, December 1994.

Greece: 1913-29 real product in international units from C. Clark, *Conditions of Economic Progress*, 3rd edition, Macmillan, London, 1957; 1929-38 GNP at factor cost from *Ekonomikos Tachydromos*, 22 May 1954;1938-50 from OEEC, *Europe and the World Economy*, Paris 1960, p. 116. 1950 onwards from OECD, *National Accounts*, various issues.

Ireland: For Ireland, there is no time series for years before 1926, and one must therefore rely on indications of the relative size of Irish income in 1831 and 1920 by British historians (Deane and Feinstein — see note above on the UK) to get a crude picture. Mokyr has recently produced a spot estimate for 1841 (see J. Mokyr, *Why Ireland Starved: A Quantitative and Analytical History of the Irish Economy 1800-1850*, Allen and Unwin, London, 1985) which shows a much lower ratio (though the first edition of his book showed a higher one). Cullen has produced a spot estimate for 1911 which is higher than one can derive from Feinstein. The Mokyr-Cullen estimates have led some Irish historians to assume faster growth than I have done — see K.A. Kennedy, T. Giblin and D. McHugh, *The Economic Development of Ireland in the Twentieth Century*, Routledge, London, 1988, pp. 17-18, and C. Ó Gráda, *Ireland Before and After the Famine*, Manchester University Press, 1988, p. 128. The present estimates refer throughout to GDP in the area of the Irish Republic (i.e. Southern Ireland). The 1920 per capita GDP level was taken to be 54 per cent of that in the UK (excluding Southern Ireland) as estimated by C.H. Feinstein, *National Income, Expenditure and Output of the United Kingdom 1855-1965*, Cambridge University Press, 1972, Table 6. This proportion was assumed to be valid for 1820, 1900 and 1913 as well. 1926-50 from K.A. Kennedy, *Productivity and Industrial Growth: The Irish Experience*, Oxford University Press, 1971, p. 3. 1950-60 from OECD *National Accounts, 1950-68*, Paris, 1970. 1960-92 from CSO, *National Income and Expenditure 1992*, Dublin, 1993, p. ix.

Portugal: 1850-1913 GDP volume estimate derived from indices of agricultural and industrial output in Pedro Lains, "How Far Can We Go? Measuring Portuguese Economic Growth (1850-1913)" and statistical annex, paper presented to the World Cliometric Congress, Santander, 1989; for the service sector population was used as a proxy indicator. The 1890 sector weights (agriculture 49.3, industry 24.7 and services 26.0) were taken from Lains. For 1913-53 I used an adjusted version of the GDP estimates of A.B. Nunes, E. Mata and N. Valerio, "Portuguese Economic Growth 1833-1985", *Journal of European Economic History*, vol. 18, 2, Fall 1989. The Nunes, Mata, Valerio estimates have been criticized by P. Lains and J. Reis, "Portuguese Economic Growth, 1833-1985: Some Doubts", *Journal of European Economic History*, vol. 20, 2, Fall 1991. The Nunes, Mata, Valerio estimates for GDP are based on 3 proxy indicators (exports, fiscal receipts, and government expenditures) at current prices, which they deflate by the cost of living index. These indicators are adjusted in the light of the relationship between their estimating technique and the official GDP series for 1947-85. Their GDP estimate was taken as representative for the material production sectors, and I used population as a proxy for service sector growth. 1938-58 from *O Rendimento Nacional Português, Estudos*, No. 34, Instituto Nacional de Estatística, Lisbon, 1960;1958-60 from R. Janes Cartado and N.E. Sequeira da Rosa, *Series Longas as Contas Nacionais Portuguesas 1958-1985*, Banco de Portugal, Lisbon, 1986. 1960 onwards from OECD, *National Accounts*, various issues. The Portuguese authorities are in process of revising the GDP level upwards to incorporate the islands of the Azores and Madeira which were previously excluded, and to provide better estimates for construction and tourism-sectors which had previously been inadequately covered. This involved an upward revision in the 1990 GDP level of 14.1545 per cent. This figure is provisional (see H. Garrido, "Portugueses mais ricos", *Diario de Noticias*, Lisbon, 11 April 1994).

Spain: A rough estimate of the real income movement for 1820-50 was derived from L. Prados, *Comercio Exterior y Crecimiento Economico en Espana, 1826-1913: Tendencias a Largo Plaza, Estudios de Historia*, No. 7, Banco de España, 1982, p. 110. This shows the movement in national product in current prices for 1832-60, which is here deflated by Sarda's wholesale price index in *Estadisticas Historicas de España*, Fundacion Banco Exterior, Madrid, 1989, p. 518. 1850-1993 GDP by category of expenditure was supplied by Leandro Prados de la Escosura. For 1850-1950 these estimates move in a similar way to those in his "Spain's Real Gross Domestic Product, 1850-1990: A New Series", Ministério de Economia y Hacienda, Madrid, March 1993, Table D.1, but for 1950-93, Prados has now made a tapered adjustment for jumps in the GDP level between successive segments of the official national accounts. The Spanish authorities have hitherto ignored these jumps and simply linked the successive indexes at the overlap year. Prados' procedure is analogous to that which I used to adjust the official Italian estimates. Prados shows his results for all years at 1980 "prices", but this is simply his numeraire, as the underlying procedure was to chain successive segments at characteristic constant prices for the relevant period.

Turkey: 1923-48 GDP by industry of origin at factor cost and by type of expenditure at 1938 market prices from T. Bulutay, Y.S. Tezel and N. Yielderim, *Turkiye Milli Geliri 1923-1948*, Ankara, 1974. 1913 per capita GDP assumed to be the same as in 1929. 1948 onwards from OECD, *National Accounts*, various issues.

East European Countries

In Eastern Europe and the USSR, the conventions for measuring macroeconomic performance in the communist period were different from those in other countries in our comparisons. The scope of the official output measure was narrower. It referred to "material product" and excluded a good many service activities. For the activities which were included, output was generally measured on a gross value rather than a value added basis, which led to some double counting. A much larger proportion of statistical reporting came from administrative sources than in Western national accounting practice. The price system and tax structure were also different from those in capitalist countries, and gave incentives to enterprises to exaggerate quality improvements when new products were introduced. Problems of comparability were further handicapped by the secretive habits of statistical agencies, and their susceptibility to official "guidance" concerning magnitudes which might throw adverse light on the achievements of the regime.

For the communist period, reliance was placed almost entirely on estimates from Western sources. Abram Bergson is the most distinguished Western student of the subject, and he concentrated his efforts on the former USSR. In his *Soviet National Income and Product in 1937*, Columbia University Press, 1953, he developed an "adjusted factor cost" framework for valuation of Soviet output, where Soviet commodity prices were adjusted to equal average cost, and imputations were made for capital costs. Later he adjusted for turnover taxes and subsidies. He adjusted the scope of the accounts so that they approximated to the Western concept of GDP, and his indicators of production volume were intended to reflect value added rather than gross output. Bergson's methods were adopted by the US Central Intelligence Agency which made the annual estimates of Soviet GDP which were presented regularly and publicly to the Joint Economic Committee of the US Congress.

Thad Alton and his colleagues in the Research Project on National Income in East Central Europe in New York prepared regular estimates for Bulgaria, Czechoslovakia, East Germany, Poland, Romania and Yugoslavia from the early 1960s, using the methodology developed originally by Bergson. This was a very ambitious project which gave greatest priority to measuring changes in real output by sector of the economy in order to measure movements in aggregate and sectoral output and productivity, but also yielded estimates of real expenditure growth and aggregate levels in dollars corrected for differences in purchasing power parity.

Their estimates rely mainly on East European sources for quantitative indicators of commodity output, and for services there was a partial reliance on official deflators. The sector and industry weights approximate to gross value added at factor cost, and although they are ultimately derived from East European sources, they involved elaborate estimates of returns to labour, the net return on fixed and working capital and agricultural land, and the depreciation of fixed capital. The weights were first established for the mid 1950s in a series of detailed country monographs and studies for the 1950-65 segment of the estimates. The base was shifted to the late 1960s for the 1965-75 segment, in Thad Alton and Associates, "Statistics on East European Economic Structure and Growth", *Occasional Paper* 48, New York, 1975. The third shift (to mid-1970s weights) was made in *Occasional Paper* 64, New York, 1981 and these weights were applied to the 1975-85 time segment. The fourth weight shift to the 1980s was made in *Occasional Paper* 120, New York, 1992 and applied to the 1985-91 segment.

The sample of quantity indicators seems quite respectable, but is smaller than would be available in an official statistical office with full access to the basic reporting system. In order to make a sensitivity test of the robustness of the sample procedure, G.J. Staller, "Comparison of Official and Recalculated Industrial Growth: Austria and Czechoslovakia", *Occasional Paper* 84, New York, 1984 recalculated Austrian output using a restricted sample analogous to the (387 item) sample used for Czechoslovak industrial output. He concluded that the sample procedure was reasonably reliable. However, this cannot be assumed to be the case for all the countries, because the openness of the statistical offices varied, as did the size of the Alton group's research input. The partial reliance on official deflators of service output may also have led to some overstatement of growth. Judging by the number of research papers, the reliability of their results seems likely to be most sound for Czechoslovakia, Hungary and Poland, somewhat weaker for Bulgaria and weakest for East Germany (only 2 *Occasional Papers*), Romania (2 *Occasional Papers*) and Yugoslavia (5 *Occasional Papers*). These three countries all showed faster growth than the three which are best documented, and in the case of East Germany, in particular, there is now very strong evidence that the Alton group overstated growth.

The Alton group gave preference to its measures by industry of origin and regarded them as more reliable than its estimates by type of expenditure which generally showed slower growth. For the first segment (ending in 1965) the Alton (1970) expenditure side estimates for Czechoslovakia and Hungary showed slower growth (as noted below). For 1965-82, the expenditure side estimates (see Alton, 1985, p. 112) showed slower growth for Bulgaria (2.9 per cent a year for 1965-82 instead of 3.5); for Czechoslovakia 2.2 per cent a year instead of 2.6; for East Germany 2.5 per cent a year instead of 2.8 and for Poland 2.0 per cent a year instead of 2.6. The only case where the expenditure side estimates showed faster growth was in Poland for 1950-65.

The Alton group's purchasing power parity converters were generally derived from studies by other researchers, e.g. those of M. Ernst in their 1970 study, and adjusted ICP estimates for 1985 and 1990.

Since 1990, the East European countries have undergone major political change and are moving away from planning and public ownership towards market prices and privatisation. They have given up the "material product" concept of total output and have widened the scope of their accounts to cover the whole of GDP. There is now much greater openness about statistical procedures and sources. The experience of East Germany in particular demonstrates the need to re-examine past estimates of comparative levels of performance and growth rates. There must also be doubt about the accuracy of the new measures for the transition period, because the statistical apparatus for monitoring the greatly expanded private sector is defective, so our measures of the decline in output since 1989 may be exaggerated.

Useful surveys of the methodological problems can be found in CIA, *Measuring Soviet GNP: Problems and Solutions*, Directorate of Intelligence, September 1990, and in P. Marer and Associates, *Historically Planned Economies: A Guide to the Data*, World Bank, Washington, D.C., 1992.

Bulgaria: The estimates for Bulgaria are not as well documented as those for Czechoslovakia and Hungary. The 1913-26 movement of real income (including imputations) in international units was derived by Colin Clark from two separate spot estimates by different authors (see his *Conditions of Economic Progress*, 3rd edition, Macmillan, London, 1957, p. 105) which were linked at 1926 to the 1924-45 movement in real national income shown by A. Chakalov, *The National Income and Outlay of Bulgaria: 1924-1945* (in Bulgarian), Knipegraph, Sofia, 1946. This was then linked at 1939 to the 1939-65 movement in GNP by industry of origin (with mid-1950s weights) shown by T.P. Alton, "Economic Structure and Growth in Eastern Europe", in *Economic Developments in Countries of Eastern Europe*, Joint Economic Committee, US Congress, 1970, p. 46. 1965-75 movement of real GNP by industry of origin (with weights of the late 1960s) from T.P. Alton, "East European GNPs: Origins of Product, Final Uses, Rates of Growth and International Comparisons", in *East European Economies: Slow Growth in the 1980s*, vol. I, *Economic Performance and Policy*, Joint Economic Committee, US Congress, October 1985, pp. 109-10. The 1975-92 movement of real GNP by industry of origin (with mid-1970s weights for 1975-85 and mid-1980s weights for 1985 onwards) is from T.P. Alton and Associates, "Economic Growth in Eastern Europe", *Occasional Papers* 120 and 124, L.W. Research Project on National Income in East Central Europe, New York, 1992 and 1993. The Alton team has produced 7 *Occasional Papers* on individual sector performance in Bulgaria.

Czechoslovakia: For 1820-1913 growth rates of per capita product by industry of origin were assumed to fall midway between the rates Kausel shows for Austria proper and for the rest of Cisleithania (the Austrian part of the Habsburg Empire). See A. Kausel, "Österreichs Volkseinkommen 1830 bis 1913", in "Geschichte und Ergebnisse der zentralen amtlichen Statistik in Österreich 1829-1979", *Beiträge zum Österreichischen Statistik*, 550, Vienna, 1979. 1913-37, GDP by industry of origin with 1929 weights from F.L. Pryor, Z.P. Pryor, M. Stadnik, and G.J. Staller "Czechoslovak Aggregate Production in the Inter-war Period", *Review of Income and Wealth*, March 1971, p. 36. 1937-65 GNP by industry of origin at 1956 adjusted factor cost from G. Lazarcik, "Czechoslovak Gross National Product by Sector of Origin and Final Use, 1937, and 1948-65", *Occasional Paper* 26, Research Project on National Income in East Central Europe, New York, 1969. Lazarcik also provides estimates of GNP growth by type of expenditure which show slower growth (1.9 per cent a year instead of 2.3 per cent) than by industry of origin. The Lazarcik estimates are based on 9 of the 12 other *Occasional Papers* on Czechoslovakia by sector, and the earlier benchmark study, T.P. Alton and Associates, *Czechoslovak National Income and Product, 1947-8 and 1955-6*, Columbia University Press, New York, 1962. 1965 onwards as for Bulgaria.

On 1 January 1993, the Czech and the Slovak republics became separate countries. The Czech republic had a population of 10 315 thousand in 1992, the Slovak republic had 5 300 thousand. Per capita product was about 15 per cent higher in the Czech republic than in Slovakia in the late 1980s.

Hungary: For 1870-1913, estimates of gross material product at 1913 prices in agriculture, transport and trade were taken from L. Katus, "Economic Growth in Hungary during the Age of Dualism (1867-1913)" in E. Pemlenyi, ed., *Social Economic Research in the History of East Central Europe*, Akademiai Kiado, Budapest, 1970, p. 108 and J. Komlos, *The Habsburg Monarchy as a Customs Union*, Princeton, 1983, pp. 291-3 for industrial production at 1913 prices. Housing and other services were assumed to grow parallel with population. 1900-42 net national product by industry of origin at 1938/9 factor cost from A. Eckstein, "National Income and Capital Formation in Hungary, 1900-50", in S. Kuznets, ed., *Income and Wealth*, series V, Bowes and Bowes, London, 1955, p. 175 (1924-38 data refer to fiscal years). The Eckstein series was linked at 1938 to estimates of GNP by industry of origin for 1938-65 at 1955 "adjusted" factor cost from L. Czirjak, "Hungarian GNP by Sectors of Origin of Product and End Uses, 1938 and 1946-67", *Occasional Paper* 43, Research Project on East Central Europe, New York, 1973. Czirjak also provides an estimate of GNP growth by type of expenditure, which shows slower growth (2.1 per cent a year instead of 2.3 per cent) than by industry of origin. The Czirjak estimates are built on 10 earlier *Occasional Papers* on Hungary by sector as well as the benchmark study showing the derivation of the 1955 adjusted factor cost weights, T.P. Alton and Associates, *Hungarian National Income and Product in 1955*, Columbia University Press, New York, 1963. 1965 onwards as for Bulgaria.

Poland: 1929-38 from K. Laski, *Akumulacja i spozycie w procesie uprzemyslowienia Polski Ludowej*, Ksiazka i Wiedza, Warsaw, 1956, pp. 86-90 as cited by N. Spulber, *The State and Economic Development in Eastern Europe*, Random House, New York, 1966, p. 59; 1937-65 from T.P. Alton (1970), p. 46, 1965 onwards as for Bulgaria. There are 9 *Occasional Papers* of Alton's team on Polish performance in individual sectors from pre-war to 1965 as well as the benchmark volume, T.P. Alton and Associates, *Polish National Income and Product in 1954*, Columbia University Press, New York, 1965. Alton (1970), p. 52 shows real expenditure for 1950-65 rising by 5.2 per cent a year which is faster than the increase using his industry of origin estimates.

Romania: 1926-38 from "Venitul National", in *Enciclopedia Romaniei*, Bucharest, 1940, vol. 4, pp. 941-966 as cited by N. Spulber, p. 54, *op. cit.*; 1938-50 from D. Grindea, *Vencital National in Republica Socialista Romania*, Stiintifica, Bucharest, 1967, p. 113; 1950-65 from Alton (1970) *op. cit.*, p. 46; 1965-75 from T.P. Alton (1985) *op. cit.*, pp. 109-10; 1975-92 as for Bulgaria. The estimates for Romania are probably the weakest for our East European group. There are only 2 *Occasional Papers* from the Alton group on Romania and no benchmark volume.

USSR: For the Tsarist period to 1928 there are two different types of estimate of GDP growth: (a) by industry of origin, where the measures of output are volume estimates based on physical indicators, mainly for agriculture and industry: (b) expenditure studies in current prices with the components (private consumption, government current spending, and investment) deflated by price indices. In the following, use was made of sources based on the first method. Alternative studies of net domestic product may be found from the expenditure side in P.R. Gregory, *Russian National Income 1885-1913*, Cambridge University Press, 1982, pp. 56-7. For the period before 1913, the two methods concord very well. Using an adjusted version of Goldsmith's industry of origin material, one gets a GDP index of 43.2 for 1890, 66.3 for 1900 and 100 for 1913. The average of Gregory's two alternatives is 43.2 for 1890, 66.3 for 1900, 100 for 1913. For the change between 1913 and 1928, Gregory (p. 113) provides two estimates of net national product at 1913 market prices, one of these showed 1928 as 94.4 percent of 1913 (which he preferred) and another showed 1928 as 106.2 percent of 1913. In our industry of origin estimate (described below) 1928 was estimated to be 99.8 percent of 1913. The 1870-1913 growth indicators were derived from R.W. Goldsmith, "The Economic Growth of Tsarist Russia 1860-1913", *Economic Development and Cultural Change*, April 1961, pp. 450, and 462-3, i.e. crop output at 1896-1900 weights, his industrial index (based on linked segments with 1887, 1900, and 1908 weights) and his indications for livestock and handicrafts. 1913 weights from M.E. Falkus, "Russia's National Income 1913: A Revaluation", *Economica*, February 1968, pp. 62 and 67 (forestry and fishing were assumed to move parallel to agriculture; construction, transport and communication parallel to industry).

For 1820-60 there is no real evidence on Russian growth rates, though there are some grounds for inference. It is unlikely that Russian growth was faster than in the Czech lands of the Austrian Empire, and it is unlikely that the Russian per capita level in 1820 was above that in Finland. I therefore simply assumed that the average growth of per capita GDP was the same as Czechoslovakia, which meant that its 1820 level would be slightly lower than in Finland in that year.

For 1913-28, the same technique of estimation was used as for 1870-1913, taking the estimate of net agricultural product from S.G. Wheatcroft in R.W. Davies, ed., *From Tsarism to the New Economic Policy*, Macmillan, London, 1990, p. 279, and industrial output from G.W. Nutter, *Growth of Industrial Production in the Soviet Union*, Princeton, 1962, p. 150, using the Falkus 1913 weights. 1928-40 and 1945-50 gross national product at 1937 prices by industry of origin from R. Moorsteen and R.P. Powell, *The Soviet Capital Stock 1928-1962*, Irwin, Illinois, 1966, p. 361 with the 1939-40 increase reduced to offset the population increase due to territorial acquisitions at that time.

1950-90 estimates of GNP at 1982 factor cost by industry of origin were supplied by the CIA. Their weighting system is an adjusted factor cost method first developed by Abram Bergson in *Soviet National Income and Product in 1937*, Columbia, New York, 1953 which is intended to correct for distortions in the Soviet pricing system. 1990-1 movement from B.M. Bolotin, "The Former Soviet Union as Reflected in National Accounts Statistics", *In Search of Answers in the Post Soviet Era*, IMEMO, Moscow, 1992. 1991-2 movement derived from information for the 15 post Soviet republics in World Bank, *World Tables 1994*, Washington, D.C., 1994.

There have recently been suggestions within Russia that Western Kremlinologists overstated growth in the communist period. The most prominent of these new Russian revisionists is Khanin, whose work is conveniently summarised in M. Harrison, "Soviet Economic Growth Since 1928: The Alternative Statistics of G.I. Khanin", *Europe-Asia Studies*, vol. 45, No. 1, 1993, pp. 141-67. Khanin finds a different time path for growth than the CIA but no net difference for the post-war period as a whole. The big difference between his estimates and those which I use is that he gets a much lower rate of growth for 1928-40. However, Khanin has not used a GDP framework for his analysis and has not produced annual estimates, so his revision needs further substantiation.

At the end of 1991, the constituent republics of the USSR became independent. Their relative size is shown in Table B-8. The biggest was Russia with 51.1 per cent of the population and 58.7 per cent of GDP.

Table B-8. **Characteristics of the 15 Constituent Republics of the USSR in 1991**

	Population (000s)	GDP (million 1990 international dollars)	GDP per capita in 1990 international dollars
Armenia	3 400	16 363	4 813
Azerbaijan	7 250	30 026	4 142
Belarus	10 300	65 619	6 371
Estonia	1 600	13 832	8 645
Georgia	5 500	29 520	5 367
Kazakhstan	16 850	98 513	5 846
Kyrgyzstan	4 500	13 158	2 924
Latvia	2 700	21 423	7 934
Lithuania	3 750	27 327	7 287
Moldova	4 400	20 242	4 600
Russia	148 800	990 360	6 656
Tajikistan	5 400	13 158	2 437
Turkmenistan	3 750	11 471	3 059
Ukraine	52 000	257 079	4 944
Uzbekistan	21 000	78 777	3 751
USSR	291 200	1 686 868	5 793

Source: Derived from B.M. Bolotin, "The Former Soviet Union as Reflected in National Accounts Statistics", in S. Hirsch, ed., *Memo 3: In Search of Answers in the Post Soviet Era*, Bureau of National Affairs, Washington, D.C., 1992. Col. 1 above is from Bolotin, pp. 182-3, col. 2 is adapted from Bolotin who presents his estimates in 1990 dollars, without giving the source for his PPPs. His total for the 15 republics is $ 1541 700 million. My estimate is 9.4 per cent higher and is derived as explained in Appendix C. However, I have used Bolotin's proportionate allocation of total GDP (pp. 184-5). Col. 3 is derived from cols. 1 and 2.

Yugoslavia: 1909-12 average, 1920-39, and 1947-54 annual GDP by industry of origin at 1953 market prices from I. Vinski, "National Product and Fixed Assets in the Territory of Yugoslavia 1900-59", in P. Deane, ed., *Income and Wealth*, Series IX, Bowes and Bowes, London, 1961, p. 221 linked at 1950 to GNP index for 1950-68 in T.P. Alton, "Economic Structure and Growth in Eastern Europe", in *Economic Developments in Countries of Eastern Europe*, Joint Economic Committee, US Congress, 1970, p. 46, 1968-75 from World Bank, *World Tables*, various issues. 1975-91 from "Economic Growth in Eastern Europe 1975-91" in T.P. Alton and Associates, *Occasional Paper*, 120, L.W. Research Project on National Income in East Central Europe, New York, 1992. I assumed a 20 per cent drop in GDP in 1992.

In the early 1990s, Yugoslavia split into five separate republics. The population in 1992 (in thousands) was Slovenia 1,990, Croatia 4,789, Bosnia-Herzegovina 4,383, the rump Yugoslav republic (Serbia and Montenegro) 10,597, and Macedonia 2,172.

Latin America

For Latin American countries, the 1990-4 GDP movements were taken from CEPAL, *Balance Preliminar de la Economia de America Latina y el Caribe 1994*, Santiago, December 1994.

Argentina: 1870-1900 per capita growth assumed to be the same as in 1900-13. 1900-1913 unpublished annual estimates supplied by CEPAL/CONADE. Buenos Aires; these served as background for the quinquennial averages published in *El Desarrollo Económico de la Argentina*, CEPAL, Mexico, 1959, p. 15; 1913-80 GDP by industry of origin at 1960 prices from IEERAL, "Estadísticas de la evolución económica de Argentina, 1913-84", *Estudios*, Buenos Aires, July-September, 1986. 1980-90 revised estimates of GDP at 1986 market prices (including 35.69 per cent upward revision in the 1980 level) from *Estimaciones anuales de la Oferta y Demanda Globales: Periodo 1980-1990*, Banco Central de la República Argentina, April 1993.

Brazil: 1820-50 per capita GDP growth assumed to be at the same rate as 1850-1913. 1850-1900 GDP by industry of origin from R.W. Goldsmith, *Desenvolvimento Financeiro sob um Secolo de Inflaçao*, Harper and Row, S. Paulo, 1986, pp. 22-3 and 82-83. 1900-85 GDP by industry of origin from A. Maddison and Associates, *The Political Economy of Poverty, Equity and Growth: Brazil and Mexico*, Oxford University Press, New York 1992; the 1900-50 estimates are based on sector weights for 1947, the 1950-85 estimates are in 1970 prices. 1985-90 GDP at 1987 market prices from World Bank, *World Tables 1993*.

Chile: 1900-80 from A.A. Hofman, "International Estimates of Capital. A 1950-1989 Comparison of Latin America and the USA", *Research Memorandum No. 509*, University of Groningen 1992. 1980-90 GDP at 1987 market prices from World Bank, *World Tables 1993*.

Colombia: 1900-13 per capita movement taken to be equal to the average for Brazil and Chile. 1913-29 from L.J. Zimmerman, *Arme en rijke landen*, The Hague, 1964. 1929-50 from CEPAL, *Series Historicas del Crecimiento de America Latina*, Santiago, 1978. 1950-80 from A. Urdinola and M. Carrizosa, *Poverty, Equity and Growth in Colombia*, processed, Bogota, 1985. 1980-90 GDP at 1987 market prices from World Bank, *World Tables 1993*.

Mexico: 1820-1900 per capita GDP movement from INEGI, *Estádisticas Historicas de Mexico*, Mexico, 1985, vol. 1, Table 9.1. 1900-80 as for Brazil. 1980-90 GDP at 1987 market prices from World Bank, *World Tables 1993*.

Peru: 1900-13 per capita GDP movement assumed equal to the average per capita movement in Brazil and Chile. 1913-41 GDP movement from C.A. Bolona Behr, "Tariff Policies in Peru, 1880-1980", Ph.D. thesis, Oxford University, 1981; 1942-5 GDP in 1950 dollars from "Cuadros del producto interno bruto en dollares de 1950", CEPAL, Santiago, October 1962, mimeographed; 1945-50 GDP at 1970 factor cost from *Series Historicas del Crecimiento de America Latina*, CEPAL, Santiago, 1978. 1950-80 GDP in 1979 prices by industry of origin and expenditure from Richard Webb, *Poverty, Equity and Growth in Peru*, processed, Lima, 1987. 1980-90 GDP at 1987 market prices from World Bank, *World Tables 1993*.

Venezuela: 1900-1920 "economic activity" in four sectors in 1936 bolivars linked to 1920-70 GDP by industry of origin in 1968 bolivars from A. Baptista, *Bases cuantativas de la economía venezolana 1830-1989*, Communicaciones Corporativas, Caracas, 1991, pp. 31-4. Baptista's indicator of economic activity in fact goes back to 1830, but as it is very volatile, his 1830-99 figures were not used. 1970-90 GDP at 1987 prices from World Bank, *World Tables 1993*, Washington, D.C.

Asia

Bangladesh: 1820 per capita product assumed equal to that in India. 1900-1950 per capita domestic product assumed to move as in pre-partition India. 1950-66 net domestic product by industry of origin at 1959 factor cost from A. Maddison, *Class Structure and Economic Growth*, Allen and Unwin, London, 1971, p. 171. 1966-70 from World Bank, *World Tables*, (1988). 1970 onwards GDP at 1987 market prices from World Bank, *World Tables*. The figures for 1967 onwards are for fiscal years.

Burma: 1901-38 net domestic product by industry of origin at 1901 prices for nine benchmark years from Aye Hlaing, "Trends of Economic Growth and Income Distribution in Burma 1870-1940", *Journal of the Burma Research Society*, 1964, p. 144 linked to 1938-59 estimates of GDP by industry of origin at 1947/8 prices in E.E. Hagen, *On the Theory of Social Change*, Dorsey, Homewood, Illinois, 1962, Table 18-1, linked at 1951 to OECD Development Centre estimates. 1972-92 from World Bank, *World Tables 1994*. All estimates are for fiscal years. 1913 is my interpolation.

China: There are a number of quantitative estimates which throw light on Chinese growth performance in the past century, but they do not always accord very well and conjectures about what rates of growth are plausible are made all the more difficult because of the wide variations in the estimates of present day (1990) Chinese income levels (see Appendix C). Over the really long term, however, there is no other country whose past has been more magisterially investigated in quantitative terms than in Dwight Perkins, *Agricultural Development in China 1368-1968*, Aldine, Chicago, 1969.

For the period from the mid 1880s to 1933, we have various spot estimates which may be compared in order to infer the intervening growth performance. Chung-Li Chang, *The Income of the Chinese Gentry*, University of Washington, Seattle, 1962, pp. 296 and 324 provides an estimate for the mid 1880s which he converts into 1933 prices for comparison with Pao-san Ou's (1947) estimate for 1933. The latter study was in Chinese, but a similar version can be found in Pao-san Ou, "A New Estimate of China's National Income", *Journal of Political Economy*, 1946, pp. 547-54, with a slight upward revision in his Harvard Ph.D. thesis (1948).

Subsequently, Chang's estimate for the 1880s was adjusted upwards (somewhat cavalierly) in A. Feuerwerker, *The Chinese Economy, ca. 1870-1911*, Michigan Papers in Chinese Studies, No. 5, 1969, p. 2; Feuerwerker (1977, p. 12) appears to favour a comparison of his revision with the 1933 estimates of Liu and Yeh (1963). Thus Feuerwerker estimates output in the mid 1880s as 49.2 per cent of that in 1933. This compares with the 61.1 per cent ratio one can derive from Chang. As a rough compromise I averaged the two ratios at 55.15 per cent.

There are more options than this as there are 6 alternatives for 1933 which we can compare either with Chang or Feuerwerker, as shown in Table B-9.

Table B-9. **Alternative Estimates (in billion 1933 yuan) of Chinese GDP in the mid 1880s and in 1933**

	mid-1880s		1933	
Chang (1962)	12 254	Ou (1947)	20 044	
Feuerwerker (1969)	14 710	Ou (1948)	21 770	
		Liu (1946)	24 190	(excluding Manchuria, Jehol, Sinkiang, Mongolia and Tibet)
		Liu (1946)	26 660	(with Manchuria, Jehol, Sinkiang, Mongolia and Tibet)
		Liu and Yeh (1965)	29 880	(including Manchuria and Outer Mongolia)
		Yeh (1979)	29 460	(coverage not specified)

Source: Chang (1962), Feuerwerker (1969) and Ou (1947 and 1948) as above: Ta-chung Liu, *China's National Income 1931-36*, Brookings, Washington, D.C., 1946, p. 10; Ta-chung Liu and Kung-chia Yeh, *The Economy of the Chinese Mainland: National Income and Economic Development 1933-1959*, Princeton University Press, 1965, p. 66; Kung-chia Yeh, "China's National Income, 1931-36" in Chi-ming Hou and Tzong-shian Yu, eds., *Modern Chinese Economic History*, Academia Sinica, Taipei, 1979, p. 98. Feuerwerker (1977) in his *Economic Trends in the Republic of China*, Michigan Papers in Chinese Studies, No. 31, 1977.

For the period 1913-52 we have three options. The one I prefer is that of D.W. Perkins, ed., *China's Modern Economy in Historical Perspective*, Stanford University Press, 1975, p. 11. He provides an estimate for 1914/18, 1933 and 1952, from which the following index can be derived: 1913 = 100, 1933 = 133.1, and 1952 = 142.1. Yeh (1979) p. 126 provides estimates for 1914/18, 1931/36 and 1952/7, which show slower interwar growth: one can derive an estimate of 1933 = 123.3 (1913 = 100) from Yeh. More recently T.G. Rawski, *Economic Growth in Prewar China*, University of California Press, Berkeley, 1989, p. 336 provided an index of aggregate output of 100 for 1914/18, 140 for 1931/36, 132 for 1946, 119 for 1949 and 166 for 1952. Unscrambling his multi-year averages, one can derive 1913 = 100, 1933 = 146.9, and 1952 = 175. Rawski has a strong bias towards establishing the case that Chinese growth was "substantial", and he reaches rather selectively towards evidence which will make the case. Perkins occupies a middle path between Rawski and Yeh. This is one reason for preferring the Perkins variant. The other is the massive scholarly effort involved in Perkins' agricultural component which is the major part of output.

In constructing a time series for China, an average of the preferred ratios of Chang (1962) and Feuerwerker (1969, 1977) was used for 1885-1933 and linked at 1933 to Perkins (1975). The annual 1931-36 movement was derived from Yeh (1979), p. 98 with inferential estimates for 1929-30, and 1936-38 as explained in A. Maddison, *Two Crises: Latin America and Asia 1929-38 and 1973-83*, OECD Development Centre, Paris, 1985, p. 85. Thus there is some documented basis for the following years:

1885	1913	1931	1932	1933	1934	1935	1936	1952
73.4	100.0	129.0	133.1	133.1	121.5	131.3	139.6	142.1

1890 and 1900 were derived by interpolating between 1885 and 1913, and 1870 by extrapolating the 1885-1913 growth back to that year. No change in per capita real income was assumed from 1820 to 1870 because of the huge population loss and damage due to the Tai-ping rebellion.

GDP movement for 1952-90 was derived from H.X. Wu, "The Real Chinese Gross Domestic Product (GDP for the Pre-Reform Period 1952-77", *Review of Income and Wealth*, March 1993. I used his estimates for agriculture and industry at 1980 prices. I assumed that half of services moved parallel to the joint product of agriculture and industry and half moved parallel to population; 1950-52 derived from A.G. Ashbrook's estimates (similarly adjusted) in Joint Economic Committee, *Chinese Economy Post-Mao*, US Congress, Washington, D.C., 1978, vol. 1, p. 231.

It should of course be stressed that the edifice is shaky and that adjustments have been made in a way which the authors may not have approved, e.g. pinpointing specific years which were originally embedded in multi-year averages.

Over the period 1967-91, the Joint Committee of the US Congress published a series of quantitative studies on the Chinese economy, where an attempt was made to estimate Chinese GDP according to Western concepts. They were the counterpart of the CIA estimates for Eastern Europe and the USSR which the Committee also published on a regular basis. Unfortunately these estimates appear to have been abandoned after 1982, when the Committee reports switched to using official Chinese concepts and sources.

It should be stressed that the official growth estimates for China are very weak. The World Bank, *China: Statistical System in Transition*, September 1992, gives a good idea of the problems of measuring both growth and levels. It makes clear that the old official MPS estimates tended to understate the level of output and exaggerate growth, and it is also clear that in moving towards the SNA concept of national accounts some of these problems are still significant. They are described in more detail in A. Keidel, "How Badly Do China's National Accounts Underestimate China's GNP?", Rock Creek Research Inc., December 1992. In the old MPS accounting system, the service sector was considered unproductive and not included; township and village industry was also neglected. Agricultural output was understated because of the exclusion of grains and vegetables directly consumed by producers. The weight of manufacturing (the most rapidly growing sector) was overstated because of the incidence of taxes and the inclusion in the weights of the value of miscellaneous in-kind allocations to those employed in this sector. The rate of growth of manufacturing was overstated by the reporting firms, and by the treatment of new products which are usually marked up excessively when they are first introduced.

India: 1870-1900 net domestic product by industry of origin in 1946-7 prices derived from A. Heston, "National Income", in D. Kumar and M. Desai, *Cambridge Economic History of India*, vol. 2, Cambridge, 1983, p. 397. For 1820-70 per capita product was assumed to rise by 0.1 per cent a year.

1900-46 net domestic product by industry of origin at 1938 factor cost from A. Maddison, "Alternative Estimates of the Real Product of India, 1900-46", *Indian Economic and Social History Review*, 22, 2, 1985. 1946-50 net domestic product by industry of origin at 1948 factor cost from A. Maddison, *Class Structure and Economic Growth: India and Pakistan Since the Moghuls*, Allen and Unwin, London, 1971, p. 169. All these figures refer to fiscal years. 1950-90, fiscal years, gross domestic product at 1980-1 market prices supplied by Central Statistical Organisation, Delhi, in May 1992. Thereafter from OECD Development Centre.

Indonesia: 1820-70 from rough estimates of real income for three ethnic groups (indigenous, foreign Asiatic, and "European") in A. Maddison, "Dutch Income In and From Indonesia", *Modern Asian Studies*, 23, 4 (1989), pp. 663-5. 1870-1992 estimates of GDP by industry of origin in 1983 prices supplied by Pierre van der Eng. They are a revision of estimates in his article, "The Real Domestic Product of Indonesia, 1880-1989", *Explorations in Economic History*, July 1992. Here his total GDP by industry of origin was used and not his variant with a shadow price for energy. The figures are not adjusted to exclude the impact of the incorporation of Irian Jaya as a 26th province in 1968 and of East Timor as the 27th province in 1976. Both provinces are now included in the official GDP estimates, but it is not clear when they were included. Irian Jaya added about 0.8 per cent to Indonesian population and East Timor about 0.38 per cent in the respective years of accession.

Pakistan: As for Bangladesh. The figures for 1966 onwards are for fiscal years.

Philippines: 1900-50 derived by interpolation of estimates of GDP in 1939 prices by industry of origin for 1902, 1918, 1938, 1948 and 1961 in R.W. Hooley, "Long Term Growth of the Philippine Economy, 1902-1961", *The Philippine Economic Journal*, First Semester, 1968. 1950-80 supplied by National Statistical Coordination Board, Manila. 1980 onwards GDP at 1987 market prices from World Bank, *World Tables*.

South Korea: 1900-1913 per capita movement assumed equal to the average for the other Asian countries. 1911-38 average of expenditure and product estimates of GDP at 1934-6 prices in T. Mizoguchi and M. Umemura, *Basic Economic Statistics of Former Japanese Colonies 1895-1938,* Toyo Keizai Shinposha, Tokyo, 1988, p. 238. 1938-40 commodity output derived from Sang-Chul Suh, *Growth and Structural Changes in the Korean Economy, 1910-40*, Cambridge, Mass., 1978, p. 171, and 1940-1953 commodity output from Kwang Suk Kim and M. Roemer, *Growth and Structural Transformation*, Cambridge, Mass., 1979, p. 35. For 1938-53 it was assumed that service output moved parallel to population. Sector weights for 1953 were taken from Kim and Roemer, p. 35. 1950-66 from A. Maddison, *Economic Progress and Policy in Developing Countries*, 1970, 1966-70 from World Bank, *World Tables*, 1988. 1970 onwards GDP at 1987 factor cost from World Bank, *World Tables*. Kim and Roemer (1979) p. 23 estimate that the South Korean area produced 54.3 per cent of the "net commodity" product of Korea in 1940 and accounted for 66.4 per cent of the population. At that time, per capita product was 66 per cent higher in North Korea than in the South.

Taiwan: 1900 estimated by backward extrapolation of 1903-13 growth rate. 1903-38 average of expenditure and product estimates at 1934-6 prices in T. Mizoguchi and M. Umemura, *Basic Economic Statistics of Former Japanese Colonies 1895-1938*, Toyo Keizai Shinposha, Tokyo, 1988, p. 234. 1938-44 movement based on Hsing's estimate as cited by S.P.S. Ho, *Economic Development of Taiwan 1860-1970*, Yale, 1978, p. 285. 1945-51 figures are interpolated assuming equal percentage growth each year. 1938-51 link from A. Maddison, *Economic Progress and Policy in Developing Countries*, Norton, New York, 1970, pp. 298-9. 1951 onwards GDP by type of expenditure at 1986 market prices from *National Income in Taiwan Area of the Republic of China*, Executive Yuan, Taipei.

Thailand: 1900-50 GDP by industry of origin estimates for a few benchmark years from Sompop Manarungsan, "Economic Development of Thailand, 1850-1950", University of Groningen, Ph.D. thesis, 1989 (his alternative procedure, using our population figures for 1950). 1950-85 GDP in 1972 prices from Oey Meesook and Associates, *The Political Economy of Poverty, Equity and Growth: Thailand, 1850-1985*, Washington, D.C., 1988, processed. 1985 onwards GDP at 1987 market prices from World Bank, *World Tables*.

Africa

Côte d'Ivoire: 1950 onwards from OECD Development Centre.

Egypt: 1913-50 GDP at 1954 prices derived from B. Hansen and G.A. Marzouk, *Development and Economic Policy in the UAR (Egypt)*, North Holland, Amsterdam, 1965, p. 3. 1950 onwards from OECD Development Centre.

Ethiopia: 1950 onwards derived from World Bank, *World Tables*, various issues. Figures for 1951-4, 1956-9, 1961-4 are interpolations.

Ghana: 1900 and 1913 derived from A. Szereszewski, *Structural Changes in the Economy of Ghana, 1891-1911*, Weidenfeld and Nicolson, London, 1965, p. 126.

Nigeria: 1950-92 annual estimates are interpolations from benchmark years as given (in the light of the 1992 census results) in « Le Recensement du Nigeria », *Populations et sociétés*, INED, Paris, October 1992.

South Africa: 1900 and 1913 derived from B.R. Mitchell, *International Historical Statistics: Africa and Asia*, Macmillan, London, 1982, p. 41. 1920-49 movement from UN, *Demographic Yearbook*, New York, 1960; 1950-60 from OECD Development Centre; 1960-70 interpolated; 1970 onwards from World Bank, *World Tables*, Washington, D.C.

Zaire: 1950 onwards from OECD Development Centre.

Table B-10a. **GDP Indices for 17 Advanced Capitalist Countries, 1820-1994**

(1913 = 100)

	Australia	Austria	Belgium	Canada	Denmark	Finland	France	Germany	Italy
1820	0.2	17.5	14.0	2.0	12.6	14.3	26.6	11.3	23.6
1850	4.5	27.8	25.4	9.4	22.7		42.4	20.3	
1870	23.2	35.9	42.5	18.3	32.4	31.3	49.9	30.4	43.8
1871	22.3	38.5	42.6	19.1	32.5	31.5	49.6	30.2	44.3
1872	24.7	38.8	45.2	18.9	34.3	32.6	54.2	32.3	43.6
1873	27.3	37.9	45.5	20.8	34.1	34.5	50.4	33.7	45.3
1874	28.2	39.6	47.0	21.3	35.1	35.3	56.8	36.2	45.2
1875	31.3	39.8	46.9	20.8	35.7	36.0	58.7	36.4	46.5
1876	31.2	40.7	47.5	19.4	36.4	38.0	53.9	36.2	45.5
1877	32.5	42.1	48.1	20.7	35.4	37.1	56.8	36.0	45.5
1878	35.6	43.5	49.5	19.9	36.8	36.4	56.1	37.7	46.1
1879	36.1	43.2	50.0	21.8	38.0	36.8	52.6	36.8	46.7
1880	38.0	43.8	52.5	22.8	38.9	37.0	57.3	36.5	48.9
1881	40.8	45.6	53.2	26.0	39.3	36.0	59.5	37.4	45.6
1882	38.5	45.9	55.0	27.2	40.7	39.5	62.3	38.0	49.6
1883	44.2	47.8	55.8	27.3	42.1	41.0	62.5	40.1	49.4
1884	44.4	49.1	56.3	29.5	42.3	41.3	61.8	41.1	49.8
1885	47.3	48.8	57.0	27.7	42.6	42.3	60.7	42.1	50.8
1886	47.9	50.4	57.7	28.0	44.3	44.4	61.7	42.4	53.1
1887	53.0	53.9	59.9	28.9	45.9	45.1	62.1	44.1	54.6
1888	53.3	53.8	60.3	31.0	46.2	46.8	62.7	45.9	54.4
1889	57.9	53.3	63.2	31.2	46.8	48.4	64.3	47.2	52.0
1890	55.9	56.2	64.6	33.5	49.6	51.1	65.8	48.7	55.4
1891	60.2	58.2	64.7	34.3	50.6	50.6	67.3	48.6	55.1
1892	52.8	59.5	66.3	34.1	51.8	49.1	69.0	50.6	52.0
1893	49.9	59.9	67.3	33.9	52.8	51.0	70.2	53.1	54.4
1894	51.6	63.4	68.3	35.5	53.9	55.0	72.8	54.4	53.7
1895	48.7	65.1	69.9	35.1	56.9	58.0	71.3	57.0	54.5
1896	52.4	66.1	71.3	34.2	59.0	61.8	74.7	59.0	56.0
1897	49.5	67.5	72.6	37.9	60.4	64.8	73.7	60.7	53.5
1898	57.2	71.3	73.8	39.4	61.4	67.6	77.3	63.3	58.3
1899	57.2	72.8	75.3	43.1	64.0	66.0	81.7	65.6	59.6
1900	60.6	73.4	77.5	45.5	66.2	69.1	80.8	68.4	63.0
1901	58.8	73.7	78.2	49.1	69.0	68.3	79.5	66.8	67.0
1902	59.4	76.6	79.8	53.9	70.6	66.9	78.2	68.4	65.2
1903	64.1	77.3	81.6	55.5	74.8	71.4	79.9	72.2	68.3
1904	68.4	78.5	83.7	56.3	76.4	74.1	80.5	75.1	68.9
1905	69.2	82.9	86.1	62.9	77.7	75.3	81.9	76.7	72.8
1906	73.9	86.1	87.9	69.2	79.9	78.3	83.4	79.0	75.5
1907	76.9	91.4	89.2	73.2	82.9	81.0	87.0	82.5	84.0
1908	79.5	91.8	90.1	69.7	85.5	81.9	86.5	83.9	86.0
1909	86.0	91.5	91.8	77.1	88.8	85.5	90.1	85.6	92.7
1910	92.0	92.8	94.2	83.7	91.5	87.4	84.6	88.7	89.3
1911	92.7	95.7	96.4	89.4	96.4	89.9	92.9	91.7	95.1
1912	94.9	100.5	98.7	95.3	96.4	94.9	100.6	95.7	95.9
1913	100.0	100.0	100.0	100.0	100.0	100.0	100.0	100.0	100.0
1914	92.3	83.5	93.7	93.3	106.3	95.6	92.9	85.2	99.9
1915	86.9	77.4	92.5	99.3	98.9	90.8	91.0	80.9	111.8
1916	93.0	76.5	97.9	109.3	103.1	92.0	95.6	81.7	125.4
1917	95.1	74.8	84.1	113.8	97.0	77.3	81.0	81.8	131.3
1918	95.6	73.3	67.8	106.5	93.8	67.0	63.9	82.0	133.3
1919	94.7	61.8	79.9	98.4	105.9	80.9	75.3	72.3	111.0
1920	101.9	66.4	92.5	97.3	110.9	90.5	87.1	78.6	101.3
1921	111.9	73.5	94.1	86.8	107.7	93.5	83.5	87.5	99.8
1922	112.7	80.1	103.3	99.5	118.6	103.4	98.5	95.2	104.9
1923	115.0	79.3	107.0	105.4	131.1	111.0	103.6	79.1	111.3
1924	123.8	88.5	110.5	107.0	131.5	113.9	116.6	92.6	112.4
1925	127.9	94.5	112.2	118.7	128.5	120.4	117.1	103.0	119.8
1926	126.3	96.1	116.0	125.1	136.0	125.0	120.2	98.8	121.1
1927	126.0	99.0	120.3	137.5	138.7	134.8	117.7	117.2	118.4
1928	124.0	103.6	126.6	149.7	143.4	143.9	125.9	119.9	126.9
1929	122.8	105.1	125.5	149.5	153.0	145.6	134.4	121.3	131.1
1930	116.8	102.2	124.3	144.5	162.1	143.9	130.5	113.9	124.6
1931	111.5	94.0	122.1	122.2	163.9	140.4	122.7	102.3	123.9
1932	115.7	84.3	116.6	113.5	159.6	139.8	114.7	92.8	127.9
1933	122.3	81.5	119.1	105.4	164.7	149.1	122.9	102.5	127.1

Table B-10a (cont. 2)

	Australia	Austria	Belgium	Canada	Denmark	Finland	France	Germany	Italy
1934	127.0	82.2	118.1	116.6	169.7	166.0	121.7	110.4	127.6
1935	132.2	83.8	125.4	126.0	173.5	173.1	118.6	120.4	139.9
1936	138.5	86.3	126.3	132.8	177.8	184.8	123.1	133.0	140.1
1937	146.4	90.9	128.0	145.3	182.1	195.3	130.2	141.0	149.7
1938	147.5	102.5	125.1	149.1	186.5	205.4	129.7	151.9	150.8
1939	147.9	116.2	133.6	158.0	195.4	196.6	139.0	166.2	161.8
1940	157.6	113.2	117.7	179.7	168.0	186.4	114.7	167.4	162.8
1941	175.2	121.3	111.5	204.8	151.4	192.5	90.7	178.0	160.8
1942	195.4	115.2	101.9	241.1	154.8	193.1	81.3	180.4	158.8
1943	202.3	118.0	99.5	252.0	171.9	215.3	77.2	184.0	143.8
1944	195.3	121.0	105.4	261.5	189.9	215.4	65.2	188.7	116.8
1945	185.5	50.0	111.7	253.4	175.6	202.9	70.7	134.2	91.5
1946	178.9	58.4	118.3	250.8	203.0	219.4	107.5	79.7	119.8
1947	183.3	64.4	125.4	261.9	214.4	224.5	116.5	89.5	140.8
1948	195.1	82.0	132.9	266.7	220.2	242.3	125.0	106.0	148.8
1949	208.0	97.5	138.3	272.5	235.4	257.0	142.0	123.5	159.8
1950	222.4	109.6	145.9	292.6	254.1	266.9	152.6	147.5	172.8
1951	231.9	117.1	154.2	309.2	255.8	289.6	162.0	162.0	185.7
1952	234.0	117.2	153.0	331.7	258.3	299.3	166.3	176.9	199.6
1953	241.3	122.3	157.9	347.2	273.0	301.4	171.1	192.5	214.0
1954	256.3	134.8	164.4	344.8	278.3	327.8	179.4	207.3	225.1
1955	270.3	149.7	172.2	377.0	281.3	344.5	189.7	232.2	238.2
1956	279.6	160.0	177.2	407.5	284.7	354.9	199.3	249.9	249.0
1957	285.2	169.8	180.5	419.3	306.3	371.6	211.3	264.6	263.7
1958	298.9	176.0	180.3	426.8	313.2	373.6	216.6	276.1	277.8
1959	317.3	181.0	186.0	444.1	336.5	395.8	222.8	297.6	295.1
1960	330.6	195.9	196.0	457.9	345.9	432.0	238.5	323.4	311.1
1961	329.4	206.3	205.8	472.4	367.9	465.0	251.6	338.0	337.3
1962	350.4	211.3	216.5	506.0	388.8	478.7	268.4	353.5	363.6
1963	373.4	219.9	225.9	532.1	391.3	494.4	282.8	363.3	389.5
1964	397.0	233.1	241.6	567.6	427.6	520.3	301.2	387.5	404.7
1965	419.0	239.8	250.2	605.1	447.1	547.9	315.6	408.3	413.8
1966	430.9	253.3	258.1	646.3	459.3	560.9	332.1	419.9	435.4
1967	460.7	261.0	268.1	666.5	475.0	573.1	347.6	418.6	466.4
1968	487.7	272.6	279.4	700.8	493.9	586.3	362.4	441.8	505.4
1969	517.2	289.7	298.0	738.3	525.1	642.5	387.8	474.7	534.3
1970	548.4	310.4	316.9	757.9	535.8	690.5	410.0	498.9	546.3
1971	580.9	326.2	328.5	801.6	550.1	705.0	429.5	513.9	555.1
1972	603.3	346.5	345.9	847.2	579.1	758.8	447.0	535.8	570.1
1973	635.3	363.4	366.3	912.5	600.1	809.7	471.2	561.9	610.5
1974	645.3	377.8	381.3	952.4	594.5	834.2	484.0	563.4	643.7
1975	663.3	376.4	375.6	977.1	590.6	842.8	482.4	555.5	626.7
1976	688.0	393.6	396.6	1 037.1	628.8	846.1	503.7	585.2	667.9
1977	694.8	411.5	398.5	1 074.2	639.0	847.0	521.5	601.8	690.4
1978	715.4	411.7	409.4	1 123.4	648.5	865.5	539.1	619.9	715.8
1979	747.7	431.3	418.1	1 167.2	671.4	928.4	556.2	645.3	758.7
1980	764.4	443.9	436.1	1 184.5	668.5	977.8	563.9	652.3	790.8
1981	792.2	442.6	431.8	1 228.2	662.5	993.3	570.7	652.9	795.2
1982	787.9	447.3	438.3	1 188.7	682.5	1 028.9	583.8	646.8	796.9
1983	796.7	456.2	440.3	1 226.7	699.7	1 059.4	588.4	658.2	804.6
1984	854.6	462.4	449.8	1 304.9	730.4	1 091.9	597.1	676.7	826.2
1985	892.8	473.8	453.5	1 366.6	761.8	1 128.3	608.0	690.4	847.7
1986	921.0	479.4	460.1	1 411.2	789.5	1 152.0	622.6	706.6	872.5
1987	955.8	487.4	469.5	1 469.7	791.8	1 197.9	636.1	717.1	899.8
1988	1 003.0	507.2	492.9	1 542.7	801.1	1 262.5	663.2	743.8	936.4
1989	1 041.6	526.6	511.6	1 579.3	805.6	1 334.1	688.2	770.7	963.9
1990	1 054.4	549.0	529.1	1 576.4	822.1	1 334.2	704.7	814.7	984.5
1991	1 055.8	563.8	539.1	1 549.2	832.2	1 240.0	707.7	851.7	996.8
1992	1 072.4	573.1	543.5	1 560.8	842.4	1 190.1	719.9	865.0	1 006.1
1993	1 113.2	571.4	534.3	1 595.1	854.2	1 166.3	712.7	855.5	999.1
1994	1 161.0	586.2	546.5	1 660.5	894.3	1 207.1	728.4	879.4	1 021.0

Table B-10a (cont. 3)

	Japan	Netherlands	New Zealand	Norway	Sweden	Switzerland	UK	USA
1820	31.7	15.1		17.5	17.8		16.2	2.4
1850		24.0		27.0	25.8		28.2	8.2
1870	37.0	39.2	15.6	40.6	39.8	35.6	44.6	19.0
1871		39.8	16.7	41.2	40.5		47.0	19.9
1872		40.6	19.5	43.8	42.4		47.1	20.7
1873		39.7	22.2	44.7	46.3		48.2	21.7
1874		41.8	24.4	46.2	48.1		49.0	21.6
1875		44.4	25.9	47.6	46.0		50.2	22.7
1876		44.0	27.2	49.0	49.0		50.7	23.0
1877		47.5	31.0	49.2	47.4		51.2	23.7
1878		50.9	34.5	47.7	47.1		51.4	24.7
1879		47.1	30.5	48.3	46.3		51.2	27.8
1880		51.8	33.7	49.8	48.5		53.6	31.1
1881		50.6	35.1	50.2	48.6		55.5	32.2
1882		51.4	35.0	50.0	50.6		57.1	34.2
1883		59.3	34.7	49.8	51.1		57.5	35.0
1884		58.1	38.3	50.8	52.5		57.6	35.7
1885	45.6	59.9	38.1	51.4	52.3		57.3	35.9
1886	49.5	60.7	39.0	51.7	52.1		58.2	37.0
1887	51.5	62.0	39.9	52.3	52.3		60.5	38.7
1888	49.3	58.5	39.9	54.6	53.7		63.2	38.5
1889	51.9	63.4	42.0	56.5	56.5		66.6	40.9
1890	56.6	58.1	43.2	58.0	57.3		66.9	41.5
1891	53.9	61.0	43.5	58.5	58.0		66.9	43.3
1892	57.5	65.3	45.1	59.8	59.2		65.3	47.5
1893	57.7	59.5	46.2	61.4	59.3		65.3	45.2
1894	64.6	66.2	44.7	61.6	60.5		69.7	43.9
1895	65.5	67.1	46.3	62.2	63.5		71.9	49.2
1896	61.9	69.0	51.6	64.1	67.2		74.9	48.2
1897	63.2	75.8	52.2	67.3	69.6		75.9	52.8
1898	75.2	76.0	53.7	67.5	71.1		79.6	53.9
1899	69.6	77.2	55.5	69.4	72.7	69.5	82.9	58.8
1900	72.6	74.6	60.0	70.6	75.3	71.7	82.3	60.4
1901	75.2	72.9	60.2	72.5	74.5	73.9	82.3	67.2
1902	71.3	76.6	64.8	74.0	74.4	76.0	84.4	67.9
1903	76.3	78.7	70.9	73.7	79.9	78.2	83.5	71.2
1904	76.9	78.0	70.6	73.6	80.7	80.4	84.0	70.3
1905	75.6	80.6	77.1	74.5	81.6	82.6	86.5	75.5
1906	85.5	84.5	84.4	77.2	86.9	84.8	89.4	84.2
1907	88.2	84.8	89.5	80.1	88.8	86.9	91.1	85.5
1908	88.8	84.7	83.3	82.7	88.6	89.1	87.4	78.5
1909	88.7	88.5	84.5	84.9	88.0	91.3	89.4	88.1
1910	90.1	89.3	96.1	87.9	93.3	93.5	92.2	89.0
1911	95.0	91.9	101.4	90.6	95.6	95.6	94.9	91.9
1912	98.4	97.0	98.4	94.7	98.3	97.8	96.3	96.2
1913	100.0	100.0	100.0	100.0	100.0	100.0	100.0	100.0
1914	97.0	97.3	102.6	102.2	99.1	100.1	101.0	92.3
1915	106.0	100.6	103.1	106.6	99.1	101.1	109.1	94.9
1916	122.4	103.3	102.3	110.0	97.8	100.7	111.5	108.0
1917	126.5	96.7	99.8	100.0	85.8	89.7	112.5	105.3
1918	127.8	90.7	98.2	96.3	84.5	89.4	113.2	114.8
1919	140.9	112.4	109.2	112.6	89.4	95.3	100.9	115.8
1920	132.1	115.8	121.1	119.7	94.6	101.5	94.8	114.7
1921	146.6	122.9	113.1	109.8	91.1	99.0	87.1	112.1
1922	146.2	129.6	109.2	122.6	99.7	108.5	91.6	118.3
1923	146.3	132.8	118.0	125.3	105.0	114.8	94.5	133.9
1924	150.4	142.5	120.1	124.7	108.3	119.1	98.4	138.0
1925	156.6	148.5	126.5	132.4	112.3	127.8	103.2	141.2
1926	158.0	160.4	119.8	135.3	118.6	134.2	99.4	150.4
1927	160.3	167.1	116.4	140.5	122.3	141.4	107.4	151.9
1928	173.4	176.0	129.3	145.1	128.1	149.3	108.7	153.6
1929	178.8	177.4	133.9	158.6	135.9	154.5	111.9	163.0
1930	165.8	177.0	128.1	170.3	138.7	153.5	111.1	148.5
1931	167.2	166.2	117.2	157.1	133.7	147.1	105.4	137.1
1932	181.2	163.9	114.3	167.6	130.1	142.1	106.2	119.0
1933	199.0	163.6	121.9	171.6	132.6	149.2	109.3	116.5

Table B-10a (cont. 4)

	Japan	Netherlands	New Zealand	Norway	Sweden	Switzerland	UK	USA
1934	199.4	160.6	128.0	177.1	142.7	149.5	116.5	125.5
1935	204.9	166.6	134.0	184.7	151.8	148.9	121.0	135.1
1936	219.8	177.1	158.9	196.0	160.6	149.4	126.5	154.3
1937	230.3	187.2	167.5	203.0	168.2	156.5	130.9	160.9
1938	245.7	182.7	179.3	208.1	171.0	162.5	132.5	154.5
1939	284.4	195.1	181.8	218.0	182.8	162.3	133.8	166.8
1940	292.7	171.9	178.3	198.6	177.4	164.0	147.2	179.7
1941	296.7	162.8	172.7	203.4	180.4	162.9	160.6	212.4
1942	295.1	148.8	191.7	195.5	191.4	158.8	164.6	254.9
1943	299.3	145.2	195.7	191.6	199.9	157.4	168.2	305.6
1944	286.4	97.4	196.5	181.6	206.7	161.2	161.6	331.2
1945	143.2	99.7	202.3	203.5	212.3	207.5	154.5	317.9
1946	155.6	168.3	217.9	225.3	235.6	221.7	147.8	252.3
1947	168.0	194.8	243.9	251.1	241.4	248.4	145.6	248.5
1948	193.0	215.6	219.7	271.1	248.9	253.4	150.2	257.9
1949	205.9	234.6	243.4	276.4	258.0	246.5	155.8	258.9
1950	227.1	243.0	279.1	291.5	271.6	258.1	160.8	281.4
1951	255.4	248.1	257.8	305.0	282.4	279.0	165.6	309.1
1952	285.0	253.1	269.0	315.9	286.4	281.3	165.3	322.3
1953	306.0	275.1	278.2	330.5	294.4	291.2	171.8	334.3
1954	323.3	293.8	316.5	346.9	306.8	307.6	178.8	332.0
1955	351.1	315.6	322.4	353.6	315.7	328.3	185.3	350.7
1956	377.5	327.2	339.1	372.1	327.7	350.1	187.6	357.7
1957	405.1	336.4	348.8	382.9	342.4	364.0	190.6	364.6
1958	428.7	335.4	362.5	379.4	344.1	356.3	190.2	362.8
1959	467.8	351.8	388.3	398.9	354.6	378.7	197.9	382.6
1960	529.2	381.4	388.3	421.8	373.4	405.2	209.3	390.4
1961	592.9	382.5	410.5	448.3	394.8	438.0	216.2	400.2
1962	645.8	408.7	426.3	460.9	411.4	459.0	218.4	424.8
1963	700.5	423.5	445.4	478.3	433.3	481.5	226.8	443.4
1964	782.3	458.6	468.4	502.3	462.9	506.8	238.8	470.0
1965	827.8	482.6	497.3	528.8	480.6	522.9	245.0	499.5
1966	915.9	495.9	528.4	548.9	490.6	535.7	249.7	531.9
1967	1 017.4	522.0	504.1	583.2	507.2	552.1	255.3	545.7
1968	1 148.4	555.5	503.9	596.4	525.6	571.9	265.7	570.3
1969	1 291.7	591.3	555.2	623.2	551.9	604.1	271.2	588.0
1970	1 430.0	624.9	547.4	635.7	587.7	642.7	277.4	588.0
1971	1 491.0	651.3	575.7	664.8	593.2	668.8	282.9	607.7
1972	1 613.6	672.9	600.4	699.1	606.8	690.3	292.7	642.1
1973	1 736.7	704.4	643.0	727.9	630.9	711.3	314.3	679.4
1974	1 725.9	732.4	681.4	765.7	651.0	721.7	309.0	675.5
1975	1 775.3	731.7	673.5	797.6	667.7	664.5	306.7	669.6
1976	1 850.1	769.1	689.9	851.9	674.7	659.7	315.1	706.0
1977	1 937.3	787.0	656.3	882.4	664.0	675.8	322.4	742.4
1978	2 031.6	806.3	659.0	922.5	675.6	678.5	333.7	780.7
1979	2 144.0	825.4	672.4	969.2	701.5	695.4	343.1	803.3
1980	2 221.9	832.5	677.0	1 010.0	713.2	727.4	335.5	803.3
1981	2 301.4	826.7	709.9	1 018.9	713.1	737.9	331.2	825.0
1982	2 374.2	815.0	722.6	1 022.3	720.3	731.1	336.9	809.2
1983	2 438.3	826.5	742.2	1 069.6	732.9	738.4	349.6	840.7
1984	2 542.4	852.6	778.9	1 131.1	762.6	751.5	358.3	896.7
1985	2 669.1	875.1	786.0	1 190.7	797.3	779.3	370.8	926.2
1986	2 739.2	899.1	806.1	1 240.5	795.1	801.7	386.8	952.8
1987	2 851.7	909.7	812.1	1 265.2	820.1	817.9	405.2	983.3
1988	3 028.7	933.5	803.0	1 258.8	838.6	841.7	425.4	1 020.6
1989	3 171.5	977.2	813.2	1 266.3	858.5	874.2	434.7	1 046.2
1990	3 324.2	1 017.4	810.0	1 287.4	870.2	894.3	436.4	1 055.0
1991	3 458.7	1 038.8	796.8	1 307.7	860.5	894.0	426.5	1 042.3
1992	3 503.7	1 053.3	819.5	1 350.8	844.0	893.5	424.5	1 063.8
1993	3 507.2	1 057.5	855.6	1 380.5	826.3	885.5	433.0	1 096.8
1994	3 542.3	1 084.0	898.3	1 430.2	845.3	900.5	448.1	1 139.6

Table B-10b. **GDP Indices for 5 South European Countries, 1820-1994**

(1913 = 100)

	Greece	Ireland	Portugal	Spain	Turkey
1820		56.9		28.4	
1850			51.6	37.1	
1870		80.9	58.1	48.8	
1890		88.4	77.0	71.8	
1900		93.9	94.4	82.9	
1901				87.8	
1902				84.3	
1903				86.3	
1904				84.5	
1905				83.9	
1906				88.5	
1907				89.4	
1908				91.7	
1909				93.9	
1910				91.1	
1911				97.3	
1912				95.9	
1913	100.0	100.0	100.0	100.0	100.0
1914				96.2	
1915				97.5	
1916				101.2	
1917				99.5	
1918				99.4	
1919				100.9	
1920				107.3	
1921				111.3	
1922				115.0	
1923				118.1	61.2
1924				123.3	73.2
1925				131.1	81.5
1926		92.3		131.0	94.6
1927				141.7	86.0
1928				141.2	95.3
1929	170.2	100.2	127.2	149.7	110.5
1930	166.1			143.8	115.5
1931	159.2	105.3		140.6	122.4
1932	172.7			145.0	115.0
1933	182.8	100.2		142.3	130.1
1934	187.3			149.1	133.1
1935	195.1			150.2	135.8
1936	195.8	109.4		120.1	161.6
1937	223.6	105.3		112.0	167.0
1938	218.9	108.3	159.1	111.9	181.7
1939	218.6			118.8	196.8
1940				129.0	184.9
1941				129.0	168.2
1942	134.2			136.3	175.5
1943				139.8	159.3
1944				146.0	152.5
1945	79.5			135.7	131.9
1946	119.1			143.2	170.4

Table B-10b (cont. 2)

	Greece	Ireland	Portugal	Spain	Turkey
1947	153.7	111.1	204.8	145.2	180.0
1948	161.4	116.5	209.6	142.3	204.4
1949	170.0	122.6	213.4	142.8	194.1
1950	167.8	123.6	223.3	146.2	212.3
1951	182.6	126.7	233.3	161.7	239.5
1952	183.9	129.9	233.6	174.4	268.2
1953	209.1	133.4	249.9	176.4	298.1
1954	215.6	134.6	261.9	186.5	289.6
1955	231.9	138.1	272.7	196.2	313.0
1956	251.7	136.3	284.6	210.3	323.1
1957	268.1	136.1	297.2	219.3	348.8
1958	280.5	133.3	301.1	229.1	364.8
1959	290.8	138.7	317.4	224.8	381.5
1960	303.4	146.5	338.6	230.1	392.8
1961	330.0	153.5	357.1	257.3	399.4
1962	342.4	158.2	380.8	281.3	423.8
1963	377.2	165.3	403.4	305.9	463.7
1964	408.2	173.3	430.0	324.8	482.8
1965	379.5	176.3	462.0	356.4	495.5
1966	473.8	178.1	480.8	393.4	553.5
1967	499.8	186.9	517.1	419.1	578.3
1968	533.1	200.6	563.1	455.6	617.2
1969	585.9	211.3	575.0	506.8	649.9
1970	632.6	218.2	627.3	540.6	681.7
1971	677.5	228.1	668.9	568.7	743.5
1972	738.6	242.5	722.5	616.3	792.4
1973	791.8	255.4	803.7	665.9	827.4
1974	762.9	264.3	812.8	704.4	897.9
1975	809.1	267.6	777.7	711.4	977.7
1976	860.6	273.7	831.0	734.8	1 062.8
1977	890.1	292.9	877.3	758.6	1 108.7
1978	948.0	314.6	902.3	770.9	1 140.3
1979	984.7	325.3	953.1	770.7	1 130.4
1980	1 001.8	332.3	996.9	780.6	1 121.9
1981	1 002.5	341.5	1 013.2	778.7	1 170.7
1982	1 006.4	346.0	1 034.7	788.2	1 229.3
1983	1 010.4	346.7	1 033.1	802.4	1 274.7
1984	1 038.3	359.1	1 013.6	816.8	1 347.8
1985	1 070.6	368.0	1 041.9	835.7	1 416.6
1986	1 088.1	367.7	1 085.0	863.1	1 515.9
1987	1 083.1	383.8	1 142.3	909.6	1 648.0
1988	1 131.2	401.1	1 187.0	956.4	1 712.1
1989	1 171.2	427.2	1 248.1	1 000.3	1 731.8
1990	1 158.8	461.1	1 302.7	1 037.8	1 891.4
1991	1 196.7	469.9	1 330.5	1 060.1	1 928.4
1992	1 207.8	491.6	1 344.9	1 069.2	2 042.0
1993	1 201.8	511.3	1 330.1	1 058.5	2 162.5
1994	1 213.8	536.8	1 343.4	1 076.5	2 078.1

Table B-10c. **GDP Indices for 7 East European Countries, 1820-1992**

(1913 = 100, except for Poland and Romania 1950 = 100)

	Bulgaria	Czechoslovakia	Hungary	Poland	Romania	USSR	Yugoslavia
1820		22.0				16.3	
1850		33.5					
1870		41.4	44.1			36.0	
1890		61.4				43.2	
1900		75.5	72.9			66.3	
1913	100.0	100.0	100.0			100.0	100.0
1920		90.4	82.6				93.6
1921		97.7					95.9
1922		95.1					98.7
1923		103.0					103.6
1924	69.3	113.7	95.7				110.5
1925	71.8	127.1	115.0				115.9
1926	92.9	126.6	110.2		87.4		123.4
1927	101.3	136.1	115.0		87.4		122.2
1928	99.7	148.1	125.1		87.4	99.8	132.1
1929	97.8	152.2	129.2	97.1	83.4	102.6	138.7
1930	107.8	147.2	126.4	92.6	89.4	108.6	136.5
1931	123.6	142.2	120.3	85.9	91.5	110.7	133.0
1932	124.4	136.5	117.1	79.2	86.4	109.5	122.2
1933	126.5	130.7	127.7	77.0	90.5	114.0	125.5
1934	115.7	125.7	128.5	78.1	91.5	125.2	129.7
1935	110.4	124.5	135.0	79.2	93.5	144.1	128.1
1936	134.5	134.7	144.0	81.5	94.5	155.5	143.1
1937	142.1	149.8	140.8	97.1	90.5	171.3	145.6
1938	145.8		148.0	111.6	100.5	174.4	156.4
1939	147.6		159.2			185.2	164.6
1940	143.7		148.3			180.8	
1941	146.5		149.2				
1942	139.5		156.7				
1943	143.9						
1944	133.0						
1945	103.7					143.6	
1946			94.6			143.2	
1947			97.9			159.2	147.6
1948		137.3	122.5		67.3	181.0	173.6
1949		144.9	132.4			200.4	190.4
1950	166.7	156.3	140.8	100.0	100.0	219.6	180.7
1951	201.0	159.1	154.4	104.4		220.6	187.9
1952	191.8	164.4	159.6	106.8		234.9	173.0
1953	213.3	163.7	162.5	113.0		245.0	198.9
1954	209.3	170.4	168.2	119.4		256.9	209.9
1955	224.3	185.0	183.4	125.2	141.8	278.9	223.1
1956	224.5	195.9	175.1	130.8		305.6	218.0
1957	248.3	207.9	189.6	137.7		311.8	254.3
1958	269.9	223.8	202.3	144.4		335.2	264.6
1959	291.4	233.6	210.5	148.6		331.5	297.2
1960	319.0	251.3	221.5	156.6	176.0	363.0	315.9

Table B-10c (cont. 2)

	Bulgaria	Czechoslovakia	Hungary	Poland	Romania	USSR	Yugoslavia
1961	339.8	261.3	232.7	169.1	187.9	383.8	330.2
1962	367.7	264.8	242.4	166.8	194.5	394.2	336.4
1963	384.5	259.8	255.7	176.8	208.5	385.2	371.5
1964	414.8	272.0	270.1	184.7	221.7	435.0	406.9
1965	439.7	282.0	272.2	194.9	235.5	459.7	417.9
1966	474.4	294.2	287.7	207.2	262.4	482.0	440.4
1967	499.9	306.8	304.2	214.7	274.4	503.3	448.0
1968	509.1	321.1	307.9	227.7	280.2	532.8	457.4
1969	533.9	327.0	317.1	225.4	293.1	540.3	508.5
1970	564.3	333.6	316.0	237.1	299.7	581.8	532.5
1971	582.7	345.0	330.1	254.0	342.0	597.3	593.9
1972	610.3	357.2	337.2	272.5	364.0	600.7	614.4
1973	634.4	369.1	354.7	293.0	375.6	651.2	634.9
1974	654.3	382.5	363.9	310.2	396.7	670.1	716.8
1975	708.1	393.8	371.7	324.8	414.5	672.0	716.8
1976	729.3	400.1	372.8	332.9	435.7	703.5	739.0
1977	722.3	418.2	396.2	339.1	445.6	720.1	792.8
1978	737.9	423.3	405.8	351.4	460.1	738.2	836.5
1979	766.3	426.9	406.6	344.9	473.4	734.7	893.9
1980	744.3	438.7	410.7	336.2	474.7	735.6	936.9
1981	764.1	436.5	413.6	318.3	471.8	742.3	951.9
1982	788.8	445.0	428.5	315.4	472.2	760.6	960.5
1983	773.9	451.7	424.1	331.0	468.0	784.9	969.2
1984	799.5	462.3	435.2	343.3	486.6	795.0	991.4
1985	775.4	465.9	424.5	346.9	485.8	802.1	1 000.0
1986	795.9	474.5	433.0	357.9	494.1	835.1	1 041.5
1987	797.4	476.9	439.7	353.1	483.7	845.9	1 029.4
1988	792.4	487.5	446.4	360.9	482.5	863.9	1 015.0
1989	778.2	491.5	436.4	355.3	467.1	876.8	1 002.1
1990	693.2	477.6	407.3	320.9	416.4	855.6	929.0
1991	539.0	409.6	378.0	302.1	344.0	726.0	831.5
1992	480.1	385.1	353.5	298.5	302.6	587.8	665.0

Table B-10d. **GDP Indices for 7 Latin American Countries, 1820-1994**

(1913 = 100)

	Argentina	Brazil	Chile	Colombia	Mexico	Peru	Venezuela
1820		15.2			22.8		
1850		25.9			23.3		
1870	8.1	36.5			29.8		
1890	25.0	55.2			52.9		
1900	44.5	63.8	62.6	60.6	71.7	68.8	65.8
1901	48.3	70.2	64.7		77.8		64.7
1902	47.3	70.2	66.9		72.3		70.4
1903	54.1	71.6	69.1		80.4		76.1
1904	59.9	73.0	71.5		81.8		74.3
1905	67.8	75.1	73.9		90.3		73.4
1906	71.2	82.0	76.4		89.3		68.5
1907	72.7	82.1	79.0		94.5		68.5
1908	79.8	81.5	81.6		94.4		73.2
1909	83.8	88.0	83.0		97.2		75.8
1910	89.9	89.0	89.8		98.0		78.3
1911	91.5	98.8	89.0				83.7
1912	99.0	97.7	98.9				86.6
1913	100.0	100.0	100.0	100.0	100.0	100.0	100.0
1914	89.6	98.2	93.2			90.3	87.4
1915	90.1	102.6	86.6			95.9	90.1
1916	87.5	105.6	102.7			124.9	85.0
1917	80.4	112.9	111.0			120.4	99.2
1918	95.2	110.6	111.2			117.2	98.6
1919	98.7	117.7	87.9			135.3	92.1
1920	105.9	129.3	100.4			138.0	110.6
1921	108.6	132.0	86.4		105.5	97.3	115.1
1922	117.2	141.1	92.4		108.0	110.2	118.3
1923	130.2	149.2	115.0		111.7	142.3	136.5
1924	140.3	149.1	125.4		109.9	144.3	158.1
1925	139.7	149.7	126.9	138.0	116.7	128.5	204.3
1926	146.4	152.9	123.7	151.2	123.7	143.2	247.1
1927	156.8	164.0	118.6	164.8	118.3	161.1	277.2
1928	166.6	182.9	143.9	176.9	119.0	172.4	310.4
1929	174.2	183.3	157.9	183.3	114.4	190.5	352.0
1930	167.0	179.3	148.3	181.7	107.2	169.2	358.3
1931	155.4	175.3	111.7	180.6	110.8	148.9	289.6
1932	150.3	181.4	110.5	190.7	94.2	141.4	277.4
1933	157.3	198.3	130.8	201.4	104.9	190.5	303.5
1934	169.8	211.9	148.9	197.2	112.0	222.6	323.9
1935	177.3	217.7	151.7	219.3	120.3	228.7	347.4
1936	178.5	238.6	157.5	230.9	129.9	238.9	381.6
1937	191.5	246.4	169.5	234.5	134.2	244.1	437.8
1938	192.3	256.7	166.6	249.8	136.4	237.9	473.3
1939	199.6	265.2	171.7	265.1	143.7	259.3	502.0
1940	202.9	269.5	179.2	270.8	145.7	255.2	482.5
1941	213.3	288.4	179.4	275.4	157.6	284.8	474.6
1942	215.8	277.7	189.3	275.9	168.8	255.2	415.0
1943	214.1	295.5	197.2	277.1	175.1	243.2	453.0
1944	238.4	306.5	200.0	295.8	189.4	276.8	558.8
1945	230.7	314.7	218.1	309.7	195.3	308.3	679.2
1946	251.3	347.9	231.6	337.7	208.2	320.7	815.0

Table B-10d (cont. 2)

	Argentina	Brazil	Chile	Colombia	Mexico	Peru	Venezuela
1947	279.2	360.2	216.1	351.0	215.3	330.2	974.8
1948	294.7	387.8	241.2	361.9	224.2	341.3	1 085.2
1949	290.7	412.7	239.7	381.9	236.5	365.5	1 151.6
1950	294.3	437.7	251.3	388.7	259.9	383.8	1 178.2
1951	305.8	458.6	262.1	400.7	280.0	414.9	1 260.2
1952	290.2	485.9	277.1	426.0	291.2	441.1	1 370.3
1953	305.8	509.3	291.6	452.1	292.0	464.5	1 423.1
1954	318.4	543.0	292.8	483.5	321.2	494.4	1 570.4
1955	341.1	582.8	292.4	502.2	348.4	518.2	1 701.9
1956	350.5	591.2	294.1	522.4	372.3	540.4	1 849.6
1957	368.5	640.4	324.9	541.5	400.5	576.4	2 125.0
1958	391.1	698.5	333.8	555.1	421.8	573.5	2 160.5
1959	365.8	757.1	332.0	595.1	434.4	594.2	2 290.3
1960	394.4	820.1	353.8	620.4	469.6	667.1	2 297.6
1961	422.6	881.6	370.8	651.8	488.4	716.2	2 226.8
1962	415.8	935.4	388.4	687.2	510.8	776.1	2 325.1
1963	405.8	945.1	412.9	709.8	548.9	804.9	2 431.4
1964	447.6	977.0	422.1	753.7	607.3	857.4	2 638.0
1965	488.5	996.7	425.5	780.9	646.8	900.1	2 813.0
1966	491.8	1 059.1	472.9	822.5	686.6	976.1	2 863.5
1967	505.0	1 101.7	488.3	857.1	727.4	1 013.0	3 036.6
1968	526.5	1 199.9	505.8	909.6	780.1	1 016.4	3 244.1
1969	571.5	1 304.6	524.6	967.5	825.4	1 054.5	3 360.6
1970	602.1	1 432.9	535.4	1 032.8	879.6	1 116.3	3 618.9
1971	631.3	1 578.3	583.3	1 094.2	916.3	1 163.0	3 672.1
1972	651.0	1 748.4	576.3	1 178.1	994.0	1 196.5	3 719.0
1973	690.7	1 967.7	544.2	1 257.4	1 077.6	1 260.4	3 983.2
1974	735.5	2 122.9	549.5	1 329.7	1 143.5	1 377.2	4 067.5
1975	729.0	2 233.6	478.5	1 360.5	1 207.6	1 424.0	4 183.8
1976	727.2	2 443.8	495.4	1 425.0	1 258.8	1 452.0	4 506.9
1977	771.1	2 558.1	544.2	1 484.1	1 302.2	1 457.9	4 789.0
1978	737.2	2 686.4	588.9	1 610.0	1 409.6	1 462.0	4 902.5
1979	789.9	2 877.2	637.7	1 696.3	1 538.6	1 547.0	4 941.1
1980	801.1	3 131.0	687.3	1 765.9	1 666.7	1 616.2	4 719.9
1981	755.1	2 993.4	725.5	1 803.5	1 812.7	1 689.8	4 704.7
1982	731.3	3 010.7	622.3	1 821.4	1 801.4	1 692.3	4 606.9
1983	757.1	2 908.0	618.1	1 850.5	1 725.9	1 479.4	4 434.0
1984	772.5	3 064.1	657.3	1 916.4	1 789.3	1 547.9	4 497.0
1985	721.4	3 307.4	673.4	1 979.3	1 838.5	1 583.4	4 565.7
1986	774.2	3 572.7	711.5	2 100.3	1 767.4	1 730.3	4 799.0
1987	794.2	3 692.4	752.3	2 213.1	1 800.5	1 872.1	4 970.9
1988	779.2	3 683.7	807.8	2 303.6	1 827.0	1 717.6	5 260.3
1989	730.8	3 804.4	888.3	2 378.2	1 885.7	1 520.1	4 809.5
1990	731.3	3 643.8	907.4	2 477.2	1 960.8	1 444.1	5 063.9
1991	796.4	3 676.6	960.0	2 524.3	2 031.4	1 474.4	5 580.4
1992	864.9	3 643.5	1 058.9	2 615.1	2 084.2	1 434.6	5 965.5
1993	916.8	3 792.9	1 118.2	2 743.2	2 096.7	1 527.8	5 953.6
1994	971.8	3 963.6	1 168.5	2 880.4	2 159.6	1 695.9	5 715.4

Table B-10e. **GDP Indices for 10 Asian Countries. 1820-1992**

(1913 = 100)

	Bangladesh	Burma	China	India	Indonesia	Pakistan	Philippines	South Korea	Taiwan	Thailand
1820	54.1		66.2	55.8	24.1	49.7				
1850				61.5	33.0					
1870			62.2	71.0	41.5					56.3
1890			77.6	85.4	54.4					71.6
1900	86.0		86.6	88.3	69.6	93.1	56.9	76.6	78.9	80.8
1901		86.7		88.8	68.7					
1902				95.2	67.4					
1903				94.8	71.4				83.4	
1904				92.1	72.9				78.1	
1905				90.8	74.0				79.7	
1906		75.6		97.3	76.5				88.7	
1907				89.1	78.4				88.9	
1908				93.9	78.9				88.7	
1909				103.1	83.3				97.1	
1910				103.4	88.9				113.9	
1911		87.0		101.2	94.1			91.8	106.8	
1912				102.7	94.9			93.9	97.2	
1913	100.0	100.0	100.0	100.0	100.0	100.0	100.0	100.0	100.0	100.0
1914				103.1	100.3			106.9	102.2	
1915				104.4	101.8			121.4	104.0	
1916		123.2		108.7	103.9			123.8	122.7	
1917				108.6	104.7			132.5	133.6	
1918				93.8	107.0			143.3	125.9	
1919				106.6	115.9			140.6	133.8	
1920				95.3	114.2			137.3	124.9	
1921		111.2		103.5	115.7			146.3	124.3	
1922				105.2	118.2			144.0	133.4	
1923				102.5	120.3			148.7	137.6	
1924				104.0	127.1			150.9	150.5	
1925				103.9	131.4			152.3	154.8	
1926		134.1		106.5	138.4			157.7	155.8	
1927				105.5	147.9			167.1	154.9	
1928				107.7	154.8			163.3	172.4	
1929	108.6		126.1	109.9	157.8	115.0	151.5	160.2	180.5	131.0
1930			127.7	109.2	158.5			163.4	186.3	
1931		156.7	129.0	108.9	149.9			161.1	184.5	
1932	108.9		133.1	110.2	146.6	115.3		167.9	214.4	
1933			133.1	112.9	145.0			192.1	201.0	
1934			121.5	111.8	143.7			190.0	216.2	
1935			131.3	112.7	147.2			214.9	246.1	
1936		155.9	139.6	118.4	155.5			229.5	252.8	
1937			136.2	119.2	169.4			260.6	259.1	
1938	115.8	141.4	132.8	114.9	169.1	124.2	179.3	258.6	272.0	169.5
1939				120.9	169.8			231.8	297.7	
1940				123.9	181.9			259.7	296.6	
1941				122.7	191.0			263.3	326.3	
1942				128.3	150.9			261.8	350.3	
1943				137.0	128.6			265.6	238.8	
1944				134.6	97.8			254.1	164.0	
1945				134.2	82.3			127.1	177.5	
1946				129.8	85.3			138.1	192.2	

Table B-10e (cont. 2)

	Bangladesh	Burma	China	India	Indonesia	Pakistan	Philippines	South Korea	Taiwan	Thailand
1947				132.3	99.9			148.5	208.0	
1948	123.9			125.5	121.9	155.3		159.8	225.1	
1949	114.4			127.9	137.4	157.2		171.9	243.7	
1950	121.1	91.3	111.5	128.4	150.9	167.8	195.0	184.9	263.8	224.2
1951	122.8	104.6	124.2	132.4	161.1	162.3	204.0	170.7	282.6	240.1
1952	126.4	106.9	142.1	135.8	173.0	162.9	222.1	181.7	316.4	247.3
1953	128.2	109.7	149.5	144.2	180.8	178.5	239.3	234.4	346.0	274.9
1954	130.7	102.9	155.7	151.4	192.7	182.6	252.1	251.1	379.0	269.0
1955	123.8	116.3	165.4	156.5	192.7	186.8	272.0	265.9	409.7	292.6
1956	136.8	124.0	180.0	165.2	200.3	192.3	285.7	269.1	432.2	311.9
1957	133.9	131.3	187.1	164.9	207.3	200.7	298.4	290.9	464.1	304.0
1958	131.3	127.7	208.8	177.0	212.4	203.5	310.8	309.9	495.2	315.9
1959	138.3	147.5	206.0	181.9	225.2	205.7	298.7	324.8	533.1	334.5
1960	146.2	152.4	194.6	191.1	235.3	215.8	303.2	333.4	566.7	369.0
1961	154.5	156.1	160.3	198.5	246.3	228.9	320.2	348.4	605.7	388.5
1962	153.7	169.7	158.9	204.8	246.9	245.5	335.4	360.3	653.6	420.2
1963	170.0	174.5	175.0	217.6	240.4	260.9	358.8	393.3	714.7	455.4
1964	171.8	177.6	199.4	233.7	249.1	280.6	371.3	426.3	801.9	482.5
1965	180.2	182.1	224.6	228.2	251.6	293.1	390.8	457.4	891.2	516.6
1966	182.5	174.5	250.5	227.4	249.2	317.0	408.1	516.2	970.6	581.1
1967	178.5	179.4	241.3	245.0	244.5	328.9	429.0	539.2	1 074.6	619.0
1968	195.1	191.2	232.5	253.9	263.6	351.9	453.6	587.9	1 173.1	669.5
1969	197.8	199.1	257.1	270.5	288.0	374.7	475.4	664.6	1 278.1	720.1
1970	208.5	208.1	297.0	284.5	314.0	413.6	498.4	723.8	1 423.4	776.0
1971	199.4	214.9	315.8	289.7	325.0	415.6	526.9	799.7	1 607.0	812.3
1972	175.7	216.5	323.1	287.9	361.0	418.9	554.4	855.4	1 821.0	851.3
1973	177.0	217.3	347.6	296.4	417.5	448.7	601.4	989.7	2 054.7	931.6
1974	200.7	228.8	354.5	300.0	436.3	464.0	631.4	1 073.7	2 078.6	982.2
1975	198.2	238.3	380.6	327.5	436.2	483.2	672.9	1 134.5	2 181.0	1 052.2
1976	207.0	252.8	372.8	333.4	479.9	508.7	725.8	1 279.4	2 483.3	1 143.9
1977	209.1	267.9	392.9	357.3	511.3	528.9	770.4	1 418.1	2 736.3	1 226.4
1978	224.5	285.2	429.6	378.0	537.6	571.6	813.0	1 565.8	3 108.3	1 349.9
1979	237.8	300.1	457.2	358.1	560.6	592.6	863.7	1 676.8	3 362.4	1 431.7
1980	241.1	323.7	476.6	381.8	602.4	654.3	909.7	1 606.2	3 607.9	1 514.2
1981	264.0	344.1	493.4	406.8	643.9	706.2	940.7	1 717.2	3 830.2	1 609.5
1982	273.9	363.3	530.1	422.1	630.5	752.2	974.5	1 838.7	3 966.2	1 675.4
1983	286.6	379.2	577.0	453.5	665.5	803.0	992.1	2 045.7	4 301.3	1 773.2
1984	300.2	397.3	649.8	470.2	711.2	844.1	919.4	2 253.6	4 757.2	1 883.1
1985	312.0	408.3	727.7	495.9	728.8	908.0	852.5	2 420.7	4 992.8	1 958.4
1986	325.7	404.9	779.9	520.0	771.7	957.9	881.7	2 717.8	5 574.0	2 057.4
1987	339.0	388.3	853.2	544.5	809.7	1 019.7	923.9	3 034.2	6 261.6	2 255.8
1988	348.6	343.7	946.7	598.1	856.1	1 097.6	982.2	3 374.9	6 721.3	2 558.2
1989	357.2	356.6	984.8	633.7	921.1	1 151.9	1 040.5	3 609.8	7 230.0	2 871.4
1990	379.4	366.1	1 017.2	668.7	989.0	1 213.4	1 062.8	3 945.3	7 581.9	3 166.7
1991	392.2	361.7	1 082.4	703.5	1 051.9	1 308.0	1 052.0	4 276.5	8 130.4	3 420.1
1992	408.7	402.3	1 201.5	711.9	1 116.1	1 342.1	1 069.9	4 481.8	8 667.0	3 676.6

Table B-10f. **GDP Indices for 10 African Countries, 1900-1992**

(1950 = 100)

	Cote d'Ivoire	Egypt	Ethiopia	Ghana	Kenya	Morocco	Nigeria	South Africa	Tanzania	Zaire
1900		48.9		15.8						
1913		58.4		25.4				28.6		
1950	100.0	100.0	100.0	100.0	100.0	100.0	100.0	100.0	100.0	100.0
1951	103.7	110.5	102.8	103.7	121.8	105.2	107.5	104.7	112.6	111.7
1952	107.5	110.0	105.7	101.8	108.3	107.7	115.2	108.4	114.9	121.9
1953	111.4	110.6	111.8	115.9	105.6	113.3	117.9	113.5	110.8	128.8
1954	115.5	117.6	111.8	130.5	117.9	122.8	126.6	120.2	119.8	136.6
1955	119.8	123.7	117.8	122.1	126.8	128.5	129.9	126.2	122.7	141.9
1956	124.2	127.0	121.7	129.3	133.8	123.3	126.9	133.2	124.2	151.5
1957	128.8	130.4	120.8	133.5	138.2	121.1	132.1	138.3	127.2	156.3
1958	133.6	146.6	124.8	131.3	139.7	111.3	130.6	141.2	128.3	151.8
1959	138.5	161.7	128.2	150.3	143.1	125.5	136.3	147.5	134.6	157.1
1960	150.9	173.9	134.8	161.4	148.6	121.8	142.4	153.7	140.1	160.7
1961	165.0	181.5	141.4	167.1	145.0	126.5	147.2	160.3	138.5	143.2
1962	172.3	194.0	147.2	175.2	152.8	131.5	155.6	169.3	151.1	173.6
1963	200.6	211.7	166.7	181.3	160.5	127.3	170.2	181.7	160.6	182.7
1964	236.5	228.8	174.9	185.2	176.1	143.1	177.5	193.9	169.4	178.2
1965	231.3	249.9	185.2	187.7	178.1	150.9	189.5	205.5	175.5	180.0
1966	249.6	252.4	192.4	187.9	201.0	153.7	183.4	214.4	198.0	192.2
1967	253.2	253.9	200.5	191.3	211.4	151.6	154.9	229.1	206.0	190.3
1968	292.7	260.7	203.9	194.0	226.7	161.5	153.2	239.0	216.6	198.5
1969	305.6	278.5	211.5	200.9	240.8	181.5	194.3	253.7	220.6	217.0
1970	338.8	294.1	223.5	210.6	258.4	183.1	254.1	266.9	233.4	216.5
1971	355.8	304.0	232.9	227.4	274.8	174.3	284.0	280.0	243.2	230.3
1972	375.5	310.2	244.8	220.6	289.0	178.0	294.7	285.4	259.5	230.6
1973	405.2	312.3	252.9	226.9	304.0	184.8	320.0	297.4	267.9	250.6
1974	416.9	328.3	256.0	242.5	319.0	195.5	357.1	314.1	274.1	259.2
1975	416.5	373.3	256.4	212.3	317.7	210.2	346.4	319.9	288.3	246.3
1976	466.4	402.4	263.4	204.8	330.5	235.3	384.1	327.7	308.9	232.2
1977	488.4	434.1	270.6	209.5	360.8	252.3	412.2	327.1	317.6	233.4
1978	536.8	478.8	267.6	227.3	393.3	258.0	379.7	336.8	326.8	220.2
1979	546.9	526.7	284.8	221.5	408.1	270.3	394.7	350.0	330.8	219.9
1980	589.1	573.1	297.3	214.5	430.9	280.2	406.0	372.6	333.6	224.5
1981	609.7	604.6	303.4	214.8	440.8	272.4	394.1	392.2	329.9	229.8
1982	610.9	645.1	308.2	199.9	467.4	298.6	394.1	390.6	334.2	228.7
1983	587.1	683.8	323.9	190.8	470.3	297.0	360.5	383.5	332.7	231.9
1984	567.7	766.5	317.2	207.3	478.5	309.8	340.7	403.0	341.0	244.8
1985	595.6	836.4	296.0	217.8	499.1	329.4	372.7	398.2	340.2	245.9
1986	613.4	889.8	315.2	229.2	534.9	356.8	384.4	398.4	351.3	257.5
1987	603.6	924.5	344.8	240.2	566.7	347.7	382.6	406.5	369.2	264.4
1988	592.7	952.3	351.5	253.7	600.8	383.8	420.5	423.2	384.8	265.9
1989	589.2	977.1	357.2	266.6	628.2	393.4	451.6	432.0	397.7	264.1
1990	548.5	999.5	351.6	275.5	655.2	408.1	488.6	428.0	412.0	257.7
1991	545.8	993.3	349.6	289.2	669.6	434.2	510.6	425.6	427.7	236.3
1992	546.3	996.6	323.4	305.1	676.3	415.0	532.5	415.8	440.5	211.2

Appendix C

Levels of GDP

The annual GDP levels shown in this Appendix were derived by merging the GDP Appendix B with the benchmark values of 1990 GDP levels shown below. In order to compa output or output per capita in different countries, or to add their output to form a larger regior aggregate, it is necessary to convert them into a common unit.

Three Approaches for Converting Currencies into a Common Unit

There are three basic options for converting the nominal values:

a) use the exchange rate. This is the simplest option, but exchange rates are mainly a r purchasing power over tradeable items. For these goods inter-country price diff reduced because of possibilities for trade and specialisation. In poor countries wher low, non-tradeable items, like haircuts, government services or building const generally cheaper than in high income countries, so there is a general tendenc exchange rates to understate purchasing power (see Table C-11). The other pr exchange rates is that they are often powerfully influenced by capital movements, anc 20 years have been too volatile to serve as reliable indicators of purchasing power. T see (Tables C-4 and C-5) that exchange rates in virtually all advanced OECI understated purchasing power in 1980 and 1985 (as measured by the Geary-Khamis whereas in 1990 (Table C-6) they overstated purchasing power relative to the US doll

Table C-1 provides an illustrative exchange rate conversion for 1900, i.e. a time whe rates had been stable for some years. However, it is clear that they tended to purchasing power in lower income countries.

b) the second option is to use the purchasing power parity converters (PPPs) which developed by cooperative research of national statistical offices and international age past few decades. The expenditure approach, as instituted by OEEC in the 1950s for and developed by Kravis, Heston and Summers in the ICP (International Comparis for 34 countries, was taken over by the United Nations/EUROSTAT/OECD joint pr the 1980s, and ICP estimates are now available for 87 countries for at least one year basically a highly sophisticated comparative pricing exercise. It involves the c carefully specified price information by statistical offices for representativ consumption, investment goods and government services. In the 1990 EUROST 2 553 prices were collected for specified sample items. These were allocated tc headings which were then aggregated to produce the PPP converters. The exerc reinforce the comparability of national accounts, and provides detailed eviden structure as well as the aggregate converter which is our main concern here.

For countries not covered by the ICP, Summers and Heston have devised short cut and in their latest (1993) exercise provided PPP converters and real product e 150 countries. Their estimates for countries which have never participated in necessarily rougher than for those where these exercises are available. For the lat much more limited price information from cost of living surveys (of diplomats, UN people working abroad for private business) as a proxy for the ICP specification pric

As there are ICP estimates for 49 of the 56 sample countries and the Summers figures are available for the others, I have a strong preference for ICP PPP con exchange rates. Problems do arise for 49 countries outside my sample which ha covered either by ICP or by Summers and Heston. For these countries I had to use c to derive the world total. However, they accounted for only 0.9 per cent of 1990 wor Appendix F).

c) the third option is the approach developed by the ICOP (International Comparison o Productivity) project of the University of Groningen. This involves comparison of (value added) by industry of origin using census of production material on output well as prices (for agriculture, industry and service activity). This approach is partic for analysis of productivity performance by sector. Although there are a large nun studies for agriculture and manufacturing, there are as yet few for the service sector GDP comparisons, on an ICOP basis, are feasible for only a limited number of c

A. Maddison and B. van Ark, "The International Comparison of Real Product and Productivity", *Research Memorandum,* GD-6, Groningen Growth and Development Centre, April 1994, for a confrontation of the ICOP and ICP results).

Alternative Options within the ICP PPP Approach

a) Binary Comparisons

When the ICP approach was originally developed in OEEC in the 1950s, the main emphasis was on binary comparisons. Here, the three most straightforward options are: (i) Laspeyres volume comparisons based on the prices (unit values) of the numeraire country; (ii) Paasche volume comparisons based on the prices (unit values) of the other country or countries in the comparison; or (iii) the Fisher geometric average of these two measures which is in effect a compromise measure. Conversely, the PPPs corresponding to these three volume options are: (i) the Paasche PPP (with "own" country quantity weights); (ii) the Laspeyres PPP (with the quantity weights of the numeraire country); and (iii) the Fisher geometric average of the two measures. The most generally used of the binary measures is the Fisher variant, but I myself prefer the Paasche PPP. This gives a Laspeyres volume measure which values output in all countries at US prices. Unfortunately, the Paasche and other binary measures are no longer published for non-OECD countries.

The results of binary studies can be linked to compare the situation in a number of countries, each binary being linked via a "star" country. Hence a series of binary comparisons France/USA, Germany/USA and UK/USA are linked with the USA as the star country. However, the France-Germany, UK-Germany, and France-UK comparisons which can be derived from these are inferential and will not necessarily produce the same results as direct binary comparison of France and Germany, UK and Germany or France-UK. Such star-system comparisons are not "transitive", and this is generally considered to be a substantial drawback.

b) Multilateral Comparisons

Comparisons can be made transitive if they are done on a "multilateral" rather than a "binary" basis. The Geary-Khamis approach (initiated by R.S. Geary in 1958 and developed by S.H. Khamis in 1970 and after) is an ingenious method for multilaterising the results which provides transitivity and other desirable properties (base-country invariance and additivity). It is based on twin concepts of purchasing power parity of currencies and international average prices of commodities. It was used by Kravis, Heston and Summers (1982) as a method for aggregating ICP results available at the basic heading level, and they used it in conjunction with the CPD (commodity product dummy) method (invented by Robert Summers) for filling holes in the data at the basic heading level. It should be noted that the ICP programme of the United Nations is now carried out separately for six different regions, and the estimates are subsequently "globalised", i.e. interregional links are made by using limited information for core countries. For this reason the quality of the "transitivity" is poorer than in the original Kravis-Heston-Summers approach (see *World Comparisons of Real Gross Domestic Product and Purchasing Power 1958*, UN, New York, 1994, pp. 17-19.

The Geary-Khamis approach gives a weight to countries corresponding to the size of their GDP, so that a large economy, like the USA, has a strong influence on the results. For this reason, alternative multilateral methods are sometimes used in which all countries have an equal weight, e.g. the Gerardi or EKS techniques. For our purposes, equi-country weighting systems which treat Luxemburg and the USA as equal partners are inappropriate, so the Geary-Khamis approach is my preferred multilateral measure. The Geary-Khamis PPP is usually nearest to the Paasche. The Fisher is somewhat higher and the Laspeyres shows the highest PPP. Generally speaking, the dispersion between alternative PPPs is wider, the lower the per capita income of the country concerned (see Tables C-7 and C-11).

The Estimation of 1990 Benchmark Levels of GDP in OECD Countries

The quality of the PPP information for OECD countries is now very satisfactory. There have been six ICP exercises. The latest (1990) round is the only one which is complete, and includes all 24 member countries. The latest Geary-Khamis estimates are not subject to the "fixity" constraint imposed by EUROSTAT — a device which preserves the relative standing of the 12 individual EU countries which prevailed before the EU results were merged with those for other OECD countries. Furthermore, EUROSTAT/OECD have made all the PPP binary variants available to researchers, so the transparency of the results is greater than for any other region. The full range of these converters is shown in Tables C-2 to C-6, and Table C-7 illustrates the relationship between the main PPP variants for 1990.

Table C-8 shows the variation in the level of 1990 per capita GDP according to which ICP round is used as a benchmark, and the right hand side of Table C-10 shows the range of those variations for the different OECD countries. Generally, the variance is smaller in a comparison of ICP III and ICP VI (neither of which was subject to the fixity constraint) than it is when all rounds are compared.

It is inevitable that there should be some degree of inconsistency between results of different ICP rounds, as the patterns of output and prices change, the relative size of countries varies and the procedures for calculation have undergone some modification. Nevertheless, the fact that the GDP growth rates implicit in successive ICP rounds were different from those in the national accounts estimates led Robert Summers and Alan Heston, "The Penn World Table (Mark 5): An Expanded Set of International Comparisons, 1955-1988", *Quarterly Journal of Economics*, May 1991, to devise an elaborate compromise technique which purged the inconsistencies between the four successive ICP benchmark levels for 1970, 1975, 1980 and 1985 and those recorded in the national accounts. Their (1991) estimates are shown in the penultimate column of Table C-8, updated to 1990. In most cases, their estimates fell outside the range of per capita product in all the other ICP rounds.

It is not easy to see why this should be the case, but one should keep in mind that their estimating procedures were different from mine in three very important respects:

a) they used the original basic data for countries which participated in ICP2, ICP3, ICP4 and ICP5 plus much rougher price information for 57 non-benchmark countries and reworked the Geary-Khamis PPPs on a global basis for 138 countries. Their PPPs were therefore different from those of ICP which I used;

b) their updating was done on a disaggregated basis, with separate estimates for consumption, investment, government expenditure and net foreign balance, whereas my updating is cruder and done only at the GDP level;

c) their "consistentising" procedure to eliminate the variance between successive ICP rounds involved modification of the growth rates in national prices. I have not modified these because they are likely to contain less error than the successive ICP benchmarks. Furthermore, the Summers/Heston procedure is asymmetric, because it involves modification of growth rates only for those countries for which there is more than one ICP benchmark.

My own view, as expressed in Maddison (1991, p. 201) is that the variance between successive ICP rounds is more likely to be the source of the problem than errors in the national growth measures. If an averaging procedure is used, an average of the successive ICP rounds might well be preferable to the Summers-Heston 1991 procedure which also involved adjustment of the growth rates. Summers and Heston concentrate on the situation since 1950 or 1960. Earlier than that it is impossible to use their procedure, as there are no equivalent benchmarks available.

Kravis and Lipsey also had doubts about the "consistentising" procedure because it diminishes transparency and introduces ambiguity in what is being measured: "Our view is that the best general-purpose estimates of growth rates are those derived directly from the national accounts - from domestic price deflators of the countries. They have relatively clear conceptual underpinning. (They are, to be sure, made less comparable from country to country by use of different base years.) Similarly, we think that the best estimates of real GDP per capita levels are those produced by the benchmark studies, unaltered by modifications based on a mixture of domestic and international prices." (see I.B. Kravis and R.E. Lipsey, "The International Comparison Program: Current Status and Problems", in P.E. Hooper and J.D. Richardson, *International Economic Transactions: Issues in Measurement and Empirical Research*, University of Chicago Press, Chicago, 1991.

Recently Summers and Heston (NBER diskette of June 1993) have issued new Penn World Tables: Mark 5.5, which do not involve adjustments of the national indicators of GDP growth [of the type mentioned in para. (c) above]. They now apply "consistentisation" only to the successive ICP rounds. Their (1993) results are shown in the last column of Table C-8 and are more acceptable than their (1991) results as they now generally fall within the range of the ICP results.

The Estimation of 1990 Benchmark Levels of GDP for Non-OECD Countries

ICP estimates do not yet provide PPP converters for all our 34 non-OECD countries. ICP3 covered 13 of them, ICP4 20, ICP5 16, and ICP6 only 6 of our East European countries. Altogether ICP estimates are available for 27 of our 34 countries for at least one year.

I used ICP converters for 17 of the non-OECD countries (ICP6 for 1990 for 6 East European countries, an update of ICP4 for 6 Latin American countries, and 4 Asian countries, and an update of ICP3 for Mexico).

For Bangladesh and Pakistan I used a 1950 benchmark estimate of their relative GDP levels which I linked to that of India. This was necessary for the purposes of historical consistency, and in any case the 1985 ICP estimates of Bangladeshi and Pakistani GDP seemed to me to be too high relative to the Indian level.

For the 15 other countries in my non-OECD sample (Bulgaria, Burma, China, Taiwan, Thailand and the ten African countries) I used the Summers and Heston (1993) 1990 estimates.

Table C-9 shows the full set of real per capita GDP levels which can be derived by applying ICP PPP converters in conjunction with the most recent estimates of nominal GDP and population. It also shows the variant I chose and the Summers and Heston (1993) estimates. The subsequent tables in this section show in detail how the updated estimates were established.

It should be noted that the alternative estimates from different ICP rounds for non-OECD countries show a greater variance than is the case for OECD countries (see Table C-10). This suggests that the OECD estimates are more firmly based than those for non-OECD countries. The biggest variance has been in Eastern Europe and in India where the earliest estimates generally gave higher estimates of GDP than the later results. For the OECD countries there has been a much narrower range of variance except for Italy and the UK.

Table C-11 shows the variation between the different possible PPP converters and the exchange rates for 1980, in relation to the Geary-Khamis PPP used here. This can be compared with Table C-7 for non-OECD countries. The range between the different converters is generally larger in the non-OECD countries because their price structures are more different from the USA (the numeraire country) than those in the higher income OECD countries.

Table C-11 demonstrates very clearly how misleading exchange rate conversions can be. A high ratio in the last column indicates that the exchange rate understates a country's purchasing power, whereas a figure below 1 indicates that the exchange rate overvalues the purchasing power of the currency. It can be seen in Table C-6 that the advanced capitalist countries of OECD had exchange rates that led to substantial overvaluation of their currencies' purchasing power relative to the US dollar in 1990, whereas the opposite was true of most of the non-OECD countries in 1980. It can also be seen that the relationship between PPPs and exchange rates was quite erratic between countries.

The following notes by region and country give more detail of the procedures I used and describe some of the problems in such comparisons.

Eastern Europe

Some of the East European countries have been included in all of the ICP rounds, but ICP6 was the most comprehensive in coverage and involved six of our seven sample countries. The 1990 comparisons were carried out by the United Nations Economic Commission for Europe in cooperation with the national statistical office and were compared on a binary basis with Austria. The binary real GDP ratios were multiplied by the Austrian GDP in 1990 Geary-Khamis dollars, using the results presented in ECE,

International Comparison of Gross Domestic Product in Europe 1990, Geneva, 1994. For Bulgaria, I used Summers and Heston (1993), as Bulgaria did not participate in the ECE study. The details for earlier years are shown in Tables C-12a, C-12b, and C-12c.

Estimates of 1990 GDP Level in Latin America

The ICP covered only three of our Latin American countries (Brazil, Colombia and Mexico) in 1975 and six (Argentina, Brazil, Chile, Colombia, Peru and Venezuela) in 1980. They were not included in ICP5 for 1985. I therefore used the 1980 Geary-Khamis PPPs as a benchmark for these six countries, and the 1975 Geary-Khamis PPP for Mexico. These figures were updated using the volume movement in GDP from the benchmark year to 1990, and then adjusting the result in line with the movement in the US GDP deflator over the same period.

A major problem with the national accounts of Latin American economies is the assessment of activity in the informal sector. Recent official revisions for Argentina have been very substantial. Instead of a GDP totalling 2 830 million australes in 1980, it is now estimated to have been 3 840 million (nearly 36 per cent higher). Maddison and Van Ark (1989) pointed out that the Mexican national accounts carry a very large imputation for informal activity, whereas in Brazil, the official imputation for such activity is relatively modest. Because of this, I have adjusted the official estimate of the GDP levels in national currency in conjunction with the ICP PPPs for Brazil and Mexico. For Brazil I made an upward adjustment of GDP by 3.27 per cent to correct for underestimation of GDP in agriculture. For Mexico GDP was adjusted downwards by 17.96 per cent to correct for apparent exaggeration of output levels in agriculture, manufacturing and some services (see Maddison and Van Ark, "International Comparison of Purchasing Power, Real Output and Labour Productivity: A Case Study of Brazilian, Mexican and US Manufacturing in 1975", *Review of Income and Wealth*, 1989, Maddison and H. van Ooststroom, "The International Comparison of Value Added, Productivity and Purchasing Power Parities in Agriculture", *Research Memo GD-1*, Groningen, 1993 and N. Mulder and A. Maddison, "The International Comparison of Performance in Distribution: Value Added, Labour Productivity and PPPs in Mexican and US Wholesale and Retail Trade 1975/7", *Research Memo GD-2*, Groningen, 1993).

H. de Soto, *El Otro Sendero*, Instituto Libertad y Democracia, Lima, 1987, p. 13 suggested that the official Peruvian national accounts missed a good deal of informal activity. It seems likely that the Colombian national accounts may also understate informal activity. However, I did not have an adequate basis for making adjustments to the estimates for Peru and Colombia.

Estimates of 1990 GDP Level in Asia

The 1970 ICP exercise covered three of our Asian countries (India, Korea and the Philippines), five for 1975 (India, Korea, Pakistan, Philippines and Thailand), five for 1980 (India, Indonesia, Korea, Pakistan and Philippines) and six for 1985 (Bangladesh, India, Korea, Pakistan, Philippines and Thailand). China and Taiwan do not figure in any of the ICP comparisons. The results of the different rounds are somewhat erratic, and we must necessarily use a mixture of sources. Table C-14a takes the results of ICP 3 for 1975 and updates them to 1990 using the volume indices from Appendix B, and the US GDP deflator for 1975-90. Tables C-14b and C-14c make similar adjustments to 1980 (ICP 4) and to the 1985 results (ICP 5).

The 1985 ICP results were not used because they were not available until the present study was in its final stages, and involved some methodological differences from earlier studies. For Asia, ICP contained an implausibly low figure for India relative to Bangladesh and Pakistan, so I preferred to use the 1980 ICP 4 figures. For India, Bangladesh and Pakistan I needed to have benchmarks which are compatible with the fact that the three countries were united until 1947. I assumed that Pakistan and Bangladesh combined had the same average per capita income as India in 1950, and used the careful official estimates of relative income levels in Pakistan and Bangladesh when they were two "wings" of the former Pakistan (see A. Maddison, *Class Structure and Economic Growth: India and Pakistan since the Moghuls*, Allen and Unwin, London, 1971, p. 171).

For Taiwan and Thailand the 1990 PPP estimate was taken from the June 1993 Supplement (PWT 5.5) to R. Summers and H. Heston, "The Penn World Table (Mark 5): An Expanded Set of International Comparisons, 1950-1988", *Quarterly Journal of Economics*, May 1991.

The Merits of Four Alternative Measures of the Chinese GDP Level

For China there are four significant benchmarks to choose from. The first three are binary comparisons from the expenditure side between China and the USA.

The first of these is that of Irving Kravis, "An Approximation of the Relative Real Per Capita GDP of the People's Republic of China", *Journal of Comparative Economics*, 5, 1981, pp. 60-78. This comparison relates to 1975, and was based on price and expenditure information supplied by official sources in both countries according to the standard specifications of the UN ICP. It was a "reduced information" exercise as the amount of detail on prices and expenditure in China was significantly less than normal by ICP standards. It involved the highest levels of expertise available in this field, but the publication included no detailed information by category of expenditure.

Kravis did the comparison of real GDP per capita in Chinese and US prices, and the geometric mean of the two estimates showed Chinese per capita GDP to be 10.4 per cent of that in the USA in 1975. The four-fold spread between the two basic estimates was unusually large, with per capita GDP (Chinese weights) 5 per cent of the USA, and 21 per cent with Chinese weights. This was due to the nature of the Chinese price system where important basic commodities were supplied very much below cost and some consumer durables had very heavy implicit taxes.

ICP comparisons are normally carried out at multilateral (Geary-Khamis) prices rather than the Fisher binary which Kravis estimated. Geary-Khamis comparisons yield consistently higher estimates of real GDP in poor countries than Fisher comparisons because the weight of the country's own price structure is much bigger in the latter. Kravis therefore made a rough estimate of what China's per capita product might have been on a Geary-Khamis basis. This involved raising his Fisher estimate by 18.7 per cent (which was the average ratio of the Geary-Khamis to Fisher measures for the four lowest-income countries in the ICP2 comparisons). The end result was a Kravis estimate of Chinese per capita GDP 12.3 per cent of that in the USA in 1975. One can see from Table D-1a that US per capita GDP was $16 060 in 1975 in 1990 prices. 12.3 per cent of this yields an estimate of $1 975 for China. Chinese per capita GDP in 1990 was 215.9 per cent of that in 1975, yielding a 1990 per capita product of $4 264, and a total 1990 Chinese GDP of $4 834 billion.

A significantly modified version of the Kravis estimates was used in the Penn World Tables (5.5) of Summers and Heston (1993). They estimate Chinese GDP in 1990 at 1990 prices to have been $3 061 billion. Instead of updating the Kravis benchmark with the subsequent growth recorded for China and the USA, as we have done above, they extrapolated price changes in China and the USA. For China they used the official consumption deflators, together with a geometric average of PPPs they derived from Ren and Chen (1993). These they combined in a geometric average. The Summers and Heston estimate is therefore a hybrid, and is not significantly different from what one would obtain by taking a simple geometric average of the Kravis and Ren-Chen (1993) estimates shown below. See Appendix A to A. Heston, D. Nuxoll, and R. Summers, "Issues in Comparing Relative Prices, Quantities and Real Output Among Countries", processed, World Bank, 1994.

The third estimate is that of Ren Ruoen and Chen Kai, "An Expenditure-Based Bilateral Comparison of Gross Domestic Product between China and the United States", May 1993 (processed). This estimate was made by a group of researchers in Beijing supplemented by a further two years of research by Ren Ruoen in MIT, the University of Maryland and the World Bank during 1991-3.

The basic procedure of the Ren-Chen study is binary and similar to that of Kravis, except that it is for 1986, and the research team had better access to Chinese price and expenditure detail than Kravis had. They also had prices for over 200 items compared with the 93 which Kravis had. The three-fold spread between the results at US weights ($1 818) and Chinese weights ($571) was large, but not as wide as Kravis found for 1975. The results are stated in terms of the Fisher geometric average and show Chinese GDP per capita to have been $1 044 in 1986, implying $1 114 billion for GDP. If this is adjusted for the rise in the volume of GDP (30.42 per cent) and in the US GDP deflator (15 per cent) from 1986 to 1990 this yields an estimate of GDP in 1990 at 1990 US prices of $1 670.7 billion. Ren Ruoen and Chen Kai do not make the adjustment from a Fisher to a Geary-Khamis basis, but if one applies the same (1.187) ratio as Kravis did, the end result is a Chinese GDP of $1 983 billion in 1990, or $1 749 per capita. This comparison may understate Chinese real product to some extent because it uses a shadow price for Chinese house rents (based on cost) rather than the very low rents actually charged in China. In this respect the procedure has some resemblance to the adjusted factor cost method developed by Abram Bergson in his work on USSR/USA comparisons, but it is not a normal procedure in ICP comparisons. Furthermore, the use of these shadow prices for housing should have been matched by an increase in the estimate of Chinese housing expenditure, and it is not clear that this was done. To this extent Ren and Chen understate Chinese per capita product.

An alternative way of using the Ren-Chen results is to apply their PPP for GDP to the World Bank's new estimates of nominal Chinese GDP for 1986. In *World Tables 1994* this estimate is 34 per cent higher than in *World Tables 1993*. With the new GDP figure one arrives at a figure of $1 494 billion for GDP (1 301.5 billion Yuan divided by .8709). This is 34 per cent higher than the estimate Ren-Chen derived by adding their more detailed expenditure categories to the old total for GDP. When the new figure is adjusted to produce an equivalent Geary-Khamis estimate for 1990, it raises the Ren-Chen estimate from $1 983 billion to $2 661 billion ($2 347 per capita).

The fourth significant comparison of China/USA is that of J.R. Taylor, "Dollar GNP Estimates for China," Centre for International Research, US Bureau of the Census, CIR Staff Paper, March 1991. Taylor's PPP is estimated only on a Paasche basis, at US prices. This is a comparison by industry of origin for 1981, using a double deflation approach and deriving producer price information from a variety of sources. The service sector prices are inferred by use of input-output tables. He shows 1981 GDP in 1981 prices to be $417.81 billion. If we update this to 1990 allowing for the rise in Chinese GDP (206.16 per cent of 1981) and the rise in the US GDP deflator (1.49338), we arrive at a 1990 GDP in 1990 prices of $1 286.3 billion or $1 135 on a per capita basis.

Thus we have four estimates for China which, when updated, yield the following results for 1990 in terms of 1990 prices:

	GDP billion $	GDP per capita
Kravis (1981)	4 834	4 264
Summers and Heston (1993)	3 061	2 700
Ren Ruoen and Chen Kai (1993)	1 983	1 749
Ren Ruoen and Chen Kai (1994 variant)	2 661	2 347
Taylor (1991)	1 286	1 135

Recently, the World Bank has been moving away from its previous preference for adjusted exchange rate converters towards use of ICP type estimates and in its *World Development Report 1993* adopted the estimate of Ren Ruoen and Chen Kai, which showed a Chinese per capita GDP of $1 680 for 1991. This differs from my update for two reasons: (a) it is updated from the 1986 benchmark by using the official Chinese estimate of GDP growth, which is faster than that which I use; (b) it does not adjust the Ren-Chen estimate from a Fisher to a Geary-Khamis basis.

The IMF has now adopted ICP type estimates for measuring world output. For China it used Taylor's estimate, without explaining why it made this choice, see IMF, *World Economic Outlook*, May 1993, pp. 116-9. The IMF did not show the actual figure they used. However, *Time* magazine (May 31, 1993) reported the IMF figure for China's GDP in 1991 as being $1 660 billion, which is a good deal higher than my updated version of Taylor. If *Time* magazine is correct, the IMF obviously updated Taylor's benchmark in a different way than I did.

In deciding which of these estimates to use as a benchmark, it is useful to keep two main criteria in mind. One of these is the scientific quality of the basic estimates, the second is their plausibility. On scientific grounds one must give preference to the estimates of Kravis, and Ren-Chen which are the most transparent and conform, more or less, to traditional ICP methodology. I would rate the Taylor estimates lowest of the four on these grounds as it is not very clear how they were made. The Summers and Heston estimates are clearly intended as an expedient and plausible compromise between the estimates of Kravis and Ren-Chen (1993).

The compatibility of the benchmark level with the time series estimates of growth is indeed an important consideration. If one used the Kravis benchmark with my time series, then one would have a Chinese per capita GDP 3.4 times as high as in India in 1990 and 1.7 times the Indian level in 1950 which seems unreasonably high. With the Ren-Chen estimate we have a GDP per capita about a third higher than in India in 1990 and only two thirds of that in India in 1950, which seems too low. Taylor's estimate is below that of India for 1990, and would produce an estimate for 1950 only 40 per cent of that in India, which seems unacceptable. I have therefore used the Summers and Heston version which seems the most plausible, and is rather close to the 1994 variant of Ren-Chen.

China's economy has in recent years moved towards a market system and has a substantial private sector, but it still has important features of a command economy and administered prices. Hence there is a mix of price systems which makes international comparisons of growth and level very difficult. There is a strong case for augmenting the ICP type comparisons by the industry of origin approach which Ren Ruoen has now undertaken in cooperation with A. Szirmai of Groningen University. So far this research is in a preliminary stage, but it should strengthen the basis for future assessments considerably.

Estimates of GDP Level in Africa

ICP estimates are available for 6 of our African countries (Côte d'Ivoire, Ethiopia, Kenya, Morocco, Nigeria and Tanzania) for the ICP 4 exercise. Seven countries (including Egypt as well) were included in ICP5. However, I used R. Summers and A. Heston, Penn World Table 5.5 of June 1993, for all the African countries, as they had better access to the EUROSTAT material on Africa than I did.

Table C-1. **Confrontation of My Estimate of Real GDP per Capita in 1900 in "1990 international dollars" and the 1900 levels estimated using Exchange Rates**

	1900 GDP in thousand national currency units	Exchange Rate US cents per unit of national currency	GDP in million 1990 dollars	Population 000s	GDP per capita 1990 dollars	GDP per capita index US=100	GDP per capita index using 1990 international dollars
Australia	198 300	486.60	965	3 741	258	104.5	102.8
Canada	1 030 000	100.00	1 030	5 319	194	78.5	67.0
France	26 130 000	19.30	5 043	38 940	130	52.6	68.1
Germany	35 170 000	23.82	8 377	56 046	149	60.3	71.3
India	14 343 200	32.24	4 624	284 500	16	6.5	14.9
Japan	2 422 000	50.66	1 227	44 103	28	11.3	27.1
UK	1 922 000	486.60	9 352	41 155	227	91.9	106.5
USA	18 782 000	100.00	18 782	76 094	247	100.0	100.0

Source: First column: Appendix to A. Maddison, "A Long Run Perspective on Saving", *Scandinavian Journal of Economics*, June 1992; col. 2 from A. Maddison, *The World Economy in the Twentieth Century*, OECD Development Centre, Paris, 1989, p. 145, population from Appendix H, and from A. Maddison, *Dynamic Forces in Capitalist Development*, Oxford University Press, 1991, Appendix B. Last column from Appendices H and D. All the figures above refer to countries within their 1900 boundaries.

Table C-2. **Alternative PPPs for GDP from Round II of ICP and Exchange Rates for 1970**
(units of national currency per US dollar)

	Laspeyres	Paasche	Fisher	Geary-Khamis	Exchange Rate
Belgium	46.8	35.8	40.9	38.0	50.00
France	4.87	4.13	4.49	4.40	5.55
Germany	3.44	2.90	3.16	2.99	3.66
Italy	509	407	455	458	625
Netherlands	3.21	2.45	2.81	2.67	3.62
UK	0.333	0.278	0.304	0.301	0.417
USA	1.000	1.000	1.000	1.000	1.000
Japan	279	231	254	241	360

Source: I.B. Kravis, A. Heston and R. Summers, *International Comparisons of Real Product and Purchasing Power*, Johns Hopkins, Baltimore, 1978, p. 21 for Geary-Khamis, pp. 174-96 for binaries. Exchange rates from OECD, *National Accounts 1960-1992*, vol. I, Paris 1994, p. 154.

Table C-3. **Alternative PPPs for GDP from Round III of ICP and Exchange Rates for 1975**
(units of national currency per US dollar)

	Laspeyres	Paasche	Fisher	Geary-Khamis	Exchange Rate
Austria	18.77	15.89	17.27	17.5	17.4
Belgium	45.17	39.39	42.18	41.6	36.8
Denmark	8.007	6.872	7.418	7.29	5.75
France	5.207	4.292	4.727	4.69	4.29
Germany	3.143	2.638	2.880	2.81	2.46
Italy	620.1	515.1	565.2	582.0	652.9
Netherlands	3.236	2.758	2.987	2.84	2.53
UK	0.4267	0.3533	0.3883	0.406	0.452
USA	1.0000	1.0000	1.0000	1.0000	1.0000
Japan	315.0	245.2	277.9	271.0	296.8
Ireland	0.4246	0.3404	0.3802	0.388	0.452
Spain	50.05	38.12	43.68	42.3	57.4

Source: I.B. Kravis, A. Heston and R. Summers, *World Product and Income: International Comparisons of Real Gross Product*, Johns Hopkins, Baltimore, 1982, p. 21 for Geary-Khamis, pp. 253-82 for augmented binaries. Exchange rates as for Table C-2.

Table C-4. **Alternative PPPs for GDP from Round IV of ICP and Exchange Rates for 1980**
(units of national currency per US dollar)

	Laspeyres	Paasche	Fisher	Gerardi	Geary-Khamis (OECD version)	Exchange Rate
Austria	16.863	14.598	15.690	16.463	15.40	12.94
Belgium	40.337	35.268	37.718	39.375	36.60	29.24
Denmark	8.4552	7.1606	7.7810	8.0710	7.43	5.64
Finland	n.a.	n.a.	n.a.	n.a.	4.52	3.73
France	5.8318	5.0374	5.4201	5.6110	5.24	4.23
Germany	2.6151	2.3305	2.4687	2.5276	2.37	1.82
Italy	882.04	715.78	794.57	801.94	759.00	856.45
Netherlands	2.9055	2.4523	2.6693	2.7416	2.53	1.99
Norway	7.8282	5.8672	6.7771	6.7320	6.16	4.94
UK	0.59517	0.45089	0.51803	0.52130	0.487	0.430
Canada	1.1311	1.1047	1.1178	1.0952	1.08	1.17
USA	1.0000	1.0000	1.0000	1.0000	1.0000	1.0000
Japan	282.08	218.97	248.53	251.16	240.00	226.74
Greece	47.195	33.247	39.611	38.452	35.40	42.62
Ireland	0.57343	0.43230	0.49789	0.50488	0.461	0.487
Portugal	47.280	26.629	35.483	32.115	31.70	50.06
Spain	77.165	58.766	67.340	67.083	63.70	71.70

Source: First four alternatives supplied by Hugo Krijnse Locker of EUROSTAT (1988-9 worksheets). Fifth column from Michael Ward, *Purchasing Power Parities and Real Expenditures in the OECD*, OECD, Paris, 1985, p. 13. Exchange rates as for Table C-2.

Table C-5. **Alternative PPPs for GDP from Round V of ICP and Exchange Rates for 1985**
(units of national currency per US dollar)

	Laspeyres	Paasche	Fisher	Gerardi	Geary-Khamis (OECD Version)	Exchange Rate
Austria	19.4849	15.6754	17.4767	18.180	16.60	20.69
Belgium	50.1568	41.7626	45.7677	48.587	44.60	59.38
Denmark	11.5111	9.1656	10.2716	10.7642	9.80	10.60
Finland	7.35488	5.67869	6.46267	6.5273	5.97	6.19
France	8.32432	6.75214	7.49713	7.8937	7.27	8.99
Germany	2.82225	2.37162	2.58714	2.6734	2.48	2.94
Italy	1 523.45	1 197.66	1 350.77	1 401.4	1 302.00	1 909.44
Netherlands	2.89318	2.43992	2.65691	2.7531	2.55	3.32
Norway	10.5057	8.2593	9.3150	9.3035	8.63	8.60
Sweden	9.70216	7.56799	8.56889	8.9021	8.15	8.60
UK	0.660073	0.532476	0.592851	0.61300	0.568	0.779
Australia	1.39921	1.15794	1.27287	1.3255	1.24	1.43
New Zealand	1.7218	1.2582	1.4719	1.4788	1.35	2.02
Canada	1.25866	1.20922	1.23369	1.2317	1.22	1.37
USA	1.00000	1.00000	1.00000	1.00000	1.000	1.000
Japan	298.979	201.452	245.418	239.23	222.00	238.54
Greece	101.135	66.147	81.791	84.576	77.3	138.1
Ireland	0.79803	0.70662	0.75094	0.78871	0.723	0.946
Portugal	97.339	58.377	75.381	73.066	66.20	170.40
Spain	116.635	86.411	100.392	102.575	95.30	170.04
Turkey	284.14	137.63	197.75	172.84	153.00	521.98

Source: First four alternatives supplied by Hugo Krijnse Locker of EUROSTAT (1988-89 Worksheets). The set of PPPs is also available in disaggregated form for 376 expenditure categories. Fifth column from OECD, *Purchasing Power Parities and Real Expenditures, 1985*, OECD, Paris, 1987, pp. 50-1. Exchange rates as for Table C-2.

Table C-6. **Alternative PPPs for GDP from Round VI of ICP and Exchange Rates for 1990**

(units of national currency per US dollar)

	Laspeyres	Paasche	Fisher	Geary-Khamis (OECD version)	EKS	Exchange Rate
Austria	15.118	13.492	14.282	13.899	14.091	11.370
Belgium	42.547	35.584	38.910	38.362	39.432	33.418
Denmark	10.574	8.017	9.207	8.700	9.398	6.189
Finland	7.0484	5.9736	6.4888	6.219	6.386	3.824
France	7.2861	5.9514	6.5850	6.450	6.614	5.445
Germany	2.1816	1.9263	2.0500	2.052	2.091	1.616
Italy	1 601.5	1 290.9	1 437.8	1 384.11	1 421.6	1 198.1
Netherlands	2.3269	1.9433	2.1264	2.084	2.1705	1.821
Norway	10.820	8.866	9.795	9.218	9.739	6.26
Sweden	10.288	8.310	9.246	8.979	9.341	5.919
Switzerland	2.3134	2.0731	2.1900	2.160	2.2045	1.389
UK	.66335	.55618	.60740	0.587	0.60227	0.563
Australia	1.4714	1.2968	1.3814	1.352	1.3864	1.281
New Zealand	1.7126	1.4709	1.5872	1.5574	1.6136	1.676
Canada	1.3246	1.2248	1.2737	1.274	1.3068	1.167
USA	1.0000	1.0000	1.0000	1.000	1.000	1.000
Japan	220.31	176.51	197.20	185.27	195.45	144.79
Greece	164.23	120.99	140.96	129.55	140.91	158.51
Ireland	.74827	.67363	.70997	0.688	0.69091	0.605
Portugal	126.94	85.24	104.02	91.737	103.75	142.56
Spain	125.00	100.70	112.19	105.71	109.55	101.93
Turkey	2 032.4	1 078.6	1 480.6	1 176.29	1 492.05	2 608.64

Source: First three alternatives supplied by EUROSTAT; fourth column derived from OECD *Purchasing Power Parities and Real Expenditures: GK Results*, vol. 2, Paris 1993, pp. 32-3, rebased with the US dollar as the reference currency (in line with the practice in earlier ICP rounds); last column from OECD, *Purchasing Power Parities and Real Expenditures: EKS Results, 1990*, vol. 1, Paris, 1992, pp. 30-1 (rebased as in column 4). Exchange rates from OECD, *National Accounts 1960-1992*, vol. 1, Paris, 1994, p. 155.

Table C-7. **Ratio of Paasche, Laspeyres and Fisher PPPs and Exchange Rates to Geary-Khamis PPPs Round VI of ICP for 1990 for OECD Countries**

	Geary-Khamis	Paasche	Laspeyres	Fisher	Exchange Rate
Australia	1.00	.96	1.09	1.02	.92
Austria	1.00	.97	1.09	1.03	.81
Belgium	1.00	.93	1.11	1.01	.85
Canada	1.00	.96	1.04	1.00	.89
Denmark	1.00	.92	1.22	1.06	.66
Finland	1.00	.96	1.13	1.04	.60
France	1.00	.92	1.12	1.02	.82
Germany	1.00	.94	1.06	1.00	.77
Italy	1.00	.93	1.16	1.04	.84
Japan	1.00	.95	1.19	1.06	.74
Netherlands	1.00	.93	1.12	1.02	.84
New Zealand	1.00	.94	1.10	1.02	1.04
Norway	1.00	.96	1.17	1.06	.64
Sweden	1.00	.93	1.15	1.03	.63
Switzerland	1.00	.96	1.07	1.01	.63
UK	1.00	.95	1.13	1.03	.93
USA	1.00	1.00	1.00	1.00	1.00
Advanced Capitalist Average	1.00	.95	1.11	1.03	.80
Greece	1.00	.93	1.26	1.09	1.12
Ireland	1.00	.98	1.09	1.03	.88
Portugal	1.00	.93	1.38	1.13	1.37
Spain	1.00	.95	1.18	1.06	.93
Turkey	1.00	.92	1.73	1.26	1.75
South European Average	1.00	.94	1.33	1.11	1.21

Source: Derived from Table C-6.

Table C-8. **Alternative Estimates of the Level of Real GDP per Capita in OECD Countries in 1990 using Geary-Khamis PPP Converters from Successive ICP Rounds and those of Summers and Heston (1991 and 1993)**

(USA=100.00)

	ICP3	ICP4	ICP5	ICP6	Summers and Heston	
					(1991)	(1993)
Australia	n.a.	n.a.	70.09	75.08	72.71	79.66
Austria	70.79	72.73	66.61	76.80	63.71	71.74
Belgium	77.10	80.65	67.97	76.86	65.50	77.60
Canada	n.a.	100.14	92.06	89.63	87.46	95.93
Denmark	80.26	84.56	71.96	82.10	66.42	77.32
Finland	n.a.	81.94	72.04	75.93	69.45	78.76
France	80.53	82.95	72.15	81.30	68.40	77.33
Germany	82.02	83.53	72.61	85.45	69.25	84.00
Italy[a]	62.91	75.18	66.46	72.95	64.01	67.74
Japan	82.89	85.16	79.48	84.83	71.21	82.48
Netherlands	72.31	77.76	70.85	75.79	66.16	72.06
New Zealand	n.a.	n.a.	56.33	64.00	52.97	65.76
Norway	n.a.	97.73	80.71	77.26	81.43	74.02
Sweden	n.a.	n.a.	71.06	80.92	70.57	80.29
Switzerland	n.a.	n.a.	n.a.	99.06	89.74	96.86
UK	64.41	75.60	70.22	74.55	65.46	71.27
USA	100.00	100.00	100.00	100.00	100.00	100.00
Greece	n.a.	48.50	43.61	45.96	39.84	45.82
Ireland	49.67	58.45	49.71	50.87	39.24	50.41
Portugal	n.a.	41.92	41.89	48.87	36.66	41.24
Spain	56.22	58.67	51.75	55.66	43.14	54.02
Turkey	n.a.	n.a.	23.25	19.50	20.29	20.40

Note: a) Downward adjustment of 3 per cent for reasons explained in source notes for Italy in Appendix B.

Source: The Geary-Khamis PPP converters for 1975, 1980, 1985 and 1990 (see tables C-3 to C-6) were used to make a dollar conversion of the latest available estimate of GDP in national prices for these years. These estimates were updated in volume terms, and adjusted by the change in the GDP deflator for the numeraire country (the USA). They were divided by the population estimates for the relevant years and expressed as a per cent of US GDP per capita. The fifth column is derived from Summers and Heston (1991, pp. 351-4) estimates of GDP (population x per capita GDP) levels in 1988 at 1985 prices. The sixth column is from the Penn World Tables: 5.5 diskette, of 1993. The last two columns were updated to 1990 by the same procedure as above. The results in the second and third columns had "fixity" imposed on them for EC countries, whereas the results in the other columns were established without this constraint (hence, in these other columns, the interrelationship between levels in the 12 EC countries was not necessarily the same as was estimated by EUROSTAT). In 1994, the official estimates of 1990 GDP levels for Greece and Portugal were adjusted upwards: Greece by 25.2 per cent from 10 546 billion drachma to 13 204 billion; Portugal by 14.2 per cent from 8 507 434 million escudos to 9 711 614 million in line with EUROSTAT recommendations. The estimates in this table incorporate these Greek and Portuguese revisions.

Table C-9. **Alternative Estimates of the Level of Real GDP per Capita in non-OECD Countries in 1990 using Geary-Khamis PPP Converters from Successive ICP Rounds and from Summers and Heston (1993)**

(USA = 100.00)

	ICP3	ICP4	ICP5	ICP6	Summers and Heston (1993)	Maddison's Choice
Bulgaria	n.a.	n.a.	n.a.	n.a.	26.36	26.36
Czechoslovakia	n.a.	n.a.	n.a.	38.71	33.55	38.71
Hungary	42.86	36.11	29.92	29.03	29.08	29.03
Poland	31.41	27.81	19.89	23.38	20.71	23.38
Romania	22.62	n.a.	n.a.	15.82	18.41	15.82
USSR	n.a.	n.a.	n.a.	31.42	28.02	31.42
Yugoslavia	29.75	27.87	23.81	24.96	24.65	24.96
Argentina	n.a.	30.10	n.a.	n.a.	18.73	30.10
Brazil	22.88	22.01	n.a.	n.a.	14.36	22.01
Chile	n.a.	29.18	n.a.	n.a.	21.86	29.18
Colombia	21.99	22.49	n.a.	n.a.	17.09	22.49
Mexico	22.85	n.a.	n.a.	n.a.	28.90	22.85
Peru	n.a.	13.72	n.a.	n.a.	11.02	13.72
Venezuela	n.a.	37.22	n.a.	n.a.	29.79	37.22
Bangladesh	n.a.	n.a.	4.19	n.a.	6.39	3.19
Burma	n.a.	n.a.	n.a.	n.a.	3.14	3.14
China	n.a.	n.a.	n.a.	n.a.	12.35	12.35
India	7.70	6.02	4.98	n.a.	5.73	6.02
Indonesia	n.a.	11.55	n.a.	n.a.	10.22	11.55
Pakistan	8.30	8.93	8.19	n.a.	7.31	7.20
Philippines	10.09	10.52	10.10	n.a.	9.51	10.52
South Korea	44.83	41.05	36.77	n.a.	37.55	41.05
Taiwan	n.a.	n.a.	n.a.	n.a.	47.21	47.21
Thailand	22.64	n.a.	19.93	n.a.	19.08	19.08
Côte d'Ivoire	n.a.	6.16	7.12	n.a.	5.60	5.60
Egypt	n.a.	n.a.	14.75	n.a.	9.28	9.28
Ethiopia	n.a.	1.50	1.66	n.a.	1.60	1.60
Ghana	n.a.	n.a.	n.a.	n.a.	4.42	4.42
Kenya	5.65	4.98	6.19	n.a.	4.93	4.93
Morocco	n.a.	10.83	15.26	n.a.	10.97	10.97
Nigeria	n.a.	8.47	7.01	n.a.	5.11	5.11
South Africa	n.a.	n.a.	n.a.	n.a.	17.01	17.01
Tanzania	n.a.	2.65	2.66	n.a.	2.74	2.74
Zaire	n.a.	n.a.	n.a.	n.a.	2.09	2.09

Source: ICP3 (1975) PPPs derived from I.B. Kravis, A. Heston and R. Summers, *World Product and Income*, Baltimore 1982; ICP4 (1980) from U.N., *World Comparisons of Purchasing Power and Real Product for 1980*, New York, 1986; ICP5 for 1985 from UN, *World Comparisons of Real Gross Domestic Product and Purchasing Power 1985*, New York, 1994. These PPPs were applied to the latest estimates of nominal GDP in World Bank, *World Tables*, to derive real output. Per capita levels were established by using the population figures in Appendix A. Updating procedures are shown in the following tables. Preliminary ICP6 estimates of East European GDP levels relative to Austria were kindly supplied by Gyorgy Szilagyi, and I applied the coefficients to the Geary -Khamis estimate of Austrian GDP. Summers and Heston (1993) estimates of GDP were updated to 1990 in some cases, and for countries where I adopted their figures, I used my Appendix A population figures to establish the per capita estimates.

Table C-10. **Range of Variation (highest/lowest) Between per Capita GDP Levels Shown by Different ICP Rounds**

Non-OECD Countries		OECD Countries		
	All Rounds		All Rounds	Rounds 3 and 6 only
Hungary	1.48 (4)	Australia	1.07 (2)	n.a.
Poland	1.68 (4)	Austria	1.15 (4)	1.08 (2)
Romania	1.43 (2)	Belgium	1.19 (4)	1.00 (2)
Yugoslavia	1.25 (4)	Canada	1.12 (3)	n.a.
		Denmark	1.18 (4)	1.02 (2)
East European Average	1.46	Finland	1.08 (3)	n.a.
		France	1.15 (4)	1.01 (2)
		Germany	1.18 (4)	1.04 (2)
Brazil	1.04 (2)	Italy	1.20 (4)	1.16 (2)
Colombia	1.02 (2)	Japan	1.07 (4)	1.02 (2)
		Netherlands	1.10 (4)	1.05 (2)
Latin American Average	1.03	New Zealand	1.14 (2)	n.a.
		Norway	1.26 (3)	n.a.
		Sweden	1.14 (2)	n.a.
India	1.57 (3)	UK	1.17 (4)	1.16 (2)
Pakistan	1.09 (3)			
Philippines	1.04 (3)	Advanced Capitalist Average	1.15	1.06
South Korea	1.22 (3)			
Thailand	1.14 (2)			
		Greece	1.11 (3)	n.a.
Asian Average	1.21	Ireland	1.18 (4)	1.02 (2)
		Portugal	1.17 (3)	n.a.
Côte d'Ivoire	1.16 (2)	Spain	1.13 (4)	1.04 (2)
Ethiopia	1.11 (2)	Turkey	1.19 (2)	n.a.
Kenya	1.24 (3)			
Morocco	1.41 (2)	Southern Europe Average	1.16	
Nigeria	1.21 (2)			
Tanzania	1.00 (2)			
		20 OECD	1.15	
African Average	1.19			
		11 OECD		1.05
17 Non-OECD	1.24			

NB: Figures in brackets in first and second columns show the number of available published ICP rounds since ICP3. The third column shows the variance between ICP3 and ICP6 for OECD countries. The Geary-Khamis PPPs in these two rounds had a greater methodological similarity than those from ICP4 and 5 for OECD countries and the variance in results was smaller than in col. 2 (see source note to Table C-8).

Table C-11. **Ratio of Paasche, Laspeyres, and Fisher PPPs and Exchange Rate to Geary-Khamis PPP, Round IV of ICP for 1980 for Non-OECD Countries**

	Geary-Khamis	Paasche	Laspeyres	Fisher	Exchange Rate
Hungary	1.00	.98	.94	.96	2.42
Poland	1.00	1.02	1.03	1.03	1.92
Yugoslavia	1.00	.95	.90	.92	1.28
East European Average	1.00	.98	.96	.97	1.87
Argentina	1.00	.80	1.60	1.26	0.71
Brazil	1.00	.82	1.54	1.12	1.62
Chile	1.00	.88	1.67	1.21	1.46
Colombia	1.00	.89	1.44	1.13	2.15
Peru	1.00	.87	1.74	1.23	2.23
Venezuela	1.00	1.10	1.48	1.28	1.37
Latin American Average	1.00	.89	1.58	1.21	1.59
India	1.00	.71	1.68	1.09	2.33
Indonesia	1.00	.83	1.79	1.22	2.24
Pakistan	1.00	.91	1.70	1.24	3.16
Philippines	1.00	.87	1.55	1.16	2.36
South Korea	1.00	.88	1.68	1.22	1.58
Asian Average	1.00	.84	1.68	1.19	2.33
Côte d'Ivoire	1.00	1.00	1.86	1.36	1.07
Ethiopia	1.00	.54	2.15	1.08	2.07
Kenya	1.00	.73	1.60	1.08	1.51
Morocco	1.00	.89	1.91	1.30	1.37
Nigeria	1.00	.92	2.33	1.46	0.90
Tanzania	1.00	.90	1.51	1.17	1.42
African Average	1.00	.83	1.89	1.24	1.39

Source: Unpublished Paasche, Laspeyres and Fisher variants kindly supplied by Alan Heston.

Table C-12a. **East European ICP3 (1975) Results Updated to 1990**

	1975 GDP in million national currency units	1975 ICP PPP units of national currency per dollar	1975 GDP in million 1975 Geary-Khamis $	1990 GDP in million 1975 Geary-Khamis $	1990 GDP in million 1990 Geary-Khamis $
Hungary	482 700	12.3	39 244	43 003	98 906
Poland	1 752 268	14.3	122 536	121 065	278 449
Romania	437 000	8.8	49 659	49 887	114 739
Yugoslavia	581 937	11.2	51 959	67 341	154 884

Source: Col. 1 from World Bank, *World Tables*; col. 2 from ICP3; col. 3 is col. 1 ÷ col. 2; col. 4 is col. 3 adjusted for change in GDP volume 1975-90 (from Table 2c); col. 5 is col. 4 adjusted by change in US GDP deflator 1975-90.

Table C-12b. **East European ICP4 (1980) Results Updated to 1990**

	1980 GDP in million national currency units	1980 ICP PPP units of national currency per dollar	1980 GDP in million 1980 Geary-Khamis $	1990 GDP in million 1980 Geary-Khamis $	1990 GDP in million 1990 Geary-Khamis $
Hungary	721 000	13.55	53 210	52 770	83 312
Poland	2 482 452	16.14	153 807	146 808	231 780
Yugoslavia	1 800 000	19.42	92 688	91 907	145 102

Source: Method as in Table C-12a with adjustment from 1980 to 1990.

Table C-12c. **East European ICP5 (1985) Results Updated to 1990**

	1985 GDP in million national currency units	1985 ICP PPP units of national currency per dollar	1985 GDP in million 1985 Geary-Khamis $	1990 GDP in million 1985 Geary-Khamis $	1990 GDP in million 1990 Geary-Khamis $
Hungary	1 033 700	17.27	59 855	57 430	68 901
Poland	10 400 000	69.62	149 382	138 186	165 787
Yugoslavia	12 722 797	114.4	111 213	103 317	123 953

Source: Method as in Table C-12a with adjustment from 1985 to 1990.

Table C-13. **Latin American Results of ICP 4 for 1980 for 6 Countries, and ICP 3 for 1975 for Mexico, updated to 1990**

	GDP in million national currency units	ICP PPP units of national currency per dollar	Benchmark GDP in million benchmark Geary-Khamis $	1990 GDP in million benchmark Geary-Khamis $	1990 GDP in million 1990 Geary-Khamis $
Argentina	3 840	.02604	147 465	134 607	212 518
Brazil	12 805	.03252	393 773	458 266	723 510
Chile	1 075 269	26.67	40 318	53 229	84 038
Colombia	1 579 130	21.99	71 811	100 736	159 042
Mexico	967 252[a]	7.4[a]	130 709[a]	187 208[b]	430 550
Peru	5 970 000	129.6	46 065	41 157	64 979
Venezuela	297 800	3.14	94 841	101 753	160 648

a) 1975 (other countries' figures are for 1980); b) at 1975 prices (other countries are in 1980 prices).

Source: col. 1 from World Bank, *World Tables*, with adjustments indicated above for Brazil and Mexico. Otherwise as described in text.

Table C-14a. **Asian Results of ICP 3 for 1975 updated to 1990**

	1975 GDP in million national currency units[a]	ICP PPP[b] units of national currency per dollar	1975 GDP in 1975 Geary-Khamis $ (million)	1990 GDP[c] in 1975 Geary-Khamis $ (million)	1990 GDP[d] in 1990 Geary-Khamis $ (million)
India	787 600	2.59	304 093	620 907	1 428 085
Korea	10 224 000	190.0	53 811	182 388	419 492
Pakistan	112 270	3.18	35 305	88 657	203 911
Philippines	107 950	2.89	37 353	58 997	135 693
Thailand	303 300	7.6	39 908	120 107	276 246

Table C-14b. **Asian Results of ICP 4 for 1980 updated to 1990**

	1980 GDP in million national currency units[a]	ICP PPP[b] units of national currency per dollar	1980 GDP in 1980 Geary-Khamis $ (million)	1990 GDP[c] in 1980 Geary-Khamis $ (million)	1990 GDP[d] in 1990 Geary-Khamis $ (million)
India	1 360 100	3.37	403 591	706 866	1 115 999
Indonesia	48 914 000	280.0	174 693	286 805	452 807
Korea	380 410 000	384.0	99 065	243 333	384 174
Pakistan	234 530	3.13	74 930	138 957	219 385
Philippines	243 750	3.18	76 651	89 551	141 383

a) Estimates from World Bank, *World Tables 1993*, which involve revisions from the original figures used by ICP.
b) Geary-Khamis converter.
c) Col. 3 adjusted for volume increase shown in Appendix B.
d) Col. 4 multiplied by US GDP deflator 1980-90.

Table C-14c. **Asian Results of ICP 5 for 1985 updated to 1990**

	1985 GDP in million national currency units	ICP PPP units of national currency per dollar	1985 GDP in 1985 Geary-Khamis $ (million)	1990 GDP in 1985 Geary-Khamis $ million	1990 GDP in 1990 Geary-Khamis $ (million)
Bangladesh	406 930	6.075	66 884	81 455	97 724
India	2 662 500	4.667	570 495	769 290	922 944
Korea	80 847 000	459.5	175 946	286 760	344 036
Pakistan	472 160	3.761	125 541	167 766	201 275
Philippines	571 880	6.297	90 818	113 221	135 836
Thailand	1 014 400	8.094	125 327	202 652	243 128

Source: Col. 1 from World Bank, *World Tables 1994*, Washington, D.C., 1993; col. 2 PPPs from UN, *World Comparisons of Real Gross Domestic Product and Purchasing Power 1985*, New York, 1994.

Table C-15a. **African Results of ICP4 for 1980 updated to 1990**

	GDP 1980 in million national currency units	1980 ICP4 Geary-Khamis PPP: units of national currency per dollar	1980 GDP in 1980 Geary-Khamis $ (million)	1990 GDP in 1980 Geary-Khamis $ (million)	1990 GDP in 1990 Geary-Khamis $ (million)
Côte d'Ivoire	2 149 900	197.2	10 902	10 151	16 027
Ethiopia	8 505	1.002	8 488	10 590	16 721
Kenya	53 910	4.918	10 962	16 668	26 316
Morocco	74 090	2.866	25 851	37 631	59 444
Nigeria	50 900	.605	84 132	101 249	159 853
Tanzania	42 120	5.778	7 290	4 003	14 214

Table C-15b. **African Results of ICP5 for 1985 updated to 1990**

	GDP 1985 million national currency units	1985 ICP5 Geary Khamis PPP: units of national currency per dollar	1985 GDP in 1985 Geary-Khamis $ (million)	1990 GDP in 1985 Geary-Khamis $ (million)	1990 GDP in 1990 Geary-Khamis $ (million)
Côte d'Ivoire	3 136 800	187.1	16 765	15 439	18 523
Egypt	33 130	0.2828	117 150	139 995	167 956
Ethiopia	9 890	0.7562	13 079	15 536	18 639
Kenya	100 750	4.859	20 735	27 220	32 657
Morocco	129 510	2.300	56 309	69 762	83 696
Nigeria	72 360	0.8603	84 110	110 266	132 290
Tanzania	120 600	12.31	9 797	11 865	14 234

Table C-16a. **Levels of GDP in 17 Advanced Capitalist Countries, 1820-1994**

(million 1990 Geary-Khamis Dollars)

	Australia	Austria	Belgium	Canada	Denmark	Finland	France	Germany	Italy
1820	50	4 131	4 433	662	1 415	887	38 071	16 393	22 042
1850	1 194	6 563	8 042	3 110	2 549		60 685	29 449	
1870	6 157	8 475	13 456	6 054	3 638	1 942	71 419	44 101	40 900
1871	5 918	9 089	13 488	6 319	3 649	1 955	70 990	43 811	41 348
1872	6 555	9 159	14 311	6 253	3 851	2 023	77 574	46 857	40 737
1873	7 245	8 947	14 406	6 881	3 828	2 141	72 135	48 888	42 328
1874	7 484	9 348	14 881	7 047	3 941	2 190	81 295	52 515	42 187
1875	8 307	9 395	14 849	6 881	4 008	2 234	84 014	52 805	43 395
1876	8 280	9 608	15 039	6 418	4 087	2 358	77 144	52 515	42 481
1877	8 625	9 938	15 229	6 848	3 974	2 302	81 295	52 225	42 460
1878	9 448	10 269	15 672	6 583	4 132	2 259	80 293	54 691	43 087
1879	9 581	10 198	15 831	7 212	4 266	2 283	75 284	53 385	43 587
1880	10 085	10 340	16 622	7 543	4 367	2 296	82 011	52 950	45 669
1881	10 828	10 765	16 844	8 602	4 412	2 234	85 159	54 256	42 589
1882	10 218	10 835	17 414	8 999	4 569	2 451	89 167	55 126	46 319
1883	11 731	11 284	17 667	9 032	4 727	2 544	89 453	58 172	46 185
1884	11 784	11 591	17 825	9 759	4 749	2 563	88 451	59 623	46 516
1885	12 553	11 520	18 047	9 164	4 783	2 625	86 877	61 074	47 481
1886	12 712	11 898	18 268	9 263	4 974	2 755	88 308	61 509	49 587
1887	14 066	12 724	18 965	9 561	5 153	2 798	88 881	63 975	50 951
1888	14 146	12 700	19 092	10 256	5 187	2 904	89 739	66 586	50 785
1889	15 366	12 582	20 010	10 322	5 254	3 003	92 029	68 472	48 599
1890	14 836	13 267	20 453	11 083	5 569	3 171	94 176	70 648	51 707
1891	15 977	13 739	20 485	11 347	5 681	3 140	96 323	70 503	51 497
1892	14 013	14 046	20 991	11 281	5 816	3 047	98 756	73 405	48 602
1893	13 243	14 140	21 308	11 215	5 928	3 165	100 474	77 031	50 831
1894	13 694	14 967	21 625	11 744	6 051	3 413	104 195	78 917	50 114
1895	12 925	15 368	22 131	11 612	6 388	3 599	102 048	82 689	50 889
1896	13 907	15 604	22 574	11 314	6 624	3 835	106 914	85 590	52 287
1897	13 137	15 934	22 986	12 538	6 781	4 021	105 483	88 056	49 974
1898	15 181	16 831	23 366	13 035	6 893	4 195	110 636	91 828	54 429
1899	15 181	17 186	23 841	14 259	7 185	4 095	116 933	95 165	55 699
1900	16 083	17 327	24 537	15 053	7 432	4 288	115 645	99 227	58 799
1901	15 605	17 398	24 759	16 244	7 747	4 238	113 784	96 906	62 616
1902	15 765	18 083	25 266	17 832	7 926	4 151	111 924	99 227	60 870
1903	17 012	18 248	25 835	18 361	8 398	4 430	114 357	104 739	63 770
1904	18 153	18 531	26 500	18 626	8 578	4 598	115 216	108 946	64 366
1905	18 365	19 570	27 260	20 809	8 723	4 672	117 219	111 267	67 958
1906	19 613	20 325	27 830	22 893	8 970	4 858	119 366	114 604	70 511
1907	20 409	21 576	28 242	24 217	9 307	5 026	124 519	119 681	78 460
1908	21 099	21 671	28 527	23 059	9 599	5 082	123 803	121 712	80 353
1909	22 824	21 600	29 065	25 507	9 970	5 305	128 956	124 178	86 558
1910	24 416	21 907	29 825	27 690	10 273	5 423	121 084	128 676	83 420
1911	24 602	22 591	30 521	29 576	10 823	5 578	132 963	133 028	88 852
1912	25 186	23 725	31 250	31 528	10 823	5 888	143 984	138 830	89 571
1913	26 540	23 607	31 661	33 083	11 227	6 205	143 125	145 068	93 399
1914	24 496	19 701	29 657	30 866	11 934	5 932	132 963	123 598	93 326
1915	23 063	18 275	29 300	32 851	11 104	5 634	130 244	117 360	104 396
1916	24 682	18 052	31 001	36 159	11 575	5 709	136 827	118 521	117 128
1917	25 239	17 664	26 622	37 648	10 890	4 796	115 931	118 666	122 641
1918	25 372	17 300	21 453	35 233	10 531	4 157	91 457	118 956	124 466
1919	25 133	14 599	25 306	32 553	11 890	5 020	107 773	104 884	103 662
1920	27 044	15 675	29 287	32 190	12 451	5 615	124 662	114 024	94 641
1921	29 698	17 351	29 793	28 716	12 092	5 802	119 509	126 935	93 203
1922	29 910	18 909	32 706	32 917	13 315	6 416	140 978	138 105	98 019
1923	30 521	18 720	33 877	34 869	14 719	6 887	148 277	114 749	103 942
1924	32 856	20 892	34 986	35 399	14 764	7 067	166 884	134 333	104 965
1925	33 944	22 308	35 524	39 269	14 427	7 471	167 599	149 420	111 895
1926	33 520	22 686	36 727	41 387	15 269	7 756	172 036	143 327	113 067
1927	33 440	23 370	38 088	45 489	15 572	8 364	168 458	170 020	110 621
1928	32 909	24 456	40 083	49 525	16 100	8 929	180 194	173 937	118 532
1929	32 591	24 810	39 735	49 459	17 177	9 034	192 360	175 968	122 443
1930	30 998	24 126	39 355	47 805	18 199	8 929	186 778	165 233	116 411
1931	29 592	22 190	38 658	40 427	18 401	8 712	175 614	148 405	115 735
1932	30 706	19 900	36 917	37 549	17 918	8 674	164 164	134 623	119 469

Table C-16a (cont. 2)

	Australia	Austria	Belgium	Canada	Denmark	Finland	France	Germany	Italy
1933	32 458	19 239	37 708	34 869	18 491	9 252	175 900	148 695	118 664
1934	33 705	19 405	37 392	38 575	19 052	10 300	174 183	160 155	119 162
1935	35 085	19 782	39 703	41 684	19 479	10 741	169 746	174 662	130 638
1936	36 757	20 372	39 988	43 934	19 962	11 467	176 187	192 941	130 866
1937	38 854	21 458	40 526	48 069	20 445	12 118	186 349	204 546	139 828
1938	39 146	24 197	39 608	49 326	20 939	12 745	185 633	220 359	140 833
1939	39 252	27 431	42 299	52 271	21 938	12 199	198 944	241 103	151 092
1940	41 826	26 723	37 265	59 450	18 862	11 566	164 164	242 844	152 025
1941	46 497	28 635	35 302	67 754	16 998	11 944	129 814	258 221	150 159
1942	51 858	27 195	32 263	79 763	17 380	11 982	116 361	261 703	148 294
1943	53 690	27 856	31 515	83 369	19 299	13 359	110 492	266 926	134 304
1944	51 832	28 564	33 371	86 511	21 320	13 365	93 317	273 744	109 122
1945	49 231	11 803	35 365	83 832	19 715	12 590	101 189	194 682	85 432
1946	47 479	13 786	37 455	82 972	22 791	13 614	153 859	115 619	111 920
1947	48 647	15 203	39 703	86 644	24 071	13 930	166 740	129 836	131 506
1948	51 779	19 357	42 078	88 232	24 722	15 035	178 906	153 772	138 967
1949	55 202	23 016	43 787	90 151	26 429	15 947	203 237	179 159	149 227
1950	59 024	25 873	46 194	96 800	28 528	16 561	218 409	213 976	161 351
1951	61 545	27 643	48 821	102 292	28 719	17 969	231 862	235 011	173 476
1952	62 103	27 667	48 442	109 736	29 000	18 571	238 017	256 626	186 421
1953	64 040	28 871	49 993	114 863	30 650	18 702	244 887	279 256	199 899
1954	68 021	31 822	52 051	114 069	31 245	20 340	256 766	300 726	210 270
1955	71 737	35 339	54 520	124 722	31 582	21 376	271 508	336 848	222 475
1956	74 205	37 770	56 104	134 812	31 964	22 021	285 248	362 526	232 562
1957	75 691	40 084	57 148	138 716	34 389	23 057	302 423	383 851	246 325
1958	79 327	41 548	57 085	141 197	35 163	23 182	310 008	400 533	259 449
1959	84 210	42 728	58 890	146 921	37 779	24 559	318 882	431 723	275 630
1960	87 740	46 245	62 056	151 486	38 835	26 805	341 353	469 151	290 574
1961	87 422	48 700	65 159	156 283	41 305	28 853	360 102	490 331	315 053
1962	92 995	49 881	68 546	167 399	43 651	29 703	384 147	512 816	339 591
1963	99 099	51 911	71 522	176 033	43 932	30 677	404 757	527 033	363 813
1964	105 362	55 027	76 493	187 778	48 007	32 284	431 092	562 139	377 977
1965	111 201	56 609	79 216	200 184	50 196	33 997	451 702	592 314	386 481
1966	114 359	59 795	81 717	213 814	51 566	34 803	475 318	609 142	406 657
1967	122 268	61 613	84 883	220 497	53 329	35 560	497 502	607 256	435 584
1968	129 434	64 351	88 461	231 844	55 451	36 379	518 685	640 912	472 048
1969	137 263	68 388	94 350	244 250	58 954	39 867	555 038	688 639	498 996
1970	145 543	73 275	100 334	250 734	60 155	42 845	586 812	723 745	510 200
1971	154 169	77 005	104 007	265 192	61 760	43 745	614 721	745 506	518 457
1972	160 114	81 797	109 516	280 277	65 016	47 083	639 768	777 276	532 466
1973	168 606	85 786	115 975	301 880	67 374	50 241	674 404	815 138	570 200
1974	171 260	89 186	120 724	315 080	66 745	51 761	692 724	817 314	601 208
1975	176 037	88 855	118 919	323 252	66 307	52 295	690 434	805 854	585 330
1976	182 593	92 915	125 568	343 102	70 596	52 500	720 920	848 939	623 810
1977	184 397	97 141	126 170	355 375	71 741	52 556	746 396	873 021	644 825
1978	189 865	97 188	129 621	371 652	72 808	53 704	771 586	899 278	668 514
1979	198 437	101 815	132 375	386 142	75 379	57 606	796 061	936 125	708 617
1980	202 869	104 790	138 074	391 866	75 053	60 672	807 081	946 280	738 598
1981	210 247	104 483	136 713	406 323	74 380	61 633	816 814	947 151	742 707
1982	209 106	105 592	138 771	393 255	76 625	63 842	835 563	938 301	744 295
1983	211 441	107 693	139 404	405 827	78 556	65 735	842 147	954 839	751 487
1984	226 808	109 157	142 412	431 697	82 003	67 751	854 599	981 677	771 661
1985	236 946	111 848	143 583	452 109	85 528	70 010	870 199	1 001 551	791 741
1986	244 430	113 170	145 673	466 864	88 638	71 481	891 095	1 025 052	814 904
1987	253 666	115 058	148 649	486 218	88 896	74 329	910 417	1 040 284	840 402
1988	266 193	119 732	156 058	510 368	89 940	78 337	949 204	1 079 018	874 586
1989	276 437	124 312	161 978	522 476	90 446	82 780	984 985	1 118 041	900 271
1990	279 834	129 600	167 519	521 517	92 298	82 786	1 008 601	1 181 871	919 511
1991	280 206	133 094	170 685	512 518	93 432	76 941	1 012 895	1 235 546	930 999
1992	284 611	135 289	172 078	516 356	94 577	73 845	1 030 356	1 254 840	939 685
1993	295 439	134 888	169 165	527 703	95 902	72 368	1 020 051	1 241 059	933 147
1994	308 125	138 382	173 028	549 340	100 404	74 900	1 042 522	1 275 730	953 602

Table C-16a (cont. 3)

	Japan	Netherlands	New Zealand	Norway	Sweden	Switzerland	UK	USA
1820	21 831	3 677		974	3 098		34 829	12 432
1850		5 844		1 503	4 490		60 479	42 475
1870	25 505	9 545	906	2 260	6 927	5 787	95 651	98 418
1871		9 691	970	2 293	7 049		100 798	103 080
1872		9 886	1 133	2 438	7 379		101 013	107 224
1873		9 667	1 290	2 488	8 058		103 372	112 404
1874		10 178	1 418	2 572	8 371		105 087	111 886
1875		10 811	1 505	2 650	8 006		107 661	117 584
1876		10 714	1 580	2 727	8 528		108 733	119 138
1877		11 566	1 801	2 739	8 250		109 806	122 764
1878		12 394	2 005	2 655	8 197		110 235	127 944
1879		11 469	1 772	2 688	8 058		109 806	144 001
1880		12 613	1 958	2 772	8 441		114 953	161 095
1881		12 321	2 039	2 794	8 458		119 028	166 793
1882		12 516	2 034	2 783	8 807		122 459	177 153
1883		14 439	2 016	2 772	8 894		123 317	181 297
1884		14 147	2 225	2 828	9 137		123 531	184 922
1885	31 433	14 585	2 214	2 861	9 102		122 888	185 958
1886	34 122	14 780	2 266	2 878	9 068		124 818	191 656
1887	35 500	15 097	2 318	2 911	9 102		129 751	200 462
1888	33 984	14 244	2 318	3 039	9 346		135 541	199 426
1889	35 776	15 437	2 440	3 145	9 833		142 833	211 858
1890	39 016	14 147	2 510	3 228	9 973		143 477	214 966
1891	37 155	14 853	2 527	3 256	10 094		143 477	224 290
1892	39 636	15 900	2 620	3 329	10 303		140 045	246 045
1893	39 774	14 488	2 684	3 418	10 321		140 045	234 132
1894	44 530	16 119	2 597	3 429	10 530		149 482	227 398
1895	45 151	16 338	2 690	3 462	11 052		154 200	254 851
1896	42 669	16 801	2 998	3 568	11 696		160 634	249 671
1897	43 565	18 457	3 033	3 746	12 113		162 778	273 499
1898	51 837	18 505	3 120	3 757	12 374		170 714	279 197
1899	47 977	18 798	3 225	3 863	12 653	11 299	177 791	304 578
1900	50 045	18 165	3 486	3 930	13 105	11 653	176 504	312 866
1901	51 837	17 751	3 498	4 035	12 966	12 007	176 504	348 089
1902	49 149	18 652	3 765	4 119	12 949	12 361	181 008	351 715
1903	52 596	19 163	4 119	4 102	13 906	12 715	179 078	368 809
1904	53 009	18 992	4 102	4 097	14 045	13 069	180 150	364 147
1905	52 113	19 626	4 480	4 147	14 202	13 424	185 512	391 082
1906	58 937	20 575	4 904	4 297	15 124	13 778	191 731	436 148
1907	60 799	20 648	5 200	4 459	15 455	14 132	195 377	442 881
1908	61 212	20 624	4 840	4 603	15 420	14 486	187 442	406 622
1909	61 143	21 549	4 910	4 726	15 316	14 840	191 731	456 349
1910	62 108	21 744	5 584	4 893	16 238	15 194	197 736	461 011
1911	65 486	22 377	5 892	5 043	16 638	15 549	203 527	476 033
1912	67 830	23 619	5 717	5 271	17 108	15 903	206 529	498 306
1913	68 933	24 349	5 810	5 566	17 404	16 257	214 464	517 990
1914	66 865	23 692	5 961	5 689	17 248	16 270	216 609	478 105
1915	73 069	24 495	5 990	5 934	17 248	16 430	233 981	491 573
1916	84 373	25 153	5 944	6 123	17 021	16 378	239 128	559 429
1917	87 200	23 546	5 799	5 566	14 933	14 587	241 272	545 444
1918	88 096	22 085	5 706	5 360	14 707	14 535	242 774	594 653
1919	97 126	27 369	6 345	6 268	15 559	15 491	216 394	599 832
1920	91 060	28 197	7 036	6 663	16 464	16 496	203 312	594 135
1921	101 055	29 925	6 571	6 112	15 855	16 087	186 798	580 667
1922	100 779	31 557	6 345	6 824	17 352	17 645	196 449	612 782
1923	100 848	32 336	6 856	6 974	18 274	18 666	202 669	693 589
1924	103 675	34 698	6 978	6 941	18 849	19 362	211 033	714 826
1925	107 948	36 159	7 350	7 370	19 545	20 776	221 327	731 402
1926	108 913	39 056	6 961	7 531	20 641	21 817	213 177	779 057
1927	110 499	40 688	6 763	7 820	21 285	22 987	230 335	786 827
1928	119 529	42 855	7 513	8 077	22 295	24 272	233 123	795 633
1929	123 251	43 196	7 780	8 828	23 652	25 117	239 985	844 324
1930	114 290	43 098	7 443	9 479	24 140	24 954	238 270	769 215
1931	115 255	40 469	6 810	8 744	23 269	23 914	226 045	710 164
1932	124 906	39 909	6 641	9 329	22 643	23 101	227 761	616 408

Table C-16a (cont. 4)

	Japan	Netherlands	New Zealand	Norway	Sweden	Switzerland	UK	USA
1933	137 176	39 835	7 083	9 552	23 078	24 255	234 409	603 458
1934	137 452	39 105	7 437	9 858	24 836	24 304	249 851	650 078
1935	141 243	40 566	7 786	10 281	26 420	24 207	259 502	699 805
1936	151 514	43 123	9 232	10 910	27 951	24 288	271 297	799 259
1937	158 752	45 582	9 732	11 299	29 274	25 442	280 734	833 446
1938	169 367	44 486	10 418	11 583	29 761	26 418	284 165	800 295
1939	196 044	47 506	10 563	12 134	31 815	26 385	286 953	864 007
1940	201 766	41 856	10 360	11 054	30 875	26 661	315 691	930 828
1941	204 523	39 641	10 034	11 322	31 397	26 483	344 430	1 100 211
1942	203 420	36 232	11 138	10 882	33 312	25 816	353 008	1 320 357
1943	206 315	35 355	11 371	10 665	34 791	25 588	360 729	1 582 978
1944	197 423	23 716	11 417	10 108	35 974	26 206	346 574	1 715 583
1945	98 711	24 276	11 754	11 327	36 949	33 733	331 347	1 646 690
1946	107 259	40 980	12 661	12 541	41 004	36 042	316 978	1 306 889
1947	115 807	47 432	14 171	13 977	42 014	40 382	312 260	1 287 205
1948	133 040	52 497	12 765	15 090	43 319	41 195	322 125	1 335 896
1949	141 932	57 124	14 142	15 385	44 903	40 073	334 135	1 341 076
1950	156 546	59 169	16 216	16 225	47 270	41 959	344 859	1 457 624
1951	176 054	60 411	14 979	16 977	49 149	45 355	355 153	1 601 107
1952	196 458	61 628	15 630	17 584	49 846	45 739	354 509	1 669 482
1953	210 934	66 985	16 164	18 396	51 238	47 346	368 450	1 731 641
1954	222 859	71 538	18 389	19 309	53 396	50 011	383 462	1 719 727
1955	242 022	76 846	18 732	19 682	54 945	53 371	397 402	1 816 591
1956	260 220	79 671	19 703	20 712	57 033	56 913	402 335	1 852 850
1957	279 246	81 911	20 266	21 313	59 592	59 177	408 769	1 888 592
1958	295 514	81 668	21 062	21 118	59 888	57 918	407 911	1 879 268
1959	322 466	85 661	22 561	22 203	61 715	61 569	424 425	1 981 830
1960	364 791	92 868	22 561	23 478	64 987	65 879	448 874	2 022 233
1961	408 701	93 136	23 851	24 953	68 712	71 210	463 672	2 072 996
1962	445 166	99 516	24 769	25 655	71 601	74 625	468 390	2 200 422
1963	482 873	103 119	25 879	26 623	75 412	78 276	486 405	2 296 768
1964	539 259	111 666	27 215	27 959	80 564	82 385	512 141	2 434 553
1965	570 624	117 510	28 894	29 434	83 644	85 014	525 437	2 587 360
1966	631 353	120 748	30 701	30 553	85 385	87 095	535 517	2 755 189
1967	701 320	127 103	29 289	32 462	88 274	89 761	547 527	2 826 672
1968	791 621	135 260	29 278	33 197	91 476	92 975	569 832	2 954 097
1969	890 402	143 978	32 258	34 688	96 054	98 215	581 627	3 045 781
1970	985 736	152 159	31 805	35 384	102 284	104 478	594 924	3 045 781
1971	1 027 784	158 587	33 450	37 004	103 241	108 732	606 719	3 147 826
1972	1 112 296	163 847	34 885	38 913	105 608	112 220	627 737	3 326 014
1973	1 197 152	171 517	37 360	40 516	109 803	115 634	674 061	3 519 224
1974	1 189 707	178 334	39 591	42 620	113 301	117 332	662 695	3 499 023
1975	1 223 760	178 164	39 132	44 396	116 208	108 020	657 762	3 468 461
1976	1 275 321	187 271	40 085	47 418	117 426	107 253	675 777	3 657 010
1977	1 335 430	191 629	38 133	49 116	115 564	109 864	691 433	3 845 558
1978	1 400 434	196 329	38 290	51 348	117 583	110 303	715 667	4 043 948
1979	1 477 914	200 979	39 068	53 947	122 090	113 051	735 827	4 161 014
1980	1 531 612	202 708	39 335	56 218	124 126	118 253	719 528	4 161 014
1981	1 586 414	201 296	41 247	56 714	124 109	119 960	710 306	4 273 418
1982	1 636 597	198 447	41 985	56 903	125 362	118 855	722 530	4 191 575
1983	1 680 782	201 247	43 124	59 536	127 555	120 041	749 767	4 354 742
1984	1 752 541	207 602	45 256	62 959	132 724	122 171	768 425	4 644 817
1985	1 839 879	213 081	45 669	66 277	138 763	126 690	795 233	4 797 624
1986	1 888 201	218 925	46 836	69 048	138 380	130 332	829 548	4 935 409
1987	1 965 750	221 506	47 185	70 423	142 732	132 966	869 009	5 093 396
1988	2 087 760	227 301	46 656	70 067	145 951	136 835	912 331	5 286 606
1989	2 186 196	237 942	47 249	70 485	149 415	142 118	932 276	5 419 212
1990	2 291 456	247 730	47 063	71 659	151 451	145 386	935 922	5 464 795
1991	2 384 170	252 941	46 296	72 789	149 763	145 337	914 690	5 399 010
1992	2 415 190	256 471	47 615	75 188	146 891	145 256	910 401	5 510 378
1993	2 417 603	257 494	49 712	76 841	143 811	143 955	928 630	5 681 315
1994	2 441 798	263 947	52 193	79 608	147 117	146 394	961 014	5 903 015

Table C-16b. **Levels of GDP in 5 South European Countries, 1820-1994**

(million 1990 Geary-Khamis Dollars)

	Greece	Ireland	Portugal	Spain	Turkey
1820		4 808		12 975	
1850			4 193	16 949	
1870		6 836	4 722	22 295	
1890		7 470	6 257	32 802	
1900		7 935	7 671	37 873	
1901				40 112	
1902				38 513	
1903				39 427	
1904				38 604	
1905				38 330	
1906				40 432	
1907				40 843	
1908				41 894	
1909				42 899	
1910				41 620	
1911				44 452	
1912				43 812	
1913	8 795	8 450	8 127	45 686	12 728
1914				43 950	
1915				44 543	
1916				46 234	
1917				45 457	
1918				45 411	
1919				46 097	
1920				49 021	
1921				50 848	
1922				52 538	
1923				53 955	7 790
1924				56 330	9 317
1925				59 894	10 374
1926		7 799		59 848	12 041
1927				64 736	10 946
1928				64 508	12 130
1929	14 970	8 467	10 337	68 391	14 065
1930	14 609			65 696	14 701
1931	14 002	8 898		64 234	15 580
1932	15 190			66 244	14 638
1933	16 078	8 467		65 011	16 560
1934	16 474			68 117	16 942
1935	17 160			68 620	17 285
1936	17 222	9 244		54 868	20 569
1937	19 667	8 898		51 168	21 256
1938	19 253	9 151	12 929	51 122	23 133
1939	19 227			54 274	25 049
1940				58 934	23 535
1941				58 934	21 409
1942	11 804			62 269	22 338
1943				63 868	20 276
1944				66 701	19 411
1945	6 992			61 995	16 789
1946	10 475			65 422	21 689

Table C-16b (cont. 2)

	Greece	Ireland	Portugal	Spain	Turkey
1947	13 519	9 388	16 643	66 335	22 911
1948	14 196	9 844	17 033	65 011	26 017
1949	14 952	10 360	17 342	65 239	24 706
1950	14 758	10 444	18 146	66 792	27 024
1951	16 056	10 706	18 959	73 874	30 483
1952	16 174	10 977	18 984	79 676	34 132
1953	18 388	11 272	20 308	80 589	37 942
1954	18 963	11 374	21 283	85 204	36 861
1955	20 395	11 669	22 161	89 635	39 834
1956	22 136	11 517	23 128	96 077	41 131
1957	23 583	11 500	24 152	100 188	44 401
1958	24 675	11 264	24 469	104 666	46 428
1959	25 575	11 720	25 794	102 701	48 563
1960	26 682	12 379	27 516	105 123	49 995
1961	29 028	12 971	29 020	117 549	50 833
1962	30 120	13 368	30 946	128 514	53 940
1963	33 175	13 968	32 782	139 752	59 021
1964	35 905	14 644	34 944	148 387	61 453
1965	33 381	14 897	37 544	162 823	63 075
1966	41 675	15 049	39 072	179 727	70 452
1967	43 963	15 793	42 022	191 468	73 614
1968	46 885	16 951	45 760	208 144	78 559
1969	51 533	17 855	46 727	231 535	82 721
1970	55 636	18 438	50 978	246 976	86 775
1971	59 591	19 274	54 358	259 814	94 639
1972	64 963	20 491	58 714	281 560	100 854
1973	69 641	21 581	65 313	304 220	105 313
1974	67 102	22 333	66 052	321 809	114 285
1975	71 161	22 612	63 200	325 007	124 446
1976	75 691	23 128	67 531	335 698	135 283
1977	78 289	24 750	71 294	346 571	141 120
1978	83 380	26 584	73 325	352 190	145 147
1979	86 612	27 488	77 454	352 099	143 877
1980	88 117	28 079	81 013	356 622	142 796
1981	88 176	28 857	82 338	355 754	149 011
1982	88 516	29 237	84 085	360 094	156 470
1983	88 870	29 296	83 955	366 581	162 253
1984	91 319	30 344	82 370	373 160	171 550
1985	94 168	31 096	84 670	381 794	180 306
1986	95 702	31 071	88 173	394 312	192 953
1987	95 264	32 431	92 829	415 556	209 762
1988	99 494	33 893	96 462	436 937	217 923
1989	103 013	36 098	101 427	456 993	220 430
1990	101 922	38 963	105 864	474 125	240 745
1991	105 255	39 707	108 123	484 313	245 455
1992	106 232	41 540	109 293	488 470	259 914
1993	105 704	43 205	108 091	483 582	275 252
1994	106 760	45 360	109 171	491 805	264 509

Table C-16c. **Levels of GDP in 7 East European Countries, 1820-1992**

(million 1990 Geary-Khamis Dollars)

	Bulgaria	Czechoslovakia	Hungary	Poland	Romania	USSR	Yugoslavia
1820		6 106				37 873	
1850		9 298					
1870		11 491	7 253			83 646	
1890		17 042				100 376	
1900		20 955	11 990			154 049	
1913	7 181	27 755	16 447			232 351	13 988
1920		25 091	13 585				13 093
1921		27 117					13 415
1922		26 395					13 807
1923		28 588					14 492
1924	4 976	31 558	15 740				15 457
1925	5 156	35 277	18 914				16 213
1926	6 671	35 138	18 125		16 850		17 262
1927	7 274	37 775	18 914		16 850		17 094
1928	7 160	41 106	20 576		16 850	231 886	18 479
1929	7 023	42 240	21 250	58 980	16 079	238 392	19 402
1930	7 741	40 856	20 789	56 247	17 235	252 333	19 094
1931	8 876	39 468	19 786	52 177	17 640	257 213	18 605
1932	8 933	37 886	19 260	48 107	16 657	254 424	17 094
1933	9 084	36 276	21 003	46 771	17 447	264 880	17 556
1934	8 308	34 889	21 135	47 439	17 640	290 903	18 143
1935	7 928	34 556	22 204	48 107	18 026	334 818	17 919
1936	9 659	37 387	23 684	49 504	18 218	361 306	20 018
1937	10 204	41 578	23 158	58 980	17 447	398 017	20 367
1938	10 470		24 342	67 788	19 375	405 220	21 878
1939	10 599		26 184			430 314	23 025
1940	10 319		24 391			420 091	
1941	10 520		24 539				
1942	10 018		25 773				
1943	10 334						
1944	9 551						
1945	7 447					333 656	
1946			15 559			332 727	
1947			16 102			369 903	20 647
1948		38 108	20 148		12 975	420 555	24 284
1949		40 218	21 776			465 631	26 634
1950	11 971	43 368	23 158	60 742	19 279	510 243	25 277
1951	14 434	44 159	25 395	63 414		512 566	26 284
1952	13 773	45 630	26 250	64 872		545 792	24 200
1953	15 317	45 436	26 727	68 638		569 260	27 823
1954	15 030	47 295	27 664	72 526		596 910	29 362
1955	16 107	51 348	30 164	76 049	27 337	648 027	31 208
1956	16 121	54 373	28 799	79 450		710 065	30 495
1957	17 831	57 704	31 184	83 641		724 470	35 573

Table C-16c (cont. 2)

	Bulgaria	Czechoslovakia	Hungary	Poland	Romania	USSR	Yugoslavia
1958	19 382	62 117	33 273	87 711		778 840	37 014
1959	20 926	64 837	34 622	90 262		770 244	41 574
1960	22 908	69 749	36 431	95 121	33 931	843 434	44 190
1961	24 401	72 525	38 273	102 714	36 225	891 763	46 190
1962	26 405	73 496	39 868	101 317	37 497	915 928	47 057
1963	27 611	72 109	42 056	107 391	40 196	895 016	51 967
1964	29 787	75 495	44 424	112 190	42 741	1 010 727	56 919
1965	31 575	78 270	44 770	118 386	45 402	1 068 117	58 458
1966	34 067	81 657	47 319	125 857	50 588	1 119 932	61 605
1967	35 898	85 154	50 033	130 412	52 901	1 169 422	62 668
1968	36 559	89 123	50 641	138 309	54 019	1 237 966	63 983
1969	38 340	90 760	52 155	136 912	56 506	1 255 392	71 131
1970	40 523	92 592	51 974	144 018	57 779	1 351 818	74 489
1971	41 844	95 756	54 293	154 284	65 934	1 387 832	83 078
1972	43 826	99 142	55 460	165 521	70 175	1 395 732	85 945
1973	45 557	102 445	58 339	177 973	72 411	1 513 070	88 813
1974	46 986	106 165	59 852	188 421	76 479	1 556 984	100 269
1975	50 849	109 301	61 135	197 289	79 911	1 561 399	100 269
1976	52 371	111 050	61 316	202 209	83 998	1 634 589	103 375
1977	51 869	116 073	65 164	205 975	85 906	1 673 159	110 901
1978	52 989	117 489	66 743	213 446	88 702	1 715 215	117 014
1979	55 028	118 488	66 875	209 498	91 266	1 707 083	125 043
1980	53 449	121 763	67 549	204 213	91 517	1 709 174	131 058
1981	54 870	121 153	68 026	193 341	90 957	1 724 741	133 156
1982	56 644	123 512	70 477	191 579	91 035	1 767 262	134 359
1983	55 574	125 371	69 753	201 055	90 225	1 823 723	135 576
1984	57 412	128 313	71 579	208 526	93 811	1 847 190	138 682
1985	55 682	129 313	69 819	210 713	93 657	1 863 687	139 885
1986	57 154	131 700	71 217	217 394	95 257	1 940 363	145 690
1987	57 262	132 366	72 319	214 479	93 252	1 965 457	143 997
1988	56 903	135 308	73 421	219 217	93 020	2 007 280	141 983
1989	55 883	136 418	71 776	215 815	90 051	2 037 253	140 179
1990	49 779	132 560	66 990	194 920	80 277	1 987 995	129 953
1991	38 706	113 686	62 171	183 501	66 319	1 686 868	116 314
1992	34 476	106 886	58 141	181 314	58 338	1 365 759	93 023

Table C-16d. **Levels of GDP in 7 Latin American Countries, 1820-1994**

(million 1990 Geary-Khamis Dollars)

	Argentina	Brazil	Chile	Colombia	Mexico	Peru	Venezuela
1820		3 018			5 006		
1850		5 143			5 116		
1870	2 354	7 247			6 543		
1890	7 265	10 960			11 616		
1900	12 932	12 668	5 798	3 891	15 744	3 096	2 087
1901	14 036	13 939	5 992		17 083		2 053
1902	13 746	13 939	6 196		15 876		2 233
1903	15 722	14 217	6 400		17 654		2 414
1904	17 407	14 495	6 622		17 962		2 357
1905	19 703	14 912	6 844		19 828		2 329
1906	20 691	16 282	7 076		19 608		2 173
1907	21 127	16 302	7 317		20 750		2 173
1908	23 190	16 183	7 557		20 728		2 322
1909	24 353	17 473	7 687		21 343		2 405
1910	26 125	17 672	8 317		21 519		2 484
1911	26 590	19 618	8 243				2 655
1912	28 770	19 399	9 160				2 747
1913	29 060	19 856	9 261	6 420	21 958	4 500	3 172
1914	26 038	19 499	8 632			4 063	2 773
1915	26 183	20 372	8 020			4 315	2 858
1916	25 428	20 968	9 511			5 620	2 697
1917	23 364	22 417	10 280			5 418	3 147
1918	27 665	21 961	10 299			5 274	3 128
1919	28 683	23 370	8 141			6 088	2 922
1920	30 775	25 674	9 298			6 209	3 509
1921	31 559	26 210	8 002		23 166	4 378	3 651
1922	34 059	28 017	8 558		23 715	4 959	3 753
1923	37 837	29 625	10 651		24 527	6 403	4 330
1924	40 772	29 605	11 614		24 132	6 493	5 016
1925	40 597	29 724	11 753	8 860	25 625	5 782	6 481
1926	42 544	30 360	11 456	9 707	27 162	6 443	7 839
1927	45 567	32 564	10 984	10 581	25 976	7 249	8 794
1928	48 414	36 316	13 327	11 357	26 130	7 757	9 847
1929	50 623	36 396	14 624	11 768	25 120	8 572	11 167
1930	48 531	35 602	13 735	11 666	23 539	7 613	11 367
1931	45 160	34 807	10 345	11 595	24 329	6 700	9 187
1932	43 678	36 019	10 234	12 243	20 684	6 362	8 800
1933	45 712	39 374	12 114	12 930	23 034	8 572	9 628
1934	49 344	42 075	13 790	12 661	24 593	10 016	10 275
1935	51 524	43 226	14 050	14 080	26 415	10 291	11 021
1936	51 873	47 376	14 587	14 824	28 523	10 750	12 106
1937	55 650	48 925	15 698	15 055	29 467	10 984	13 889
1938	55 883	50 970	15 430	16 038	29 951	10 705	15 015
1939	58 004	52 658	15 902	17 020	31 553	11 668	15 926
1940	58 963	53 512	16 596	17 386	31 993	11 483	15 307
1941	61 986	57 264	16 615	17 681	34 606	12 815	15 056
1942	62 712	55 140	17 532	17 713	37 065	11 483	13 166
1943	62 218	58 674	18 263	17 790	38 448	10 943	14 371
1944	69 280	60 858	18 523	18 991	41 588	12 455	17 727
1945	67 042	62 487	20 199	19 883	42 884	13 872	21 547
1946	73 029	69 079	21 449	21 681	45 716	14 430	25 855

Table C-16d (cont. 2)

	Argentina	Brazil	Chile	Colombia	Mexico	Peru	Venezuela
1947	81 136	71 521	20 014	22 535	47 275	14 858	30 925
1948	85 641	77 001	22 339	23 235	49 230	15 357	34 427
1949	84 478	81 945	22 200	24 519	51 930	16 446	36 534
1950	85 524	86 909	23 274	24 955	57 069	17 270	37 377
1951	88 866	91 059	24 274	25 726	61 482	18 669	39 979
1952	84 333	96 480	25 663	27 350	63 941	19 848	43 472
1953	88 866	101 126	27 006	29 026	64 117	20 901	45 147
1954	92 528	107 818	27 117	31 042	70 529	22 246	49 820
1955	99 125	115 720	27 080	32 242	76 501	23 317	53 991
1956	101 856	117 388	27 238	33 539	81 749	24 316	58 677
1957	107 087	127 157	30 090	34 766	87 941	25 936	67 414
1958	113 655	138 694	30 915	35 639	92 618	25 805	68 540
1959	106 303	150 329	30 748	38 207	95 385	26 737	72 658
1960	114 614	162 838	32 767	39 831	103 114	30 017	72 889
1961	122 809	175 050	34 341	41 847	107 242	32 226	70 643
1962	120 833	185 732	35 971	44 120	112 161	34 922	73 762
1963	117 927	187 658	38 240	45 571	120 527	36 217	77 134
1964	130 074	193 992	39 092	48 389	133 350	38 580	83 688
1965	141 960	197 904	39 407	50 136	142 024	40 501	89 240
1966	142 919	210 294	43 797	52 806	150 763	43 921	90 842
1967	146 755	218 753	45 223	55 028	159 722	45 581	96 334
1968	153 002	238 251	46 844	58 398	171 293	45 734	102 916
1969	166 080	259 040	48 585	62 116	181 240	47 448	106 612
1970	174 972	284 515	49 586	66 308	193 141	50 229	114 807
1971	183 458	313 386	54 022	70 250	201 200	52 331	116 494
1972	189 183	347 161	53 373	75 637	218 261	53 838	117 982
1973	200 720	390 705	50 401	80 728	236 618	56 713	126 364
1974	213 739	421 521	50 891	85 370	251 088	61 969	129 038
1975	211 850	443 502	44 316	87 347	265 163	64 075	132 728
1976	211 327	485 239	45 881	91 488	276 406	65 334	142 978
1977	224 084	507 934	50 401	95 283	285 935	65 600	151 927
1978	214 233	533 409	54 540	103 366	309 518	65 784	155 528
1979	229 547	571 295	59 060	108 906	337 844	69 609	156 752
1980	232 802	621 689	63 654	113 375	365 972	72 723	149 735
1981	219 434	594 367	67 192	115 789	398 030	76 035	149 253
1982	212 518	597 802	57 634	116 938	395 549	76 147	146 150
1983	220 016	577 410	57 245	118 806	378 971	66 567	140 665
1984	224 491	608 405	60 875	123 037	392 892	69 650	142 664
1985	209 641	656 715	62 366	127 076	403 696	71 247	144 843
1986	224 985	709 392	65 895	134 844	388 083	77 857	152 244
1987	230 797	733 160	69 674	142 086	395 352	84 237	157 698
1988	226 438	731 433	74 814	147 896	401 170	77 285	166 879
1989	212 373	755 399	82 269	152 686	414 060	68 399	152 577
1990	212 518	723 510	84 038	159 042	430 550	64 979	160 648
1991	231 436	730 023	88 909	162 066	446 052	66 342	177 034
1992	251 343	723 450	98 069	167 896	457 646	64 552	189 251
1993	266 425	753 115	103 561	176 120	460 391	68 745	188 873
1994	282 408	787 009	108 220	184 928	474 202	76 309	181 316

Table C-16e. **Levels of GDP in 10 Asian Countries, 1820-1992**

(million 1990 Geary-Khamis Dollars)

	Bangladesh	Burma	China	India	Indonesia	Pakistan	Philippines	South Korea	Taiwan	Thailand
1820	10 611		199 212	93 125	11 011	7 246				
1850				102 638	15 086					
1870			187 175	118 492	19 000					4 140
1890			233 517	142 525	24 907					5 265
1900	16 868		260 600	147 365	31 866	13 574	7 569	7 459	2 173	5 941
1901		6 783		148 199	31 454					
1902				158 880	30 859					
1903				158 213	32 690				2 297	
1904				153 706	33 377				2 151	
1905				151 537	33 880				2 196	
1906		5 915		162 385	35 025				2 443	
1907				148 700	35 895				2 449	
1908				156 710	36 124				2 443	
1909				172 064	38 138				2 675	
1910				172 565	40 702				3 138	
1911		6 807		168 894	43 083			8 939	2 942	
1912				171 397	43 449			9 144	2 678	
1913	19 614	7 824	300 924	166 891	45 784	14 580	13 303	9 738	2 755	7 353
1914				172 064	45 922			10 409	2 815	
1915				174 234	46 608			11 821	2 865	
1916		9 639		181 410	47 570			12 055	3 380	
1917				181 243	47 936			12 902	3 680	
1918				156 544	48 989			13 954	3 468	
1919				177 906	53 064			13 691	3 686	
1920				159 047	52 286			13 370	3 441	
1921		8 700		172 732	52 972			14 246	3 424	
1922				175 569	54 117			14 022	3 675	
1923				171 063	55 079			14 480	3 790	
1924				173 566	58 192			14 694	4 146	
1925				173 400	60 161			14 830	4 264	
1926		10 492		177 739	63 366			15 356	4 292	
1927				176 070	67 715			16 271	4 267	
1928				179 741	70 874			15 901	4 749	
1929	21 301		379 465	183 413	72 248	16 767	20 154	15 599	4 972	9 633
1930			384 280	182 245	72 568			15 911	5 132	
1931		12 260	388 192	181 744	68 631			15 687	5 082	
1932	21 360		400 530	183 914	67 120	16 811		16 349	5 906	
1933			400 530	188 420	66 387			18 706	5 537	
1934			365 623	186 584	65 792			18 501	5 956	
1935			395 113	188 086	67 395			20 926	6 779	
1936		12 197	420 090	197 599	71 195			22 348	6 964	
1937			409 859	198 934	77 559			25 376	7 137	
1938	22 713	11 063	399 627	191 758	77 421	18 108	23 852	25 181	7 493	12 464
1939				201 771	77 742			22 572	8 201	
1940				206 778	83 282			25 288	8 170	
1941				204 775	87 448			25 639	8 989	
1942				214 121	69 089			25 493	9 650	
1943				228 640	58 879			25 863	6 578	
1944				224 635	44 777			24 743	4 518	
1945				223 967	37 681			12 376	4 890	
1946				216 624	39 054			13 448	5 295	

Table C-16e (cont. 2)

	Bangladesh	Burma	China	India	Indonesia	Pakistan	Philippines	South Korea	Taiwan	Thailand
1947				220 797	45 739			14 460	5 730	
1948	24 302			209 448	55 811	22 643		15 561	6 201	
1949	22 439			213 453	62 908	22 920		16 739	6 713	
1950	23 753	7 143	335 530	214 288	69 089	24 465	25 941	18 005	7 267	16 486
1951	24 086	8 184	373 748	220 963	73 759	23 664	27 138	16 622	7 785	17 655
1952	24 793	8 364	427 613	226 638	79 207	23 751	29 546	17 693	8 716	18 185
1953	25 146	8 583	449 882	240 657	82 778	26 025	31 834	22 825	9 531	20 214
1954	25 636	8 051	468 539	252 673	88 226	26 623	33 537	24 451	10 440	19 780
1955	24 283	9 099	497 728	261 184	88 226	27 236	36 184	25 892	11 286	21 516
1956	26 832	9 702	541 663	275 704	91 706	28 038	38 006	26 204	11 906	22 935
1957	26 264	10 273	563 029	275 203	94 911	29 262	39 696	28 326	12 785	22 354
1958	25 754	9 991	628 330	295 397	97 246	29 671	41 345	30 177	13 641	23 229
1959	27 127	11 540	619 904	303 574	103 106	29 991	39 736	31 627	14 685	24 597
1960	28 676	11 923	585 598	318 928	107 731	31 464	40 334	32 465	15 611	27 134
1961	30 304	12 213	482 381	331 278	112 767	33 374	42 596	33 925	16 685	28 568
1962	30 147	13 277	478 168	341 792	113 042	35 794	44 618	35 084	18 005	30 899
1963	33 344	13 653	526 617	363 154	110 066	38 039	47 731	38 298	19 688	33 487
1964	33 698	13 895	600 043	390 024	114 049	40 912	49 394	41 511	22 090	35 480
1965	35 345	14 247	675 876	380 845	115 193	42 734	51 988	44 539	24 550	37 987
1966	35 796	13 653	753 815	379 510	114 095	46 219	54 289	50 265	26 737	42 730
1967	35 012	14 036	726 130	408 883	111 943	47 954	57 069	52 505	29 602	45 517
1968	38 268	14 959	699 649	423 736	120 687	51 307	60 342	57 247	32 315	49 231
1969	38 797	15 577	773 676	451 440	131 859	54 632	63 242	64 715	35 208	52 951
1970	40 896	16 281	893 745	474 804	143 763	60 303	66 302	70 480	39 210	57 062
1971	39 111	16 813	950 318	483 483	148 799	60 595	70 093	77 871	44 268	59 731
1972	34 462	16 939	972 286	480 479	165 281	61 076	73 751	83 295	50 163	62 599
1973	34 717	17 001	1 046 012	494 664	191 150	65 421	80 004	96 372	56 601	68 504
1974	39 366	17 901	1 066 776	500 672	199 757	67 652	83 994	104 552	57 259	72 224
1975	38 876	18 644	1 145 317	546 567	199 711	70 451	89 515	110 472	60 080	77 372
1976	40 602	19 779	1 121 845	556 414	219 719	74 169	96 552	124 582	68 408	84 115
1977	41 014	20 960	1 182 331	596 301	234 095	77 114	102 485	138 088	75 377	90 181
1978	44 034	22 314	1 292 770	630 847	246 137	83 340	108 152	152 470	85 625	99 263
1979	46 643	23 479	1 375 825	597 636	256 667	86 402	114 897	163 279	92 624	105 278
1980	47 290	25 326	1 434 204	637 189	275 805	95 398	121 016	156 404	99 387	111 344
1981	51 782	26 922	1 484 760	678 912	294 805	102 965	125 140	167 213	105 511	118 352
1982	53 724	28 424	1 595 199	704 446	288 670	109 672	129 637	179 044	109 257	123 198
1983	56 215	29 668	1 736 332	756 850	304 695	117 078	131 978	199 200	118 488	130 389
1984	58 882	31 084	1 955 405	784 721	325 618	123 071	122 307	219 445	131 047	138 471
1985	61 197	31 945	2 189 825	827 612	333 676	132 387	113 407	235 716	137 537	144 008
1986	63 884	31 679	2 346 907	867 832	353 318	139 663	117 291	264 646	153 547	151 287
1987	66 493	30 380	2 567 484	908 721	370 716	148 673	122 905	295 456	172 489	165 876
1988	68 376	26 890	2 848 849	998 174	391 960	160 031	130 661	328 631	185 152	188 113
1989	70 063	27 900	2 963 501	1 057 587	421 719	167 948	138 416	351 505	199 165	211 144
1990	74 417	28 643	3 061 000	1 115 999	452 807	176 915	141 383	384 174	208 859	232 858
1991	76 928	28 299	3 257 203	1 174 077	481 605	190 708	139 946	416 425	223 969	251 491
1992	80 164	31 475	3 615 603	1 188 096	510 999	195 680	142 328	436 416	238 750	270 353

Table C-16f. **Levels of GDP in 10 African Countries, 1900-1992**

(million 1990 Geary Khamis Dollars)

	Cote d'Ivoire	Egypt	Ethiopia	Ghana	Kenya	Morocco	Nigeria	South Africa	Tanzania	Zaire
1900		5 171		824						
1913		6 175		1 324				8 926		
1950	2 656	10 574	5 088	5 213	3 979	14 750	19 755	31 211	3 562	6 316
1951	2 754	11 684	5 231	5 406	4 846	15 517	21 236	32 678	4 011	7 055
1952	2 855	11 631	5 378	5 307	4 309	15 885	22 757	33 833	4 093	7 700
1953	2 959	11 694	5 689	6 042	4 201	16 711	23 291	35 424	3 947	8 135
1954	3 068	12 435	5 689	6 803	4 691	18 112	25 009	37 516	4 267	8 628
1955	3 182	13 080	5 994	6 365	5 045	18 953	25 661	39 388	4 371	8 963
1956	3 299	13 429	6 193	6 740	5 323	18 186	25 069	41 573	4 424	9 569
1957	3 421	13 788	6 147	6 959	5 498	17 862	26 096	43 165	4 531	9 872
1958	3 548	15 501	6 350	6 845	5 558	16 416	25 800	44 070	4 570	9 588
1959	3 679	17 098	6 523	7 835	5 693	18 511	26 926	46 036	4 795	9 923
1960	4 008	18 388	6 859	8 414	5 912	17 965	28 131	47 971	4 991	10 150
1961	4 382	19 191	7 195	8 711	5 769	18 658	29 079	50 031	4 934	9 045
1962	4 576	20 513	7 490	9 133	6 079	19 396	30 738	52 840	5 382	10 965
1963	5 328	22 384	8 482	9 451	6 386	18 776	33 622	56 710	5 721	11 540
1964	6 281	24 193	8 900	9 655	7 006	21 107	35 064	60 518	6 034	11 256
1965	6 143	26 424	9 424	9 785	7 086	22 257	37 435	64 139	6 252	11 369
1966	6 629	26 688	9 790	9 795	7 997	22 670	36 230	66 916	7 053	12 140
1967	6 725	26 847	10 202	9 973	8 411	22 360	30 600	71 504	7 338	12 020
1968	7 774	27 566	10 375	10 113	9 020	23 821	30 264	74 594	7 716	12 538
1969	8 117	29 448	10 762	10 473	9 581	26 770	38 383	79 182	7 858	13 706
1970	8 998	31 097	11 373	10 979	10 281	27 006	50 196	83 302	8 314	13 675
1971	9 450	32 144	11 851	11 855	10 933	25 709	56 103	87 391	8 663	14 546
1972	9 973	32 800	12 457	11 500	11 498	26 254	58 217	89 076	9 244	14 565
1973	10 762	33 022	12 869	11 828	12 095	27 257	63 215	92 821	9 543	15 829
1974	11 073	34 713	13 026	12 642	12 692	28 835	70 544	98 034	9 764	16 372
1975	11 062	39 472	13 047	11 067	12 640	31 004	68 430	99 844	10 270	15 557
1976	12 387	42 549	13 403	10 676	13 149	34 706	75 877	102 278	11 003	14 666
1977	12 972	45 900	13 769	10 921	14 355	37 213	81 428	102 091	11 313	14 742
1978	14 257	50 627	13 617	11 849	15 648	38 054	75 008	105 119	11 641	13 908
1979	14 526	55 692	14 492	11 547	16 237	39 868	77 971	109 238	11 784	13 889
1980	15 646	60 598	15 128	11 182	17 144	41 328	80 204	116 292	11 883	14 180
1981	16 193	63 929	15 438	11 198	17 538	40 178	77 853	122 409	11 751	14 515
1982	16 225	68 211	15 683	10 421	18 596	44 042	77 853	121 910	11 905	14 445
1983	15 593	72 303	16 481	9 947	18 712	43 806	71 215	119 694	11 851	14 647
1984	15 078	81 047	16 141	10 807	19 038	45 694	67 304	125 780	12 147	15 462
1985	15 819	88 438	15 062	11 354	19 857	48 585	73 625	124 282	12 118	15 532
1986	16 292	94 085	16 039	11 948	21 282	52 626	75 937	124 345	12 514	16 264
1987	16 031	97 754	17 545	12 522	22 547	51 284	75 581	126 873	13 151	16 700
1988	15 742	100 693	17 886	13 226	23 904	56 609	83 068	132 085	13 707	16 795
1989	15 649	103 315	18 176	13 898	24 994	58 025	89 212	134 831	14 167	16 681
1990	14 568	105 684	17 891	14 362	26 068	60 193	96 521	133 583	14 676	16 277
1991	14 496	105 028	17 789	15 076	26 641	64 043	100 867	132 834	15 235	14 925
1992	14 510	105 377	16 456	15 905	26 907	61 211	105 193	129 775	15 691	13 340

Appendix D

Levels of GDP Per Capita

The annual GDP per capita estimates were derived from Appendix B for GDP and Appendix A for population.

Table D-1a. **Levels of GDP Per Capita in 17 Advanced Capitalist Countries, 1820-1994**

(1990 Geary-Khamis Dollars)

	Australia	Austria	Belgium	Canada	Denmark	Finland	France	Germany	Italy
1820	1 528	1 295	1 291	893	1 225	759	1 218	1 112	1 092
1850	3 070	1 661	1 808	1 280	1 700		1 669	1 476	
1870	3 801	1 875	2 640	1 620	1 927	1 107	1 858	1 913	1 467
1871	3 533	1 992	2 626	1 662	1 917	1 094	1 881	1 891	1 473
1872	3 807	1 989	2 764	1 616	2 008	1 112	2 059	2 011	1 443
1873	4 096	1 926	2 760	1 745	1 979	1 159	1 904	2 082	1 491
1874	4 108	1 994	2 828	1 756	2 017	1 169	2 137	2 213	1 480
1875	4 433	1 986	2 800	1 690	2 031	1 176	2 198	2 198	1 516
1876	4 293	2 013	2 814	1 555	2 049	1 223	2 009	2 159	1 473
1877	4 324	2 064	2 823	1 637	1 968	1 176	2 107	2 120	1 461
1878	4 582	2 114	2 880	1 551	2 022	1 139	2 071	2 194	1 473
1879	4 504	2 082	2 882	1 673	2 067	1 134	1 935	2 117	1 481
1880	4 590	2 093	3 000	1 721	2 099	1 122	2 100	2 078	1 546
1881	4 772	2 159	3 005	1 932	2 100	1 078	2 173	2 114	1 435
1882	4 352	2 154	3 070	1 998	2 155	1 168	2 267	2 134	1 549
1883	4 794	2 223	3 078	1 981	2 212	1 194	2 266	2 237	1 534
1884	4 610	2 263	3 070	2 114	2 199	1 184	2 232	2 274	1 532
1885	4 737	2 230	3 071	1 964	2 188	1 196	2 187	2 314	1 549
1886	4 638	2 283	3 086	1 966	2 247	1 239	2 216	2 310	1 607
1887	4 962	2 420	3 181	2 009	2 304	1 239	2 228	2 377	1 641
1888	4 825	2 395	3 178	2 131	2 298	1 265	2 248	2 447	1 625
1889	5 085	2 353	3 307	2 122	2 309	1 288	2 301	2 488	1 544
1890	4 775	2 460	3 355	2 254	2 427	1 341	2 354	2 539	1 631
1891	4 999	2 523	3 323	2 282	2 458	1 311	2 409	2 508	1 615
1892	4 280	2 552	3 369	2 246	2 499	1 243	2 469	2 585	1 514
1893	3 972	2 542	3 382	2 211	2 529	1 302	2 511	2 686	1 574
1894	4 034	2 662	3 395	2 293	2 557	1 359	2 601	2 721	1 541
1895	3 735	2 706	3 437	2 246	2 665	1 449	2 545	2 814	1 557
1896	3 947	2 719	3 476	2 168	2 728	1 525	2 660	2 872	1 591
1897	3 663	2 748	3 510	2 380	2 754	1 577	2 614	2 909	1 511
1898	4 168	2 874	3 538	2 448	2 761	1 620	2 734	2 987	1 635
1899	4 113	2 905	3 579	2 649	2 840	1 561	2 884	3 049	1 663
1900	4 299	2 901	3 652	2 758	2 902	1 620	2 849	3 134	1 746
1901	4 112	2 883	3 640	2 934	2 986	1 589	2 800	3 016	1 848
1902	4 095	2 965	3 660	3 156	3 022	1 545	2 749	3 040	1 782
1903	4 367	2 960	3 692	3 159	3 165	1 637	2 804	3 162	1 852
1904	4 600	2 975	3 740	3 107	3 199	1 681	2 820	3 242	1 854
1905	4 587	3 110	3 799	3 375	3 219	1 692	2 867	3 265	1 941
1906	4 828	3 197	3 834	3 644	3 273	1 743	2 915	3 317	1 998
1907	4 945	3 360	3 849	3 671	3 354	1 782	3 041	3 416	2 204
1908	5 027	3 342	3 849	3 385	3 417	1 776	3 016	3 427	2 238
1909	5 335	3 298	3 887	3 647	3 504	1 830	3 137	3 449	2 390
1910	5 581	3 312	3 978	3 852	3 564	1 852	2 937	3 527	2 281
1911	5 467	3 388	4 060	3 991	3 710	1 883	3 219	3 602	2 407
1912	5 404	3 528	4 117	4 147	3 668	1 964	3 481	3 715	2 411
1913	5 505	3 488	4 130	4 213	3 764	2 050	3 452	3 833	2 507
1914	4 966	2 895	3 840	3 814	3 954	1 943	3 206	3 227	2 487
1915	4 639	2 671	3 776	4 011	3 635	1 827	3 217	3 038	2 749
1916	4 981	2 645	3 994	4 402	3 744	1 838	3 431	3 098	3 071
1917	5 099	2 603	3 444	4 549	3 479	1 535	2 951	3 118	3 229
1918	5 042	2 572	2 801	4 207	3 327	1 330	2 373	3 151	3 317
1919	4 840	2 274	3 318	3 808	3 713	1 610	2 785	2 763	2 783
1920	5 047	2 428	3 878	3 659	3 840	1 792	3 196	2 986	2 531
1921	5 438	2 668	3 970	3 181	3 681	1 830	3 046	3 288	2 473
1922	5 366	2 897	4 320	3 594	4 008	1 999	3 576	3 558	2 574
1923	5 357	2 861	4 437	3 767	4 386	2 124	3 718	2 937	2 703
1924	5 646	3 184	4 539	3 768	4 356	2 160	4 140	3 417	2 705
1925	5 712	3 389	4 567	4 112	4 212	2 261	4 127	3 772	2 857
1926	5 528	3 436	4 682	4 261	4 423	2 323	4 209	3 592	2 862
1927	5 404	3 529	4 819	4 593	4 481	2 483	4 115	4 235	2 776
1928	5 220	3 682	5 030	4 900	4 604	2 629	4 390	4 308	2 950
1929	5 095	3 723	4 947	4 799	4 883	2 639	4 666	4 335	3 026
1930	4 792	3 610	4 873	4 558	5 138	2 589	4 489	4 049	2 854
1931	4 534	3 309	4 757	3 793	5 156	2 506	4 195	3 618	2 814
1932	4 667	2 959	4 510	3 479	4 973	2 476	3 922	3 267	2 884
1933	4 895	2 852	4 581	3 193	5 090	2 624	4 199	3 591	2 842
1934	5 044	2 871	4 526	3 497	5 197	2 902	4 152	3 846	2 831
1935	5 212	2 926	4 790	3 743	5 272	3 004	4 047	4 165	3 079
1936	5 419	3 015	4 809	3 908	5 363	3 184	4 204	4 571	3 061

Table D-1a (cont. 2)

	Australia	Austria	Belgium	Canada	Denmark	Finland	France	Germany	Italy
1937	5 680	3 177	4 856	4 239	5 453	3 342	4 444	4 809	3 247
1938	5 670	3 583	4 730	4 307	5 544	3 486	4 424	5 126	3 244
1939	5 631	4 123	5 040	4 518	5 766	3 310	4 748	5 549	3 444
1940	5 940	3 985	4 465	5 086	4 922	3 128	4 004	5 545	3 429
1941	6 539	4 245	4 266	5 733	4 400	3 226	3 278	5 862	3 357
1942	7 230	4 009	3 912	6 664	4 453	3 231	2 953	5 892	3 295
1943	7 420	4 092	3 824	6 881	4 887	3 590	2 833	6 046	2 973
1944	7 092	4 180	4 025	7 052	5 333	3 578	2 399	6 249	2 409
1945	6 663	1 736	4 241	6 758	4 874	3 350	2 549	4 326	1 880
1946	6 353	1 969	4 477	6 567	5 557	3 577	3 819	2 503	2 448
1947	6 420	2 181	4 699	6 716	5 806	3 610	4 099	2 763	2 856
1948	6 711	2 783	4 917	6 694	5 900	3 843	4 352	3 187	2 996
1949	6 971	3 315	5 083	6 693	6 248	4 024	4 900	3 642	3 193
1950	7 218	3 731	5 346	7 047	6 683	4 131	5 221	4 281	3 425
1951	7 311	3 985	5 625	7 282	6 673	4 440	5 500	4 651	3 658
1952	7 193	3 993	5 548	7 573	6 691	4 540	5 606	5 046	3 911
1953	7 260	4 164	5 695	7 718	7 015	4 518	5 728	5 438	4 168
1954	7 561	4 585	5 901	7 445	7 091	4 858	5 963	5 797	4 354
1955	7 797	5 087	6 147	7 929	7 115	5 047	6 252	6 431	4 575
1956	7 877	5 433	6 287	8 361	7 157	5 143	6 506	6 839	4 754
1957	7 852	5 754	6 358	8 318	7 662	5 332	6 825	7 154	5 008
1958	8 060	5 946	6 306	8 248	7 788	5 317	6 922	7 377	5 244
1959	8 374	6 092	6 469	8 385	8 236	5 588	7 049	7 867	5 531
1960	8 539	6 561	6 779	8 459	8 477	6 051	7 472	8 463	5 789
1961	8 320	6 872	7 095	9 606	8 956	6 468	7 801	8 729	6 236
1962	8 691	6 996	7 436	8 993	9 393	6 614	8 174	9 023	6 679
1963	9 086	7 235	7 705	9 282	9 379	6 782	8 465	9 184	7 106
1964	9 473	7 617	8 166	9 717	10 171	7 097	8 923	9 697	7 325
1965	9 805	7 786	8 384	10 173	10 552	7 449	9 264	10 104	7 434
1966	9 859	8 167	8 595	10 665	10 750	7 597	9 668	10 299	7 771
1967	10 363	8 352	8 882	10 802	11 021	7 720	10 041	10 243	8 271
1968	10 778	8 679	9 224	11 185	11 393	7 864	10 391	10 772	8 943
1969	11 193	9 191	9 815	11 615	12 049	8 622	11 031	11 465	9 359
1970	11 637	9 813	10 410	11 758	12 204	9 302	11 558	11 933	9 508
1971	11 798	10 266	10 752	12 280	12 444	9 485	11 994	12 161	9 598
1972	12 035	10 843	11 278	12 829	13 024	10 147	12 374	12 603	9 788
1973	12 485	11 308	11 905	13 644	13 416	10 768	12 940	13 152	10 409
1974	12 480	11 736	12 354	14 017	13 230	11 034	13 205	13 171	10 905
1975	12 671	11 724	12 133	14 158	13 104	11 098	13 101	13 034	10 558
1976	13 012	12 281	12 790	14 901	13 916	11 109	13 626	13 797	11 199
1977	12 993	12 836	12 816	15 242	14 097	11 090	14 045	14 219	11 571
1978	13 223	12 852	13 130	15 717	14 259	11 299	14 456	14 664	11 911
1979	13 670	13 487	13 457	16 246	14 731	12 089	14 850	15 257	12 588
1980	13 805	13 881	14 022	16 280	14 645	12 693	14 979	15 370	13 092
1981	14 089	13 811	13 875	16 676	14 522	12 840	15 075	15 355	13 145
1982	13 771	13 947	14 080	15 983	14 969	13 226	15 337	15 223	13 141
1983	13 736	14 260	14 146	16 362	15 361	13 537	15 388	15 545	13 225
1984	14 559	14 452	14 451	17 271	16 041	13 878	15 553	16 047	13 542
1985	15 008	14 799	14 565	17 954	16 724	14 282	15 773	16 412	13 859
1986	15 260	14 960	14 771	18 399	17 309	14 534	16 086	16 786	14 241
1987	15 597	15 189	15 061	18 960	17 339	15 071	16 366	17 032	14 659
1988	16 115	15 765	15 730	19 676	17 532	15 838	16 985	17 559	15 226
1989	16 452	16 305	16 299	19 901	17 620	16 676	17 457	18 015	15 650
1990	16 417	16 792	16 807	19 599	17 953	16 604	17 777	18 685	15 951
1991	16 204	17 013	17 060	18 982	18 128	15 299	17 755	19 339	16 112
1992	16 237	17 160	17 165	18 159	18 293	14 646	17 959	19 351	16 229
1993	16 627	16 978	16 841	18 300	18 492	14 316	17 680	18 856	16 084
1994	17 107	17 285	17 225	18 350	19 305	14 779	17 968	19 097	16 404

Table D-1a (cont. 3)

	Japan	Netherlands	New Zealand	Norway	Sweden	Switzerland	UK	USA
1820	704	1 561		1 004	1 198		1 756	1 287
1850		1 888		1 080	1 289		2 362	1 819
1870	741	2 640	3 115	1 303	1 664	2 172	3 263	2 457
1871		2 655	3 171	1 314	1 684		3 421	2 508
1872		2 677	3 541	1 389	1 746		3 394	2 545
1873		2 588	3 850	1 408	1 885		3 441	2 604
1874		2 679	3 863	1 442	1 938		3 463	2 531
1875		2 829	3 707	1 469	1 835		3 511	2 599
1876		2 771	3 641	1 491	1 935		3 508	2 574
1877		2 958	4 003	1 479	1 851		3 503	2 594
1878		3 134	4 292	1 415	1 818		3 479	2 646
1879		2 867	3 587	1 413	1 769		3 428	2 915
1880		3 120	3 765	1 444	1 846		3 556	3 193
1881		3 012	3 784	1 453	1 851		3 649	3 223
1882		3 023	3 664	1 450	1 924		3 725	3 341
1883		3 447	3 512	1 444	1 937		3 726	3 338
1884		3 337	3 721	1 466	1 976		3 704	3 326
1885	818	3 401	3 605	1 472	1 952		3 654	3 269
1886	883	3 406	3 620	1 470	1 929		3 681	3 295
1887	913	3 437	3 622	1 478	1 926		3 797	3 372
1888	866	3 205	3 572	1 537	1 971		3 936	3 284
1889	901	3 433	3 720	1 585	2 065		4 115	3 416
1890	974	3 113	3 774	1 617	2 086		4 099	3 396
1891	920	3 228	3 750	1 618	2 106		4 065	3 471
1892	974	3 414	3 820	1 643	2 144		3 933	3 732
1893	970	3 072	3 808	1 677	2 143		3 897	3 482
1894	1 077	3 376	3 597	1 667	2 171		4 120	3 318
1895	1 081	3 346	3 660	1 662	2 257		4 211	3 648
1896	1 011	3 434	4 008	1 689	2 367		4 345	3 509
1897	1 022	3 726	3 970	1 749	2 429		4 360	3 774
1898	1 201	3 690	4 005	1 728	2 457		4 528	3 784
1899	1 100	3 703	4 061	1 753	2 491	3 463	4 670	4 056
1900	1 135	3 533	4 320	1 762	2 561	3 531	4 593	4 096
1901	1 161	3 400	4 245	1 790	2 515	3 594	4 551	4 469
1902	1 086	3 516	4 461	1 811	2 496	3 653	4 628	4 426
1903	1 147	3 556	4 751	1 793	2 669	3 709	4 540	4 556
1904	1 143	3 471	4 594	1 784	2 680	3 764	4 528	4 415
1905	1 113	3 535	4 875	1 796	2 691	3 879	4 623	4 648
1906	1 248	3 653	5 184	1 853	2 845	3 870	4 736	5 085
1907	1 275	3 616	5 367	1 914	2 885	3 921	4 784	5 071
1908	1 268	3 564	4 859	1 962	2 853	3 972	4 550	4 566
1909	1 251	3 689	4 795	1 996	2 809	4 021	4 612	5 023
1910	1 254	3 684	5 343	2 052	2 980	4 068	4 715	4 970
1911	1 304	3 739	5 522	2 100	3 002	4 118	4 815	5 052
1912	1 332	3 892	5 236	2 175	3 064	4 164	4 868	5 207
1913	1 334	3 950	5 178	2 275	3 096	4 207	5 032	5 307
1914	1 276	3 774	5 215	2 301	3 048	4 175	5 038	4 805
1915	1 375	3 830	5 200	2 375	3 028	4 231	5 408	4 870
1916	1 568	3 860	5 146	2 428	2 968	4 218	5 506	5 465
1917	1 602	3 539	5 034	2 182	2 584	3 752	5 544	5 254
1918	1 605	3 271	4 936	2 079	2 533	3 746	5 583	5 666
1919	1 758	4 022	5 309	2 408	2 669	4 004	4 980	5 687
1920	1 631	4 117	5 670	2 529	2 802	4 255	4 651	5 559
1921	1 789	4 324	5 154	2 291	2 674	4 150	4 238	5 329
1922	1 762	4 488	4 866	2 532	2 906	4 555	4 427	5 546
1923	1 741	4 523	5 171	2 571	3 047	4 807	4 545	6 171
1924	1 767	4 777	5 169	2 543	3 130	4 970	4 698	6 240
1925	1 814	4 909	5 318	2 683	3 233	5 314	4 912	6 290
1926	1 801	5 228	4 930	2 726	3 404	5 549	4 713	6 610
1927	1 799	5 371	4 706	2 818	3 500	5 811	5 075	6 584
1928	1 917	5 581	5 167	2 900	3 657	6 086	5 115	6 577
1929	1 949	5 551	5 289	3 158	3 869	6 245	5 255	6 907
1930	1 780	5 467	4 985	3 377	3 937	6 160	5 195	6 220
1931	1 768	5 059	4 498	3 096	3 782	5 861	4 906	5 698
1932	1 887	4 913	4 349	3 283	3 666	5 632	4 916	4 914
1933	2 042	4 836	4 599	3 342	3 722	5 884	5 039	4 783
1934	2 019	4 688	4 792	3 430	3 992	5 871	5 354	5 120
1935	2 040	4 810	4 984	3 559	4 233	5 826	5 537	5 473
1936	2 159	5 064	5 869	3 757	4 466	5 827	5 762	6 211

Table D-1a (cont. 4)

	Japan	Netherlands	New Zealand	Norway	Sweden	Switzerland	UK	USA
1937	2 227	5 301	6 132	3 871	4 664	6 087	5 937	6 438
1938	2 356	5 122	6 495	3 945	4 725	6 302	5 983	6 134
1939	2 709	5 409	6 492	4 108	5 029	6 273	5 979	6 568
1940	2 765	4 714	6 332	3 718	4 858	6 309	6 546	7 018
1941	2 764	4 421	6 160	3 786	4 914	6 225	7 143	8 215
1942	2 711	4 007	6 796	3 616	5 179	6 023	7 294	9 753
1943	2 714	3 884	6 963	3 517	5 360	5 919	7 394	11 532
1944	2 558	2 585	6 903	3 303	5 484	6 005	7 071	12 348
1945	1 295	2 621	6 963	3 665	5 568	7 646	6 737	11 722
1946	1 389	4 348	7 198	4 010	6 103	8 068	6 440	9 207
1947	1 482	4 925	7 886	4 416	6 176	8 926	6 306	8 896
1948	1 660	5 357	6 964	4 714	6 293	8 991	6 441	9 075
1949	1 731	5 738	7 559	4 757	6 455	8 637	6 641	8 954
1950	1 873	5 850	8 495	4 969	6 738	8 939	6 847	9 573
1951	2 072	5 886	7 689	5 151	6 951	9 551	7 022	10 338
1952	2 277	5 936	7 830	5 284	6 996	9 499	6 987	10 596
1953	2 412	6 383	7 889	5 472	7 145	9 708	7 242	10 810
1954	2 511	6 739	8 778	5 688	7 403	10 146	7 509	10 549
1955	2 695	7 148	8 757	5 740	7 566	10 717	7 759	10 948
1956	2 868	7 317	9 025	5 983	7 797	11 281	7 823	10 970
1957	3 051	7 429	9 076	6 100	8 089	11 545	7 913	10 981
1958	3 200	7 300	9 214	5 991	8 077	11 140	7 864	10 746
1959	3 459	7 549	9 662	6 244	8 279	11 707	8 137	11 145
1960	3 879	8 085	9 491	6 549	8 688	12 286	8 571	11 193
1961	4 307	8 002	9 827	6 903	9 137	12 919	8 780	11 285
1962	4 647	8 429	9 967	7 050	9 468	13 171	8 789	11 796
1963	4 990	8 618	10 201	7 260	9 917	13 522	9 070	12 137
1964	5 514	9 208	10 512	7 569	10 515	13 994	9 486	12 687
1965	5 771	9 560	10 966	7 906	10 815	14 305	9 668	13 316
1966	6 327	9 695	11 443	8 141	10 937	14 526	9 800	14 017
1967	6 954	10 090	10 737	8 576	11 218	14 805	9 962	14 225
1968	7 757	10 625	10 631	8 693	11 562	15 162	10 320	14 719
1969	8 625	11 180	11 604	9 008	12 055	15 811	10 487	15 028
1970	9 448	11 670	11 278	9 122	12 717	16 671	10 694	14 854
1971	9 726	12 020	11 679	9 481	12 749	17 142	10 852	15 158
1972	10 378	12 292	11 976	9 894	13 003	17 532	11 194	15 846
1973	11 017	12 763	12 575	10 229	13 494	17 953	11 992	16 607
1974	10 800	13 166	13 058	10 695	13 885	18 163	11 787	16 362
1975	10 973	13 037	12 676	11 080	14 185	16 868	11 701	16 060
1976	11 309	13 596	12 864	11 778	14 282	16 936	12 023	16 773
1977	11 727	13 830	12 191	12 148	14 006	17 395	12 308	17 461
1978	12 186	14 082	12 237	12 647	14 209	17 417	12 742	18 168
1979	12 754	14 317	12 450	13 245	14 720	17 800	13 087	18 489
1980	13 113	14 326	12 511	13 755	14 935	18 520	12 777	18 270
1981	13 484	14 129	13 065	13 833	14 910	18 659	12 599	18 569
1982	13 817	13 865	13 190	13 825	15 055	18 379	12 826	18 027
1983	14 093	14 008	13 368	14 422	15 315	18 519	13 299	18 547
1984	14 602	14 393	13 891	15 204	15 920	18 781	13 603	19 597
1985	15 237	14 704	13 957	15 959	16 618	19 392	14 046	20 050
1986	15 542	15 024	14 292	16 562	16 533	19 828	14 614	20 426
1987	16 101	15 104	14 281	16 820	16 996	20 088	15 265	20 880
1988	17 028	15 400	14 066	16 647	17 301	20 509	15 988	21 463
1989	17 757	16 024	14 189	16 675	17 593	21 381	16 288	21 783
1990	18 548	16 569	13 994	16 897	17 695	21 661	16 302	21 866
1991	19 240	16 784	13 592	17 079	17 380	21 398	15 867	21 366
1992	19 425	16 898	13 947	17 543	16 927	21 036	15 738	21 558
1993	19 379	16 845	14 527	17 829	16 456	20 506	15 915	21 972
1994	19 505	17 152	15 085	18 372	16 710	20 830	16 371	22 569

Table D-1b. **Levels of GDP per Capita in 5 South European Countries, 1820-1994**

(1990 Geary-Khamis Dollars)

	Greece	Ireland	Portugal	Spain	Turkey
1820		954		1 063	
1850			1 100	1 147	
1870		1 773	1 085	1 376	
1890		2 225	1 227	1 847	
1900		2 495	1 408	2 040	
1901				2 150	
1902				2 050	
1903				2 084	
1904				2 026	
1905				2 003	
1906				2 093	
1907				2 100	
1908				2 139	
1909				2 175	
1910				2 096	
1911				2 223	
1912				2 177	
1913	1 621	2 733	1 354	2 255	979
1914				2 155	
1915				2 169	
1916				2 236	
1917				2 184	
1918				2 168	
1919				2 186	
1920				2 309	
1921				2 375	
1922				2 429	
1923				2 470	561
1924				2 552	667
1925				2 687	738
1926		2 625		2 658	851
1927				2 846	768
1928				2 808	838
1929	2 386	2 883	1 536	2 947	956
1930	2 300			2 802	985
1931	2 174	3 034		2 713	1 027
1932	2 331			2 772	950
1933	2 439	2 859		2 695	1 058
1934	2 463			2 798	1 065
1935	2 526			2 792	1 070
1936	2 501	3 116		2 304	1 252
1937	2 820	3 018		2 043	1 271
1938	2 727	3 116	1 707	2 022	1 359
1939	2 687			2 127	1 430
1940				2 288	1 321
1941				2 269	1 189
1942	1 608			2 378	1 227
1943				2 420	1 102
1944				2 508	1 044
1945	955			2 313	893
1946	1 412			2 422	1 129

Table D-1b (cont. 2)

	Greece	Ireland	Portugal	Spain	Turkey
1947	1 796	3 157	2 015	2 270	1 167
1948	1 832	3 298	2 038	2 369	1 297
1949	1 903	3 475	2 056	2 359	1 205
1950	1 951	3 518	2 132	2 397	1 299
1951	2 096	3 616	2 218	2 630	1 409
1952	2 092	3 717	2 217	2 812	1 536
1953	2 352	3 822	2 365	2 821	1 663
1954	2 403	3 867	2 473	2 957	1 573
1955	2 560	3 995	2 560	3 085	1 655
1956	2 756	3 974	2 659	3 273	1 660
1957	2 913	3 986	2 764	3 378	1 741
1958	3 019	3 948	2 784	3 493	1 769
1959	3 097	4 118	2 919	3 393	1 797
1960	3 204	4 368	3 095	3 437	1 801
1961	3 457	4 601	3 245	3 804	1 787
1962	3 565	4 724	3 438	4 125	1 850
1963	3 912	4 901	3 626	4 446	1 975
1964	4 219	5 113	3 860	4 675	2 006
1965	3 904	5 180	4 173	5 075	2 009
1966	4 838	5 218	4 404	5 538	2 188
1967	5 044	5 446	4 776	5 829	2 230
1968	5 364	5 819	5 234	6 262	2 320
1969	5 874	6 102	5 373	6 898	2 383
1970	6 327	6 250	5 885	7 291	2 437
1971	6 748	6 472	6 303	7 599	2 589
1972	7 308	6 776	6 798	8 162	2 689
1973	7 799	7 023	7 568	8 739	2 739
1974	7 487	7 149	7 439	9 156	2 901
1975	7 867	7 117	6 790	9 151	3 084
1976	8 257	7 165	7 182	9 341	3 306
1977	8 410	7 564	7 498	9 530	3 373
1978	8 842	8 022	7 631	9 576	3 393
1979	9 071	8 161	7 973	9 488	3 289
1980	9 139	8 256	8 251	9 539	3 192
1981	9 062	8 381	8 358	9 424	3 249
1982	9 041	8 401	8 513	9 486	3 328
1983	9 025	8 358	8 487	9 601	3 366
1984	9 224	8 598	8 317	9 732	3 471
1985	9 479	8 784	8 548	9 915	3 559
1986	9 605	8 775	8 904	10 197	3 737
1987	9 542	9 156	9 379	10 733	3 977
1988	9 944	9 580	9 754	11 259	4 038
1989	10 262	10 270	10 355	11 752	3 989
1990	10 051	11 123	10 685	12 170	4 263
1991	10 250	11 267	11 017	12 410	4 254
1992	10 314	11 711	11 130	12 498	4 422
1993	10 163	12 102	10 969	12 354	4 542
1994	10 165	12 624	11 083	12 544	4 266

Table D-1c. **Levels of GDP per Capita in 7 East European Countries, 1820-1992**

(1990 Geary-Khamis Dollars)

	Bulgaria	Czechoslovakia	Hungary	Poland	Romania	USSR	Yugoslavia
1820		849				751	
1850		1 069					
1870		1 164	1 269			1 023	
1890		1 505				925	
1900		1 729	1 682			1 218	
1913	1 498	2 096	2 098			1 488	1 029
1920		1 933	1 709				1 054
1921		2 085					1 064
1922		2 006					1 079
1923		2 151					1 116
1924	909	2 353	1 912				1 173
1925	922	2 606	2 279				1 212
1926	1 169	2 575	2 162		1 258		1 271
1927	1 255	2 752	2 237		1 241		1 240
1928	1 219	2 977	2 415		1 225	1 370	1 321
1929	1 180	3 042	2 476	2 117	1 152	1 386	1 367
1930	1 284	2 926	2 404	1 994	1 219	1 448	1 325
1931	1 454	2 809	2 268	1 823	1 229	1 462	1 273
1932	1 444	2 680	2 192	1 658	1 144	1 439	1 154
1933	1 450	2 552	2 374	1 590	1 184	1 493	1 169
1934	1 309	2 443	2 370	1 593	1 182	1 630	1 191
1935	1 236	2 410	2 471	1 597	1 196	1 864	1 161
1936	1 493	2 599	2 618	1 625	1 194	1 991	1 279
1937	1 567	2 882	2 543	1 915	1 130	2 156	1 284
1938	1 595		2 655	2 182	1 242	2 150	1 360
1939	1 603		2 838			2 237	1 412
1940	1 548		2 626			2 144	
1941	1 567		2 626				
1942	1 479		2 743				
1943	1 513						
1944	1 387						
1945	1 073						
1946			1 721			1 913	
1947			1 774			2 126	1 324
1948		3 088	2 200		816	2 402	1 535
1949		3 259	2 354			2 623	1 660
1950	1 651	3 501	2 480	2 447	1 182	2 834	1 546
1951	1 989	3 524	2 695	2 509		2 798	1 585
1952	1 893	3 598	2 762	2 519		2 928	1 441
1953	2 085	3 544	2 786	2 614		3 004	1 632
1954	2 025	3 652	2 850	2 710		3 098	1 699
1955	2 148	3 922	3 070	2 788	1 578	3 304	1 781
1956	2 128	4 110	2 906	2 856		3 557	1 724
1957	2 330	4 320	3 169	2 954		3 566	1 992

Table D-1c (cont. 2)

	Bulgaria	Czechoslovakia	Hungary	Poland	Romania	USSR	Yugoslavia
1958	2 508	4 610	3 367	3 049		3 768	2 054
1959	2 683	4 780	3 484	3 087		3 660	2 283
1960	2 912	5 108	3 649	3 218	1 844	3 935	2 401
1961	3 072	5 263	3 817	3 428	1 951	4 088	2 482
1962	3 295	5 303	3 963	3 341	2 007	4 130	2 501
1963	3 418	5 168	4 169	3 499	2 137	3 976	2 731
1964	3 658	5 370	4 390	3 600	2 258	4 430	2 961
1965	3 850	5 528	4 409	3 759	2 386	4 626	3 008
1966	4 125	5 734	4 646	3 970	2 643	4 796	3 136
1967	4 320	5 953	4 894	4 083	2 743	4 955	3 159
1968	4 368	6 206	4 934	4 281	2 739	5 194	3 195
1969	4 546	6 296	5 062	4 206	2 825	5 218	3 520
1970	4 773	6 460	5 028	4 428	2 853	5 569	3 657
1971	4 902	6 654	5 238	4 703	3 221	5 663	4 038
1972	5 110	6 854	5 336	5 005	3 396	5 640	4 137
1973	5 284	7 036	5 596	5 334	3 477	6 058	4 237
1974	5 414	7 229	5 716	5 593	3 637	6 175	4 738
1975	5 831	7 384	5 805	5 799	3 761	6 136	4 693
1976	5 979	7 444	5 791	5 885	3 917	6 366	4 792
1977	5 891	7 722	6 126	5 936	3 966	6 459	5 092
1978	6 012	7 761	6 253	6 097	4 059	6 565	5 326
1979	6 235	7 790	6 251	5 947	4 139	6 480	5 641
1980	6 031	7 978	6 307	5 740	4 122	6 437	5 876
1981	6 180	7 911	6 350	5 385	4 069	6 442	5 926
1982	6 369	8 038	6 580	5 288	4 050	6 544	5 937
1983	6 238	8 133	6 519	5 498	4 001	6 692	5 946
1984	6 433	8 300	6 703	5 649	4 146	6 715	6 040
1985	6 228	8 343	6 551	5 664	4 121	6 715	6 050
1986	6 381	8 479	6 693	5 804	4 174	6 924	6 261
1987	6 383	8 504	6 809	5 695	4 065	6 943	6 148
1988	6 336	8 675	6 929	5 790	4 035	7 032	6 026
1989	6 217	8 729	6 787	5 685	3 890	7 078	5 917
1990	5 764	8 464	6 348	5 113	3 460	6 871	5 458
1991	4 516	7 244	6 010	4 798	2 887	5 793	4 861
1992	4 054	6 845	5 638	4 726	2 565	4 671	3 887

Table D-1d. **Levels of GDP per Capita in 7 Latin American Countries, 1820-1994**

(1990 Geary-Khamis Dollars)

	Argentina	Brazil	Chile	Colombia	Mexico	Peru	Venezuela
1820		670			760		
1850		711			668		
1870	1 311	740			710		
1890	2 152	772			990		
1900	2 756	704	1 949	973	1 157	817	821
1901	2 880	758	1 990		1 242		797
1902	2 717	742	2 033		1 142		856
1903	2 992	741	2 074		1 256		913
1904	3 191	740	2 120		1 264		876
1905	3 479	745	2 164		1 380		861
1906	3 518	797	2 210		1 351		799
1907	3 459	781	2 257		1 414		793
1908	3 657	760	2 303		1 397		841
1909	3 699	803	2 313		1 423		865
1910	3 822	795	2 472		1 435		886
1911	3 746	865	2 420				937
1912	3 904	837	2 656				962
1913	3 797	839	2 653	1 236	1 467	1 037	1 104
1914	3 302	807	2 440			927	956
1915	3 244	826	2 238			974	980
1916	3 091	832	2 620			1 255	921
1917	2 790	871	2 794			1 198	1 069
1918	3 248	836	2 763			1 154	1 057
1919	3 307	871	2 155			1 318	983
1920	3 473	937	2 430			1 331	1 173
1921	3 471	937	2 064		1 555	926	1 214
1922	3 636	982	2 179		1 567	1 035	1 241
1923	3 898	1 017	2 676		1 596	1 318	1 420
1924	4 055	996	2 880		1 546	1 318	1 630
1925	3 919	980	2 876	1 255	1 616	1 157	2 081
1926	3 994	981	2 767	1 340	1 687	1 272	2 487
1927	4 156	1 031	2 618	1 424	1 588	1 410	2 761
1928	4 291	1 127	3 136	1 490	1 573	1 487	3 057
1929	4 367	1 106	3 396	1 505	1 489	1 619	3 426
1930	4 080	1 061	3 143	1 474	1 371	1 417	3 444
1931	3 712	1 016	2 333	1 448	1 392	1 228	2 754
1932	3 522	1 030	2 274	1 511	1 163	1 148	2 613
1933	3 621	1 104	2 652	1 577	1 272	1 524	2 831
1934	3 845	1 156	2 976	1 526	1 333	1 753	2 995
1935	3 950	1 164	2 987	1 677	1 406	1 772	3 181
1936	3 912	1 250	3 056	1 744	1 363	1 822	3 449
1937	4 125	1 265	3 241	1 751	1 382	1 832	3 896
1938	4 072	1 291	3 139	1 843	1 380	1 757	4 144
1939	4 148	1 307	3 178	1 905	1 428	1 884	4 305
1940	4 161	1 302	3 259	1 895	1 556	1 823	4 045
1941	4 304	1 361	3 205	1 877	1 636	1 998	3 903
1942	4 284	1 280	3 322	1 832	1 703	1 757	3 347
1943	4 182	1 331	3 400	1 792	1 716	1 643	3 575
1944	4 579	1 348	3 388	1 863	1 804	1 835	4 309
1945	4 356	1 352	3 630	1 899	1 808	2 005	5 102
1946	4 665	1 460	3 786	2 017	1 873	2 046	5 948

Table D-1d (cont. 2)

	Argentina	Brazil	Chile	Colombia	Mexico	Peru	Venezuela
1947	5 089	1 477	3 470	2 042	1 882	2 066	6 894
1948	5 252	1 553	3 806	2 050	1 904	2 094	7 394
1949	5 047	1 614	3 715	2 107	1 952	2 199	7 544
1950	4 987	1 673	3 827	2 089	2 085	2 263	7 424
1951	5 080	1 702	3 906	2 094	2 185	2 384	7 646
1952	4 727	1 751	4 041	2 164	2 208	2 475	8 010
1953	4 884	1 782	4 162	2 232	2 151	2 540	7 995
1954	4 986	1 845	4 089	2 321	2 296	2 633	8 455
1955	5 237	1 923	3 997	2 343	2 416	2 689	8 775
1956	5 290	1 894	3 927	2 367	2 503	2 732	9 140
1957	5 468	1 992	4 238	2 382	2 609	2 835	10 083
1958	5 705	2 110	4 254	2 371	2 663	2 745	9 869
1959	5 245	2 220	4 134	2 469	2 656	2 768	10 077
1960	5 559	2 335	4 304	2 499	2 781	3 023	9 726
1961	5 865	2 440	4 404	2 548	2 802	3 153	9 073
1962	5 682	2 516	4 504	2 608	2 839	3 320	9 122
1963	5 459	2 471	4 675	2 614	2 955	3 347	9 194
1964	5 929	2 482	4 667	2 694	3 166	3 463	9 615
1965	6 371	2 461	4 593	2 709	3 265	3 531	9 887
1966	6 321	2 542	5 001	2 773	3 355	3 722	9 715
1967	6 397	2 570	5 060	2 808	3 441	3 758	9 935
1968	6 573	2 721	5 135	2 895	3 572	3 665	10 247
1969	7 033	2 875	5 218	2 993	3 659	3 698	10 268
1970	7 302	3 067	5 217	3 104	3 774	3 807	10 827
1971	7 535	3 297	5 581	3 212	3 805	3 857	10 609
1972	7 642	3 564	5 417	3 384	3 993	3 859	10 370
1973	7 970	3 913	5 028	3 539	4 189	3 953	10 717
1974	8 344	4 120	4 995	3 667	4 305	4 201	10 559
1975	8 132	4 230	4 282	3 674	4 408	4 226	10 480
1976	7 978	4 516	4 366	3 766	4 460	4 193	10 896
1977	8 322	4 613	4 728	3 838	4 481	4 098	11 176
1978	7 828	4 727	5 043	4 072	4 714	4 001	11 051
1979	8 256	4 940	5 381	4 197	5 004	4 126	10 771
1980	8 245	5 246	5 711	4 274	5 254	4 205	9 966
1981	7 655	4 894	5 933	4 272	5 582	4 292	9 637
1982	7 306	4 803	5 005	4 222	5 421	4 201	9 167
1983	7 456	4 527	4 887	4 199	5 078	3 591	8 580
1984	7 503	4 654	5 109	4 259	5 150	3 674	8 467
1985	6 912	4 902	5 145	4 310	5 141	3 676	8 364
1986	7 320	5 167	5 345	4 485	4 847	3 928	8 557
1987	7 413	5 211	5 557	4 636	4 846	4 156	8 631
1988	7 183	5 091	5 869	4 737	4 828	3 729	8 897
1989	6 655	5 139	6 347	4 804	4 893	3 228	7 928
1990	6 581	4 812	6 380	4 917	4 997	3 000	8 139
1991	7 089	4 766	6 655	4 930	5 079	2 997	8 768
1992	7 616	4 637	7 238	5 025	5 112	2 854	9 163
1993	7 985	4 739	7 536	5 187	5 045	2 975	8 939
1994	8 373	4 862	7 764	5 359	5 098	3 232	8 389

Table D-1e. **Levels of GDP per Capita in 10 Asian Countries, 1820-1992**

(1990 Geary-Khamis Dollars)

	Bangladesh	Burma	China	India	Indonesia	Pakistan	Philippines	South Korea	Taiwan	Thailand
1820	531		523	531	614	531				
1850				547	657					
1870			523	558	657					717
1890			615	608	663					789
1900	581		652	625	745	687	1 033	850	759	812
1901		647		625	727					
1902				666	704					
1903				659	737				770	
1904				636	743				712	
1905				623	745				712	
1906		525		663	762				778	
1907				604	771				772	
1908				632	767				764	
1909				690	801				828	
1910				688	844				958	
1911		562		671	883			898	882	
1912				681	880			904	787	
1913	617	635	688	663	917	729	1 418	948	794	846
1914				683	909			996	798	
1915				691	912			1 116	804	
1916		762		719	920			1 120	943	
1917				718	920			1 180	1 016	
1918				620	936			1 256	948	
1919				704	1 001			1 213	998	
1920				629	973			1 167	921	
1921		658		679	974			1 219	902	
1922				684	984			1 176	950	
1923				659	989			1 191	962	
1924				662	1 033			1 185	1 034	
1925				655	1 055			1 175	1 041	
1926		754		664	1 098			1 199	1 023	
1927				652	1 159			1 251	995	
1928				658	1 198			1 205	1 082	
1929	619		779	665	1 207	735	1 564	1 164	1 107	799
1930			786	654	1 198			1 173	1 112	
1931		836	788	643	1 116			1 137	1 072	
1932	600		807	642	1 076	705		1 165	1 213	
1933			801	649	1 049			1 311	1 109	
1934			727	635	1 024			1 275	1 161	
1935			782	632	1 034			1 420	1 290	
1936		777	827	655	1 076			1 498	1 293	
1937			803	651	1 155			1 681	1 291	
1938	572	685	778	619	1 136	680	1 497	1 649	1 320	832
1939				643	1 124			1 460	1 409	
1940				650	1 187			1 618	1 365	
1941				637	1 226			1 649	1 458	
1942				658	953			1 600	1 522	
1943				696	803			1 607	1 011	
1944				675	609			1 484	693	
1945				665	514			687	748	
1946				636	527			694	809	

Table D-1e (continued 2)

	Bangladesh	Burma	China	India	Indonesia	Pakistan	Philippines	South Korea	Taiwan	Thailand
1947				641	609			727	903	
1948	585			602	732	631		777	926	
1949	530			604	810	623		828	922	
1950	551	393	614	597	874	650	1 293	876	922	848
1951	534	443	670	605	916	614	1 313	808	943	882
1952	539	446	752	609	965	602	1 387	855	1 020	882
1953	537	450	774	635	990	645	1 450	1 093	1 080	951
1954	537	415	787	655	1 036	644	1 482	1 153	1 143	904
1955	499	461	818	665	1 016	644	1 552	1 197	1 191	955
1956	541	483	872	688	1 037	648	1 581	1 177	1 212	988
1957	520	502	883	673	1 053	660	1 603	1 237	1 262	935
1958	500	479	962	707	1 059	654	1 620	1 281	1 304	943
1959	517	543	931	713	1 102	646	1 511	1 305	1 359	970
1960	536	549	878	735	1 131	661	1 488	1 302	1 399	1 029
1961	554	550	731	746	1 162	684	1 521	1 327	1 450	1 051
1962	539	585	718	753	1 142	716	1 542	1 348	1 518	1 103
1963	584	589	772	783	1 090	743	1 597	1 426	1 612	1 159
1964	577	586	859	823	1 107	780	1 600	1 508	1 757	1 191
1965	592	588	945	785	1 096	795	1 630	1 578	1 899	1 237
1966	586	552	1 025	767	1 064	840	1 647	1 738	2 013	1 350
1967	561	555	962	808	1 024	851	1 676	1 771	2 174	1 395
1968	600	578	903	818	1 082	888	1 716	1 884	2 317	1 464
1969	595	589	972	853	1 159	923	1 740	2 078	2 468	1 527
1970	613	602	1 092	878	1 239	995	1 766	2 208	2 692	1 596
1971	570	608	1 130	873	1 257	968	1 813	2 389	2 978	1 619
1972	488	599	1 128	847	1 363	945	1 854	2 504	3 313	1 647
1973	478	589	1 186	853	1 538	981	1 956	2 840	3 669	1 750
1974	527	606	1 185	844	1 569	983	1 999	3 021	3 645	1 794
1975	508	618	1 250	900	1 531	992	2 077	3 131	3 755	1 871
1976	518	641	1 205	897	1 643	1 013	2 187	3 475	4 189	1 982
1977	513	665	1 253	941	1 708	1 021	2 270	3 792	4 524	2 072
1978	540	693	1 352	972	1 753	1 071	2 343	4 124	5 044	2 226
1979	560	713	1 420	900	1 783	1 078	2 434	4 350	5 352	2 306
1980	557	756	1 462	938	1 870	1 155	2 504	4 103	5 634	2 384
1981	596	788	1 494	978	1 957	1 210	2 526	4 318	5 871	2 480
1982	604	816	1 582	994	1 876	1 250	2 552	4 553	5 971	2 528
1983	617	835	1 697	1 045	1 938	1 294	2 535	4 991	6 372	2 621
1984	631	858	1 886	1 062	2 028	1 320	2 292	5 431	6 944	2 730
1985	641	865	2 084	1 096	2 034	1 376	2 073	5 777	7 187	2 786
1986	654	836	2 200	1 127	2 116	1 408	2 094	6 426	7 932	2 873
1987	665	782	2 369	1 158	2 181	1 453	2 143	7 107	8 817	3 094
1988	669	676	2 586	1 246	2 265	1 516	2 225	7 829	9 357	3 449
1989	671	684	2 649	1 296	2 394	1 542	2 303	8 294	9 955	3 808
1990	698	687	2 700	1 316	2 525	1 575	2 300	8 977	10 324	4 173
1991	707	676	2 832	1 360	2 639	1 650	2 232	9 645	10 957	4 437
1992	720	748	3 098	1 348	2 749	1 642	2 213	10 010	11 590	4 694

Table D-1f. **Levels of GDP per Capita in 10 African Countries, 1900-1992**

(1990 Geary-Khamis Dollars)

	Cote d'Ivoire	Egypt	Ethiopia	Ghana	Kenya	Morocco	Nigeria	South Africa	Tanzania	Zaire
1900		509		462						
1913		508		648				1 451		
1950	859	517	277	1 193	609	1 611	547	2 251	427	636
1951	873	557	279	1 183	724	1 651	577	2 293	472	694
1952	886	542	281	1 110	629	1 648	606	2 309	473	742
1953	880	532	292	1 154	586	1 651	598	2 288	440	770
1954	913	553	286	1 299	655	1 789	642	2 423	475	799
1955	927	569	295	1 162	690	1 829	646	2 474	478	812
1956	941	570	298	1 173	708	1 704	619	2 540	475	849
1957	956	571	289	1 159	712	1 627	633	2 565	478	855
1958	971	626	293	1 091	701	1 454	614	2 548	473	809
1959	985	675	294	1 199	700	1 596	629	2 589	487	816
1960	1 051	712	302	1 232	717	1 511	645	2 624	498	808
1961	1 108	722	310	1 243	692	1 527	653	2 681	478	719
1962	1 115	753	315	1 269	703	1 545	677	2 774	506	800
1963	1 251	801	349	1 279	713	1 455	726	2 916	522	807
1964	1 422	844	358	1 272	755	1 592	742	3 049	534	754
1965	1 340	899	370	1 255	737	1 633	777	3 165	537	729
1966	1 394	884	375	1 231	802	1 625	737	3 235	588	746
1967	1 364	869	381	1 228	814	1 566	610	3 387	594	707
1968	1 519	872	378	1 219	842	1 630	592	3 461	606	707
1969	1 528	911	382	1 237	864	1 790	736	3 599	599	740
1970	1 633	941	393	1 275	894	1 764	944	3 709	615	711
1971	1 646	955	400	1 335	919	1 636	1 034	3 798	624	735
1972	1 667	958	410	1 258	933	1 629	1 052	3 778	650	717
1973	1 727	947	412	1 260	947	1 651	1 120	3 844	655	757
1974	1 706	976	406	1 314	958	1 705	1 219	3 965	653	762
1975	1 638	1 088	396	1 125	920	1 792	1 153	3 946	668	704
1976	1 760	1 147	396	1 065	922	1 961	1 247	3 951	693	644
1977	1 771	1 210	396	1 073	970	2 056	1 305	3 856	690	627
1978	1 873	1 302	381	1 148	1 017	2 057	1 173	3 884	685	571
1979	1 838	1 398	395	1 100	1 015	2 107	1 189	3 949	673	545
1980	1 909	1 483	401	1 041	1 031	2 132	1 193	4 114	657	538
1981	1 908	1 524	399	1 015	1 013	2 022	1 129	4 238	629	533
1982	1 848	1 585	394	917	1 032	2 161	1 101	4 132	617	514
1983	1 718	1 636	403	847	998	2 094	982	3 971	595	504
1984	1 604	1 787	384	888	977	2 127	905	4 080	592	516
1985	1 622	1 901	347	900	981	2 202	965	3 937	573	501
1986	1 607	1 974	358	914	1 013	2 318	971	3 842	574	516
1987	1 520	2 003	379	926	1 036	2 194	943	3 821	585	514
1988	1 434	2 017	374	946	1 060	2 363	1 011	3 876	592	502
1989	1 369	2 026	367	963	1 071	2 366	1 059	3 854	595	484
1990	1 224	2 030	350	966	1 079	2 399	1 118	3 719	599	458
1991	1 176	1 961	336	983	1 065	2 489	1 140	3 613	604	407
1992	1 134	1 927	300	1 007	1 055	2 327	1 152	3 451	601	353

Appendix E

Regional Totals for the 56 Sample Countries and the Degree of Conjecture in the Estimates

The tables in this Appendix provide totals/averages for the 7 major world regions and for the 56 countries combined. Annual figures are provided for 1950-92, as well as for the earlier benchmark years, 1820, 1870, 1900, 1913, 1929, and 1938.

These estimates were mainly derived by summing the individual country entries in Appendix A for population (Table E-1) and Appendix C entries for GDP levels (Table E-2). The Table E-3 figures for per capita GDP are weighted regional averages derived by dividing the Table E-2 entries by the corresponding Table E-1 entries. Japan was included in the Asian region throughout.

As the regional totals in this Appendix are the first step towards estimation of world totals, it was necessary to fill the holes in the data-sets in Appendices A and C. This gap-filling exercise involved the following process of conjecture. The general principle followed when information was lacking, was to assume a movement parallel to the average for the countries in the same region for which information was available.

Population

a) for Western Europe there were no gaps;

b) for Western offshoots, the individual country estimates in Appendix A for 1820 did not include indigenous population, but a rough estimate of their size is given in the country notes for Australia, Canada, New Zealand, and the USA. These indigenous peoples were included in Table E-1;

c) for Southern Europe, there was no information for Greece and Turkey for 1820 and 1870. It was assumed that the 1820-1900 proportional movement for these two countries was the same as the average for the other three countries in the region;

d) for Eastern Europe, there were gaps for four countries for 1820, and two for 1870. It was assumed that the 1820-90 movement in the missing countries was the same as the average for the countries for which estimates were available;

e) for Latin America there were no gaps;

f) for Asian countries there were gaps for Burma, South Korea and Taiwan for 1820 and for the two latter countries in 1870. It was assumed that the 1820-90 movement in the missing countries was the same as the average for the countries for which estimates were available;

g) for Africa, no indications were available for 1820 except a rough estimate of Egyptian population at the time of the Napoleonic occupation at the beginning of the nineteenth century. The estimates for 1820 and 1870 were derived from the proportionate movements for the region given by A.M. Carr-Saunders, *World Population: Past Growth and Present Trends*, Cass, London, 1964, p. 42. The Carr-Saunders estimates were also used by S. Kuznets, *Modern Economic Growth*, Yale University Press, New Haven, 1966, p. 38.

The population gaps represented 13.9 per cent of the estimated 56 country total for 1820, and 11.7 per cent of the 1870 total.

Per Capita Product

For per capita GDP, there were more holes in the data-set than for population. The same general principle was followed — i.e. the assumption of a movement parallel to the average for the countries in the same region, for which information was available.

a) for Western Europe the only gap was for Switzerland in 1820. I assumed that the proportionate change for 1820-70 was the same as in Germany.

b) For Western offshoots, the only gaps were for the indigenous population in 1820. I assumed that their per capita GDP was $500 in all four countries.

c) for Southern Europe, there were gaps for Greece, Portugal, and Turkey in 1820, and for Greece and Turkey in 1870 and 1900. It was assumed that the 1820-1913 per capita movement for the missing countries was the same as the average for the countries in the region for which estimates were available.

d) for Eastern Europe, there are gaps for five of the seven countries for 1820, for four in 1870 and 1900, and for two in 1913. For 1820, I assumed that the regional average was the same as for Russia. For the other years, I assumed a movement for the missing countries parallel to the average for the countries for which estimates were available. There were also gaps for Romania for eight years in the 1950s, which I filled by interpolation between the years which were available.

e) for Latin America, there were gaps for five countries in 1820, and I assumed that the average level was the same as that for Brazil and Mexico. There were gaps for four countries for 1870, and I assumed that average regional per capita GDP was nearer to that for Brazil and Mexico than it was to that of Argentina.

f) for Asia, there were gaps for five countries in 1820 and four in 1870. I assumed that the movement for the missing countries was proportionate to the average for the countries for which estimates were available.

g) for Africa, I assumed that the proportionate movement for 1900-50 for the missing countries was the same as the average movement for the countries for which estimates were available. For 1820-1900 I assumed per capita growth was somewhat slower than the average for Asia.

GDP

The GDP gaps were filled by multiplying the conjectural estimates for population and per capita GDP. The GDP conjectures for 1820 represented 15.9 per cent of the estimated 56 country total, 12.5 per cent of the 1870 total, 5.3 per cent of 1900, and 3.5 per cent of 1913.

It should be noted that the degree of conjecture in the GDP estimates for 1820 is not fully measured by counting the gaps in the table for sample countries, because there is also a degree of country-specific conjecture in the 1820 entries for some countries. The country notes in Appendix B are fully transparent in showing this conjectural element, whose proportionate importance was greatest in the 1820 estimates for China, India and Russia.

Table E-1. **Regional and World Totals: Population, 1820-1992: Sample (56 countries)**

(thousands at mid-year)

	Western Europe (12)	Western Offshoots (4)	Southern Europe (5)	Eastern Europe (7)	Latin America (7)	Asia (11)	Africa (10)	Total Sample (56)
1820	102 691	11 255	33 277	83 979	15 754	670 721	42 648	960 325
1870	144 131	45 708	39 545	131 509	29 406	699 518	48 365	1 138 182
1900	178 050	86 396	44 058	195 875	49 589	807 803	55 645	1 417 416
1913	197 715	111 401	47 784	234 898	62 182	886 591	64 081	1 604 652
1929	210 316	140 417	53 856	256 436	82 041	1 000 682	87 082	1 830 830
1932	214 093	144 336	55 779	264 311	86 661	1 031 377	92 237	1 888 794
1938	220 534	150 436	59 868	281 579	98 241	1 097 458	103 480	2 011 596
1948	233 838	169 931	66 585	259 417	120 942	1 205 286	125 344	2 181 343
1950	238 228	176 094	67 724	266 509	127 160	1 235 327	130 243	2 241 285
1951	240 022	179 291	68 887	270 736	130 688	1 259 595	133 258	2 282 477
1952	241 456	182 674	69 800	275 043	134 326	1 284 586	136 286	2 324 171
1953	243 062	185 936	70 742	279 411	138 118	1 310 665	141 370	2 369 304
1954	244 808	189 438	71 686	283 866	142 062	1 338 583	142 517	2 412 960
1955	246 576	193 001	72 665	288 692	146 136	1 365 918	145 719	2 458 707
1956	248 536	196 630	73 753	293 449	150 322	1 393 929	149 217	2 505 836
1957	250 586	200 534	74 873	297 996	154 648	1 425 055	152 786	2 556 478
1958	252 668	204 130	76 023	302 628	159 087	1 457 274	156 441	2 608 251
1959	254 822	207 743	77 229	307 430	163 665	1 485 669	160 133	2 656 691
1960	256 814	211 232	78 390	312 221	168 405	1 502 787	163 805	2 693 654
1961	259 299	212 895	79 512	317 045	173 190	1 514 236	167 396	2 723 573
1962	262 130	218 338	80 594	321 508	178 112	1 537 994	172 300	2 770 976
1963	264 720	221 651	81 683	325 751	183 168	1 573 482	176 786	2 827 241
1964	267 103	224 925	82 796	329 782	188 386	1 608 497	181 399	2 882 888
1965	269 447	227 957	83 899	333 370	193 767	1 645 569	186 135	2 940 144
1966	271 506	230 890	85 014	336 666	199 221	1 685 033	191 007	2 999 337
1967	273 153	233 651	86 277	339 908	204 833	1 724 769	195 901	3 058 492
1968	274 507	236 198	87 492	343 400	210 613	1 766 651	200 947	3 119 808
1969	276 640	238 748	88 680	346 517	216 531	1 809 269	206 122	3 182 507
1970	278 584	241 703	89 887	349 068	222 558	1 853 778	211 325	3 246 903
1971	280 762	245 187	91 177	352 221	228 393	1 900 958	216 450	3 315 148
1972	282 524	247 961	92 550	355 400	234 369	1 947 195	221 693	3 381 692
1973	284 077	250 510	93 893	358 508	240 473	1 992 566	227 084	3 447 111
1974	285 125	253 088	95 511	361 851	246 691	2 036 506	232 935	3 511 707
1975	285 605	255 784	97 394	365 156	253 008	2 078 929	238 991	3 574 867
1976	285 885	258 209	98 660	368 407	259 421	2 118 347	245 351	3 634 280
1977	286 161	260 875	100 291	371 637	265 949	2 157 094	251 894	3 693 901
1978	286 900	263 720	101 905	374 713	272 587	2 196 786	258 805	3 755 416
1979	287 508	266 477	103 479	377 599	279 320	2 236 777	266 148	3 817 308
1980	288 410	269 666	104 985	380 459	286 399	2 276 375	273 527	3 879 821
1981	289 186	272 584	106 639	383 353	293 063	2 316 292	281 117	3 942 234
1982	289 688	275 491	108 128	386 348	299 813	2 358 288	288 991	4 006 747
1983	290 037	278 221	109 629	389 488	306 640	2 401 098	297 156	4 072 269
1984	290 402	280 843	111 095	392 628	313 550	2 442 510	305 668	4 136 696
1985	290 899	283 520	112 548	395 683	321 123	2 485 714	314 568	4 204 055
1986	291 594	286 294	113 706	398 915	328 092	2 529 186	323 245	4 271 032
1987	292 341	289 154	114 887	402 281	335 132	2 574 242	332 604	4 340 641
1988	293 510	292 081	116 211	405 113	341 732	2 620 795	342 105	4 411 547
1989	295 122	295 168	117 491	407 844	348 711	2 665 944	351 772	4 482 052
1990	297 322	296 942	118 983	409 330	355 734	2 725 523	361 611	4 565 445
1991	299 123	300 386	120 325	410 957	362 190	2 769 172	372 116	4 634 269
1992	301 134	304 989	121 527	411 852	368 766	2 817 206	382 684	4 708 158

Table E-2. **Regional and World Totals: GDP Level, 1820-1992: Sample (56 countries)**

(million 1990 Geary-Khamis Dollars)

	Western Europe (12)	Western Offshoots (4)	Southern Europe (5)	Eastern Europe (7)	Latin America (7)	Asia (11)	Africa (10)	Total Sample (56)
1820	132 629	13 557	26 813	62 984	11 264	368 750	19 192	635 189
1870	304 101	111 535	43 924	135 415	23 525	405 866	23 215	1 047 581
1900	550 612	347 488	69 389	247 306	56 216	550 243	27 820	1 849 074
1913	732 332	583 423	83 786	365 753	94 230	657 699	36 852	2 554 075
1929	922 306	934 153	116 230	403 366	158 269	858 323	57 501	3 450 149
1932	824 408	691 304	114 767	402 361	138 020	879 635	62 502	3 112 547
1938	1 040 726	899 185	115 588	586 493	193 991	959 048	73 845	3 868 875
1948	1 047 063	1 488 672	132 101	576 465	307 230	833 378	97 524	4 482 433
1950	1 220 373	1 629 665	137 165	694 037	332 379	898 513	103 103	5 015 234
1951	1 290 547	1 779 923	150 078	706 926	350 055	969 657	110 418	5 357 605
1952	1 334 048	1 856 950	159 942	742 687	361 087	1 060 962	113 748	5 629 424
1953	1 404 671	1 926 708	168 500	776 974	376 189	1 128 408	118 094	5 899 544
1954	1 480 936	1 920 207	173 685	814 280	401 099	1 180 815	126 218	6 097 240
1955	1 575 895	2 031 782	183 694	880 240	427 977	1 244 656	131 002	6 475 247
1956	1 644 859	2 081 570	193 989	947 848	444 764	1 332 916	133 805	6 779 751
1957	1 718 039	2 123 265	203 824	980 208	480 391	1 381 348	137 339	7 024 415
1958	1 755 470	2 120 854	211 501	1 049 458	505 865	1 490 294	138 247	7 271 689
1959	1 845 765	2 235 522	214 352	1 054 959	520 366	1 528 354	147 018	7 546 336
1960	1 971 104	2 284 020	221 695	1 145 764	556 071	1 564 656	152 788	7 896 098
1961	2 071 185	2 340 552	239 400	1 212 091	584 159	1 532 793	156 995	8 137 175
1962	2 168 120	2 485 585	256 888	1 241 569	607 500	1 585 993	167 113	8 512 768
1963	2 263 481	2 597 779	278 698	1 236 346	623 275	1 706 950	178 401	8 884 930
1964	2 397 734	2 754 909	295 333	1 372 283	667 166	1 880 353	190 014	9 557 792
1965	2 491 554	2 927 640	311 721	1 444 978	701 171	1 993 928	200 313	10 071 305
1966	2 578 297	3 114 064	345 976	1 521 024	735 342	2 148 462	205 909	10 649 074
1967	2 660 855	3 198 726	366 860	1 586 489	767 395	2 229 970	205 980	11 016 274
1968	2 799 027	3 344 653	396 299	1 670 600	816 440	2 339 362	213 780	11 580 161
1969	2 958 794	3 459 553	430 371	1 701 196	871 122	2 572 499	234 280	12 227 815
1970	3 086 595	3 473 865	458 802	1 813 192	933 559	2 848 582	255 222	12 869 817
1971	3 179 484	3 600 635	487 676	1 883 020	991 141	2 978 867	268 645	13 389 468
1972	3 301 247	3 801 290	526 582	1 915 802	1 055 435	3 112 627	275 584	13 988 567
1973	3 490 650	4 027 071	566 068	2 058 607	1 142 248	3 347 598	289 241	14 921 483
1974	3 553 946	4 024 955	591 583	2 135 155	1 213 616	3 399 861	307 694	15 226 809
1975	3 512 545	4 006 883	606 427	2 160 152	1 248 980	3 580 765	312 392	15 428 144
1976	3 670 394	4 222 789	637 331	2 248 907	1 318 653	3 681 505	330 696	16 110 275
1977	3 769 455	4 423 463	662 024	2 309 048	1 381 164	3 893 377	344 706	16 783 237
1978	3 883 928	4 643 754	680 626	2 371 598	1 436 378	4 165 385	349 728	17 531 398
1979	4 033 873	4 784 661	687 529	2 373 281	1 533 013	4 340 643	365 244	18 118 245
1980	4 091 381	4 795 084	696 627	2 378 723	1 619 949	4 534 975	383 585	18 500 325
1981	4 096 264	4 931 235	704 136	2 386 245	1 620 099	4 742 774	391 002	18 871 756
1982	4 125 086	4 835 921	718 402	2 434 867	1 602 738	4 957 866	399 291	19 074 172
1983	4 198 007	5 015 134	730 955	2 501 278	1 559 680	5 261 676	394 250	19 660 980
1984	4 303 141	5 348 578	748 743	2 545 514	1 622 014	5 642 591	408 498	20 619 078
1985	4 414 506	5 532 348	772 034	2 562 755	1 675 583	6 047 188	424 673	21 429 086
1986	4 536 247	5 693 540	802 211	2 658 775	1 753 301	6 378 255	441 331	22 263 660
1987	4 654 672	5 880 465	845 842	2 679 131	1 813 003	6 814 942	449 988	23 138 044
1988	4 839 361	6 109 823	884 709	2 727 131	1 825 915	7 414 597	473 714	24 275 251
1989	4 995 048	6 265 374	917 961	2 747 376	1 837 762	7 795 144	488 948	25 047 613
1990	5 134 334	6 313 209	961 619	2 642 474	1 835 285	8 168 511	499 823	25 555 255
1991	5 189 112	6 238 030	982 853	2 267 565	1 901 863	8 624 820	506 936	25 711 179
1992	5 234 878	6 358 960	1 005 450	1 897 938	1 952 206	9 125 053	504 367	26 078 852

Table E-3. **Regional and World Averages: GDP per Capita, 1820-1992: Sample (56 countries)**

(in 1990 Geary-Khamis Dollars)

	Western Europe (12)	Western Offshoots (4)	Southern Europe (5)	Eastern Europe (7)	Latin America (7)	Asia (11)	Africa (10)	Average (56)
1820	1 292	1 205	806	750	715	550	450	661
1870	2 110	2 440	1 111	1 030	800	580	480	920
1900	3 092	4 022	1 575	1 263	1 134	681	500	1 305
1913	3 704	5 237	1 753	1 557	1 515	742	575	1 592
1929	4 385	6 653	2 158	1 573	1 929	858	660	1 884
1932	3 851	4 790	2 057	1 522	1 593	853	678	1 648
1938	4 719	5 977	1 931	2 083	1 975	874	714	1 923
1948	4 478	8 760	1 984	2 222	2 540	691	778	2 055
1950	5 123	9 255	2 025	2 604	2 614	727	792	2 238
1951	5 377	9 928	2 179	2 611	2 679	770	829	2 347
1952	5 525	10 165	2 291	2 700	2 688	826	835	2 422
1953	5 779	10 362	2 382	2 781	2 724	861	835	2 490
1954	6 049	10 136	2 423	2 869	2 823	882	886	2 527
1955	6 391	10 527	2 528	3 049	2 929	911	899	2 634
1956	6 618	10 586	2 630	3 230	2 959	956	897	2 706
1957	6 856	10 588	2 722	3 289	3 106	969	899	2 748
1958	6 948	10 390	2 782	3 468	3 180	1 023	884	2 788
1959	7 243	10 761	2 776	3 432	3 179	1 029	918	2 841
1960	7 675	10 813	2 828	3 670	3 302	1 041	933	2 931
1961	7 988	10 994	3 011	3 823	3 373	1 012	938	2 988
1962	8 271	11 384	3 187	3 862	3 411	1 031	970	3 072
1963	8 550	11 720	3 412	3 795	3 403	1 085	1 009	3 143
1964	8 977	12 248	3 567	4 161	3 541	1 169	1 047	3 315
1965	9 247	12 843	3 715	4 334	3 619	1 212	1 076	3 425
1966	9 496	13 487	4 070	4 518	3 691	1 275	1 078	3 550
1967	9 741	13 690	4 252	4 667	3 746	1 293	1 051	3 602
1968	10 197	14 160	4 530	4 865	3 876	1 324	1 064	3 712
1969	10 695	14 490	4 853	4 909	4 023	1 422	1 137	3 842
1970	11 080	14 372	5 104	5 194	4 195	1 537	1 208	3 964
1971	11 324	14 685	5 349	5 346	4 340	1 567	1 241	4 039
1972	11 685	15 330	5 690	5 391	4 503	1 599	1 243	4 137
1973	12 288	16 075	6 029	5 742	4 750	1 680	1 274	4 329
1974	12 465	15 903	6 194	5 901	4 920	1 669	1 321	4 336
1975	12 299	15 665	6 227	5 916	4 937	1 722	1 307	4 316
1976	12 839	16 354	6 460	6 104	5 083	1 738	1 348	4 433
1977	13 172	16 956	6 601	6 213	5 193	1 805	1 368	4 543
1978	13 538	17 609	6 679	6 329	5 269	1 896	1 351	4 668
1979	14 030	17 955	6 644	6 285	5 488	1 941	1 372	4 746
1980	14 186	17 782	6 635	6 252	5 656	1 992	1 402	4 768
1981	14 165	18 091	6 603	6 225	5 528	2 048	1 391	4 787
1982	14 240	17 554	6 644	6 302	5 346	2 102	1 382	4 761
1983	14 474	18 026	6 668	6 422	5 086	2 191	1 327	4 828
1984	14 818	19 045	6 740	6 483	5 173	2 310	1 336	4 984
1985	15 175	19 513	6 860	6 477	5 218	2 433	1 350	5 097
1986	15 557	19 887	7 055	6 665	5 344	2 522	1 365	5 213
1987	15 922	20 337	7 362	6 660	5 410	2 647	1 353	5 331
1988	16 488	20 918	7 613	6 732	5 343	2 829	1 385	5 503
1989	16 925	21 226	7 813	6 736	5 270	2 924	1 390	5 588
1990	17 269	21 261	8 082	6 456	5 159	2 997	1 382	5 598
1991	17 348	20 767	8 168	5 518	5 251	3 115	1 362	5 548
1992	17 384	20 850	8 273	4 608	5 294	3 239	1 318	5 539

Appendix F

GDP, Population and Per Capita GDP in 143 Non-Sample Countries and the Degree of Conjecture in the Estimates

In order to get a picture for the world as a whole, the estimates for the 56 country sample were supplemented with estimates for 143 non-sample countries. For 1950-92, I relied mainly on information in the OECD Development Centre's data files. For 1820-1950, I had very little information on individual countries within this group and I made crude estimates by region as explained below. The 143 non-sample countries represented 6.8 per cent of world output in 1992, and 13.5 per cent of population.

The Development Centre data bank was started in 1964 and covers the years since 1950. It is based on questionnaires sent annually since then to the countries on which it reports. It has been established longer than the data set collected by the World Bank for its publication *World Tables* (which goes back to 1960 at best). The United Nations Statistical Office also has such a data bank, with data from 1960 onwards. There are discrepancies between the three data banks, but as the Development Centre bank has better coverage, is better documented, has had continuity of management and was more accessible, there were considerable advantages in using it for the majority of countries.

The Nature of the Evidence for 1950-92 (see Table F-4)

The 199 countries included in my world estimates can be divided into 4 groups:

a) Group 1 consists of the 56 country sample for which the basic source material is laid out fully in Appendices A-D, together with some degree of conjecture to fill data gaps and arrive at regional totals (as noted in Appendix E);

b) Group 2 consists of 94 countries for which more or less complete annual information was available on population and GDP movements for 1950-92. For these countries estimates of the 1990 benchmark level of GDP in 1990 Geary-Khamis dollars were derived from the Penn World Tables 5.5 of Summers and Heston (1993). This group represented 5.7 per cent of world GDP in 1990, and 10.4 per cent of world population. The reliability of this information is on a par with that for the 10 African countries in our sample;

c) Group 3 consists of 22 countries where more or less complete annual information was available for population and GDP movements for 1950-92, but where estimates of the GDP level in Geary-Khamis dollars were not available. For 16 of these countries, per capita GDP levels in the benchmark year 1990 were assumed to be the same as the average for the Group 1 countries in the region to which they belonged (except that, for Asian countries, a Group 1 average excluding Japan was used). For the other 6 countries, there were special circumstances likely to make their GDP per capita differ from the regional average, and for these an *ad hoc* assumption was made. For Cuba, it was assumed that GDP per capita was likely to be about the same as the Group 2 average for Latin America; for Afghanistan, Kampuchea and Vietnam it was assumed that war conditions had reduced their 1990 per capita GDP to $1 000; for Macao, per capita GDP was assumed to be half of that in Hong Kong; and for Libya to be the same as in Algeria. These 22 countries represented 0.6 per cent of world GDP in 1990, and 2.2 per cent of population;

d) Group 4 consists of 27 countries for which some information on population was available, but where there were no indications of GDP movement or of per capita levels. For these countries, which represented only 0.3 per cent of world GDP and 0.6 per cent of population, the estimates were therefore highly conjectural. In most cases it was assumed that per capita GDP movement in these countries corresponded to the Group 1 average for their respective regions. Their level of GDP per capita was assumed to correspond with the average for their region, except for Albania, Gaza and the West Bank, where the level was assumed to be below the regional average.

Nature of the Conjectures for Non-Sample Countries for 1820-1929

For the 143 non-sample countries, there was virtually no information for 1820-1929. Regional GDP estimates were derived by using separate hypotheses for the movement of population and GDP in extrapolating backwards from 1950.

Population

For population 1820-1950, regional movements were generally assumed to be proportionally the same as those for Group 1 countries in the same region. For Latin America there is information on population in the non-sample countries for 1929 from the *Cambridge History of Latin America*. Table F-1 shows the relative importance of the non-sample countries in the 199 country total. It also illustrates the assumptions that were made for each region. Except for East Germany, where 1820-1929 population was assumed to move with that in the rest of Germany, the proportionate adjustment for the non-sample countries was the same for each region for the whole period 1820-1929. The non-sample share was biggest in Africa and Latin America. The 143 country total was derived as the sum of the estimates for each region. As the growth rates were different from region to region, the percentages in the bottom row are not stable.

Per Capita Product

The next step was to assess the likely level of per capita income in each of the non-sample regions. Here again, I generally assumed the change in levels to correspond with those for Group 1 countries in the same region, with some adjustments.

a) The 1820-1929 per capita product of the 11 small countries of Western Europe was assumed to have been the same as the average for the Group 1 countries in that region. The higher income of the small countries in 1950-92 was due to special tax haven features;

b) Cyprus and Malta were assumed to have had 1820-1929 per capita income levels which bore the same relation to the average for Group 1 Southern European countries as they had in 1950;

c) For Albania the 1820-1929 per capita income movement was assumed to be the same as for the corresponding Group 1 region. For East Germany the movement was assumed to be the same as the average for the rest of Germany;

d) For Latin America, it was assumed that the 1950 proportionate differences between sample and non-sample per capita GDP also prevailed in 1820-1929;

e) For non-sample Asia and Africa it was assumed that 1820-1929 per capita product was the same as the average for the respective Group 1 countries. The substantial per capita advantage of the Asian non-sample group in 1950-92 was due in major part to the oil revenue of selected countries, which either did not exist or was much smaller in 1820-1929.

GDP

The estimates for GDP for the non-sample countries were derived from the assumptions for population and for per capita product. Table F-3 shows the GDP shares of non-sample countries in each of the regional totals.

Table F-1. **Percentage Share of Non-Sample Countries in the Regional and World Population Totals**

	1820	1870	1900	1913	1929	1950	1973	1992
Western Europe (11 countries)	0.3	0.3	0.3	0.3	0.3	0.3	0.3	0.4
Western Offshoots (0 countries)	0.0	0.0	0.0	0.0	0.0	0.0	0.0	0.0
Southern Europe (2 countries)	1.1	1.1	1.1	1.1	1.1	1.1	0.9	0.9
Eastern Europe (2 countries)	6.5	6.5	6.0	6.0	5.9	6.9	5.1	4.4
Latin America (37 countries)	22.4	22.4	22.4	22.4	22.4	21.7	20.3	20.0
Asia and Oceania (45 countries)	9.0	9.0	9.0	9.0	9.0	9.0	9.6	10.9
Africa (46 countries)	41.6	41.6	41.6	41.6	41.6	41.6	40.7	41.7
Total (143 countries)	10.1	9.7	9.4	9.4	10.6	10.8	11.5	13.5

Source: See text for 1820-1929; 1950-92 from OECD data files (see Table F-4 for country detail).

Table F-2. **Average Level of GDP per Capita in Non-Sample Countries as a Percent of Regional and World Averages**

	1820	1870	1900	1913	1929	1950	1973	1992
Western Europe (11 countries)	100	100	100	100	100	122	103	105
Southern Europe (2 countries)	80	80	80	80	80	80	76	119
Eastern Europe (2 countries)	142	173	224	223	246	114	101	126
Latin America (37 countries)	82	82	82	82	82	82	68	53
Asia and Oceania (45 countries)	100	100	100	100	100	149	163	103
Africa (46 countries)	100	100	100	100	100	106	104	96
Total (143 countries)	85	74	69	67	63	62	59	51

Source: See text for 1820-1929; 1950-92 from OECD data files (see Table F-4 for country detail).

Table F-3. **Percentage Share of Non-Sample Countries in the Regional and World GDP Totals**

	1820	1870	1900	1913	1929	1950	1973	1992
Western Europe (11 countries)	0.3	0.3	0.3	0.3	0.3	0.4	0.3	0.4
Western Offshoots (0 countries)	0.0	0.0	0.0	0.0	0.0	0.0	0.0	0.0
Southern Europe (2 countries)	0.9	0.9	0.9	0.9	0.9	0.9	0.7	1.0
Eastern Europe (2 countries)	9.2	11.3	13.6	13.4	14.6	7.8	5.2	5.6
Latin America (37 countries)	18.3	18.3	18.3	18.3	18.3	17.7	13.7	12.2
Asia (45 countries)	9.0	9.0	9.0	9.0	9.0	13.4	15.6	11.3
Africa (46 countries)	41.6	41.6	41.6	41.6	41.6	44.3	42.4	40.1
Total (143 countries)	8.6	7.2	6.5	6.3	8.5	6.6	7.1	6.8

Table F-4. **Estimates of GDP, Population and Per Capita GDP for 143 Non-Sample Countries in 1950 and 1990**

	1950			1990		
	GDP (million $)	Population (000s)	GDP per capita ($)	GDP (million $)	Population (000s)	GDP per capita ($)
			Western Europe			
Iceland	717	143	5 014	4 432	255	17 380
Luxembourg	2 344	296	7 919	7 655	380	20 145
Total group 2	*3 061*	*439*	*6 973*	*12 087*	*635*	*19 035*
Andorra	31	6	5 123	898	52	17 269
Channel Islands	533	104	5 123	2 383	138	17 269
Faeroe Islands	159	31	5 123	812	47	17 269
Gibraltar	128	25	5 123	535	31	17 269
Greenland	118	23	5 123	967	56	17 269
Isle of Man	272	53	5 123	1 088	63	17 269
Liechtenstein	72	14	5 123	484	28	17 269
Monaco	108	21	5 123	484	28	17 269
San Marino	67	13	5 123	397	23	17 269
Total group 4	*1 486*	*290*	*5 123*	*8 047*	*466*	*17 269*
Total non-sample	*4 547*	*729*	*6 237*	*20 134*	*1 101*	*18 287*
Total sample	*1 220 373*	*238 228*	*5 123*	*5 134 334*	*297 322*	*17 269*
			Western Offshoots			
Total sample	*1 629 665*	*176 094*	*9 255*	*6 313 209*	*296 942*	*21 261*
			Southern Europe			
Cyprus	930	450	2 067	6 651	700	9 501
Malta	279	296	943	2 987	350	8 534
Total group 2	*1 209*	*746*	*1 621*	*9 638*	*1 050*	*9 179*
Total sample	*134 194*	*67 724*	*1 981*	*941 102*	*118 983*	*7 910*
			Eastern Europe			
DDR	57 499	18 388	3 127	91 897	16 111	5 704
Total group 2	*57 499*	*18 388*	*3 127*	*91 897*	*16 111*	*5 704*
Albania	1 228	1 219	1 007	8 125	3 250	2 500
Total group 4	*1 228*	*1 219*	*1 007*	*8 125*	*3 250*	*2 500*
Total non-sample	*58 727*	*19 607*	*2 995*	*100 022*	*19 361*	*5 166*
Total sample	*693 724*	*266 509*	*2 603*	*2 642 474*	*408 963*	*6 461*

Table F-4 (continued). **Estimates of GDP, Population and Per Capita GDP for 143 Non-Sample countries in 1950 and 1990**

	1950			1990		
	GDP (million $)	Population (000s)	GDP per capita ($)	GDP (million $)	Population (000s)	GDP per capita ($)
			Latin America			
Bahamas	756	80	9 451	3 946	260	15 177
Barbados	448	197	2 276	2 138	260	8 223
Belize	110	65	1 689	735	190	3 868
Bolivia	4 940	2 622	1 884	12 908	7 400	1 744
Costa Rica	1 698	863	1 968	11 730	2 990	3 923
Dominica	82	51	1 615	279	80	3 488
Dominican Rep.	2 590	2 136	1 212	16 794	7 170	2 342
Ecuador	4 440	3 340	1 329	32 744	10 780	3 037
El Salvador	2 830	1 859	1 522	10 296	5 250	1 961
Grenada	71	78	906	310	111	2 793
Guatemala	4 823	2 876	1 677	22 643	9 200	2 461
Guyana	462	423	1 092	1 159	1 032	1 123
Haiti	2 959	3 008	984	5 939	5 725	1 037
Honduras	1 568	1 513	1 036	7 714	5 110	1 510
Jamaica	1 548	1 403	1 103	7 452	2 420	3 079
Nicaragua	1 864	1 052	1 772	5 513	3 662	1 505
Panama	1 335	816	1 636	8 424	2 420	3 481
Paraguay	1 864	1 391	1 340	11 428	4 280	2 670
Puerto Rico	4 309	2 207	1 952	39 496	3 599	10 974
St. Lucia	61	75	815	449	150	2 993
St. Vincent	79	56	1 404	392	120	3 267
Suriname	315	213	1 477	1 094	420	2 605
Trinidad & Tobago	2 677	590	4 537	11 926	1 281	9 310
Uruguay	8 096	2 062	3 926	15 974	3 100	5 153
Total group 2	*49 926*	*28 976*	*1 723*	*231 483*	*77 010*	*3 006*
Antigua & Barbuda	82	45	1 828	413	80	5 159
Bermuda	65	34	1 913	310	60	5 159
Cuba	20 139	5 516	3 651	31 920	10 640	3 000
Guadeloupe	359	214	1 676	1 801	349	5 159
Guyana (French)	138	32	4 303	516	100	5 159
Martinique	293	213	1 376	1 857	360	5 159
Netherlands Ant.	393	162	2 428	980	190	5 159
St. Kitts-Nevis	68	44	1 546	258	50	5 159
Total group 3	*21 537*	*6 260*	*3 440*	*38 054*	*11 829*	*3 217*
Aruba	52	20	2 614	310	60	5 159
Falkland Islands	5	2	2 614	10	2	5 159
St. Pierre & Miquelon	13	5	2 614	31	6	5 159
Turks & Caicos Islands	18	7	2 614	52	10	5 159
Virgin Islands	86	33	2 614	666	129	5 159
Total group 4	175	67	2 614	1 068	207	5 159
Total non-sample	71 638	35 303	2 029	270 605	89 046	3 039
Total sample	332 378	127 160	2 614	1 835 285	355 734	5 159

Table F-4 (continued). **Estimates of GDP, Population and Per Capita GDP for 143 Non-Sample countries in 1950 and 1990**

	1950			1990		
	GDP (million $)	Population (000s)	GDP per capita ($)	GDP (million $)	Population (000s)	GDP per capita ($)
			Asia			
Bahrain	613	113	5 424	5 209	500	10 418
Bhutan	369	750	492	1 407	1 520	926
Hong Kong	3 747	1 910	1 962	97 584	5 700	17 120
Iran	32 676	17 270	1 892	199 977	54 610	3 662
Iraq	5 407	5 171	1 046	34 238	18 192	1 882
Israel	3 107	1 267	2 452	47 047	4 660	10 096
Jordan	952	1 156	824	12 618	4 010	3 147
Kuwait	3 915	150	26 097	12 276	2 140	5 736
Laos	2 238	1 944	1 151	11 041	4 665	2 367
Malaysia	9 877	5 824	1 696	100 129	17 760	5 638
Nepal	6 358	8 720	729	22 240	18 920	1 175
Oman	287	401	716	10 839	1 500	7 226
Qatar	1 375	47	29 257	5 906	375	15 749
Saudi Arabia	9 061	4 137	2 190	151 996	14 870	10 222
Singapore	2 093	1 027	2 038	39 736	2 710	14 663
Sri Lanka	7 424	7 658	969	46 761	16 990	2 752
Syria	6 961	3 459	2 012	58 623	12 120	4 837
U. Arab Emirates	996	94	10 594	22 473	1 590	14 134
Yemen	3 285	4 195	783	21 294	10 647	2 000
Total group 2	*100 740*	*65 293*	*1 543*	*901 394*	*193 479*	*4 659*
Afghanistan	11 983	8 776	1 365	20 203	20 203	1 000
Brunei	79	46	1 712	587	260	2 259
Kampuchea	2 155	3 645	591	8 235	8 235	1 000
Lebanon	3 313	1 443	2 296	6 099	2 700	2 259
Macao	127	160	796	4 109	480	8 560
Maldives	43	82	528	497	220	2 259
Vietnam	10 451	29 274	357	66 230	66 230	1 000
Total group 3	*28 150*	*43 426*	*648*	*105 961*	*98 328*	*1 078*
Gaza	198	198	1 000	700	700	1 000
Guam	38	59	643	267	118	2 259
Mongolia	592	920	643	4 947	2 190	2 259
North Korea	5 842	9 083	643	49 178	21 773	2 259
West Bank	453	453	1 000	1 600	1 600	1 000
Total group 4	*7 122*	*10 713*	*665*	*56 691*	*26 381*	*2 149*
Total non-sample	*136 012*	*119 432*	*1 139*	*1 064 046*	*318 188*	*3 344*
Total sample	*897 300*	*1 235 327*	*726*	*8 168 511*	*2 725 523*	*2 997*

Table F-4 (continued). **Estimates of GDP, Population and Per Capita GDP for 143 Non-Sample countries in 1950 and 1990**

	1950			1990		
	GDP (million $)	Population (000s)	GDP per capita ($)	GDP (million $)	Population (000s)	GDP per capita ($)
			Oceania			
Fiji	851	294	2 895	3 440	730	4 712
Papua New Guinea	1 356	1 476	919	5 865	3 700	1 585
Solomon Islands	136	100	1 360	670	320	2 094
Tonga	41	47	872	210	90	2 333
Vanuatu	70	49	1 429	250	150	1 667
Western Samoa	85	63	1 349	299	160	1 869
Total group 2	*2 539*	*2 029*	*1 251*	*10 734*	*5 150*	*2 084*
Kiribati-Tuvalu	145	38	3 820	146	70	2 084
New Caledonia	97	59	1 649	354	170	2 084
Pacific Islands	104	54	1 923	354	170	2 084
Polynesia (French)	36	59	608	438	210	2 084
Total group 3	*382*	*210*	*1 820*	*1 292*	*620*	*2 084*
American Samoa	24	19	1 251	81	39	2 084
Marshall Islands	29	23	1 251	96	46	2 084
Micronesia	60	48	1 251	206	99	2 084
Wallis & Futuna	10	8	1 251	35	17	2 084
Total group 4	*123*	*98*	*1 251*	*419*	*201*	*2 084*
Total non-sample	*3 044*	*2 337*	*1 302*	*12 445*	*5 971*	*2 084*

Table F-4 (continued). **Estimates of GDP, Population and Per Capita GDP for 143 Non-Sample countries in 1950 and 1990**

	1950			1990		
	GDP (million $)	Population (000s)	GDP per capita ($)	GDP (million $)	Population (000s)	GDP per capita ($)
			Africa			
Algeria	11 557	8 358	1 383	70 407	25 010	2 815
Angola	3 941	3 997	986	6 554	10 020	654
Benin	1 779	1 636	1 087	5 248	4 740	1 107
Botswana	169	434	390	5 479	1 300	4 215
Burkina Faso	1 706	3 394	503	5 545	9 000	616
Burundi	718	2 244	320	3 272	5 460	599
Cameroon	3 900	4 855	803	17 115	11 830	1 447
Cape Verde	83	143	580	542	370	1 465
Centr. Afr. Rep.	957	1 314	729	1 952	3 033	644
Chad	1 160	2 583	449	2 374	5 680	418
Comoros Is.	83	157	528	294	550	535
Congo	1 096	824	1 330	5 972	2 270	2 631
Djibouti	83	159	523	490	405	1 210
Gabon	1 045	866	1 207	3 639	1 273	2 859
Gambia	124	271	459	629	730	862
Guinea	733	2 819	260	3 087	6 892	448
Guinea Bissau	157	559	280	751	960	782
Lesotho	231	712	324	1 818	1 770	1 027
Liberia	823	729	1 129	2 126	2 460	864
Madagascar	4 338	4 514	961	9 093	11 971	760
Malawi	858	2 802	306	4 840	8 290	584
Mali	1 411	3 441	410	5 059	9 396	538
Mauretania	479	779	615	1 873	2 020	927
Mauritius	1 129	465	2 428	7 211	1 050	6 868
Mozambique	6 753	6 749	1 001	13 445	15 660	859
Namibia	869	569	1 528	4 009	1 873	2 140
Niger	1 819	2 448	743	3 865	7 111	544
Reunion	452	244	1 854	2 514	590	4 261
Rwanda	1 168	1 927	606	5 360	7 234	741
Senegal	3 114	2 805	1 110	9 351	7 371	1 269
Seychelles	53	36	1 471	308	70	4 400
Sierra Leone	1 277	1 809	706	4 041	4 011	1 007
Somalia	2 290	2 411	950	6 429	7 500	857
Sudan	9 452	9 322	1 014	28 308	25 200	1 123
Swaziland	147	259	566	1 580	770	2 052
Togo	645	1 178	547	2 688	3 530	761
Tunisia	3 782	3 335	1 134	26 421	8 170	3 234
Uganda	6 487	5 644	1 149	17 457	18 494	944
Zambia	1 819	2 481	733	6 935	8 473	818
Zimbabwe	2 167	2 118	1 023	14 913	9 370	1 592
Total group 2	*80 853*	*91 390*	*885*	*312 994*	*251 907*	*1 242*
Equat. Guinea	114	197	578	576	417	1 382
Libya	824	1 029	801	12 780	4 540	2 815
S. Tome Principe	49	56	868	166	120	1 382
Total group 3	*986*	*1 282*	*769*	*13 522*	*5 077*	*2 663*
Mayotte	22	28	792	105	76	1 382
St. Helena	4	5	792	10	7	1 382
Western Sahara	53	67	792	246	178	1 382
Total group 4	*79*	*100*	*792*	*361*	*261*	*1 382*
Total non-sample	*81 919*	*92 772*	*792*	*326 877*	*257 245*	*1 271*
Total sample	*103 104*	*130 243*	*792*	*499 823*	*361 611*	*1 382*

Table F-5. **World and Regional Totals: Population, 1820-1992: Non-Sample (143 countries)**

(thousands at mid-year)

	Western Europe (11)	Western Offshoots	Southern Europe (2)	Eastern Europe (2)	Latin America (37)	Asia & Oceania (45)	Africa (46)	Total Non-Sample (143)
1820	314		367	5 842	4 553	66 115	30 378	107 569
1870	441		436	9 180	8 499	68 954	34 450	121 960
1900	545		485	12 610	14 330	79 627	39 636	147 233
1913	605		527	15 070	17 971	87 394	45 645	167 212
1929	644		594	16 166	23 710	112 869	62 029	216 012
1950	729		746	19 607	35 303	121 769	92 772	270 926
1951	736		754	19 589	36 155	124 256	94 528	276 019
1952	745		765	19 625	37 024	126 808	96 394	281 361
1953	753		774	19 599	38 163	129 528	98 375	287 193
1954	762		785	19 423	39 095	132 345	100 695	293 105
1955	772		788	19 334	40 038	135 242	102 728	298 902
1956	780		797	19 182	41 013	138 901	104 829	305 502
1957	789		810	18 967	42 011	142 088	107 019	311 684
1958	799		821	18 794	43 048	145 492	109 259	318 212
1959	807		833	18 724	44 156	149 011	111 569	325 100
1960	817		841	18 736	45 208	152 754	114 030	332 386
1961	828		845	18 671	46 274	156 535	116 629	339 782
1962	839		847	18 591	47 400	160 625	118 939	347 240
1963	849		849	18 697	48 591	164 708	121 772	355 465
1964	861		849	18 790	49 843	168 801	124 806	363 950
1965	871		848	18 890	51 069	173 035	127 683	372 397
1966	881		849	18 982	52 333	177 291	131 055	381 392
1967	888		855	19 062	53 573	181 718	134 243	390 339
1968	896		860	19 121	54 833	186 273	137 452	399 436
1969	905		864	19 172	56 076	190 853	140 721	408 592
1970	912		870	19 215	57 310	196 011	144 140	418 458
1971	922		873	19 281	58 649	200 915	147 909	428 548
1972	933		879	19 327	59 952	206 044	151 789	438 923
1973	943		885	19 330	61 351	211 204	155 754	449 467
1974	957		891	19 320	62 787	216 544	160 078	460 576
1975	968		902	19 291	64 264	221 880	164 350	471 655
1976	975		914	19 274	65 707	226 543	169 127	482 541
1977	983		925	19 301	67 208	231 778	174 371	494 566
1978	988		930	19 341	68 643	237 839	180 123	507 865
1979	998		939	19 380	70 097	243 674	185 360	520 448
1980	1 006		948	19 423	71 474	249 959	191 024	533 834
1981	1 015		957	19 473	72 925	256 731	197 604	548 705
1982	1 023		966	19 522	74 628	264 000	203 426	563 565
1983	1 031		978	19 544	76 323	271 603	209 579	579 059
1984	1 040		992	19 570	77 935	279 091	215 559	594 187
1985	1 047		1 005	19 598	79 585	286 877	222 120	610 232
1986	1 057		1 010	19 636	81 351	294 695	228 982	626 732
1987	1 067		1 020	19 711	83 318	303 581	235 777	644 474
1988	1 077		1 040	19 795	85 011	310 640	242 983	660 547
1989	1 091		1 040	19 588	86 897	318 047	250 282	676 945
1990	1 101		1 050	19 361	89 046	324 159	257 245	691 962
1991	1 120		1 070	19 222	90 981	334 959	264 670	712 022
1992	1 122		1 080	19 105	92 749	345 619	273 520	733 195

Table F-6. **World and Regional Totals: GDP Level, 1820-1992: Non-Sample (143 countries)**

(million 1990 Geary-Khamis Dollars)

	Western Europe (11)	Western Offshoots	Southern Europe (2)	Eastern Europe (2)	Latin America (37)	Asia & Oceania (45)	Africa (46)	Total Non-Sample (143)
1820	406		237	6 385	2 522	36 363	13 670	59 583
1870	931		388	17 268	5 269	39 903	16 536	80 295
1900	1 685		612	38 851	12 610	54 226	19 818	127 802
1913	2 241		739	56 784	21 134	64 846	26 246	171 990
1929	2 824		1 026	68 883	35 494	96 842	40 939	246 008
1950	4 547		1 209	58 727	71 638	139 057	81 919	357 096
1951	4 448		1 201	59 026	74 783	145 214	84 402	369 075
1952	4 745		1 305	60 812	77 916	151 564	88 195	384 538
1953	4 894		1 420	59 329	79 412	161 672	91 458	398 184
1954	5 077		1 456	60 481	83 018	171 789	94 745	416 566
1955	5 404		1 505	64 484	85 917	176 129	98 493	431 932
1956	5 650		1 672	66 914	89 525	186 663	104 268	454 693
1957	5 877		1 758	69 355	92 966	196 609	108 512	475 077
1958	6 042		1 744	73 116	95 503	206 591	112 640	495 635
1959	6 269		1 830	75 385	97 770	219 527	120 991	521 771
1960	6 594		1 750	80 411	101 184	235 903	126 696	552 539
1961	6 851		1 892	82 379	104 370	249 527	127 635	572 653
1962	7 108		2 004	82 544	109 156	265 734	128 422	594 969
1963	7 465		2 101	80 948	113 493	281 831	136 655	622 494
1964	8 033		1 950	84 377	118 766	300 524	143 895	657 546
1965	8 338		2 318	87 217	123 362	324 592	152 721	698 548
1966	8 642		2 482	90 748	129 301	344 481	156 968	732 623
1967	8 748		2 785	94 420	134 128	366 345	164 177	770 603
1968	9 011		2 943	98 524	139 770	399 496	176 572	826 315
1969	9 659		3 200	100 093	146 535	434 815	187 822	882 124
1970	10 044		3 359	102 797	153 190	473 547	197 854	940 792
1971	10 531		3 715	106 030	157 784	516 226	201 138	995 424
1972	11 115		3 954	109 255	164 688	571 144	211 080	1 071 237
1973	11 900		4 062	111 938	181 707	620 546	212 838	1 142 991
1974	12 378		3 606	114 659	185 505	673 199	217 719	1 207 065
1975	12 056		3 284	116 641	189 666	697 155	221 495	1 240 298
1976	12 597		3 869	117 270	199 113	786 138	235 788	1 354 775
1977	13 100		4 432	121 437	209 366	838 880	246 769	1 433 984
1978	13 712		4 823	122 114	219 023	823 929	255 175	1 438 776
1979	14 266		5 309	122 613	224 878	849 052	263 899	1 480 018
1980	14 646		5 643	125 547	232 842	856 552	270 217	1 505 449
1981	14 828		5 821	124 701	236 201	873 090	275 352	1 529 992
1982	15 142		6 107	126 733	234 593	910 138	286 021	1 578 734
1983	15 303		6 310	128 113	235 344	935 433	292 346	1 612 849
1984	16 021		6 707	130 565	239 750	963 306	294 642	1 650 991
1985	16 570		6 979	131 181	244 086	965 864	301 651	1 666 331
1986	17 358		7 248	133 272	248 777	935 194	304 774	1 646 623
1987	18 169		7 693	133 927	253 659	967 493	308 751	1 689 692
1988	18 872		8 346	136 882	260 300	978 998	314 410	1 717 808
1989	19 629		8 925	135 681	266 394	1 006 694	324 416	1 761 740
1990	20 134		9 638	100 022	270 605	1 076 491	326 877	1 803 767
1991	20 548		9 905	93 055	268 026	1 119 048	331 450	1 842 032
1992	20 548		11 607	112 656	272 468	1 161 741	338 048	1 916 068

Table F-7. **World and Regional Averages: GDP per Capita, 1820-1992: Non-Sample (143 countries)**

(1990 Geary-Khamis Dollars)

	Western Europe (11)	Western Offshoots	Southern Europe (2)	Eastern Europe (2)	Latin America (37)	Asia & Oceania (45)	Africa (46)	Average (143)
1820	1 292		645	1 093	554	550	450	554
1870	2 110		889	1 881	620	580	480	658
1900	3 092		1 261	3 081	880	681	500	868
1913	3 704		1 403	3 768	1 176	742	575	1 029
1929	4 385		1 727	4 261	1 497	858	660	1 139
1950	6 237		1 621	2 995	2 029	1 142	883	1 318
1951	6 040		1 593	3 013	2 068	1 169	893	1 337
1952	6 371		1 706	3 099	2 104	1 195	915	1 367
1953	6 496		1 834	3 027	2 081	1 248	930	1 386
1954	6 663		1 854	3 114	2 124	1 298	941	1 421
1955	7 004		1 910	3 335	2 146	1 302	959	1 445
1956	7 242		2 098	3 488	2 183	1 344	995	1 488
1957	7 450		2 170	3 657	2 213	1 384	1 014	1 524
1958	7 565		2 124	3 890	2 219	1 420	1 031	1 558
1959	7 765		2 197	4 026	2 214	1 473	1 084	1 605
1960	8 070		2 081	4 292	2 238	1 544	1 111	1 662
1961	8 274		2 238	4 412	2 255	1 594	1 094	1 685
1962	8 473		2 366	4 440	2 303	1 654	1 080	1 713
1963	8 794		2 475	4 330	2 336	1 711	1 122	1 751
1964	9 331		2 297	4 491	2 383	1 780	1 153	1 807
1965	9 574		2 733	4 617	2 416	1 876	1 196	1 876
1966	9 809		2 923	4 781	2 471	1 943	1 198	1 921
1967	9 850		3 257	4 953	2 504	2 016	1 223	1 974
1968	10 053		3 422	5 153	2 549	2 145	1 285	2 069
1969	10 678		3 704	5 221	2 613	2 278	1 335	2 159
1970	11 015		3 861	5 350	2 673	2 416	1 373	2 248
1971	11 420		4 256	5 499	2 690	2 569	1 360	2 323
1972	11 919		4 499	5 653	2 747	2 772	1 391	2 441
1973	12 619		4 590	5 791	2 962	2 938	1 367	2 543
1974	12 940		4 047	5 935	2 955	3 109	1 360	2 621
1975	12 452		3 641	6 046	2 951	3 142	1 348	2 630
1976	12 921		4 233	6 084	3 030	3 470	1 394	2 808
1977	13 331		4 791	6 292	3 115	3 619	1 415	2 899
1978	13 872		5 186	6 314	3 191	3 464	1 417	2 833
1979	14 290		5 654	6 327	3 208	3 484	1 424	2 844
1980	14 555		5 953	6 464	3 258	3 427	1 415	2 820
1981	14 605		6 082	6 404	3 239	3 401	1 393	2 788
1982	14 796		6 322	6 492	3 144	3 447	1 406	2 801
1983	14 837		6 452	6 555	3 084	3 444	1 395	2 785
1984	15 410		6 761	6 672	3 076	3 452	1 367	2 779
1985	15 828		6 944	6 693	3 067	3 367	1 358	2 731
1986	16 419		7 176	6 787	3 058	3 173	1 331	2 627
1987	17 035		7 542	6 794	3 044	3 187	1 310	2 622
1988	17 524		8 025	6 915	3 062	3 152	1 294	2 601
1989	17 984		8 582	6 927	3 066	3 165	1 296	2 602
1990	18 287		9 179	5 166	3 039	3 321	1 271	2 607
1991	18 346		9 257	4 841	2 945	3 341	1 252	2 587
1992	18 313		9 821	5 897	2 938	3 361	1 236	2 613

Appendix G

Regional and World Totals

Tables G-1, G-2 and G-3 show the regional and world totals for population, GDP and GDP per capita for 199 countries for the benchmark years 1820, 1870, 1900, 1913, 1929 and annual figures for 1950-92.

Table G-1 is the sum of the estimates for the sample and non-sample countries in Tables E-1 and F-5. Table G-2 is the sum of the estimates in Tables E-2 and F-6. Table G-3 is derived by dividing the GDP estimates in Table G-2, by the population figures in Table G-1.

Table G-1. **World and Regional Totals: Population, 1820-1992: Sample and Non-Sample (199 countries)**

(thousands at mid-year)

	Western Europe (23)	Western Offshoots (4)	Southern Europe (7)	Eastern Europe (9)	Latin America (44)	Asia & Oceania (56)	Africa (56)	World (199)
1820	103 005	11 255	33 644	89 821	20 307	736 836	73 026	1 067 894
1870	144 572	45 708	39 981	140 689	37 905	768 472	82 815	1 260 142
1900	178 595	86 396	44 543	208 485	63 919	887 430	95 281	1 564 649
1913	198 320	111 401	48 311	249 968	80 153	973 985	109 726	1 771 864
1929	210 960	140 417	54 450	272 602	105 751	1 113 551	149 111	2 046 842
1950	238 957	176 094	68 470	286 116	162 463	1 357 096	223 015	2 512 211
1951	240 758	179 291	69 641	290 325	166 843	1 383 851	227 786	2 558 496
1952	242 201	182 674	70 565	294 668	171 350	1 411 394	232 680	2 605 532
1953	243 815	185 936	71 516	299 010	176 281	1 440 193	239 745	2 656 497
1954	245 570	189 438	72 471	303 289	181 157	1 470 928	243 212	2 706 065
1955	247 348	193 001	73 453	308 026	186 174	1 501 160	248 447	2 757 609
1956	249 316	196 630	74 550	312 631	191 335	1 532 830	254 046	2 811 338
1957	251 375	200 534	75 683	316 963	196 659	1 567 143	259 805	2 868 162
1958	253 467	204 130	76 844	321 422	202 135	1 602 766	265 700	2 926 463
1959	255 629	207 743	78 062	326 154	207 821	1 634 680	271 702	2 981 791
1960	257 631	211 232	79 231	330 957	213 613	1 655 541	277 835	3 026 040
1961	260 127	212 895	80 357	335 716	219 464	1 670 771	284 025	3 063 355
1962	262 969	218 338	81 441	340 099	225 512	1 698 619	291 239	3 118 216
1963	265 569	221 651	82 532	344 448	231 759	1 738 190	298 558	3 182 706
1964	267 964	224 925	83 645	348 572	238 229	1 777 298	306 205	3 246 838
1965	270 318	227 957	84 747	352 260	244 836	1 818 604	313 818	3 312 541
1966	272 387	230 890	85 863	355 648	251 554	1 862 324	322 062	3 380 729
1967	274 041	233 651	87 132	358 970	258 406	1 906 487	330 144	3 448 831
1968	275 403	236 198	88 352	362 521	265 446	1 952 924	338 399	3 519 244
1969	277 545	238 748	89 544	365 689	272 607	2 000 122	346 843	3 591 099
1970	279 496	241 703	90 757	368 283	279 868	2 049 789	355 465	3 665 361
1971	281 684	245 187	92 050	371 502	287 042	2 101 873	364 359	3 743 696
1972	283 457	247 961	93 429	374 727	294 321	2 153 239	373 482	3 820 615
1973	285 020	250 510	94 778	377 838	301 824	2 203 770	382 838	3 896 578
1974	286 082	253 088	96 402	381 171	309 478	2 253 050	393 013	3 972 283
1975	286 573	255 784	98 296	384 447	317 272	2 300 809	403 341	4 046 522
1976	286 860	258 209	99 574	387 681	325 128	2 344 890	414 478	4 116 821
1977	287 144	260 875	101 216	390 938	333 157	2 388 872	426 265	4 188 467
1978	287 888	263 720	102 835	394 054	341 230	2 434 625	438 928	4 263 281
1979	288 506	266 477	104 418	396 979	349 417	2 480 451	451 508	4 337 756
1980	289 416	269 666	105 933	399 882	357 873	2 526 334	464 551	4 413 655
1981	290 201	272 584	107 596	402 826	365 988	2 573 023	478 721	4 490 939
1982	290 711	275 491	109 094	405 870	374 441	2 622 288	492 417	4 570 312
1983	291 068	278 221	110 607	409 032	382 963	2 672 701	506 735	4 651 328
1984	291 442	280 843	112 087	412 198	391 485	2 721 601	521 227	4 730 883
1985	291 946	283 520	113 553	415 281	400 708	2 772 591	536 688	4 814 287
1986	292 651	286 294	114 716	418 551	409 443	2 823 881	552 227	4 897 764
1987	293 408	289 154	115 907	421 992	418 450	2 877 823	568 381	4 985 115
1988	294 587	292 081	117 251	424 908	426 743	2 931 435	585 088	5 072 094
1989	296 213	295 168	118 531	427 432	435 608	2 983 991	602 054	5 158 997
1990	298 423	296 942	120 033	428 691	444 780	3 049 682	618 856	5 257 407
1991	300 243	300 386	121 395	430 179	453 171	3 104 131	636 786	5 346 291
1992	302 256	304 989	122 607	430 957	461 515	3 162 825	656 204	5 441 353

Table G-2. **World and Regional Totals: GDP Level, 1820-1992: Sample and Non-Sample (199 countries)**

(million 1990 Geary Khamis Dollars)

	Western Europe (23)	Western Offshoots (4)	Southern Europe (7)	Eastern Europe (9)	Latin America (44)	Asia & Oceania (56)	Africa (56)	World (199)
1820	133 035	13 557	27 050	69 369	13 786	405 113	32 862	694 772
1870	305 032	111 535	44 312	152 683	28 794	445 769	39 751	1 127 876
1900	552 297	347 488	70 001	286 157	68 826	604 469	47 638	1 976 876
1913	734 573	583 423	84 525	422 537	115 364	722 545	63 098	2 726 065
1929	925 130	934 153	117 256	472 249	193 763	955 165	98 440	3 696 156
1950	1 224 919	1 629 665	138 374	752 764	404 016	1 037 569	185 022	5 372 330
1951	1 294 995	1 779 923	151 280	765 952	424 839	1 114 871	194 820	5 726 680
1952	1 338 793	1 856 950	161 246	803 499	439 004	1 212 526	201 944	6 013 962
1953	1 409 565	1 926 708	169 919	836 303	455 601	1 290 079	209 552	6 297 728
1954	1 486 013	1 920 207	175 141	874 761	484 118	1 352 604	220 963	6 513 807
1955	1 581 299	2 031 782	185 200	944 724	513 894	1 420 786	229 495	6 907 179
1956	1 650 509	2 081 570	195 662	1 014 762	534 289	1 519 579	238 073	7 234 444
1957	1 723 916	2 123 265	205 582	1 049 563	573 357	1 577 957	245 852	7 499 492
1958	1 761 512	2 120 854	213 245	1 122 574	601 369	1 696 884	250 887	7 767 324
1959	1 852 034	2 235 522	216 182	1 130 344	618 136	1 747 882	268 009	8 068 108
1960	1 977 698	2 284 020	223 445	1 226 175	657 255	1 800 559	279 484	8 448 637
1961	2 078 036	2 340 552	241 292	1 294 470	688 529	1 782 320	284 630	8 709 828
1962	2 175 229	2 485 585	258 892	1 324 113	716 657	1 851 727	295 535	9 107 737
1963	2 270 946	2 597 779	280 799	1 317 294	736 768	1 988 781	315 057	9 507 424
1964	2 405 767	2 754 909	297 283	1 456 660	785 932	2 180 878	333 908	10 215 338
1965	2 499 892	2 927 640	314 039	1 532 194	824 533	2 318 520	353 034	10 769 853
1966	2 586 939	3 114 064	348 458	1 611 771	864 643	2 492 943	362 877	11 381 696
1967	2 669 603	3 198 726	369 645	1 680 909	901 523	2 596 315	370 157	11 786 877
1968	2 808 038	3 344 653	399 242	1 769 124	956 210	2 738 858	390 352	12 406 476
1969	2 968 453	3 459 553	433 571	1 801 289	1 017 657	3 007 314	422 102	13 109 939
1970	3 096 639	3 473 865	462 162	1 915 989	1 086 749	3 322 129	453 076	13 810 608
1971	3 190 015	3 600 635	491 392	1 989 050	1 148 925	3 495 093	469 782	14 384 892
1972	3 312 362	3 801 290	530 537	2 025 057	1 220 123	3 683 771	486 664	15 059 804
1973	3 502 550	4 027 071	570 131	2 170 545	1 323 955	3 968 144	502 079	16 064 474
1974	3 566 324	4 024 955	595 189	2 249 814	1 399 121	4 073 059	525 414	16 433 875
1975	3 524 601	4 006 883	609 711	2 276 793	1 438 646	4 277 921	533 887	16 668 442
1976	3 682 991	4 222 789	641 200	2 366 177	1 517 766	4 467 643	566 484	17 465 050
1977	3 782 555	4 423 463	666 456	2 430 485	1 590 530	4 732 256	591 475	18 217 221
1978	3 897 641	4 643 754	685 449	2 493 711	1 655 402	4 989 314	604 903	18 970 175
1979	4 048 139	4 784 661	692 838	2 495 894	1 757 891	5 189 696	629 143	19 598 262
1980	4 106 027	4 795 084	702 271	2 504 270	1 852 792	5 391 527	653 803	20 005 773
1981	4 111 092	4 931 235	709 957	2 510 945	1 856 301	5 615 864	666 354	20 401 748
1982	4 140 228	4 835 921	724 508	2 561 600	1 837 331	5 868 004	685 312	20 652 906
1983	4 213 310	5 015 134	737 265	2 629 391	1 795 024	6 197 108	686 596	21 273 829
1984	4 319 162	5 348 578	755 451	2 676 078	1 861 764	6 605 897	703 140	22 270 069
1985	4 431 076	5 532 348	779 013	2 693 936	1 919 669	7 013 051	726 325	23 095 417
1986	4 553 605	5 693 540	809 459	2 792 047	2 002 078	7 313 449	746 105	23 910 283
1987	4 672 840	5 880 465	853 535	2 813 059	2 066 662	7 782 435	758 739	24 827 735
1988	4 858 233	6 109 823	893 055	2 864 013	2 086 215	8 393 595	788 124	25 993 059
1989	5 014 677	6 265 374	926 887	2 883 057	2 104 156	8 801 838	813 364	26 809 353
1990	5 154 468	6 313 209	971 257	2 742 496	2 105 890	9 245 002	826 700	27 359 022
1991	5 209 660	6 238 030	992 758	2 360 620	2 169 889	9 743 868	838 386	27 553 211
1992	5 255 426	6 358 960	1 016 057	2 010 594	2 224 674	10 286 794	842 415	27 994 920

Table G-3. **World and Regional Averages: GDP per Capita, 1820-1992: Sample and Non-Sample (199 countries)**

(1990 Geary Khamis Dollars)

	Western Europe (23)	Western Offshoots (4)	Southern Europe (7)	Eastern Europe (9)	Latin America (44)	Asia & Oceania (56)	Africa (56)	Average (199)
1820	1 292	1 205	804	772	679	550	450	651
1870	2 110	2 440	1 108	1 085	760	580	480	895
1900	3 092	4 022	1 572	1 373	1 077	681	500	1 263
1913	3 704	5 237	1 750	1 690	1 439	742	575	1 539
1929	4 385	6 653	2 153	1 732	1 832	858	660	1 806
1950	5 126	9 255	2 021	2 631	2 487	765	830	2 138
1951	5 379	9 928	2 172	2 638	2 546	806	855	2 238
1952	5 528	10 165	2 285	2 727	2 562	859	868	2 308
1953	5 781	10 362	2 376	2 797	2 585	896	874	2 371
1954	6 051	10 136	2 417	2 884	2 672	920	909	2 407
1955	6 393	10 527	2 521	3 067	2 760	946	924	2 505
1956	6 620	10 586	2 625	3 246	2 792	991	937	2 573
1957	6 858	10 588	2 716	3 311	2 915	1 007	946	2 615
1958	6 950	10 390	2 775	3 493	2 975	1 059	944	2 654
1959	7 245	10 761	2 769	3 466	2 974	1 069	986	2 706
1960	7 676	10 813	2 820	3 705	3 077	1 088	1 006	2 792
1961	7 989	10 994	3 003	3 856	3 137	1 067	1 002	2 843
1962	8 272	11 384	3 179	3 893	3 178	1 090	1 015	2 921
1963	8 551	11 720	3 402	3 824	3 179	1 144	1 055	2 987
1964	8 978	12 248	3 554	4 179	3 299	1 227	1 090	3 146
1965	9 248	12 843	3 706	4 350	3 368	1 275	1 125	3 251
1966	9 497	13 487	4 058	4 532	3 437	1 339	1 127	3 367
1967	9 742	13 690	4 242	4 683	3 489	1 362	1 121	3 418
1968	10 196	14 160	4 519	4 880	3 602	1 402	1 154	3 525
1969	10 695	14 490	4 842	4 926	3 733	1 504	1 217	3 651
1970	11 079	14 372	5 092	5 202	3 883	1 621	1 275	3 768
1971	11 325	14 685	5 338	5 354	4 003	1 663	1 289	3 842
1972	11 686	15 330	5 679	5 404	4 146	1 711	1 303	3 942
1973	12 289	16 075	6 015	5 745	4 387	1 801	1 311	4 123
1974	12 466	15 903	6 174	5 902	4 521	1 808	1 337	4 137
1975	12 299	15 665	6 203	5 922	4 534	1 859	1 324	4 119
1976	12 839	16 354	6 439	6 103	4 668	1 905	1 367	4 242
1977	13 173	16 956	6 584	6 217	4 774	1 981	1 388	4 349
1978	13 539	17 609	6 666	6 328	4 851	2 049	1 378	4 450
1979	14 031	17 955	6 635	6 287	5 031	2 092	1 393	4 518
1980	14 187	17 782	6 629	6 263	5 177	2 134	1 407	4 533
1981	14 166	18 091	6 598	6 233	5 072	2 183	1 392	4 543
1982	14 242	17 554	6 641	6 311	4 907	2 238	1 392	4 519
1983	14 475	18 026	6 666	6 428	4 687	2 319	1 355	4 574
1984	14 820	19 045	6 740	6 492	4 756	2 427	1 349	4 707
1985	15 178	19 513	6 860	6 487	4 791	2 529	1 353	4 797
1986	15 560	19 887	7 056	6 671	4 890	2 590	1 351	4 882
1987	15 926	20 337	7 364	6 666	4 939	2 704	1 335	4 980
1988	16 492	20 918	7 617	6 740	4 889	2 863	1 347	5 125
1989	16 929	21 226	7 820	6 745	4 830	2 950	1 351	5 197
1990	17 272	21 261	8 092	6 397	4 735	3 031	1 336	5 204
1991	17 351	20 767	8 178	5 488	4 788	3 139	1 317	5 154
1992	17 387	20 850	8 287	4 665	4 820	3 252	1 284	5 145

Appendix H

Impact of Frontier Changes

The annual population and GDP series in this volume have been adjusted to eliminate the impact of frontier changes. In this way the underlying movements in economic growth are clearer and it is much easier to add the individual country figures into a regional or world total if they are free of a large number of non-synchronous frontier changes. It was assumed that the impact of boundary changes on GDP would be the same proportionately as that on population, except in cases where separate estimates were available of the GDP effect. In general the adjustment to a constant frontier basis was made by applying the coefficient for the year where the break occurred to all the preceding years. In most cases the constant frontier estimates are counterfactuals which probably correspond reasonably well with the situation one would find if one were able to recalculate the whole annual series backwards. Such recalculations are rare. One such case is that for Austria where Kausel (1979) made estimates for Austria within its present frontiers as well as for the Austrian half of the Austro-Hungarian dual monarchy for the whole period 1830-1913. The estimates for Italy are also of this nature. In the general case, one has to link separate segments, each of which refers to the territory of the epoch concerned, e.g. France with and without Alsace-Lorraine, Belgium with and without Eupen and Malmedy, Denmark with and without South Slesvig. The most serious problem arose in adjusting the figures for the UK for the loss of Southern Ireland (see UK country note in Appendix A).

Table G-1 shows the effect of frontier changes on 22 countries. Most of those in Europe occurred as a result of the first and second world wars and the events of the early 1990s. The changes in Canada and the USA were due to the accession of Newfoundland, and of Alaska and Hawaii respectively.

Decolonisation had a major impact in Asia after the second world war and Table H-1 shows the major cases of frontier change as they affected the sample countries.

In the case of Africa, most of the countries which exist today were colonies of Belgium, France, Germany, Portugal, Spain and the UK. The colonial powers created most of the present frontiers, so it is not possible to carry the history of these national entities into the nineteenth century. There have been some changes since independence in Morocco and Ethiopia, but I was not able to document these.

In making the adjustments to a constant frontier basis, my major consideration was to ensure that the corrected population and GDP estimates were congruent.

Tables H-2 and H-3 show population, GDP, and GDP per capita for France, Germany, Italy, the UK, India and Russia/USSR for selected years 1820-1992. The country notes in Appendix B provide GDP coefficients for other countries where they are available separately from the population coefficients (Austria, Canada, Denmark, and Korea).

Table H-1. **Impact of Frontier Changes on Population**

(000s)

	1913 situation		1939 situation		1992 situation	
	Within 1913 frontiers	Within 1990 frontiers	Within 1938 frontiers	Within 1990 frontiers	Within 1990 frontiers	Within new frontiers
Austria	29 193	6 767				
Belgium	7 605	7 666				
Bulgaria	4 497	4 794	6 244	6 564		
Czechoslovakia	-	13 245	15 427	14 603	15 615	10 315
Denmark	2 833	2 983				
France	39 770	41 463				
Germany	66 978	37 843	68 558	42 990	64 846	80 576
Greece	2 728	5 425				
Ireland	-	3 092				
Italy	36 167	37 248				
Hungary	21 325	7 840	9 159	9 167		
Poland	-	26 710	34 662	31 062		
Romania	7 353	12 527	19 750	15 601		
Russia/USSR	154 099	156 192	168 587	188 498	292 375	149 400
UK	45 649	42 622				
Yugoslavia	3 032	13 590	15 384	16 084	23 931	10 597
Canada	7 653	7 852	11 162	11 452		
USA	97 227	97 606	129 969	130 476		
Bangladesh	-	31 786	-	39 716		
India	303 700	251 906	376 100	309 740		
Pakistan	-	20 008	-	26 644		
Korea	15 470	10 277	23 002	15 275		

Sources: See Appendix A, also A. Maddison, *Dynamic Forces in Capitalist Development*, Oxford, 1991, Appendix B, and I. Svennilson, *Growth and Stagnation in the European Economy*, ECE, Geneva, 1954, pp. 236-7.

Table H-2. **Confrontation of Actual and Adjusted Estimates of Population, GDP and GDP per Capita for France, Germany and Italy, 1820-1992**

	Situation Within Actual Boundaries			Situation Adjusted to 1990 Frontiers		
	Population (000s)	GDP (million 1990 $)	GDP per capita (1990 $)	Population (000s)	GDP (million 1990 $)	GDP per capita (1990 $)
			France			
1820	30 698	37 397	1 218	31 250	38 071	1 218
1870	38 440	71 419	1 858	38 440	71 419	1 858
1900	38 940	110 927	2 849	40 598	115 645	2 849
1913	39 770	137 286	3 452	41 463	143 125	3 452
1929	41 230	192 360	4 666	41 230	192 360	4 666
1950	41 836	218 409	5 221	41 836	218 409	5 221
1973	52 118	674 404	12 940	52 118	674 404	12 940
1992	57 372	1 030 356	17 959	57 372	1 030 356	17 959
			Germany			
1820	11 214	11 864	1 058	14 747	16 393	1 112
1870	39 231	71 440	1 821	23 055	44 101	1 913
1900	56 046	167 177	2 983	31 666	99 227	3 134
1913	66 978	244 347	3 648	37 843	145 068	3 833
1929	64 739	273 549	4 225	40 595	175 968	4 335
1950	49 983	213 976	4 281	49 983	213 976	4 281
1973	61 976	815 138	13 152	61 976	815 138	13 152
1992	80 576	1 358 485	16 860	64 846	1 254 840	19 351
			Italy			
1820				20 176	22 042	1 092
1870	26 262	38 618	1 470	27 888	40 900	1 467
1900	32 695	57 676	1 764	33 672	58 799	1 746
1913	36 167	91 702	2 536	37 248	93 399	2 507
1929	41 076	124 072	3 021	40 469	122 443	3 026
1950	47 105	161 351	3 425	47 105	161 351	3 425
1973	54 779	570 200	10 409	54 779	570 200	10 409
1992	57 900	939 685	16 229	57 900	939 685	16 229

Source: See country notes in Appendices A and B. For Germany, the Saar is included in the 1929 estimates.

Table H-3. **Confrontation of Actual and Adjusted Estimates of Population, GDP and GDP per Capita for the UK, India and Russia/USSR, 1820-1992**

	Situation Within Actual Boundaries			Situation Adjusted to 1990 Frontiers		
	Population (000s)	GDP (million 1990 $)	GDP per capita (1990 $)	Population (000s)	GDP (million 1990 $)	GDP per capita (1990 $)
			United Kingdom			
1820	21 240	36 164	1 703	19 832	34 829	1 756
1870	31 393	99 318	3 164	29 312	95 651	3 263
1900	41 155	183 270	4 453	38 426	176 504	4 593
1913	45 649	222 686	4 878	42 622	214 464	5 032
1929	45 672	239 985	5 255	45 672	239 985	5 255
1950	50 363	344 859	6 847	50 363	344 859	6 847
1973	56 210	674 061	11 992	56 210	674 061	11 992
1992	57 848	910 401	15 738	57 848	910 401	15 738
			India			
1820	209 000	110 982	531	175 349	93 125	531
1870	253 000	141 282	558	212 189	118 492	558
1900	284 500	177 807	625	235 729	147 365	625
1913	303 700	201 085	663	251 906	166 891	663
1929	333 100	221 481	665	275 861	183 413	665
1950	359 000	214 288	597	359 000	214 288	597
1973	580 000	494 664	853	580 000	494 664	853
1992	881 200	1 188 096	1 348	881 200	1 188 096	1 348
			Russia/USSR			
1820	45 005	33 799	751	50 398	37 873	751
1870	79 630	81 480	1 023	81 747	83 646	1 023
1900	124 749	151 984	1 218	126 444	154 049	1 218
1913	154 099	229 238	1 488	156 192	232 351	1 488
1929	153 847	213 211	1 386	172 017	238 392	1 386
1950	180 050	510 243	2 834	180 050	510 243	2 834
1973	249 747	1 513 070	6 058	249 747	1 513 070	6 058
1992	149 400	801 837	5 367	292 375	1 365 759	4 671

Source: See country notes in Appendices A and B.

Appendix I

Exports

The individual countries in this exercise constitute a "world" economy because of their interrelationships. One fundamental aspect of this is their involvement in world trade. This includes both imports and exports, but this appendix only covers exports. Tables I-1 and I-2 present estimates of exports for the 56 individual sample countries for 1870-1992 in current and constant dollars as far as they are available. The 56 sample countries accounted for 87 per cent of world exports in 1992, and 89 per cent in 1870.

Table I-3 provides estimates of total world exports in dollars at current prices and exchange rates for the year 1870, and annual figures for 1880-1992.

Table I-4 presents estimates of world export volume for the years 1820 and 1870, and annually for 1881-1913, 1924-38, and 1950-92. These estimates (like those of Table I-2) are in 1990 prices, with conversion of the volume indices into dollars at the exchange rate of that year. Thus the numeraire is different from the total for world GDP in Table G-2. Nevertheless it is reasonable to compare the relationship between the world export and world GDP aggregates, as exchange rates are a fair proxy for purchasing power for traded goods. From such a comparison it emerges that world exports were 1 per cent of world product in 1820, 5 per cent in 1870, 8.7 per cent in 1913, 9 per cent in 1929, 7 per cent in 1950, 11.2 per cent in 1973, and 13.5 per cent in 1992.

Table I-1. **Value of Merchandise Exports at Current Prices (56 Sample Countries), 1870-1992**

(million dollars at current exchange rates)

	1870	1913	1929	1950	1973	1992
Austria	160	561	308	326	9 559	44 415
Belgium	133	717	884	1 652	22 455	122 976
Denmark	42[a]	171	433	665	6 248	39 633
Finland	9	78	162	390	3 836	23 982
France	541	1 328	1 965	3 082	36 635	235 772
Germany	424	2 454	3 212	1 993	67 563	422 271
Italy	208	485	783	1 206	22 223	178 156
Netherlands	158[b]	413	800	1 413	23 496	139 933
Norway	22	105	199	390	4 725	35 178
Sweden	41	219	486	1 103	12 201	56 115
Switzerland	132[b]	226	404	894	9 528	61 377
UK	971	2 555	3 550	6 325	29 637	190 002
Total	2 841	9 352	13 186	19 439	243 830	1 549 810
Australia	98	382	592	1 668	9 559	42 542
Canada	58	421	1 141	3 020	26 437	134 056
New Zealand	12	112	259	514	2 596	9 824
USA	403	2 380	5 157	10 282	71 404	448 164
Total	571	3 295	7 149	15 484	109 996	634 586
Greece	7	23	91	90	1 456	9 512
Ireland	-	-	225	203	2 131	28 834
Portugal	22	38	48	186	1 842	18 295
Spain	76	183	407	389	5 198	56 115
Turkey	49[b]	94	139	159	1 317	14 716
Total	154	338	910	1 027	11 944	127 472
Bulgaria	5[b]	94	46	116	3 301	5 093
Czechoslovakia	-	-	606	779	6 035	10 939[c]
Hungary	-	-	182	329	3 354	10 296
Poland	-	-	316	634	6 374	13 324
Romania	32[b]	130	173	300	3 691	4 299
USSR	216	783	482	1 801	21 458	40 800
Yugoslavia	6[b]	18	139	154	2 853	13 953[c]
Total	259	1 025	1 944	4 113	47 066	98 704

Table I-1 (continued)

	1870	1913	1929	1950	1973	1992
Argentina	29	515	908	1 178	3 266	12 235
Brazil	76	317	462	1 359	6 199	36 103
Chile	27	149	283	281	1 231	9 986
Colombia	18	34	124	394	1 177	6 916
Mexico	28[a]	150	285	532	2 261	27 618
Peru	25[a]	43	117	193	1 112	3 484
Venezuela	15[a]	28	149	929	4 680	13 348
Total	218	1 236	2 328	4 866	19 926	109 690
Bangladesh	-	-	-	303	358	2 098
Burma	-	-	-	139	140	536
China	102	299	660	550	5 876	80 517
India	255	786	1 177	1 145	2 917	19 554
Indonesia	31	270	582	800	3 211	29 322
Japan	15	315	969	825	37 017	339 885
Pakistan	-	-	-	330	955	7 317
Philippines	29	48	163	331	1 885	9 790
South Korea	0	15	159	23	3 225	76 632
Taiwan	-	26	125	73	4 483	81 419
Thailand	7	43	94	304	1 564	32 473
Total	439	1 802	3 929	4 823	61 631	679 543
Côte d'Ivoire	-	-	-	79	857	6 220
Egypt	66[a]	156	253	504	1 121	3 050
Ethiopia	n.a.	n.a.	n.a.	37	239	169
Ghana	2	26	60	217	628	942
Kenya	n.a.	n.a.	34	57	516	1 339
Morocco	n.a.	n.a.	48	190	910	3 977
Nigeria	4	36	86	253	3 462	11 886
South Africa	14	342	454	1 158	6 114	23 892
Tanzania	n.a.	n.a.	18	68	61	400
Zaire	n.a.	n.a.	40	261	1 013	437
Total	n.a.	n.a.	n.a.	2 824	14 921	52 512

a) 1874; b) 1872; c) 1991.

Source: Maddison (1962 and 1989); League of Nations, *Review of World Trade 1938*, Geneva, 1939; UN, *Yearbook of International Trade Statistics*, New York, various issues; IMF, *International Financial Statistics*, Washington, D.C., various issues; World Bank, *World Tables 1994*, Washington, D.C., 1994.

Table I-2. **Value of Merchandise Exports at Constant Prices (24 Sample Countries), 1820-1992**

(million 1990 dollars)

	1820	1870	1913	1929	1950	1973	1992
Austria	47	467	2 024	1 746	1 348	13 899	45 788
Belgium	92	1 237	7 318	7 845	8 182	61 764	122 416
Denmark	n.a.	314	1 494	2 705	3 579	16 568	39 507
Finland	n.a.	310	1 597	2 578	3 186	15 641	26 328
France	487	3 512	11 292	16 600	16 848	104 161	236 056
Germany	n.a.	6 761	38 200	35 068	13 179	194 171	409 084
Italy	339	1 788	4 621	5 670	5 846	72 749	178 037
Netherlands	n.a.	1 727[a]	4 329	7 411	7 411	71 522	141 849
Norway	n.a.	223	854	1 427	2 301	11 687	39 197
Sweden	n.a.	713	2 670	4 167	7 366	34 431	56 776
Switzerland	147	1 107	5 735	5 776	6 493	38 972	64 300
UK	1 125	12 237	39 348	31 990	39 348	94 670	194 535
Total	n.a.	30 396	119 482	122 983	115 087	730 235	1 553 873
Australia	n.a.	455	3 392	3 636	5 383	18 869	47 987
Canada	n.a.	724	4 044	7 812	12 576	60 214	140 294
USA	251	2 495	19 196	30 368	43 114	174 548	451 026
Total	n.a.	3 674	26 632	41 816	61 073	253 631	639 307
Spain	137	850	3 697	3 394	2 018	15 295	65 691
USSR	n.a.	n.a.	6 666	3 420	6 472	58 015	40 800
Argentina	n.a.	222	1 963	3 096	2 079	4 181	12 282
Brazil	n.a.	854	1 888	2 592	3 489	9 998	36 707
Chile	n.a.	166	702	1 352	1 166	2 030	10 862
Colombia	n.a.	114	267	811	1 112	2 629	8 092
Mexico	n.a.	242	2 363	3 714	1 999	5 238	30 494
Peru	n.a.	202	409	1 142	1 172	4 323	3 530
Venezuela	n.a.	n.a.	1 374	2 593	9 722	23 779	18 442
Total	n.a.	2 126	8 966	15 300	20 739	52 178	120 409

Table I-2 (continued)

	1870	1913	1929	1950	1973	1992
Bangladesh	-	-	-	284	445	2 122
Burma	-	-	-	269	235	597
China	1 398	4 197	6 262	6 339	11 679	84 940
India	3 466	9 480	8 209	5 489	9 679	20 105
Indonesia	172	989	2 609	2 254	9 605	38 045
Japan	51	1 684	4 343	3 538	95 105	299 489
Pakistan	-	-	-	720	1 626	7 945
Philippines	55	180	678	697	2 608	9 468
South Korea	0	171	1 292	112	7 894	77 800
Taiwan	-	70	261	180	5 761	82 213
Thailand	88	495	640	1 148	3 081	30 841
Total	5 230	17 266	24 294	21 030	147 733	653 565

a) 1872.

Source: Volume movement in Western Europe, Western Offshoots and Japan from A. Maddison, *Dynamic Forces in Capitalist Development*, OUP, 1991, Appendix F, updated from OECD, *Economic Outlook*, December 1994. Spain 1826-1980 from A. Carreras, ed., *Estadisticas Historicas de España: Siglos XIX-XX*, Fundacion Banco Exterior, Madrid, 1989, pp. 346-7. USSR, Latin America and Asia from sources cited in A. Maddison, *The World Economy in the Twentieth Century*, OECD Development Centre, 1989, p. 140, updated with volume movements derivable from IMF, *International Financial Statistics*, various issues. Brazil 1870-1913 from R.W. Goldsmith, *Brasil 1850-1984: Desenvolvimento Financeiro Sob um Secolo de Inflacâo*, Harper and Row, Sao Paulo, 1986, pp. 54-5 and 110-111; Peru 1870-1950 from S.J. Hunt, "Price and Quantum Estimates of Peruvian Exports, 1830-1962", Discussion Paper 33, Research Program in Economic Development, Princeton University, January 1973, (1929 weights for 1900-50, 1900 weights for 1870-1900); Venezuela 1913-29 from A. Baptista, *Bases Cuantitativas de la Economia Venezolana 1830-1989*, C. Corporativas, Caracas, 1991, and 1929-92 from ECLAC sources. 1973-92 movements from OECD and ECLAC sources, and IMF *International Financial Statistics*.

Table I-3. **Value of World Exports in Current Prices, 1870-1992**

(million dollars at exchange rates of year cited)

1870	5 132	1910	15 193	1960	128 275
		1911	15 919	1961	134 000
1880	6 481	1912	17 714	1962	141 600
1881	6 435	1913	18 401	1963	154 100
1882	6 846			1964	172 400
1883	6 827	1924	27 595	1965	187 010
1884	6 635	1925	31 261	1966	204 000
1885	6 207	1926	29 653	1967	214 500
1886	6 211	1927	31 245	1968	239 100
1887	6 339	1928	32 452	1969	272 600
1888	6 857	1929	32 746	1970	313 792
1889	7 380	1930	26 188	1971	348 100
1890	7 567	1931	18 580	1972	412 400
1891	7 611	1932	12 557	1973	578 698
1892	6 965	1933	14 757	1974	840 019
1893	7 066	1934	18 629	1975	876 065
1894	6 940	1935	19 188	1976	991 585
1895	7 186	1936	20 675	1977	1 128 085
1896	7 806	1937	25 480	1978	1 300 818
1897	8 097	1938	22 490	1979	1 643 975
1898	8 191			1980	1 993 845
1899	8 992	1950	61 372	1981	1 976 754
1900	9 437	1951	82 456	1982	1 838 110
1901	9 467	1952	80 049	1983	1 817 954
1902	9 874	1953	82 097	1984	1 921 326
1903	10 536	1954	85 654	1985	1 931 861
1904	10 978	1955	93 277	1986	2 120 524
1905	12 018	1956	103 309	1987	2 485 129
1906	13 012	1957	111 449	1988	2 813 960
1907	13 616	1958	107 617	1989	3 037 324
1908	13 012	1959	115 306	1990	3 432 253
1909	13 891	1960	127 929	1991	3 407 890
				1992	3 721 263

Sources: 1870-1960 from Maddison (1962), 1960-92 from UN, *Yearbook of International Trade Statistics*, various issues. There are two entries for 1960, as there is a break in the series.

Table I-4. **Value of World Exports at Constant Prices, 1820-1992**
(million 1990 dollars)

1820	7 255	1912	229 477	1965	979 110
		1913	236 330	1966	1 000 990
1870	56 247			1967	1 061 881
		1924	253 819	1968	1 195 500
1881	81 534	1925	273 671	1969	1 323 301
1882	86 261	1926	282 179	1970	1 446 046
1883	89 333	1927	305 339	1971	1 520 087
1884	90 987	1928	318 810	1972	1 676 423
1885	91 696	1929	334 408	1973	1 797 199
1886	94 296	1930	311 956	1974	1 858 449
1887	96 423	1931	287 378	1975	1 798 901
1888	102 331	1932	244 838	1976	1 995 141
1889	107 058	1933	251 456	1977	2 085 185
1890	110 366	1934	260 909	1978	2 168 030
1891	111 548	1935	275 089	1979	2 305 715
1892	108 476	1936	287 378	1980	2 291 776
1893	108 712	1937	324 009	1981	2 295 882
1894	116 747	1938	302 976	1982	2 249 829
1895	122 183			1983	2 348 778
1896	129 745	1950	375 765	1984	2 538 079
1897	134 945	1951	415 705	1985	2 614 156
1898	137 072	1952	417 596	1986	2 771 927
1899	142 980	1953	441 702	1987	2 916 818
1900	139 671	1954	467 934	1988	3 112 788
1901	146 525	1955	513 310	1989	3 326 751
1902	152 669	1956	556 085	1990	3 432 253
1903	158 814	1957	592 480	1991	3 498 860
1904	163 777	1958	590 826	1992	3 785 619
1905	174 412	1959	646 364		
1906	181 265	1960	700 956		
1907	181 265	1961	730 245		
1908	185 519	1962	771 663		
1909	195 209	1963	828 495		
1910	205 844	1964	907 368		
1911	211 516				

Sources: 1820-70 volume movement from A. Maddison, *Phases of Capitalist Development*, Oxford University Press, 1982, p. 254. 1870-1960 volume movement from A. Maddison, "Growth and Fluctuation in the World Economy, 1870-1960", *Banca Nazionale del Lavoro Quarterly Review*, June 1962. 1960-92 derived by linking estimates of world trade value in UN, *Yearbook of International Trade Statistics* (1992, 1985, 1980, 1972-3, and 1965 editions) with deflation by the world unit value indices in the same publication.

Appendix J

Employment, Working Hours and Labour Productivity

Measurement of labour input is a first step in constructing growth accounts. Its importance is clear if we consider the wide intercountry variation in labour inputs. In 1992, labour input per head of population varied from 543 hours a year in Ireland to 1 048 in Taiwan. The two countries had a very similar GDP per capita, but Irish labour productivity was nearly twice that of Taiwan. Similarly, we find that the Dutch worked 587 hours per head of population, and the Japanese 970. Japanese per capita GDP is significantly higher than that in the Netherlands, but Dutch labour productivity is more than 40 per cent higher than Japanese.

These differences are also important in assessing growth over time. West European working hours were about 3 000 a year in 1820. By 1992 they had fallen to an average of 1 540. The length of the working day has been lowered as a result of legislation, trade union pressures, and a realisation by employers that a 60-hour week was counterproductive because of worker fatigue. Annual vacations, weekend breaks and sick leave are modern inventions. There have also been big changes in age structure and activity rates.

The main factors determining labour supply are: a) the size of the population; b) demographic structure, in particular, the proportion of people below or above working age; c) activity rates, which depend on the willingness, incentives or legal rights of potential workers to seek employment; d) annual working hours per person.

Actual labour input will differ from potential, because of variations in the level of demand, or labour market frictions. Variations in the use of potential are most obviously reflected by unemployment, but weak demand in labour markets may also cause working hours, activity rates, migration or productivity to fall below trend levels.

Any satisfactory measure of labour input usually requires a merger of information from several different sources, as there are very few countries like Sweden which provide a careful accounting of labour input in their national accounts.

The data situation is most satisfactory for OECD countries, which have supplemented census and administrative statistics with labour force sample surveys and generally follow the standardised ILO guidelines (1954 and 1982) for measuring labour force and employment. The annual OECD publication *Labour Force Statistics* is a gold mine of information in this respect. Standardised measurement of working hours has made less progress, but it is possible to make reasonable estimates for a large number of OECD countries in the lines suggested in Maddison (1982), and it is possible to cover selected benchmark years backwards to 1870 (see Maddison 1991).

One problem which became important from the 1960s onwards was the growing incentive which tax and social security arrangements gave to conceal work activity. This phenomenon was particularly important in Italy, where evidence on its likely magnitude is available. I therefore adjusted Italian official employment statistics upward by 17.6 per cent. There are other Southern European countries where the official estimates may understate employment, but I was not able to get enough evidence to estimate its incidence.

For non-OECD countries, measurement of labour input is more difficult, partly because of the smaller statistical effort which they have been able to mount, and also because it is inherently more difficult to define the boundaries of economic activity when a large proportion of the population is engaged in activities where the production unit is the family. Social habits may also affect statistical practice. Thus in Muslim countries such as Bangladesh, Pakistan, Egypt or Morocco, female activity rates are undoubtedly low, but the fact that female activity is frowned upon, may also influence census takers to understate female activity, just as it influenced US census takers to understate female agricultural participation in the nineteenth century.

The ILO *Yearbooks* are a useful source of information on non-OECD countries. They summarise census information on age structures and activity rates, and provide figures on registered unemployment and working hours. There is also a major ILO study in several volumes *Economically Active Population 1950-2025* (1986), which provides a detailed analysis of activity rates by age and sex and major economic sector at decade intervals for 1950-80.

For Latin America, André Hofman has done a great deal of work, merging information from different sources to produce labour market accounts. For Asian countries, there are reasonably good official statistics only for Japan, Korea and Taiwan. For Africa, any estimate is bound to be rough. For Latin America and Asia I show estimates of labour inputs only for the years 1950, 1973 and 1992, and for Africa only for 1992 (employment only).

In spite of the shortcomings of the estimates for non-OECD countries, some of the broad differences between regions which can be seen in Table J-1 are reasonably valid. It is clear that the age structure of most OECD countries and Eastern Europe is more propitious for economic activity than in many countries of Latin America, Asia and Africa, where the proportion of children is much higher. Another characteristic difference is the proportion of women in the labour force. This is related to the share of the child population, but it also reflects a rise in women's aspirations and social pressures to give them better access to jobs, part-time work, etc. Women were about 43 per cent of the labour force in Western Europe and the Western Offshoots in 1992. In Eastern Europe the share was 47 per cent. In Southern Europe, Latin America, Asia and Africa, women were a third of the labour force or less.

The ratio of employment to population averaged 46 per cent in Western Europe in 1992 (in spite of large-scale unemployment). It was not too different from this in the Western Offshoots and Eastern Europe, but distinctly lower in Southern Europe, Latin America and Africa. In Asia, the regional average was 41 per cent, but there were countries like Bangladesh and Pakistan where participation was very low, and others like China, Japan, Taiwan and Thailand where it was above the European average.

In terms of total labour input (working hours) the ratios were lowest in Southern Europe and Latin America with averages around 640 hours per head of population. The West European average was below 700 hours. It was somewhat higher in the Western Offshoots. In Eastern Europe the figure was distinctly higher at 800 hours, and highest in Asia at over 900 hours. For Africa, it was not possible to assess the situation in terms of hours.

For Eastern Europe, I assumed that the level and movement of working hours was the same as in the USSR. Although the evidence is not very systematic, there is enough to justify this rough assumption, and official policy in this domain was rather similar in these countries.

For Asian countries, the information on hours is reasonably good for Japan, Korea and Taiwan, and quite negligible elsewhere. The evidence for the three countries shows working hours which were extremely long by European or American standards. In most Asian countries, intensive use of labour has been a long-term characteristic because land scarcity has been greater than in Africa or Latin America, and family discipline is strong. On these grounds I assumed an average work year of 2 200 hours for 1950, 1973 and 1992 for the eight Asian countries for which hours information were lacking.

I have presented two estimates of labour productivity. The first (Table J-5) relates to GDP per hour worked. This is the measure I prefer for measuring intertemporal and intercountry differences, though the estimates are weak for most Asian countries and non-existent for Africa.

The estimates of GDP per person employed (Table J-6) are less interesting analytically, but free of the problems of measuring hours. However, they are also weakest for most Asian countries, and poor for Africa.

Table J-1. Characteristics Affecting Labour Inputs in 1992

	Persons Aged 15-64 as per cent of Population	Females as per cent of Labour Force	Ratio of Employment to Population	Labour Input per head of Population (hours)
Austria	67.3	41.6	45.0	709
Belgium	66.5	42.3	37.9	601
Denmark	67.5	46.6	51.2	839
Finland	67.1	46.9	43.6	716
France	65.6	44.1	39.3	606
Germany	69.2	41.7	44.9	702
Italy	68.7	37.2	44.3	660
Netherlands	68.7	40.0	43.8	587
Norway	64.6	45.3	58.7	685
Sweden	62.9	47.9	48.3	733
Switzerland	68.2	38.3	50.4	834
UK	64.9	43.1	44.0	656
Arith.Average	66.8	42.9	46.0	694
Australia	66.9[a]	41.6	44.1	720
Canada	67.7	44.9	43.3	717
New Zealand	65.4	43.4	43.2	705
USA	65.5	45.0	46.6	741
Arith.Average	66.4	43.7	44.3	721
Greece	67.3[a]	35.7	35.3[a]	609[a]
Ireland	61.8	32.2	31.9[a]	543[a]
Portugal	66.9	43.9	46.6	792
Spain	67.6	36.0	32.3	618
Turkey	60.5	29.2	32.5	n.a.
Arith.Average	64.8	35.4	35.7	641
Czechoslovakia	66.7	43.0[b]	49.3	837
Hungary	70.0	45.0	45.1	767
Poland	65.8	46.0	45.3	770
Russia	66.4	53.0	48.6	825
Arith.Average	67.2	46.8	47.1	800

a) 1991; b) Slovak Republic.

Table J-1 (continued)

	Persons Aged 15-64 as per cent of Population	Females as per cent of Labour Force	Ratio of Employment to Population	Labour Input per head of Population (hours)
Argentina	60.6	28.0	35.2	642
Brazil	61.7	28.0	37.5	697
Chile	64.3	29.0	33.9	679
Colombia	60.6	22.0	33.2	648
Mexico	58.8	27.0	29.5	608
Peru	59.1	24.0	33.4	643
Venezuela	60.0	28.0	29.3	548
Arith.Average	60.7	26.6	33.1	638
Bangladesh	55.3	8.0	30.5	671
Burma	56.8	37.0	n.a.	n.a.
China	67.1	43.0	50.5	1 110
India	59.6	25.0	38.7	852
Indonesia	60.3	31.0	37.4	822
Japan	69.7	40.7	51.8	970
Pakistan	52.9	13.0	29.0	638
Philippines	57.8	31.0	35.3	777
South Korea	70.5	34.0	42.1	1 180
Taiwan	68.0	37.7	41.9	1 048
Thailand	63.8	44.0	49.2	1 083
Arith.Average	62.0	32.2	41.0	924
Côte d'Ivoire	46.2	34.0	39.0	n.a.
Egypt	56.4	10.0	28.0	n.a.
Ethiopia	47.3	37.0	41.0	n.a.
Ghana	50.0	40.0	38.0	n.a.
Kenya	50.0	39.0	40.0	n.a.
Morocco	57.7	21.0	31.0	n.a.
Nigeria	51.0	34.0	31.0	n.a.
South Africa	57.5	36.0	39.0	n.a.
Tanzania	50.0	47.0	47.0	n.a.
Arith.Average	51.8	32.0	37.0	n.a.

Source: First three columns for OECD countries from OECD *Labour Force Statistics 1972-1992*, Paris, 1994. Other countries first three columns from World Bank, *World Development 1994*, Tables 25 and 29, except col. 2 for Russia which is from *Narodnoe Khoziastvo Rossiskoi Federatii*, Goskomstat Rossii, Moscow, 1992. Total hours derived from Table J-4.

Table J-2. **Total Employment, OECD Countries and Eastern Europe, 1870-1992**

(000s at mid-year)

	1870	1913	1929	1938	1950	1973	1992
Austria	2 077	3 122	3 282	3 113	3 215	3 160	3 546
Belgium	2 141	3 376	3 636	3 316	3 341	3 748	3 802
Denmark	820	1 277	1 476	1 739	1 978	2 426	2 648
Finland	785	1 323	1 654	1 917	1 959	2 194	2 198
France	17 800	19 373	20 170	18 769	19 663	21 434	22 557
Germany	9 511	16 039	17 647	19 656	21 164	27 160	29 141
Italy	13 770	17 644	19 016	19 287	18 875	22 708	25 652
Netherlands	1 382	2 330	3 023	3 169	4 120	5 150	6 655
Norway	706	984	1 132	1 267	1 428	1 676	2 004
Sweden	1 923	2 602	3 146	3 159	3 422	3 879	4 195
Switzerland	1 285	1 904	1 995	1 984	2 237	3 277	3 481
UK	12 285	18 566	18 936	20 818	22 400	25 076	25 465
Australia	630	1 943	2 355	2 592	3 459	5 838	7 736
Canada	1 266	3 014	3 960	4 183	5 030	8 843	12 316
New Zealand	n.a.	n.a.	n.a.	n.a.	n.a.	1 154	1 476
USA	14 720	38 821	47 915	44 917	61 651	86 838	119 164
Japan	18 684	25 751	29 332	32 290	35 683	52 590	64 360
Greece	n.a.	2 018	n.a.	n.a.	2 600	3 232	3 634[a]
Ireland	n.a.	1 278	n.a.	n.a.	1 220	1 067	1 125[a]
Portugal	n.a.	2 550	n.a.	n.a.	3 196	3 486	4 573
Spain	n.a.	7 613	n.a.	n.a.	11 662	13 031	12 642
Turkey	n.a.	n.a.	n.a.	n.a.	11 800	14 409	19 100
Bulgaria	n.a.	2 397	n.a.	n.a.	4 114	4 411	n.a.
Czechoslovakia	n.a.	5 854	n.a.	n.a.	5 972	7 092	7 691
Hungary	n.a.	3 285	n.a.	n.a.	4 379	5 008	4 652
Poland	n.a.	14 049	n.a.	n.a.	12 718	17 319	17 374
Romania	n.a.	6 877	n.a.	n.a.	9 710	10 015	n.a.
USSR	n.a.	64 664	n.a.	n.a.	85 246	128 278	141 971

a) 1991.

Source: OECD countries from Maddison (1991) Appendix C, updated and revised. Southern Europe from OECD, *Labour Force Statistics*, and Maddison (1976). Eastern Europe 1913 and 1950 from Maddison (1976) with revisions. 1973 derived by interpolation from *East European Economies: Slow Growth in the 1980s*, Joint Economic Committee, US Congress, October 1985, p. 100. USSR 1992 from Bolotin (1992), 1992 for Czechoslovakia, Hungary and Poland from EC Employment Observatory, *Central and Eastern Europe: Employment Trends and Developments*, Brussels, October 1994. All figures in this table are adjusted to exclude the impact of frontier changes.

Table J-3. **Employment in Latin America, Asia and Africa, 1950-92**
(000s at mid-year)

	1950	1973	1992
Argentina	6 821	9 402	11 603
Brazil	17 657	33 164	58 505
Chile	2 256	2 896	4 588
Colombia	3 844	6 418	11 101
Mexico	8 563	15 044	26 412
Peru	2 788	4 464	7 544
Venezuela	1 571	3 331	6 055
Bangladesh	15 438	20 925	33 991
China	184 984	362 530	588 960
India	161 386	239 645	341 226
Indonesia	30 863	46 655	69 436
Pakistan	14 009	20 144	34 582
Philippines	8 525	14 195	22 701
South Korea	6 377	11 140	18 376
Taiwan	2 872	5 327	8 632
Thailand	10 119	18 576	28 347
Côte d'Ivoire			4 992
Egypt			15 310
Ethiopia			22 464
Ghana			6 004
Kenya			10 200
Morocco			8 153
Nigeria			28 303
South Africa			14 664
Tanzania			12 267

Source: Maddison (1989) updated from ECLAC sources for Latin America, from Pilat (1994) for Korea, from national sources for China and Taiwan. Other Asian countries from Maddison (1989) updated generally with labour force movement from 1986 shown in World Bank, *World Tables 1994*. Africa derived from ratios in Table J-1.

Table J-4. **Annual Hours Worked Per Person Employed, 1870-1992**

	1870	1913	1929	1938	1950	1973	1992
Austria	2 935	2 580	2 281	2 312	1 976	1 778	1 576
Belgium	2 964	2 605	2 272	2 267	2 283	1 872	1 581
Denmark	2 945	2 553	2 279	2 267	2 283	1 742	1 638
Finland	2 945	2 588	2 123	2 183	2 035	1 707	1 643
France	2 945	2 588	2 297	1 848	1 926	1 771	1 542
Germany	2 941	2 584	2 284	2 316	2 316	1 804	1 563
Italy	2 886	2 536	2 228	1 927	1 997	1 612	1 490
Netherlands	2 964	2 605	2 260	2 244	2 208	1 751	1 338
Norway	2 945	2 588	2 283	2 128	2 101	1 721	1 465
Sweden	2 945	2 588	2 283	2 204	1 951	1 571	1 515
Switzerland	2 984	2 624	2 340	2 257	2 144	1 930	1 645
UK	2 984	2 624	2 286	2 267	1 958	1 688	1 491
Australia	2 945	2 588	2 139	2 110	1 838	1 708	1 631
Canada	2 964	2 605	2 399	2 240	1 967	1 788	1 656
USA	2 964	2 605	2 342	2 062	1 867	1 717	1 589
Greece					2 200	2 000	1 720
Ireland					2 250	2 010	1 700
Portugal					2 200	1 900	1 700
Spain					2 200	2 150	1 911
USSR					1 947	1 791	1 700
Argentina					2 034	1 996	1 826
Brazil					2 042	2 096	1 858
Chile					2 212	1 955	2 005
Colombia					2 323	2 141	1 949
Mexico					2 154	2 061	2 062
Peru					2 157	2 036	1 928
Venezuela					2 179	1 965	1 868
Japan	2 945	2 588	2 364	2 391	2 166	2 042	1 876
Korea					2 200	2 683	2 800
Taiwan					2 200	2 570	2 500
Other Asia					2 200	2 200	2 200

Source: Western Europe, Western Offshoots and Japan from Maddison (1991) Appendix C updated. Southern Europe from sources cited in Maddison (1995b). Latin America (except Peru) derived with some extrapolation from André Hofman, "Twentieth Century Economic Growth in Latin America", Ph.D. thesis, University of Groningen, forthcoming. For Peru I used the average for the other 6 Latin American countries. Korea from Pilat (1994), Taiwan from *Statistical Yearbook*, Taipei. Russia from Joint Economic Committee, *Gorbachev's Economic Plans*, US Congress, 1987 p. 210-11.

Table J-5. **Labour Productivity (GDP Per Hour Worked), 1870-1992**

(1990 dollars per hour)

	1870	1913	1929	1938	1950	1973	1992
Austria	1.39	2.93	3.31	3.36	4.07	15.27	24.21
Belgium	2.12	3.60	4.81	5.27	6.06	16.53	28.55
Denmark	1.51	3.40	5.11	5.31	5.85	15.94	21.81
Finland	0.84	1.81	2.57	3.07	4.00	13.42	20.45
France	1.36	2.85	4.15	5.35	5.65	17.77	29.62
Germany	1.58	3.50	4.37	4.84	4.37	16.64	27.55
Italy	1.03	2.09	2.89	3.79	4.28	15.58	24.59
Netherlands	2.33	4.01	6.32	6.26	6.50	19.02	28.80
Norway	1.09	2.19	3.42	4.30	5.41	14.05	25.61
Sweden	1.22	2.58	3.29	4.27	7.08	18.02	23.11
Switzerland	1.75	3.25	5.38	5.90	8.75	18.28	25.37
UK	2.61	4.40	5.54	5.98	7.86	15.92	23.98
Australia	3.32	5.28	6.47	7.16	8.68	16.87	22.56
Canada	1.61	4.21	5.21	5.26	9.78	19.09	25.32
USA	2.26	5.12	7.52	8.64	12.66	23.45	29.10
Japan	0.46	1.03	1.78	2.19	2.03	11.15	20.02
Greece					2.58	10.77	16.84[a]
Ireland					3.80	10.06	20.76[a]
Portugal					2.58	9.86	14.06
Spain					2.60	10.86	20.22
Bulgaria					1.49	5.77	n.a.
Czechoslovakia					3.73	8.07	8.17
Hungary					2.72	6.50	7.35
Poland					2.45	5.74	6.14
Romania					1.02	4.04	n.a.
USSR					3.07	6.59	5.66
Argentina					6.16	10.70	11.86
Brazil					2.41	5.62	6.66
Chile					4.66	8.90	10.66
Colombia					2.79	5.87	7.76
Mexico					3.09	7.63	8.40
Peru					2.87	6.24	4.44
Venezuela					9.01	19.31	16.73
Bangladesh					0.70	0.75	1.07
China					0.82	1.31	2.79
India					0.60	0.94	1.58
Indonesia					1.02	1.86	3.35
Pakistan					0.79	1.48	2.57
Philippines					1.38	2.56	2.85
South Korea					1.28	3.22	8.48
Taiwan					1.17	4.13	11.06
Thailand					0.74	1.68	4.34

a) 1991.

Source: Appendix C for GDP; Tables J-2, J-3 and J-4 for labour input.

Table J-6. **GDP Per Person Employed, 1950-92**

(1990 international dollars)

	1950	1973	1992		1950	1973	1992
Austria	8 048	27 147	38 153	Argentina	12 538	21 349	21 662
Belgium	13 826	30 943	45 260	Brazil	4 922	11 781	12 366
Denmark	14 423	27 772	35 716	Chile	10 316	17 404	21 375
Finland	8 454	22 899	33 596	Colombia	6 492	12 578	15 124
France	11 108	31 464	45 678	Mexico	6 665	15 728	17 327
Germany	10 110	30 012	43 061	Peru	6 194	12 705	8 557
Italy	8 548	25 110	36 632	Venezuela	23 791	37 936	31 255
Netherlands	14 361	33 304	38 538				
Norway	11 362	24 174	37 519	Bangladesh	1 539	1 659	2 358
Sweden	13 814	28 307	35 016	China	1 814	2 885	6 139
Switzerland	18 757	35 287	41 728	India	1 328	2 064	3 482
UK	15 395	26 882	35 751	Indonesia	2 239	4 097	7 359
				Japan	4 387	22 764	37 526
Australia	17 063	28 881	36 790	Pakistan	1 746	3 248	5 658
Canada	19 245	34 138	41 926	Philippines	3 043	5 636	6 270
New Zealand	n.a.	32 374	32 259	South Korea	2 823	8 651	23 749
USA	23 643	40 526	46 242	Taiwan	2 530	10 625	27 659
				Thailand	1 629	3 688	9 537
Greece	4 582	21 547	29 233				
Ireland	8 561	20 226	36 924	Côte d'Ivoire	n.a.	n.a.	2 907
Portugal	5 678	18 736	23 900	Egypt	n.a.	n.a.	6 883
Spain	5 727	23 346	38 639	Ethiopia	n.a.	n.a.	733
Turkey	2 290	7 309	13 608	Ghana	n.a.	n.a.	2 649
				Kenya	n.a.	n.a.	2 638
Czechoslovakia	7 262	14 445	13 898	Morocco	n.a.	n.a.	7 508
Hungary	5 288	11 649	12 498	Nigeria	n.a.	n.a.	3 717
Poland	4 776	10 276	10 436	South Africa	n.a.	n.a.	8 850
USSR	5 986	11 795	9 620	Tanzania	n.a.	n.a.	1 279

Source: Appendix C for GDP, Tables J-2 and J-3 for employment.

Appendix K

Growth Accounts for Selected Countries

Appendix K

Growth Accounts for Selected Countries

The estimates in the preceding appendices provide a skeleton framework for analysing the growth of the world economy and the performance of individual countries. In order to explore the causal factors which influenced or determined intercountry or intertemporal variations in performance, one also needs an analytical schema for explaining growth, and an additional array of empirical evidence, structured in a way which permits the theoretical schema to be tested.

Although a good deal of progress has been made in constructing articulate growth accounts in the past three decades, they usually do not extend very far back in time and are not yet available for most countries. This appendix presents the basic elements of such accounts for the whole period 1820-1992 for the two successive lead countries — the UK and the USA — and for the most successful of the "follower" countries — Japan — which has increased its per capita product more than 27-fold since 1820. These accounts do a good deal to illuminate the nature of the growth process since 1820, and illustrate clearly the value of further research to provide similar estimates for a much wider range of countries.

Table K-1 covers the main magnitudes which are important in implementing this approach. They are also key ingredients for econometric interpretations. Table K-2 provides summary growth accounts which can be derived from this material. It should be noted that the figures in Table K-1 and K-2 are not adjusted to exclude the impact of territorial change.

The purpose and characteristics of the growth accounting approach are analysed in A. Maddison, "Growth and Slowdown in Advanced Capitalist Economies: Techniques of Quantitative Assessment". *Journal of Economic Literature*, June 1987.

The estimates in Tables K-1 are derived from the above article, from A. Maddison, *Dynamic Forces in the World Economy*, Oxford University Press, 1991, and from A. Maddison, *Explaining the Economic Performance of Nations: Essays in Time and Space*, Elgar, London, 1995. For education, the estimate for 1820 for the UK is from R.C.O. Matthews, C.H. Feinstein and J.C. Odling-Smee, *British Economic Growth 1856-1973*, Oxford University Press, 1982, p. 573. For the USA, 1820, I assumed the education level to be higher than in the UK (2.5 years) for the free population, and zero for the 30 per cent of the labour force which consisted of slaves. For Japan, the 1820 education level was derived from A. Maddison, *Economic Growth in Japan and the USSR*, Allen and Unwin, London, 1969, p. 16. The figures for 1870, 1890, 1929 and 1938 are interpolations. The totals for educational levels were derived by giving years of primary education a weight of 1, secondary 1.4, and higher 2. These differentials are intended to allow for variations in earning capacity of those with such education. As education is not only an investment in human capital, but also an aspect of consumption, and as the earnings associated with education represent rewards for intelligence, family connections or the impact of credentialist rules, as well as for cognitive ability, I have followed the normal practice in growth accounts and compressed the weight given to education by .6.

Table K-1. **Basic Components of Growth Accounts USA, UK and Japan, 1820-1992**

	Total Population 000s	Employment 000s	Total Hours Worked million	Average Years of education Per Person Employed	Land Area 000 ha.	Per cent of Employment in: Agriculture Forestry & Fisheries	Industry	Services
				USA				
1820	9 618	3 105	9 315	1.75	463 061	70.0	15.0	15.0
1870	39 905	14 411	42 714	3.92	934 646	50.0	24.4	25.6
1890	63 056	23 842	66 495	5.43	934 646	38.3	23.9	37.8
1913	97 227	38 711	100 842	7.86	937 289	27.5	29.7	42.8
1929	121 770	47 718	111 756	9.11	937 323	21.1	29.4	49.5
1938	129 969	44 732	92 237	9.93	937 323	17.9	31.2	50.9
1950	151 683	61 413	114 658	11.27	939 669	12.9	33.6	53.5
1973	211 909	86 838	149 101	14.58	939 669	4.1	31.2	64.7
1992	255 610	119 164	189 352	18.04	939 669	2.8	23.3	74.0
				UK				
1820	21 240	8 160	24 480	2.00	31 427	37.6	32.9	29.5
1870	31 393	12 593	37 578	4.44	31 427	22.7	42.3	35.0
1890	37 485	15 361	43 118	6.11	31 427	16.1	43.2	40.7
1913	45 649	19 823	52 016	8.82	31 427	11.7	44.1	44.2
1929	45 672	18 936	43 288	9.55	24 410	7.7	45.2	47.1
1938	47 494	20 818	47 194	9.99	24 410	5.9	44.0	50.1
1950	50 363	22 400	43 859	10.60	24 410	5.1	44.9	50.0
1973	56 210	25 076	42 328	11.66	24 410	2.9	40.3	56.8
1992	57 848	25 465	37 968	14.09	24 410	2.2	26.2	71.6
				Japan				
1820	31 000	16 819	49 532	1.50	38 256	n.a.	n.a.	n.a.
1870	34 437	18 684	55 024	1.50	38 256	70.1	n.a.	n.a.
1890	40 077	20 305	56 245	2.71	38 256	69.0	n.a.	n.a.
1913	51 672	25 751	66 644	5.36	38 256	60.1	17.5	22.4
1929	63 244	29 332	69 341	6.74	38 256	50.3	20.9	28.8
1938	71 879	32 290	77 205	7.67	38 256	45.2	24.1	30.7
1950	83 563	35 683	77 289	9.11	36 848	48.3	22.6	29.1
1973	108 660	52 590	107 389	12.09	37 780	13.4	37.2	49.4
1992	124 336	64 360	120 611	14.87	37 780	6.4	34.6	59.0

Table K-1 (continued)

	GDP	Gross Stock of Machinery & Equipment	Gross Stock of Non-Residential Structures	Total Stock of Gross Non-Residential Fixed Capital	Commodity Exports	GDP Per Capita	GDP Per Hour Worked
	1990 $ million	1990 $ million	1990 $ million	1990 $ million	1990 $ million	1990 $	1990 $
			USA				
1820	12 396	873	10 876	11 749	251	1 289	1.33
1870	98 129	19 695	148 343	168 038	2 495	2 459	2.30
1890	214 336	98 120	554 811	652 930	7 755	3 399	3.22
1913	516 472	268 359	1 434 437	1 702 796	19 196	5 312	5.12
1929	841 849	485 301	2 174 926	2 660 227	30 368	6 913	7.53
1938	797 949	444 826	2 432 557	2 877 382	24 129	6 140	8.65
1950	1 453 351	930 386	2 620 695	3 551 081	43 114	9 582	12.68
1973	3 519 378	2 280 288	5 163 463	7 443 690	174 548	16 608	23.60
1992	5 510 378	4 723 222	8 654 232	13 377 454	451 026	21 558	29.10
			UK				
1820	36 164	1 943	22 793	24 736	1 125	1 703	1.48
1870	99 318	10 786	78 756	89 542	12 237	3 164	2.64
1890	148 977	17 118	107 740	124 858	21 681	3 974	3.46
1913	222 685	40 071	146 775	186 846	39 348	4 878	4.28
1929	239 985	64 678	152 594	217 272	31 990	5 255	5.54
1938	284 165	86 853	170 945	257 797	22 546	5 983	5.98
1950	344 859	106 884	171 863	278 747	39 348	6 847	7.86
1973	674 061	348 786	538 886	887 672	94 670	11 992	15.92
1992	910 401	588 103	1 064 379	1 652 482	194 535	15 738	23.98
			Japan				
1820	21 831	n.a.	n.a.	n.a.	n.a.	704	0.44
1870	25 505	n.a.	n.a.	n.a.	51	741	0.46
1890	39 016	3 946	23 767	27 712	222	974	0.69
1913	68 933	16 979	44 010	60 989	1 684	1 334	1.03
1929	123 251	55 344	88 416	143 760	4 343	1 949	1.78
1938	169 367	64 967	133 085	198 052	9 907	2 356	2.19
1950	156 546	115 409	161 223	276 632	3 538	1 873	2.03
1973	1 197 152	698 778	1 388 481	2 087 259	95 105	11 017	11.15
1992	2 415 190	2 590 014	4 706 820	7 296 834	299 489	19 425	20.02

Table K-2. **Comparative Growth Performance of the USA, UK and Japan, 1820-1992**

(annual average compound growth rates)

		1820-70	1870-1913	1913-50	1950-73	1973-92	1820-1992
GDP	USA	4.22	3.94	2.84	3.92	2.39	3.61
	UK	2.04	1.90	1.19	3.00	1.59	1.89
	Japan	0.31	2.34	2.24	9.25	3.76	2.77
Population	USA	2.89	2.09	1.21	1.46	0.99	1.93
	UK	0.78	0.87	0.27	0.48	0.15	0.58
	Japan	0.21	0.95	1.31	1.15	0.71	0.81
GDP Per Capita	USA	1.30	1.81	1.61	2.42	1.38	1.65
	UK	1.25	1.01	0.92	2.47	1.44	1.30
	Japan	0.10	1.38	0.92	8.01	3.03	1.95
GDP Per Hour Worked	USA	1.10	1.88	2.48	2.74	1.11	1.81
	UK	1.16	1.13	1.66	3.12	2.18	1.63
	Japan	0.09	1.89	1.85	7.69	3.13	2.24
Total Factor Productivity	USA	-0.15	0.33	1.59	1.72	0.18	0.63
	UK	0.15	0.31	0.81	1.48	0.69	0.57
	Japan	n.a.	-0.31[a]	0.36	5.08	1.04	1.38[b]
Natural Resources	USA	1.41	0.01	0.01	0.00	0.00	0.41
	UK	0.00	0.00	-0.68	0.00	0.00	-0.15
	Japan	0.00	0.00	-0.03	0.11	0.00	-0.01
Total Hours	USA	3.09	2.02	0.35	1.15	1.27	1.77
	UK	0.85	0.76	-0.46	-0.15	-0.57	0.26
	Japan	0.21	0.45	0.40	1.44	0.61	0.52
Non-Residential Capital Stock	USA	5.46	5.53	2.01	3.27	3.13	4.18
	UK	2.61	1.73	1.09	5.17	3.32	2.47
	Japan	**n.a.**	3.49[a]	4.17	9.18	6.18	5.62[c]

a) 1890-1913;

b) 1890-1992, for the corresponding period, the rate was 1.18 for the USA, 0.78 for the UK;

c) 1890-1992, for the corresponding period the rate was 3.00 for the USA and 2.56 for the UK.

Source: Table K-1. In calculating total factor productivity, crude labour input (hours) was given a weight of 0.7, education was given a weight of .42, non-residential capital 0.27, and natural resources 0.03. Surface area was taken as a proxy for natural resources.

MAIN SALES OUTLETS OF OECD PUBLICATIONS
PRINCIPAUX POINTS DE VENTE DES PUBLICATIONS DE L'OCDE

ARGENTINA – ARGENTINE
Carlos Hirsch S.R.L.
Galería Güemes, Florida 165, 4° Piso
1333 Buenos Aires Tel. (1) 331.1787 y 331.2391
Telefax: (1) 331.1787

AUSTRALIA – AUSTRALIE
D.A. Information Services
648 Whitehorse Road, P.O.B 163
Mitcham, Victoria 3132 Tel. (03) 873.4411
Telefax: (03) 873.5679

AUSTRIA – AUTRICHE
Gerold & Co.
Graben 31
Wien I Tel. (0222) 533.50.14
Telefax: (0222) 512.47.31.29

BELGIUM – BELGIQUE
Jean De Lannoy
Avenue du Roi 202
B-1060 Bruxelles Tel. (02) 538.51.69/538.08.41
Telefax: (02) 538.08.41

CANADA
Renouf Publishing Company Ltd.
1294 Algoma Road
Ottawa, ON K1B 3W8 Tel. (613) 741.4333
Telefax: (613) 741.5439
Stores:
61 Sparks Street
Ottawa, ON K1P 5R1 Tel. (613) 238.8985
211 Yonge Street
Toronto, ON M5B 1M4 Tel. (416) 363.3171
Telefax: (416)363.59.63

Les Éditions La Liberté Inc.
3020 Chemin Sainte-Foy
Sainte-Foy, PQ G1X 3V6 Tel. (418) 658.3763
Telefax: (418) 658.3763

Federal Publications Inc.
165 University Avenue, Suite 701
Toronto, ON M5H 3B8 Tel. (416) 860.1611
Telefax: (416) 860.1608

Les Publications Fédérales
1185 Université
Montréal, QC H3B 3A7 Tel. (514) 954.1633
Telefax: (514) 954.1635

CHINA – CHINE
China National Publications Import
Export Corporation (CNPIEC)
16 Gongti E. Road, Chaoyang District
P.O. Box 88 or 50
Beijing 100704 PR Tel. (01) 506.6688
Telefax: (01) 506.3101

CHINESE TAIPEI – TAIPEI CHINOIS
Good Faith Worldwide Int'l. Co. Ltd.
9th Floor, No. 118, Sec. 2
Chung Hsiao E. Road
Taipei Tel. (02) 391.7396/391.7397
Telefax: (02) 394.9176

CZEÇH REPUBLIC – RÉPUBLIQUE TCHEQUE
Artia Pegas Press Ltd.
Narodni Trida 25
POB 825
111 21 Praha 1 Tel. 26.65.68
Telefax: 26.20.81

DENMARK – DANEMARK
Munksgaard Book and Subscription Service
35, Nørre Søgade, P.O. Box 2148
DK-1016 København K Tel. (33) 12.85.70
Telefax: (33) 12.93.87

EGYPT – ÉGYPTE
Middle East Observer
41 Sherif Street
Cairo Tel. 392.6919
Telefax: 360-6804

FINLAND – FINLANDE
Akateeminen Kirjakauppa
Keskuskatu 1, P.O. Box 128
00100 Helsinki

Subscription Services/Agence d'abonnements :
P.O. Box 23
00371 Helsinki Tel. (358 0) 12141
Telefax: (358 0) 121.4450

FRANCE
OECD/OCDE
Mail Orders/Commandes par correspondance:
2, rue André-Pascal
75775 Paris Cedex 16 Tel. (33-1) 45.24.82.00
Telefax: (33-1) 49.10.42.76
Telex: 640048 OCDE

Orders via Minitel, France only/
Commandes par Minitel, France exclusivement :
36 15 OCDE

OECD Bookshop/Librairie de l'OCDE :
33, rue Octave-Feuillet
75016 Paris Tel. (33-1) 45.24.81.81
(33-1) 45.24.81.67

Documentation Française
29, quai Voltaire
75007 Paris Tel. 40.15.70.00

Gibert Jeune (Droit-Économie)
6, place Saint-Michel
75006 Paris Tel. 43.25.91.19

Librairie du Commerce International
10, avenue d'Iéna
75016 Paris Tel. 40.73.34.60

Librairie Dunod
Université Paris-Dauphine
Place du Maréchal de Lattre de Tassigny
75016 Paris Tel. (1) 44.05.40.13

Librairie Lavoisier
11, rue Lavoisier
75008 Paris Tel. 42.65.39.95

Librairie L.G.D.J. - Montchrestien
20, rue Soufflot
75005 Paris Tel. 46.33.89.85

Librairie des Sciences Politiques
30, rue Saint-Guillaume
75007 Paris Tel. 45.48.36.02

P.U.F.
49, boulevard Saint-Michel
75005 Paris Tel. 43.25.83.40

Librairie de l'Université
12a, rue Nazareth
13100 Aix-en-Provence Tel. (16) 42.26.18.08

Documentation Française
165, rue Garibaldi
69003 Lyon Tel. (16) 78.63.32.23

Librairie Decitre
29, place Bellecour
69002 Lyon Tel. (16) 72.40.54.54

Librairie Sauramps
Le Triangle
34967 Montpellier Cedex 2 Tel. (16) 67.58.85.15
Tekefax: (16) 67.58.27.36

GERMANY – ALLEMAGNE
OECD Publications and Information Centre
August-Bebel-Allee 6
D-53175 Bonn Tel. (0228) 959.120
Telefax: (0228) 959.12.17

GREECE – GRÈCE
Librairie Kauffmann
Mavrokordatou 9
106 78 Athens Tel. (01) 32.55.321
Telefax: (01) 32.30.320

HONG-KONG
Swindon Book Co. Ltd.
Astoria Bldg. 3F
34 Ashley Road, Tsimshatsui
Kowloon, Hong Kong Tel. 2376.2062
Telefax: 2376.0685

HUNGARY – HONGRIE
Euro Info Service
Margitsziget, Európa Ház
1138 Budapest Tel. (1) 111.62.16
Telefax: (1) 111.60.61

ICELAND – ISLANDE
Mál Mog Menning
Laugavegi 18, Pósthólf 392
121 Reykjavik Tel. (1) 552.4240
Telefax: (1) 562.3523

INDIA – INDE
Oxford Book and Stationery Co.
Scindia House
New Delhi 110001 Tel. (11) 331.5896/5308
Telefax: (11) 332.5993
17 Park Street
Calcutta 700016 Tel. 240832

INDONESIA – INDONÉSIE
Pdii-Lipi
P.O. Box 4298
Jakarta 12042 Tel. (21) 573.34.67
Telefax: (21) 573.34.67

IRELAND – IRLANDE
Government Supplies Agency
Publications Section
4/5 Harcourt Road
Dublin 2 Tel. 661.31.11
Telefax: 475.27.60

ISRAEL
Praedicta
5 Shatner Street
P.O. Box 34030
Jerusalem 91430 Tel. (2) 52.84.90/1/2
Telefax: (2) 52.84.93

R.O.Y. International
P.O. Box 13056
Tel Aviv 61130 Tel. (3) 49.61.08
Telefax: (3) 544.60.39

Palestinian Authority/Middle East:
INDEX Information Services
P.O.B. 19502
Jerusalem Tel. (2) 27.12.19
Telefax: (2) 27.16.34

ITALY – ITALIE
Libreria Commissionaria Sansoni
Via Duca di Calabria 1/1
50125 Firenze Tel. (055) 64.54.15
Telefax: (055) 64.12.57
Via Bartolini 29
20155 Milano Tel. (02) 36.50.83

Editrice e Libreria Herder
Piazza Montecitorio 120
00186 Roma Tel. 679.46.28
Telefax: 678.47.51

Libreria Hoepli
Via Hoepli 5
20121 Milano Tel. (02) 86.54.46
Telefax: (02) 805.28.86

Libreria Scientifica
Dott. Lucio de Biasio 'Aeiou'
Via Coronelli, 6
20146 Milano Tel. (02) 48.95.45.52
Telefax: (02) 48.95.45.48

JAPAN – JAPON
OECD Publications and Information Centre
Landic Akasaka Building
2-3-4 Akasaka, Minato-ku
Tokyo 107 Tel. (81.3) 3586.2016
Telefax: (81.3) 3584.7929

KOREA – CORÉE
Kyobo Book Centre Co. Ltd.
P.O. Box 1658, Kwang Hwa Moon
Seoul Tel. 730.78.91
Telefax: 735.00.30

MALAYSIA – MALAISIE
University of Malaya Bookshop
University of Malaya
P.O. Box 1127, Jalan Pantai Baru
59700 Kuala Lumpur
Malaysia Tel. 756.5000/756.5425
Telefax: 756.3246

MEXICO – MEXIQUE
Revistas y Periodicos Internacionales S.A. de C.V.
Florencia 57 - 1004
Mexico, D.F. 06600 Tel. 207.81.00
Telefax: 208.39.79

NETHERLANDS – PAYS-BAS
SDU Uitgeverij Plantijnstraat
Externe Fondsen
Postbus 20014
2500 EA's-Gravenhage Tel. (070) 37.89.880
Voor bestellingen: Telefax: (070) 34.75.778

NEW ZEALAND
NOUVELLE-ZÉLANDE
Legislation Services
P.O. Box 12418
Thorndon, Wellington Tel. (04) 496.5652
Telefax: (04) 496.5698

NORWAY – NORVÈGE
Narvesen Info Center – NIC
Bertrand Narvesens vei 2
P.O. Box 6125 Etterstad
0602 Oslo 6 Tel. (022) 57.33.00
Telefax: (022) 68.19.01

PAKISTAN
Mirza Book Agency
65 Shahrah Quaid-E-Azam
Lahore 54000 Tel. (42) 353.601
Telefax: (42) 231.730

PHILIPPINE – PHILIPPINES
International Book Center
5th Floor, Filipinas Life Bldg.
Ayala Avenue
Metro Manila Tel. 81.96.76
Telex 23312 RHP PH

PORTUGAL
Livraria Portugal
Rua do Carmo 70-74
Apart. 2681
1200 Lisboa Tel. (01) 347.49.82/5
Telefax: (01) 347.02.64

SINGAPORE – SINGAPOUR
Gower Asia Pacific Pte Ltd.
Golden Wheel Building
41, Kallang Pudding Road, No. 04-03
Singapore 1334 Tel. 741.5166
Telefax: 742.9356

SPAIN – ESPAGNE
Mundi-Prensa Libros S.A.
Castelló 37, Apartado 1223
Madrid 28001 Tel. (91) 431.33.99
Telefax: (91) 575.39.98

Libreria Internacional AEDOS
Consejo de Ciento 391
08009 – Barcelona Tel. (93) 488.30.09
Telefax: (93) 487.76.59

Llibreria de la Generalitat
Palau Moja
Rambla dels Estudis, 118
08002 – Barcelona
(Subscripcions) Tel. (93) 318.80.12
(Publicacions) Tel. (93) 302.67.23
Telefax: (93) 412.18.54

SRI LANKA
Centre for Policy Research
c/o Colombo Agencies Ltd.
No. 300-304, Galle Road
Colombo 3 Tel. (1) 574240, 573551-2
Telefax: (1) 575394, 510711

SWEDEN – SUÈDE
Fritzes Customer Service
S–106 47 Stockholm Tel. (08) 690.90.90
Telefax: (08) 20.50.21

Subscription Agency/Agence d'abonnements :
Wennergren-Williams Info AB
P.O. Box 1305
171 25 Solna Tel. (08) 705.97.50
Telefax: (08) 27.00.71

SWITZERLAND – SUISSE
Maditec S.A. (Books and Periodicals - Livres et périodiques)
Chemin des Palettes 4
Case postale 266
1020 Renens VD 1 Tel. (021) 635.08.65
Telefax: (021) 635.07.80

Librairie Payot S.A.
4, place Pépinet
CP 3212
1002 Lausanne Tel. (021) 341.33.47
Telefax: (021) 341.33.45

Librairie Unilivres
6, rue de Candolle
1205 Genève Tel. (022) 320.26.23
Telefax: (022) 329.73.18

Subscription Agency/Agence d'abonnements :
Dynapresse Marketing S.A.
38 avenue Vibert
1227 Carouge Tel. (022) 308.07.89
Telefax: (022) 308.07.99

See also – Voir aussi :
OECD Publications and Information Centre
August-Bebel-Allee 6
D-53175 Bonn (Germany) Tel. (0228) 959.120
Telefax: (0228) 959.12.17

THAILAND – THAÏLANDE
Suksit Siam Co. Ltd.
113, 115 Fuang Nakhon Rd.
Opp. Wat Rajbopith
Bangkok 10200 Tel. (662) 225.9531/2
Telefax: (662) 222.5188

TURKEY – TURQUIE
Kültür Yayinlari Is-Türk Ltd. Sti.
Atatürk Bulvari No. 191/Kat 13
Kavaklidere/Ankara Tel. 428.11.40 Ext. 2458
Dolmabahce Cad. No. 29
Besiktas/Istanbul Tel. 260.71.88
Telex: 43482B

UNITED KINGDOM – ROYAUME-UNI
HMSO
Gen. enquiries Tel. (071) 873 0011
Postal orders only:
P.O. Box 276, London SW8 5DT
Personal Callers HMSO Bookshop
49 High Holborn, London WC1V 6HB
Telefax: (071) 873 8200
Branches at: Belfast, Birmingham, Bristol, Edinburgh, Manchester

UNITED STATES – ÉTATS-UNIS
OECD Publications and Information Center
2001 L Street N.W., Suite 650
Washington, D.C. 20036-4910 Tel. (202) 785.6323
Telefax: (202) 785.0350

VENEZUELA
Libreria del Este
Avda F. Miranda 52, Aptdo. 60337
Edificio Galipán
Caracas 106 Tel. 951.1705/951.2307/951.1297
Telegram: Libreste Caracas

Subscription to OECD periodicals may also be placed through main subscription agencies.

Les abonnements aux publications périodiques de l'OCDE peuvent être souscrits auprès des principales agences d'abonnement.

Orders and inquiries from countries where Distributors have not yet been appointed should be sent to: OECD Publications Service, 2 rue André-Pascal, 75775 Paris Cedex 16, France.

Les commandes provenant de pays où l'OCDE n'a pas encore désigné de distributeur peuvent être adressées à : OCDE, Service des Publications, 2, rue André-Pascal, 75775 Paris Cedex 16, France.

5-1995

OECD PUBLICATIONS, 2 rue André-Pascal, 75775 PARIS CEDEX 16
PRINTED IN FRANCE
(41 95 09 1) ISBN 92-64-14549-4 - No. 48139 1995